To Michael
With thanks
for your
inspiration

EQUALITY IN EDUCATION

Equality in Education

KATHLEEN LYNCH

GILL & MACMILLAN

Gill & Macmillan Ltd
Goldenbridge
Dublin 8
with associated companies throughout the world
www.gillmacmillan.ie

© Kathleen Lynch 1999
0 7171 2834 2

Index compiled by Helen Litton
Print origination by
Carrigboy Typesetting Services, County Cork

The paper used in this book is made from the wood pulp of managed forests. For every tree felled, at least one tree is planted, thereby renewing natural resources.

A catalogue record is available for this book from the British Library.

CONTENTS

SECTION 1: THE EQUALITY DEBATE

SECTION 2: INEQUALITY IN EDUCATION: ISSUES FOR PARTICULAR GROUPS

SECTION 3: INSTITUTIONAL ISSUES

SECTION 4: CONCLUSION

PREFACE

This collection of essays is an important addition to the literature on equality in education and is intended to provide a framework for analysing the role of education in the promotion of equality. Its author, Kathleen Lynch, acknowledges the contribution made by other researchers in the production of the book and, in particular, researchers in the Equality Studies Centre at University College Dublin.

The book is set out in four sections. Section One of the book examines theoretical issues while Sections Two and Three present an analysis of equality issues for particular groups and within educational institutions. The final section presents a critique of liberal perspectives on equality in education.

Many traditional views and attitudes are challenged in these essays. The assumption held by some that the system of education is as it is because of inevitable evolution is shattered in Chapter Four. The author argues that 'structures do not operate as a system of abstract rules dictating behaviour in a robot-like manner, rather they are mediated by collectivities and individuals . . .'. She goes on to state: 'These structural agents are not invisible; they can be named and targeted for action especially in a State such as Ireland which has a highly centralised and corporatist system of governance'.

Some readers may feel uncomfortable with this language; all readers will feel challenged in some way. In some cases the challenges are formidable; in others they are straightforward and should have been tackled long ago. For example, the low level of participation of students from working class backgrounds in higher education is not always the result of complex difficult-to-tackle factors. For some families, the inadequacy of the higher education grant is the key obstacle to participation. To quote one student: 'There is no way you can survive on it'. Another states: 'The grants are not satisfactory at all. As it is people cannot make ends meet, never mind say extending the ends and then trying to make them meet. It is a joke'. Quotations such as these make it clear that no further research is required to redress at least one of the inequalities facing young people from disadvantaged backgrounds, i.e. that of finance. This issue has been addressed in a number of reports before but in this book we hear the voices of the disadvantaged themselves highlighting the issue.

The author is committed to providing an opportunity for those who were previously voice-less to make their views heard. This is particularly true in Chapter Eight where she prioritises the voices of young people themselves in

vii

naming equality agendas in schools. According to these young people, school-ing needs to recognise and respect difference if it is to treat all people with equality of respect. It should not be assumed that all people will fit one mould. The author states that students are critical of the lack of effective democratic structures in the organisation of schooling and of the lack of respect shown by teachers to them as young persons with equal human rights.

Chapter Six also focuses on the voice of children and emphasises the importance of listening to children. Legislative and policy provisions relating to children in the context of the UN Convention on the Rights of the Child of 1989 are analysed and discussed. Not surprisingly, the analysis carried out in this chapter finds that children in Ireland are seen as subordinate to adults and as a result children are denied the right to self-determination, even in situations when such self-determination might be both feasible and desirable.

Chapter Five examines the position of women in Irish education both as learners and as educators. It brings together a range of statistics which show that although females are increasingly participating on at least an equal basis with males in education at all levels, they remain underrepresented in the labour force particularly at senior levels. Chapter Seven examines the position of mature students in Irish education. The paper shows once again that Ireland has a low rate of mature student participation in higher education and iden-tifies a number of strategies and procedures to address the disadvantages experienced by mature students generally.

Chapters Eight and Nine look at issues of stratification in education in Ireland. The author suggests that stratification by social class seems to be taking place between schools rather than within them. On the other hand, stratification by so-called 'ability grouping' is wide-spread within second-level schools in Ireland. The author wonders why so few professionals ask the basic question: What is ability? In this as in some of her previous work, Dr Lynch challenges the extent to which only particular forms of knowledge have been legitimated within western education. A range of intelligences are either ignored or dis-missed as unimportant and as a result many young people are labelled as failures and schooling does little to prepare them for the challenges of life. Moreover, for many of these young people school is an alienating and disrespectful expe-rience and the author points out that this is not only undesirable in terms of a lost opportunity for experiential democratic learning, it is also undesirable because it is a negative experience in a formative period of a young person's life. This is increasingly recognised in recent international literature on education. For example, a 1997 publication from the OECD, *Education Policy Analysis*, states:

> Policies to increase equity and efficiency in education and training should consider carefully not only the incentives for pursuing further studies, but also the quality of and attitudes to learning in a lifetime perspective. They should aim to ensure that as many young adults as possible gain positive

and constructive experiences of learning, on which they can continue to build throughout adulthood.

This is an original, courageous and often challenging book. Familiar data is analysed and dissected in such a way that the previously familiar becomes unfamiliar. Assumptions which for so long have been accepted are questioned. The system is the way it is because of conscious policy decisions made over decades and generations by people, it can equally be changed by people. After reading this book, it will be more difficult for decision makers to avoid the uncomfortable or unpalatable decisions. The author has performed an important task in bringing together a wide range of research on various aspects of inequality in Irish education. Those who read this book will view equality issues through a more informed lens from now on.

Áine Hyland
University College Cork

ACKNOWLEDGMENTS

There are many people who have contributed to the writing of this book, both directly and indirectly. First, I want to express my deepest appreciation to those researchers who worked with me in the co-authored chapters: Anne Lodge for her Trojan fieldwork which contributed so much to chapter 8; Cathleen O'Neill for her continued inspiration in preparing chapter 2; and Claire O'Riordan for her important contribution in undertaking the interviews for our study reported in chapter 4. Other people have also contributed both directly and indirectly to different chapters. Marjorie Fitzpatrick and Eileen O'Reilly played an important role in collecting data on mature students while my colleagues in Equality Studies, John Baker, Sara Cantillon, Alpha Connelly, Mary Kelly and Máire Nic Ghiolla Phádraig, have been a constant fount of support and wisdom in preparing the theoretical arguments which underpin the book.

I also wish to thank the many people with whom I have worked in UCD over the years, and in particular my colleague Pat Clancy in the Sociology Department, who has given me so much encouragement in my work. Teresa Brannick in the Business School has been a constant friend during the writing of this book, as indeed has Sheelagh Drudy of the National University of Ireland, Maynooth. Margaret Larminie, Nora Clancy, Margaret Healy and Susan Gibbons of the Equality Studies Centre also deserve much thanks for their kindness and support. My thanks too to the Library Staff of UCD and the many other staff who run the support services which make academic work possible.

This book could not have been written without the funding which was made available to the Equality Studies Centre by a private donor and the grants which were received from the Department of Education Research and Development Committee for a study on 'Equality and the Social Climate of Schools', some of which we report on in chapter 8. I wish to acknowledge and thank both for their support. My thanks also to the three anonymous reviewers for taking the time to read the manuscript so carefully, and for their helpful comments and suggestions on the earlier drafts.

I am keenly aware of the space and time which have been given to me by my family to enable me to write this book. Thank you to Nora and John for their loving hugs and support, and to my husband, John, who gives so generously always to enable me to write; he is my greatest friend. I also wish to express my deepest appreciation to Maura Walsh, who has been such a wonderful support to John and me in caring for the children over the years.

Finally, I would like to dedicate this book to my mother and to the memory of my father. My mother remains a great friend and ally to me in my work. I learned from her and my father the independence of mind and spirit that has sustained me in writing this book. For that I am for ever grateful.

INTRODUCTION

The purpose of this book is to provide a framework for analysing the role of education in the promotion of equality. It is hoped that it will stimulate and inform debates about equality generally, and in relation to education in particular. While there has been much discussion of equality in education, there have been very few publications, either nationally or internationally, which focus on the issue of equality in the more generic sense. Drawing in particular on the work being undertaken with my colleagues[1] at the Equality Studies Centre at the National University of Ireland, Dublin, the book attempts to marry normative and analytical frameworks in the study of education. At a policy level, it sets out to clarify the implications of pursuing equality objectives within different intellectual frameworks.

While section 1 of the book examines theoretical issues pertaining to equality in education within academic discourse and research in higher education, sections 2 and 3 present, respectively, an analysis of equality issues for particular groups, and within educational institutions. There is a strong focus throughout on policy and change, and in particular on the limits of liberal education policies for the promotion of substantive equality in education.

As writing about equality in education generally has been dominated by sociologists, the book opens in chapter 1 with an extensive critical review of how sociologists have analysed inequality. It examines the dominant method-ologies and conceptual frameworks for researching equality in education and explores the limits of liberal discourse, which has dominated so much of empirical research in the field. It suggests that normative and analytical frameworks should be integrated more closely in the context of developing a truly emancipatory approach to research and theory in education. One of the claims which I am making here is that it is not sufficient to critique the world and to assume that this critique will inevitably lead to transformative action, be that at policy or at classroom level. We need to identify more egalitarian and educationally enlight-ened practices at many levels. If we are to develop such a transformative paradigm we must move outside the academy and develop institutionalised procedures for dialogue not only with teachers, educators and policy-makers who manage education, but most importantly and crucially, with those who are marginalised and excluded from education at different levels. In terms of the equality debate, the latter groups, be they working-class communities, disabled people, women, Travellers, refugees, or other minorities, are often peoples about whom we write and speak but whose lifeworlds remain largely removed from our experience. Chapter 2 focuses on how a truly emancipatory research and teaching paradigm demands that excluded groups become agents and major partners in education and research practice; they need to be given the space and place to define the purposes and procedures by which their worlds are named and known. Collaborative and collegiate forms of research and teaching practice must replace dysfunctional and oppressive hierarchical procedures.

In the last fifteen years, social-class-related inequalities in education have often been ignored in the international literature. Chapter 4 reports on a national study showing how social class inequalities in education are still pervasive, despite being 'out of academic fashion' as a subject for research and theory. It examines the barriers experienced by low-income working-class students in accessing and succeeding in higher education while identifying strategies for change as seen from the perspectives of educationalists, and those directly affected by class inequalities. Working within a broadly structuralist framework, the study identified three principal barriers facing working-class students: namely, economic, social and cultural, and educational barriers; the economic barriers were found to be the most persistent and pervasive. The research challenges the view of both resistance and rational action theorists as to the value of structuralist analysis. It argues for a dynamic view of structures as sets of institutions and social relations which are visible, accountable and open to transformation. It is suggested that the dynamic role of the state, and its collective and individual actors, in creating and maintaining inequality needs to be more systematically addressed, especially in strongly (state-) centralised education systems. Through the clarification of how the state and other education mediators create inequalities, it is possible to identify both the actors and the contexts where resistance is possible.

Chapter 5 examines the position of women in Irish education both as learners and as educators. It highlights the great irony that although women are increasingly academically successful, they remain occupationally subordinate, both within education itself and within the labour market generally. Drawing on the work of Nancy Fraser, the chapter examines the limitations of employing a liberal distributive model of social justice to examine the position of women; it argues for the development of a radical distributive perspective, one which focuses on substantive economic and political distribution, in conjunction with a model which recognises culturally generated differences between women, whether they arise from ethnicity, race, religion, age, dis/ability, sexual orientation or other values.

Chapter 6 is devoted to analysing the position of children and young people in education and society generally. It examines legislative and policy provisions relating to children in the context of the rights-oriented perspective of the UN Convention on the Rights of the Child, 1989. What is clear from this analysis is that children in Ireland are defined as subordinate to adults in both the public and the private institutions of the state. While a narrowly defined developmentalism informs thinking about children within education, this perspective is encased within a strong caretaking and protectionist framework which denies children rights to self-determination even when self-determination is both feasible and/or desirable. The chapter also addresses the issue of difference between children, focusing especially on how differences arising from social class, disability, marital status and ethnicity create inequalities between children which are inextricably linked to inequalities between adults.

The position of mature students in Irish education is examined in chapter 7. This chapter reports on studies of mature students undertaken by the author for the Technical Working Group to the Steering Committee on the Future of Higher Education in 1994/5. It highlights the limitations of adopting a 'laissez-faire' approach to adult education generally and to adult education within higher education in particular. The paper shows that Ireland has a very low rate of mature student participation in higher education and it identifies a number of strategies and procedures to address the disadvantages experienced by mature students generally, and by mature students from disadvantaged backgrounds particularly.

There are two chapters devoted to analysing equality issues within schools in section 3. In 'Essays on School' Anne Lodge and I attempt to name the equality agenda within schools from the perspective of young people themselves. Taking essays on equality within school, written by over 1,200 young people in twelve second-level schools, chapter 8 outlines their views on inequality within school. It analyses these concerns in the light of current debates about equality and difference. In taking their perspectives seriously, we identified a more varied set of equality concerns among young people on schooling than that which is addressed generally in the research literature. Although they are concerned about gender, social class and other 'adult-acknowledged' equality concerns, what young people define as equality issues are not synonymous with those of adults. The unequal power relations between schoolchildren and adults, and the ordering of educational relations through ability-related grouping and signification practices, leads to the development of equality concerns among young persons which are rarely discussed in public debates about equality in education.

The stratification of students and knowledge is the subject of chapter 9. It reviews research on ability grouping in Irish schools and also identifies major gaps in our research knowledge, especially at primary level. One of the principal themes of this paper is that the issue of 'ability grouping' needs to be reinterpreted in the light of recent research and theory about human intelligences. There is a need to move from a hierarchical to a lateral view of human ability, one which both recognises the multiple forms of human ability which exist, and realises that the 'problem' of ability grouping may have more to do with the non-recognition of different abilities than with the failure to mix so-called 'high and low' abilities in the one class, as is commonly supposed.

The final chapter in the book presents a critique of liberal perspectives on equality in education. It is suggested that liberalism consigns us to a narrow reformist view of educational change — one which, at best, will bring limited gain for the relatively advantaged among the disadvantaged. In a global context of structured inequality, the promise of liberal equal opportunities policies is therefore realisable only for a small minority of relatively advantaged people within a given disadvantaged group. Moreover, the internal logic of liberal policies does not allow for anything more radical. It treats education as an autonomous site with an ability to promote equality internally irrespective of external forces. By ignoring economic and power inequalities outside of education in particular, it endorses social and economic systems which perpetuate inequality within education. It is proposed that the radical egalitarian perspective offers an alternative to the liberal model, one which confronts inequalities both within and without education in distributive terms, and one which focuses also on radical policies to promote equality of respect, in terms of how schools, curricula, planning and policies in education are planned and negotiated.

NOTES

1   I am especially indebted to John Baker, Sara Cantillon, Alpha Connelly, Mary Kelly and Máire Nic Ghiolla Phádraig.

SECTION 1

THE EQUALITY DEBATE

CHAPTER 1

EQUALITY IN EDUCATION:
A CRITIQUE OF RESEARCH AND THEORY
IN THE SOCIOLOGY OF EDUCATION

INTRODUCTION: SOCIOLOGISTS AND EQUALITY

Sociologists have dominated the debate about equality in education over the last twenty-five years. The work of sociologists has been influential throughout a wide range of equality debates in all the countries where they are active in the field of education. They have challenged the psychological reductionism which so often overwhelms educational analysis in teacher education departments; they have problematised the concept of truth itself in an education system where absolutism and certainty is all too frequently the normative code. In the Netherlands, Wesselingh (1996:216) has observed how sociologists were the most critical and reflective members of the university education departments in Dutch universities. Dale (1992:203) has made a similar observation about the UK, noting how the perceived radicalism of sociologists of education was regarded as 'dangerous' at the height of Conservative rule in the 1980s and early 1990s. In Ireland too, sociologists have been among the minority of critical voices in an educational academy which is fundamentally consensual and conservative in its approach to politics and problems in education (Lynch, 1987; O'Sullivan, 1989; Drudy, 1991). The work of Bourdieu and his colleagues in France has also been central to the development of a critical class-based analysis of educational practice not only in France but in a number of other European countries, while 'critical' sociology of education has been an important voice of challenge to the dominant educational paradigms in Canada (Livingstone, 1985), the United States (Apple, 1996), Australia (Connell, 1993) and Latin America (Torres and Rivera, 1994).

There is, however, no one sociology of education. Major reviews of work in the field display great differences in what is defined as sociological analysis in education (Karabel and Halsey, 1977; Hurn, 1978; Trent et al., 1985; Blackledge and Hunt, 1985; Arnot and Barton, 1992; Torres and Rivera, 1994; Pink and Noblit, 1995). In their review, Trent et al. (1985) equated sociological research in education with statistical studies from large databases and ignored important qualitative work (Mehan, 1992). Arnot and Barton's review (1992) represented a totally different tradition, focusing as it did on qualitative studies of policy changes in the UK, while Pink and Noblit's review (1995) is more eclectic, incorporating an analysis of quantitative and qualitative research, critical studies, policy studies and postmodernist critiques.

Given the disparate traditions within which research has been undertaken, it is inevitable that there is great diversity in the way in which equality has been interpreted and defined. It is indeed because of its theoretical diversity that sociology has had the capacity to be a critical and generative force for the development of an equality-related analysis in education.

The aim of this chapter is to analyse research and theory in the sociology of education in the context of key questions emanating from egalitarian theory. It examines the methodological and conceptual tools used in the analysis of inequality; the normative aspects of sociological work; the equality objectives informing research; the influence of positivist and transformative epistemological assumptions on conceptual frameworks; the attention given to the identification of policies and strategic practices promoting change; and the role of marginalised groups in defining the nature and purpose of equality research focused on themselves.

It is suggested that research in sociology of education over the last twenty years has been dominated by liberalism. The focus has been on modification and adjustment rather than on radical egalitarian reform. Although feminists and critical theorists have been highly critical of the education system, both as process and product, and have problematised the concept of education as an unmitigated good, they have not developed proposals which are sufficiently coherent and plausible to challenge seriously the powerful position of liberalism within educational theory.

The same issue arises in relation to Marxist critiques of the relationship between the politico-economic system and education. Critique is not substantiated with viable alternative proposals. It is suggested that theories of egalitarian-focused change, ones which are grounded in the institutional and political structures of educational reality, can be successfully developed only in a dialogical context. This dialogue should take place not only with a wide range of educationalists and academics in cognate disciplines, but with the marginalised and excluded groups who are the subjects of equality-based research in education.

THE DOMAIN ASSUMPTIONS OF THE RESEARCHER

As Bourdieu (1993:37) has observed, intellectuals 'tend to leave out of play their own game and their own stakes'. Although academic writing creates virtual, textual, ethnographic and statistical realities about the nature of inequality in education, intellectuals are disinclined, for the most part, to subject their own analysis to reflexive critique. While there are exceptions to this, especially in the critical, feminist and postmodern traditions (Wexler, 1987; Lather, 1991; Van

Galen and Baker, 1995; Apple, 1996), such analysis is not typical of work undertaken in sociology of education. Yet theoretical knowledge about equality in education has serious limitations imposed upon it by the conditions of its own performance.

Therefore, before engaging in a closer analysis of the different traditions in sociology of education, I wish to comment on the relations of research production, in terms of how they impact both on this chapter, and, more importantly, on sociology of education generally. The relations of cultural production, within which theories of educational inequality are produced, are no different to those that operate for the study of nuclear physics or corporate law. The context within which research is undertaken in universities does vary considerably cross-culturally, particularly in terms of resources; it varies far less in terms of the normative principles and frameworks which underpin it.

Academics do not work out of paradigmatic allegiances alone, important though these may be; they also work with a set of domain assumptions[1] arising from their unique biographical, linguistic and cultural experiences (Gouldner, 1970:29–35). These sub-theoretical beliefs are often internalised before the academics ever engage in intellectual work. While they may be modified by subsequent socialisation, they nonetheless form an important set of background assumptions against which academics appraise the validity of particular theories. Whether a theory is accepted or rejected is influenced, in part, by the background assumptions embedded in it. The idea that we accept or reject theories on purely rational terms is untenable; many theories are either rejected or accepted before the evidence is presented, depending on whether or not their background assumptions accord with those of the listener.

Whether we can ever know or name such sub-theoretical beliefs, in any comprehensive sense, is doubtful. There are limits to self-reflexivity; many of the values and assumptions which we hold most dearly are those that are least likely to be subjected to critical reflection. However, what we can do is to name the conditions and contexts in which we write. By identifying the parameters of our intellectual 'domain', we can at least identify some of the limiting conditions of our own analysis. Such a practice highlights the limitations of one's own knowledge, which is a precondition for deeper understanding.

Writing out of a neocolonial context in Western Europe, I am keenly aware of the importance of language. The first language of my country is Irish although English is the vernacular for over 90% of the population. Knowing and naming the world through English is very different from knowing and naming the world through Irish, or indeed any other language. What is visible about equality in one language is not necessarily as visible with another.

The sociological discourse into which I and many other minority language speakers have been socialised is that of a majority language, English in my case. Consequently, like many other sociologists, I remain quite ignorant of socio-logical debates taking place *exclusively* within minority languages, even within

European minority languages. Much of what many of us in Europe know about minority-language-speaking sociologists is what is translated into majority languages, usually English, sometimes French, German or Spanish. It is obvious therefore that with some few exceptions, the intellectual discourse of much of sociology, including sociology of education, is dominated by sociologists who either live in, or are part of, dominant cultural traditions. The limitations of operating out of a majoritarian linguistic and cultural perspective has to be acknowledged. The extent to which cultural dominance is linked to economic dominance also needs to be investigated, especially in terms of how this affects the analysis of equality issues in education. Such questions could be the subject of an international research project in the sociology of knowledge itself.

This chapter does not purport therefore to examine the vast array of sociological literature on equality in education which is produced by the global community of sociologists working in this field. Such an undertaking could be the subject of a major study in its own right. What will be examined primarily is a range of literature which is written in or translated into English. That this type of analysis can underpin and support forms of global cultural colonisation within the academy itself is a significant weakness of such an approach. It can reinforce the power of certain speakers to define what is or is not the important international question in sociological debates about equality. It privileges one cultural and linguistic tradition over others.

While recognising the impossibility of overcoming the aforesaid limitations, I will try to address the problem of bias by identifying gaps and limitations in the analysis of equality issues within the dominant traditions. This will be done by framing the analysis in terms of a series of questions which could be regarded as canonical or foundational in the study of equality (Baker, 1997). They could be raised in relation to any discipline or field of study and do not arise simply for sociologists. Addressing them specifically in relation to sociology of education, however, is an attempt to locate the equality debate in this field in a wider egalitarian context.

Key Questions

Question 1: How have sociologists described and explained inequality in education? Conceptual and methodological issues

Question 2: Is there a normative orientation within the discipline?

Question 3: Which equality objectives inform the analysis within the discipline?

Question 4: Is knowledge of equality defined in positivist terms or is there an emancipatory dimension to research and theory?

Question 5: Does the discipline identify policy frameworks or strategic practices for the realisation of equality?

Question 6: Do marginalised groups about whom the discipline speaks have a means of defining themselves within the discipline?

1. How Have Sociologists Described and Explained Inequality in Education? Conceptual and Methodological Issues

As most sociologists working in the field of education would broadly classify themselves as social *scientists*, the first and most obvious question to ask is, 'How have sociologists described and explained inequality in education?'

THE WORK OF THE EQUALITY EMPIRICISTS

In their analysis of the work undertaken in the sociology of education in the preceding twenty years, Karabel and Halsey (1977) identified the research of the 'methodological empiricists' as being a core part of the work of sociologists in the field of education. The methodological empiricists were primarily 'equality empiricists' in the sense that much of their research was centred on educational inequality. This tradition has continued to flourish since the late 1970s using large (often national) databases to determine either a) the relationship between education and status attainment for different social groups (mostly lower socio-economic or other working-class groups, or racial groups); or b) the effects of schooling on the educational opportunities of particular social groups.

Among the studies examining the links between education and various forms of status attainment were those of Sewell et al. (1976), Eckland and Alexander (1980) and Mare (1981) in the US; Halsey et al. (1980) in the UK; Jonsson (1987) in Sweden; Dronkers (1983) in the Netherlands; Gambetta (1987) in Italy; Blossfeld and Shavit (1993) in Germany; Euriat and Thelot (1995) in France; McPherson and Willms (1987) in Scotland; and Clancy (1988, 1995) in Ireland. Moreover, the work of the equality empiricists within education was paralleled by the work of stratification theorists who documented patterns of social mobility (among white men especially): Goldthorpe et al. (1980); Whelan and Whelan (1984); Ganzeboom et al. (1989); Raftery and Hout (1993). While the focus of stratification research was not on the dynamics of education per se, it nonetheless had implications for the work of egalitarian-focused sociologists of education as it documented the relative success or failure of different education strategies for the promotion of equality in society (Shavit and Blossfeld, 1993). Numerous writers have noted how sociology of education was closely tied to stratification research, in its early days especially (Rowan, 1995; Apple, 1996; Mac an Ghaill, 1996).

Equality empiricism not only focuses on the mobility of various social groups between different sectors and fields of education, it examines equality patterns within schools themselves. School-specific research examined the effects of schooling (especially tracking or streaming) on student outcomes, highlighting social class, racial and gender inequalities in access to curricula. The work of Alexander et al. (1978), Hallinan and Sorensen (1983), Oakes (1985), Hannan and Boyle (1987), Hallinan (1992), Oakes et al. (1992) and Gamoran (1996) exemplify this tradition, which has been especially developed in the US. Duru-Bellat et al. (1993, 1996) have undertaken related research on school effects in France.

A number of critiques and evaluations of the methodological and theoretical assumptions of the equality empiricists have been presented elsewhere (Young, 1971; Bourdieu, 1973; Apple and Weiss, 1983; Wexler, 1987; Pink and Noblit, 1995; Weiss, 1995; Apple, 1996). The issues which have been raised include the conceptual limitations and depoliticising implications of equating socio-economic status (of fathers mostly) with social class; the atheoretical approach of much of the research; the atomistic representation of individuals divorced from structural relations; the representation of the researchers themselves as detached and independent observers without due regard for either their para-digmatic or domain assumptions; the relative neglect of cultural politics and the role of the state; and the lack of a systematic analysis of the internal life of the school institution itself in terms of educational outcomes. The status attainment research has been especially critiqued for its failure to explain educational outcomes for women and racial minorities (Kerchoff, 1984; Alexander et al., 1987). Inequalities arising from disability or sexual orientation have also been generally ignored in this research.

CONCLUSION

The parameters within which the debate about equality in education takes place have been set by large-scale empirical studies on the effects of schooling on life chances. Although these studies are not as dominant in the US and Britain as they were in the 1970s (Weiss, 1995), they form the intellectual and political backdrop for much of contemporary research and thinking about equality in education. These are the kinds of studies which tend to be funded by governments, and they are often regarded in policy terms, if not in academic terms, as of central importance. The dominant intellectual paradigm which has been employed to interpret and explain these research findings has been structural-functionalism (ibid.). There is little critique of the many social hierarchies which underpin stratification in a class-based society within such a model. Rather, equality is equated with proportionate social mobility for different social groups; it is defined in terms of achieving 'a more equitable redistribution of life chances' (Breen et al., 1990:139). Debates about method-ologies rather than the purpose or value of the research often dominate the discourse, especially in status attainment research. This has meant that many assumptions about the role of the research in challenging inequalities in society have not been addressed.

EQUALITY-ORIENTED QUALITATIVE RESEARCH

Interpretative sociology has a large following among educators in teacher education departments (which is where most sociology of education is disseminated in the UK and Ireland, for example). Classroom- and school-based studies are especially interesting for teachers as they help to decode the internal dynamics of classroom and school life. Within this tradition there is a range of studies which are focused on the dynamics of interaction in schools and classrooms per se, including the work of symbolic interactionists; these do not address issues of equality in any direct sense (Cusick, 1973; Woods, 1980, 1983; Ball, 1981, 1987; Delamont, 1983; Denscombe, 1985).

There is equality-focused work within the interpretative tradition, however, which analyses systems of power, control and influence both in the micro-processes of school life and in the macro-processes of educational systems. Unequal access to power is a central theme in the work of Collins (1979), Archer (1984) and Blackledge and Hunt (1985). Work by Bernstein (1971), DiMaggio (1982), Heath (1982), Oakes (1985), Mehan et al. (1985) and Lareau (1987, 1989) illustrates the value of interpretative studies in highlighting how the operation of inequality in schools takes place in the micro-processes of school life. And some, including the work of Oakes et al. (1992) on tracking, attempts to define policy alternatives to present practice.

Interpretative approaches have also been adopted in the analysis of education policies, tracing the histories of particular policies and their implications for different groups (Arnot and Barton, 1992). While works such as the latter highlight the failure of particular policies to promote egalitarian outcomes for particular groups, they do not engage with egalitarian theory, nor do they specify what lies beyond critique in terms of policy alternatives. Often what is lacking is a set of clearly defined alternatives or counterfactuals (Sayer, 1995) to present educational policies.

CRITICAL SOCIOLOGY OF EDUCATION, FEMINISM AND POSTMODERNISM

The lacunae presented by the distributive, generally macroscopic focus of much of the equality-oriented studies of the 1960s and 1970s stimulated the development of the so-called new sociology of education in Britain in the early 1970s (Young, 1971; Keddie, 1971; Bernstein, 1971; Whitty, 1974, 1985), and a closely associated Marxist debate (Sarup, 1978; Sharp, 1980). A related critical tradition developed in the United States (Apple, 1979, 1982; Anyon, 1980; Giroux, 1983). These perspectives were paralleled by participatory action research which was broadly equality-oriented (Carr and Kemmis, 1986; Torres, 1990). Almost all of the early work within the critical tradition was focused on social-class-related inequalities in education.

Working originally within a neo-Marxist framework (and subsequently with a strong feminist orientation in certain cases), writers within the critical tradition refocused the debate about equality in education from concerns about 'equal rates of consumption' to questions about the nature of knowledge and patterns of power and control *within* education itself. Education was no longer defined as an unproblematic good; 'the more you got the better off you were'. Critical theorists and researchers problematised both the content of education, and the processes of influence and control within it. This tradition has remained a minority one within the US and a number of other countries (Drudy, 1991; Apple, 1996; Wesselingh, 1996) although it was a powerful force in academic discourse in the UK for a number of years. Despite its pervasive impact on intellectual debate, Dale (1992:214) claims that this tradition did not exercise much influence on public policy. He suggests that the relatively utopian character of much of the policy critique meant that change, in terms of what was proposed, was almost impossible to achieve. Even classroom-focused studies did not have an impact, he believes, as they did not answer the questions which concerned educational practitioners.

Whether this outcome is a function of the national conservative canvas against which sociology of education in Britain had to function for most of the last twenty years, or whether it is a function of the nature and quality of the work in which critical educationalists in the UK were engaged needs to be empirically investigated. The scope for radical sociologists of education to influence policy is dependent on a host of political and cultural circumstances which cannot be easily predicted in any given context. The nature of what academics write is by no means the only factor determining their level of influence. The impact of the work of Freire and his colleagues (on adult education especially) in the post-revolutionary states of Nicaragua and Cuba, for example (Torres, 1990, 1991), is no doubt related to the favourable political climate in these countries at that time.[2]

Apart from the critical neo-Marxist tradition which developed in association with the 'new sociology of education', neo-Marxism also flourished within the more traditional empirical fields of research with strong structuralist orientations (Bowles and Gintis, 1976; Willis, 1977). Within France, Bourdieu and Passeron's work (1977) focused on cultural reproduction within a broadly structuralist and Marxist paradigm. A feminist tradition also developed at this time informed by both socialist and radical feminism (Wolpe, 1977; McRobbie, 1978; Spender, 1980; Deem, 1980; Stanworth, 1981; Anyon, 1983; Walker and Barton, 1983; Arnot and Weiner, 1987; Acker, 1987, 1994; Weiler, 1988).

The critical tradition which persisted within sociology of education into the 1990s was very different in its intellectual orientation to what was defined as critical thought in the 1970s and early 1980s. First, it began to challenge the simple correspondence models of reproduction exemplified in the work of Bowles and Gintis in the 1970s; it incorporated notions of agency and resistance into debates. Secondly, it recognised the importance of non-class forms of social exclusion (gender, ethnicity, race, etc.) for understanding the patterning of domination and inequality in education (Morrow and Torres, 1995).

The rise in interests in issues of gender and ethnicity was paralleled by a gradual decline in the volume of empirical research being undertaken on social-class-related inequalities. Although dual-systems theory (Hartman, 1976) emphasised the equal importance of class and gender, increasingly it was the gender part of the dualism which was investigated within education. Even the language of the debate changed from inequality to difference; the focus was on identity, culture, recognition, rather than on stratification, selection and allocation. Postmodernist and post-structuralist analysis influenced both the language and the substance of educational thought (Mac an Ghaill, 1996). Issues of race, ethnicity, sexuality and disability, so long neglected by sociologists in education, found a new and welcome prominence in educational analysis (hooks, 1982; Barton and Tomlinson, 1984; Troyna and Williams, 1986; Verma and Ashworth, 1986; Wolpe, 1988; Verma, 1989; Oliver, 1990; Donald and Rattansi, 1992; Singh, 1993; Epstein, 1994; Barton, 1996). It was not that issues of race, disability or ethnicity had been completely ignored in the past, as they were not — especially in the US, where race was such a crucial issue (Coleman et al., 1966; Rist, 1972; Rosenbaum, 1976). But they had been defined as 'attributes' of persons whose core was defined often in socio-economic terms (in functionalist analysis) or in social class terms (within the critical tradition). In the 1990s, however, race, ethnicity, gender and/or disability were regarded as defining and essential identities, shaping the nature of all social experience. They were not defined as 'attributes', which people 'wore' on the surface of some other more fundamental social class or socio-economic identity.

The emphasis on identity politics emerging from postmodernist and post-structural influences on education analysis has inevitably focused greater attention on the process and curricula of schooling. The move from structuralism (be it of the functionalist or neo-Marxist kind) to post-structuralism has centred debate on process rather than outcome, on individual experience rather than on systems such as the state, or political operators and mediators within the education system.

Although postmodernism and post-structuralism (including feminists within these traditions) have exerted a certain influence on contemporary writing in sociology of education as exemplified in the work of Weiler (1988), Aronowitz and Giroux (1991), Giroux (1992) and McLaren (1995), there are many publications within the sociology of education which one could read without ever realising that there were significant new developments in sociology in structuration theory and postmodernism (Shilling, 1993).

CONCLUSION

What is or is not sociology of education is a contested issue. The critical tradition within the field is viewed by many of those within the positivist research tradition with methodological distrust (Hammersley, 1995). Critical theorists view with equal scepticism the claims to value neutrality of strong positivists (Abraham, 1996). The divergence between the critical/feminist/ poststructuralist traditions and the positivist tradition is exemplified in the difference in intellectual orientation between the principal British and North American journals in sociology of education. Over the last twenty years published material in these journals has varied greatly in both theoretical and methodological perspective; the main US journal, *Sociology of Education*, has relied heavily on research within the positivist tradition while the *British Journal of Sociology of Education* has had a strong critical orientation. While critical theorists regard much of the empirical work undertaken as deterministic and atheoretical, leading ultimately to the continued oppression and marginalisation of groups such as women and working-class people, the equality empiricists view critical sociological analysis as speculative, methodologically weak and lacking theoretical rigour.

Education is an extremely complex and multi-layered social practice; it can be understood at multiple levels in terms of its processes, structures and meanings. The work of the equality empiricists, interpretative researchers and critical theorists each contributes in a unique way to our understanding of education and the realisation of change within it. No one paradigm exercises a monopoly on understanding (indeed no discipline has the complete and comprehensive answer to any particular question) in the social realm.

The empirical work of both quantitative and ethnographic researchers provides essential empirical documentation of patterns of inequality at both macro- and micro-levels of social action. Without such documentation, challenges and 'resistance' to particular policies and practices would take place in an informational void and would be all the more ineffective for that. For its part, critical analysis plays an important role in highlighting questions of value in research, and in introducing debates about the transformative potential of research in education. Such work is crucial for identifying the areas of education which can be used to challenge inequality, even if at times it suffers from a certain naivety about the change-related potential of particular social actions. The feminist and postmodernist traditions, on the other hand, force educationalists and sociologists to engage in critical reflexivity about their own research, thereby making the social relations of research production in education itself a subject of critique and investigation. Such reflexivity is vital for the development of new approaches to research and theory in the study of equality.

2. Is There a Normative Orientation within the Sociology of Education?

DEFINITIONS OF EQUALITY IN THE SOCIOLOGY OF EDUCATION

Baker (1998) has identified three basic conceptions of equality in contemporary egalitarian theory: basic equality, liberal equality and radical equality. Basic equality is the principle which is fundamental to all egalitarian theory. It is the idea that all human beings are equal in dignity and worth, and are therefore equally worthy of concern and respect. It upholds the prohibition of inhuman or degrading treatment, and gives some recognition to the idea that all human beings have basic needs. It defines equality in fundamentally negative terms therefore, in terms of *freedom from*, rather than *freedom to*. Basic equality is hence a rather minimalist view of equality.

While accepting the value of basic equality, liberal egalitarians move beyond this and espouse the protection of basic civil and political rights, including freedom of speech, freedom of movement, equality before the law, freedom to own property, etc. It is the fundamental philosophical premise underpinning the Universal Declaration of Human Rights and the European Convention on Human Rights. Liberal equality is most commonly associated in the policy field with the principle of equality of opportunity (Hall, 1986). It recognises that society is stratified and proposes that equality policies should be directed towards equalising opportunities for various types of mobility (educational, occupational, career, intergenerational, etc.) within a stratified system. The best-known proponent of this tradition is Rawls (1971).

Radical egalitarians do not accept that major structural inequalities are inevitable in the way that liberal and basic egalitarians do. They argue for a radical change in the way that institutions and society are structured to promote equality. They focus especially on the importance of substantive economic and political equality, suggesting that liberals are merely concerned about ways in which to redistribute inequality across various groups, rather than how to eliminate major inequalities and hierarchies in the first place (Nielsen, 1985; Baker, 1987; Young, 1990; Cohen, 1995).

POLITICAL LIBERALISM AT THE HEART OF THE DISCIPLINE

Education was and is an ethical enterprise. Even for those who do not subscribe to the modernist and enlightenment project of which education is such a central part, there is no denial that education is essentially about the realisation of change in terms of some predefined sense of an 'educational good'. It is not surprising therefore that what Shilling (1993) calls the 'redemptive tradition' should be so strong in education.

Given its normative orientation, it is somewhat surprising that egalitarian theory emanating from political philosophy has had very little direct bearing on equality-related research in education. Yet this is not unique to education; Roemer (1996) has identified a similar phenomenon in economics, his own work being written especially to fill this void. While the lack of daily interface between political theorists and educationalists generally (especially in education departments, where political theorists are rarely employed) is undoubtedly a contributing factor, the fact that much of what is written in egalitarian theory is highly individualist in focus, and does not engage with institutional and structural issues in a way that is familiar to sociologists (Young, 1990:3–7), may also be significant. A deeper engagement with normative political theorists could, I believe, help to develop the conceptual frameworks utilised by sociologists in the analysis of inequality, many of which remain vague and ill-defined.

The absence of a clear link between egalitarian theory and the sociological analysis of equality in education does not mean that sociologists have remained apolitical in their research. There is, I would suggest, a deep liberalism underpinning much of the analysis of equality within the sociology of education.

As the development of the sociology of education, especially in Europe and the US, has been most evident since the 1950s, it is not too surprising that the normative principles which inspired work in the sociology of education were strongly influenced by the political culture of the post-war years. The aims of the post-war settlement were not only to promote full employment and prosperity but to ensure that all benefited in some way from this prosperity. Education was seen as a key instrument in this social design; it was a tool of social engineering (Finch, 1984). The goal in most welfare capitalist states was neither to reorder the structures of power and control, nor to reconstitute the ownership of industrial, agricultural or service capital. The goal was to redistribute rather than restructure (Arnot, 1992:43). Education was central to the redistributive project as it combined the goal of personal fulfilment with the goal of economic development. Expenditure on education met workers' demands for a greater equalisation of opportunity, and capital's demand for a skilled labour force. Education was also seen as the ideal tool in the realisation of the modernist project of 'progressive development'.

Most Western sociologists of education are working within capitalist states pursuing liberal democratic politics both within and without education for the last twenty years. Sociological work has inevitably been influenced by the politico-cultural contexts in which it developed, not least because of its heavy reliance on state funding for major empirical studies. The research themes which are funded by the state are inevitably those which interest the state[3] in terms of its own policy implementation. Reliance on such funding creates an interdependence between the state's project and the research preoccupations of academic sociologists, the dangers of which have been documented by Karabel and Halsey (1977). While this does not hold true for all sociologists, especially those who are writing in a critical mode, or who are employing research methodologies which do not visibly answer the types of questions that concern education decision-makers, it does apply to a significant number of researchers, especially those undertaking large-scale survey research. The cost of this is such that researchers were, and are, largely dependent, either directly or indirectly, on governments to fund it. Proof of the extent of sociologists' involvement in researching the state's educational reform project was evident in Britain in the eighteen years of Conservative government up to 1997. The equality project, even in its weak liberal form, was not the state project at that time. Consequently, sociology of education, which was seen by some to be synonymous with critical thought, was poorly funded over the period. It worked under siege (Dale, 1992), being characterised by its critics as irrelevant, politically biased and demonstrating weak scholarship (Dawson, 1981; Cox and Marks, 1982).

The normative egalitarian orientation which has dominated Western sociology of education has therefore been political liberalism (Middleton, 1990; Arnot, 1991; Lynch, 1995a). With the exception of the work of the more radical of the critical theorists, educational reformism not radicalism underpins most of the writing in the field. The proof of how liberal reformism dominates educational thinking is evident from the way in which sociologists define (or fail to define) egalitarian objectives in education.

3. WHICH EQUALITY OBJECTIVES[4] INFORM THE ANALYSIS WITHIN THE DISCIPLINE?

Equality empiricists within both quantitative and qualitative traditions work out of similar assumptions regarding the nature of inequality in society. It is a fundamentally liberal political perspective on equality[5] Equality objectives are defined in basically three different ways within this literature (although definitions are rarely used and equality terms are not clarified). The minimalist conception is one where equality is defined in terms of *equalising access* to different levels of education for relatively disadvantaged groups within a stratified society and educational system. Moving from this, certain researchers focus on *equal participation*, although participation has been largely measured and interpreted in access terms. In other words, access to different sectors of education was, and is, a central concern. Equality of participation is assessed, not so much in terms of the quality of educational experience available to students, but rather in terms of movement up to a given stage of the educational or social ladder.

Equality empiricists have therefore implicitly endorsed the meritocratic model of education. They assume that success should be measured on the basis of achieved rather than ascribed qualities — ability and effort, rather than social class, family connections, gender, race, etc. Equality is measured in terms of how far any given disadvantaged group has progressed in accessing a hitherto inaccessible 'educational good', and in particular, by examining what proportion of the disadvantaged group have accessed a particular education sector or position relative to their proportion in the general population and/or relative to some appropriate comparator group. Equality is deemed to be promoted if social class, gender, racial or other inequalities/advantages in education are proportionately distributed across social groups; the closer the participation or success ratio is to one, the greater the equality achieved. Thus whether one is measuring the progression of women into positions of management in education, or the progression of lower socio-economic groups to higher education, *the criterion for measuring equality is essentially proportionate representation for the target group* at given stages of education, or in terms of given outcomes. As lengthy participation in second-level education has become almost universal in Western countries, **proportionate access** to different levels and types of **higher education** has become the commonest measure for assessing racial, religious, social-class (more often socio-economic) and occasionally gender inequality in education.

In so far as equality empiricists focus on differences between social groups in terms of educational attainment, they move from a weaker to a stronger conception of equality; from a concern with equality of access and participation to *equality of outcome*. Studies which focus on levels of performance (measured in terms of years of schooling completed, grades attained, job obtained, etc.) highlight the fact that equalising formal rights to education, or proportionate patterns of participation, does not equate with equal rates of success or outcomes for disadvantaged groups. Data documenting high drop-out rates, poor academic performance or poor employment opportunities show the limits of weaker notions of equality, in particular conceptions of equality which focus on equal access.

The liberal model of equality which informs the work of equality empiricists operates along a continuum. In its weakest form, it focuses on issues of equal formal rights and access, while in its more radical mode, it addresses the question of differences in educational outcome for particular social groups. This model of analysis has, and will continue to have, an important contribution to make to sociological thought as it provides a clear map, over time, of how educationally stratified our society is in gender, social class, racial or other terms. It lays down the empirical (generally, but not always, statistical) floor on which other analyses can build. Without such work, it would be very difficult to have a clear profile of what progress (or lack of it) is taking place in educational opportunities for various groups vis-à-vis more advantaged groups.

But the liberal definitions of equality are but one possible set of definitions. A radical perspective suggests that equality be defined as equality of respect and/or equality of economic and political condition.

LIMITATIONS OF THE DISTRIBUTIVE MODEL OF JUSTICE: EQUALITY OF RESPECT

Equality empiricists operate out of a distributive model of justice and tend to regard education as an unproblematic 'good'. Education is defined as a 'primary good' (even though few use this Rawlsian phrase, this is effectively how education is understood) which can be distributed to greater or lesser degrees of equality between social groups in society. The most fundamental underlying weakness of this distributive model of justice is its failure to question what kind of education is being provided; its indifference to the nature of education itself. As Connell (1993:18) observes, 'education is a social process in which the "how much" cannot be separated from the "what". There is an inescapable link between distribution and content.'

What the equality empiricists have not addressed is the role of curriculum itself in the perpetuation of inequality. Yet as other sociologists have shown (Young, 1971; Bourdieu and Passeron, 1977; Anyon, 1980; Arnot, 1982; Lather, 1991; Connell, 1993), the school or college curriculum is not neutral. It is classed, gendered and raced in its orientation. It perpetuates particular cultural traditions at the expense of others, and in so doing reinforces images of what is or is not culturally valuable in a given society. If one's cultural traditions and practices are not a valued part of the education one receives, if they are denigrated or omitted, then schooling itself becomes a place where one's identity is denied or one's voice is silenced. Women have experienced this in mainstream education for centuries, as have many minority racial and ethnic groups within different societies. On a global scale, colonised peoples have experienced it through the suppression of their language, their fundamental beliefs and their cultural practices through schooling. The process of schooling therefore can itself create a sense of being inferior regardless of individual mobility outcomes. It can and does fail to provide *equality of respect* for all social groups, either by denying their identity in curricular selection or organisation, or by adopting authoritarian forms of pedagogical relations which define learners as subordinate and passive recipients of knowledge. Indeed one may learn through schooling that the only way in which to succeed in the so-called meritocratic system is to adopt the intellectual and cultural interests of the dominant culture.

Debates developing around identity politics (especially through feminist writing) have challenged traditional assumptions about the benefits of a simple distributive model of justice, especially when applied to a complex institution such as education (Weiler, 1988; Young, 1990). Critical feminist and post-modernist analyses have problematised not just the content of education, but the organisation of pedagogical relations. Drawing on the work of Freire (1972a, 1972b, 1973) especially, they note how the process of schooling cannot be divorced from the outcome.

Even if schools may appear to have relative success in terms of the pro-portionality test mentioned above (and it is clear that they are having that effect especially for women), this signifies the realisation of just one form of equality, namely distributive equality. It does not address the question of equality of respect. If educational relations are organised around 'banking principles' where education is defined as a product to be distributed across groups, and if systems of hierarchy, teacher control and uncritical consumption order the patterns of pedagogical relations, then the possibilities for developing the type of critical egalitarian consciousness which Freire espoused seem rather remote. Learning within a hierarchical set of pedagogical relations in which the student is defined as a subordinate learner contradicts other egalitarian messages which may be given through the formal curriculum itself. The absence of dialogue in pedagogical practice presents learning as a top-down rather than a partnership process; it presents the learner as passive and subordinate, thereby reinforcing hierarchy which is anathema to the principle of equality itself. The code for pedagogical practice also extends beyond hierarchy; it generally involves exclusionary (social closure) mechanisms (whereby only the suitably qualified for a course are allowed to learn, for example) and assumptions about appropriate linguistic expression and modes of learning. In other words, the pedagogic act has a number of hidden or implicit messages about appropriate contexts for learning which can be quite distinct from the curriculum itself. These can be and are often anti-egalitarian (Bourdieu and Passeron, 1977). Such issues are not named as equality concerns within most of the empirical research literature on classrooms.

This is not to suggest that all mainstream education in schools is, to use Bourdieu's phrase, a system of 'symbolic violence' for it is patently not; there are aspects of curricula which are generalisable to all groups (literacy, numeracy, scientific method, etc.), and systems and a certain amount of order are necessary in a group learning context. Rather it is to suggest that there is little debate in most countries about the ordering of pedagogical relations and the effects of hierarchical relations on equality-related attitudes and processes. Moreover, equality of respect is rarely shown for minority and marginalised cultures and traditions within mainstream education.[6]

Neither is it being suggested that we engage in the naive possibilitarianism which has characterised much of the writing about teachers as transformative agents (Ellsworth, 1989). Rather, it is to note the need to restructure the learning environment so that its hidden curriculum of pedagogical practice does not defeat those egalitarian objectives schools may uphold, either through support programmes for equality of access, participation or outcome, or through curricular reform.

LIMITS OF LIBERAL POLICIES: EQUALITY OF ECONOMIC CONDITION

Critical theorists and feminists have been key players in moving the debate about equality beyond the question of distribution. Working out of a radical conception of equality, they have argued for *equality of condition*, focusing especially on equality of respect in the organisation of schooling itself — in terms of the structures of decision-making, the organisation of curricular selection and pedagogical relations.

Neo-Marxists have also addressed the problem of equality of condition, albeit from a more emphatically economistic perspective. While other critical theorists view equality of condition not only in economic terms but also in terms of equalising power and status relations *within the education system*, neo-Marxists emphasise the role of *equality of economic condition outside of schooling* for realising all other equality objectives. They argue that substantive equality in education, especially between social classes, is impossible in a highly class-stratified society (Althusser, 1972; Sharp and Green, 1975; Bowles and Gintis, 1976; Sarup, 1978; Sharp, 1980). Unlike liberal educationalists, they do not believe that education (however it be defined and restructured internally) can be egalitarian without radical changes in the social relations of production, distribution and exchange.

In so far as neo-Marxism tends to define education as a desirable 'good' which should be distributed equally across classes, it remains within the distributive tradition of social justice. Increasingly, however, neo-Marxists have moved beyond this position, to argue for the integration of principles of equality of economic condition with equality of respect (Apple, 1982; Arnot, 1992).

While few now subscribe to the strong economic determinism of the structural Marxists, there is validity to their more general argument regarding the importance of wider economic equality for the realisation of equality within education. This has been borne out by a range of studies in industrialised countries (Shavit and Blossfeld, 1993). This research shows how various educational reforms, with a broadly egalitarian remit, have not altered the nature of the relationship between social origins and educational attainment in most of the thirteen countries reviewed. There are only two exceptions, Sweden and the Netherlands. The country which showed the weakest link between social origin and attainment was Sweden, where there has been a consistent policy of equalising socio-economic conditions (through high taxation) between social groups (Blossfeld and Shavit, 1993:21). In effect, the equalisation of life chances *outside* of schools had a direct effect on improving educational chances *within* schools.

What this demonstrates is that inequality in education cannot be understood independently of other institutions and systems in society; in particular that it cannot be understood independently of the politico-economic subsystem. While equality of respect (in terms of restructuring curricula, school organisation and pedagogical relations) is undoubtedly a logical possibility in schools without a radical redistribution of wealth and power outside of schools — given the relative autonomy of schools as social institutions — nevertheless if substantive change is sought, this must be paralleled by comparable changes in the related politico-economic realms. If education alone is made the principal site of change within the state, this allows powerful interests and classes, which may be disadvantaged by change, to use other politico-economic contexts of action to subvert the outcomes of egalitarian-oriented state policies.[7] Moreover, education-specific groups who manage and mediate the education service[8] are also able to resist change to the detriment of equality values (Lynch, 1990).

While there is no neat synchrony between education mediators and the owners and controllers of power and wealth in society, the reality is that education decision-makers are much more likely to be drawn from the same social groups as the economic and political elite than they are likely to be drawn from marginalised groups (Lynch, 1996).[9] Their own class and status position is frequently dependent on maintaining the existing order of cultural relations in education (not least of which is the substantial income differential that exists between so-called mental workers and manual workers) in most Western countries.

CONCLUSION

The distributive model of justice, most strongly espoused by the equality empiricists, has focused on *education as product*, while interpretative sociologists, critical theorists and feminists have emphasised the role of *education as process*. The latter have focused attention on *equality of respect (status)* especially, but also on *equality of power*. They have moved the debate about equality objectives from a simple concern with *equalising quantities of education* attained, to concern for *equality as quality of experience* in education. In so doing, they have critiqued some of the most dearly held assumptions about what is defined as valuable education, be it in terms of curricula, school organisation or pedagogical practice. While certain neo-Marxists have remained within the distributive paradigm in their definition of equality objectives, others have gone beyond both the class-based meta-narrative and simple economic determinism; they have attempted to analyse gendered, racial and other forms of social exclusion in conjunction with social class *within* and *without* schools. Some have incorporated critical postmodernist thinking into their work in an attempt to address the limitations of the distributive perspective (Giroux, 1992). The principal contribution of neo-Marxist scholars has been their articulation of the role played by institutions and structures extraneous to education in promoting inequality within education in a stratified society.

4. Is Knowledge Defined in Traditional Positivist Terms or is there an Emancipatory Dimension to the Research and Theory?

and

5. Does the Discipline Identify Policy Frameworks or Strategic Practices for the Realisation of Equality?

Although there is considerable dissent as to how it should be defined and interpreted, equality remains a core value in Western democracies. It is enshrined in international treaties (including the EU Amsterdam Treaty of 1997), in the constitutional provisions of different states, in legislation and in public policies. Moreover, treating people equally is a fundamental premise of most ethical theories pertaining to the organisation of society (Sen, 1992:130). By implication therefore, *inequality* is construed in political theory and practice as both politically and morally undesirable. This has profound implications for the study of inequality in the social sciences, including inequality in education.

In studying inequality (and this is what most sociologists study rather than equality) we are investigating a social phenomenon which is itself in need of 'transformation'. Researchers have to ask therefore if their work plays a role in either domesticating this inequality or changing it. Not to ask the question is to ignore a fundamental reality of the phenomenon under study itself, namely its ethical dimension. The study of inequality is not like the study of social phenomena which are morally neutral in character; inequality is not a morally neutral subject, not least because of the various forms of human misery experienced by those who are subjected to it. Posing questions regarding the transformative dimensions of particular research approaches is justifiable therefore given the nature of the subject under study.

The epistemological stance adopted by equality empiricists has proved valuable in describing patterns of inequality in education. It has systematically documented the extent and nature of inequality in a wide range of different contexts; the empirical work undertaken in both the quantitative and qualitative traditions has kept the issue of equality in the public domain as an issue of ongoing concern for public policy-makers.

The extent to which research within the empirical traditions has successfully developed explanatory theories regarding the nature and persistence of inequality is much more debatable. Many of the major statistical studies document patterns of association but they often do not offer plausible sociological explanations for such patterns. So much emphasis is placed on developing appropriate method-ologies for documenting inequality that the underlying causes are oftentimes not systematically addressed. Interpretative studies have, to some extent, filled the explanatory gaps left by the 'scientific arithmetic' approaches which have dominated the analysis of equality issues within the empirical field. Mehan (1992:2) has identified three particular contributions made by ethnographic researchers to the understanding of inequality: '(1) introducing cultural elements into highly deterministic macrotheories, (2) injecting human agency into theories accounting for social inequality, and (3) opening the black box of schooling to examine the reflexive relations between institutional practices and students' careers.'

Both those working out of the interpretative and out of the quantitative research traditions have not generally adopted a critical theoretical stance in their approach to knowledge and understanding. Knowledge is not defined in the transformative sense as *knowledge as praxis*. It is presented as a set of facts about the world, be these interpretative or statistical facts. What is not recognised (overtly at least) within these traditions is that knowledge has *consequential* as well as existential correlations. That is to say, little attention is given to identifying the change-related possibilities and limitations of particular frameworks or theories of inequality. The world is presented as a given with a past, but only occasionally as a place with a future which is open to change and intervention.

Moreover, reflexivity is not encouraged within this tradition. It largely ignores the extent to which the documentation of particular realities in the symbolic systems of academic discourse creates new realities, not least of which is the new reality of the written and spoken word itself. By defining and naming particular perspectives on selected worlds, such worlds and perspectives become more real. The way in which the worlds and stories are interpreted or defined, the perspectives on which they are based, create particular emphases and pose certain policy options as more inevitable, feasible and desirable than others. The naming of certain realities creates silences around those particular realities which are not named. The silence problem is greatest in relation to those social realities which are difficult to document or even observe using the conventional methods of the social sciences, and among these 'hidden' realities are the relational systems of inequality. For inequality is fundamentally a relative phenomenon, and it is only through an understanding of relational systems (of wealth, power, control, definitions, etc.) that we can understand how it is produced and reproduced. Yet many relational systems are not overtly visible, not least because those living at different ends of the relational spectrum have no direct ties to each other which can be socially documented. Besides, much of the powerful decision-making in both educational and financial life goes on in arenas to which social scientists are not and will not be given access. If realities are presented as reified entities, created and structured in time and place, most of these complex questions about the limitations of empiricism, the use of knowledge, the potential of knowledge to realise or forestall change, will not be addressed.

As inequality is a morally undesirable phenomenon, exclusive reliance on research methodologies which have not facilitated emancipatory change (knowledge as praxis) must be challenged. Attempts to isolate questions regarding the validity of scientific theories from moral or political values (in the name of value freedom, Abraham, 1996) lead to the analytical neglect of the transformative potential of research and theorising.

This is not to suggest that empirical research in the social sciences cannot and does not influence policy and promote equality of treatment in certain contexts. There is no doubt that it does, although most sociologists of education have not incorporated the analysis of the transformative potential of their work into the research design. However, what has also to be noted is that there is no necessary or inevitable change-specific outcome from much research on inequality (Chambers, 1983; Oliver, 1992). And realising change has not been an explicit (although I have no doubt it has been an implicit) concern of sociologists in the empirical traditions. (The failure of sociologists of education and others analysing issues of inequality to 'come out' on this issue is indeed one of the reasons for setting up a separate field of Equality Studies in our own university (Lynch, 1995b).

Critical theorists and feminist writers have departed from the dominant epistemological standpoint in sociology of education and have explored the transformative potential of their own writing. They have attempted to identify routes for action, even though their efforts are, at times, construed as either naive or redundant (Dale, 1992). One of the reasons why critical theorists and feminists have been challenged in intellectual discourse is, I would suggest, because they have been more effective on critique than they have been in identifying strategies for action and change.

Identifying the sources of 'unwanted determinations' (Bhaskar, 1991) that produce problems or inequalities is not sufficient to guide the way for their removal. Within education, the identification of sites of resistance (Giroux, 1983) or 'counter hegemony' (Weiler, 1988) does not provide a systematic guide for action. We may know the context in which a problem or inequality emerges but we do not know how to change it. Or, more accurately perhaps, some ideas are developed about how to change certain aspects of it without any clear vision as to how to successfully introduce systemic and inter-systemic change.

At present, for example, much emphasis has been placed on the notion of counter-hegemonic resistance through a radical pedagogy of transformation (Aronowitz and Giroux, 1991; Giroux, 1992). Based largely on a Freirean model of education as conscientisation, educationalists assume that teachers can and will become agents of transformative action. As noted previously (Lynch, 1990) this thesis ignores the particular cultural and political configuration of relationships within which Freire's thesis emerged. It also oversimplifies the nature of power relations in education and the dynamics of change. It is a critical theory which has not systematically addressed the issue of *feasibility* in particular *cultural and political* contexts.

But critical theory in education also fails to address the *wholeness* of the education system. Transformative education could not occur without a simultaneous transformation of all the education subsystems including curriculum structures, management structures, organisational systems, teacher education, the state, educational mediators, etc. Yet little serious attention is given to addressing the way in which changes in pedagogical practices might interface with other systems. The fact that a change in one subsystem may have little overall effect on other systems is not really recognised. Neither is the interface of interests between the politico-economic sites and the educational sites adequately understood in the context of realising change.

It is rather simplistic to assume that the mechanisms that produce good and bad outcomes are always separable or indeed determinable in advance (Sayer,

1994). It is quite conceivable that the transformative action by teachers may well instigate a reactionary response. Instead of mobilising the left to action, it may well provoke the right to counter-resistance and attempts at domestication and incorporation (as has happened to trade unions who have become incorporated in the decision-making machinery of the state). This could, in turn, make radical change even less likely to happen.

Researchers may or may not engage with policy institutions or systems but there is no procedure built into research practice on inequality whereby the institutional frameworks or the strategic practices necessary for the realisation of greater equality can be developed. Universities and research institutes generally operate at polite distances from the very communities about whom they speak. While dialogues with named marginalised subjects can and do take place they are usually of a personal or ad hoc nature, they are not institutionalised in the structure of our research practice (Lynch and O'Neill, 1994).

CONCLUSION

In so far as sociologists of education work out of an epistemological framework of 'research as praxis', this largely occurs within the critical Marxist and feminist traditions. The work undertaken tends to be strong on the critique of inequality but weak on the theorisation of counterfactuals (specific alternatives). Few conceptions of alternative institutions and systems are systematically analysed and explored. While a normative utopian vision does inform and vivify the analysis, what would constitute a desirable alternative is far from clear. One of the reasons for the intellectual void in the analysis, is, I would tentatively suggest, the very distance which exists between researchers on inequality and those with ongoing direct experience of major inequalities, especially in low-income working-class, ethnic or other marginalised communities. The other is the lack of engagement with other practice-oriented researchers in the educational field, especially in fields such as developmental psychology or curriculum design, whose work is much more directly engaged with developing structures and systems for change.

6. TO WHAT EXTENT HAS RESEARCH AND THEORY IN THE SOCIOLOGY OF EDUCATION INVOLVED MARGINALISED OR OPPRESSED GROUPS IN DEFINING ITS NATURE AND PURPOSE?

DOMAINS OF PRIVILEGE: FREEDOM FROM NECESSITY AND URGENCY TO WRITE

Much of the early, and a considerable amount of the more recent, work of sociologists of education has been inspired by social reformism if not by radical politics. In Europe and in the United States, 'educational sociology'; as it was often known in its early days, was tied closely to the analysis of education-related social reforms. Sociologists themselves were often central to the reform movement, and sociology of education was strongly focused on policy (Karabel and Halsey, 1977; Trent et al., 1985; Drudy, 1991; Dale, 1992; Noblit and Pink, 1995; Wesselingh, 1996). In more recent times, sociology of education has become more diverse, and there is a large body of work which is not especially concerned with issues of equality. Nonetheless there is a strong critical sociological tradition within education in the US, in Europe and in Australia, and an equally critical feminist tradition (Apple, 1979, 1982, 1986; Arnot, 1982; Arnot and Weiner, 1987; Aronowitz and Giroux, 1991; Lather, 1991; Giroux, 1992; Casey, 1993; Connell, 1993; McLaren, 1995).

What is not often problematised within sociology of education, however, is the position of academics themselves. Although sociologists of education writing about equality may view themselves as radical, reforming, feminist or emancipatory, the structural conditions of their own writing have not been subjected to much analysis and critique. Yet professional academics, no matter how radical their private political orientations, occupy a particular location within the class system (Bourdieu, 1993:36–48). The concept of the 'free-floating, disinterested intellectual' may be part of the ideology of academia but it is not grounded in any sociological reality. Being part of the cultural elite in society, academics have interests. No matter how uncomfortable radical intellectuals may feel with this mantle of cultural elitism, it is the one which provides them with the structural conditions to write; it gives them credibility over other voices and reinforces the perception of superiority which maintains the salary differentials between themselves and other workers. Being granted 'the freedom from necessity to write and discuss' is a privilege which academics in well-funded universities are rarely asked to reflect upon.

Bourdieu (1993:45) seems to suggest that there is no easy resolution to this dilemma for radical intellectuals. He proposes a radical, ongoing reflexivity wherein one prepares 'the conditions for a critical knowledge of the limits of knowledge which is the precondition for true knowledge' as the principal protection available so that researchers know where they themselves stand in the classification system.

Even if academics do engage in ongoing reflexivity, this does not alter the structural conditions under which they work. Intellectuals work in institutions which lay down working conditions according to the dominant meritocratic ideology of our time — promotion is based on merit. The way in which merit is measured, for the most part, is in terms of conformity to the dominant norms of intellectual and academic discourses. This includes not only writing within the dominant paradigm (Kuhn, 1961) but writing about what is currently intellectually fashionable. Without at least a nodding recognition of the importance of the dominant discourses, then one's work is not likely to be published. And it is through their publications that intellectuals in universities are generally assessed.

Not only does the academy generally recognise only those who conform to the intellectual norms of the day, it penalises those who attempt to redefine the purpose of the academy. This acts as a very effective control on academic work, limiting and containing interests within the safe confines of the university. It also works effectively to preclude intellectuals from involving themselves, and the university, in radicalising initiatives due to the time commitments involved (Olson and Shopes, 1991). Research involving genuine partnership and dialogue is time-consuming and unpredictable in its outcomes; it must also be accessible to those about whom it is conducted. Accessibility is not valued in most academic circles. Time spent in 'dialogue' with marginalised groups does not produce career-rewarded publications unless it can be reconstituted for that purpose.

Thus, it is not surprising to find that marginalised groups have rarely been documented as being partners in research about themselves. (Even teachers and pupils, who are so often the subjects of research, are rarely partners in research projects and virtually never in theoretical expositions (Van Galen and Eaker, 1995).) Where sociologists have been involved in partnerships, it has mostly been (with the exception of a small number of activist writers) in a personal rather than a university capacity. The university itself has not been a major site of resistance.

The question of partnership is especially problematic for marginalised groups or communities who are structurally excluded from the academy by virtue of their class position. Unlike debates about other equality issues in education, including gender, race or disability, there has been no indigenous class-based analysis of educational inequalities (Lynch and O'Neill, 1994). Working-class children, men and women have all remained dependent on middle-class sponsors (be they middle-class by origin or by destination) to tell their story. In many respects, a form of intellectual and cultural colonisation has continued in the social class field, which has been partially superseded in the race and gender areas (and, but to a lesser degree, in other areas, such as disability) by oppressed groups talking and researching for themselves about themselves.

If there is to be a move to create more egalitarian, emancipatory research methodologies involving genuine partnership, academic institutions will have to reorganise radically the relations of research production (Lather, 1986). It would involve, at the very least, setting up Structures for Research Dialogue (whereby those directly affected by inequality are given formal status to participate in the research process) which would fundamentally challenge the view of academic as 'expert witness' on issues of equality/inequality. Such initiatives have implications for the operation of research programmes and university life generally which extend far beyond issues of research methodology. They involve an equalisation of perspectives on equality issues, rather than placing the academic voice as the leading 'expert' one (Lynch, 1999, forthcoming).

To date there has been little discussion of how to involve research subjects in defining the nature and purposes of research and theory in education with the exception of work by feminist educators and philosophers (Weiler, 1988; Stanley, 1990; Lather, 1991; Humphries and Truman, 1994; Humphries, 1997). Nor have there been many attempts to identify the kinds of institutional and strategic practices required to implement a truly participatory methodology. Such elaboration is essential, however, if those who are prescribing dialogue are to be taken seriously. Otherwise they will face the continued challenge posed by Sayer (1995) about the limits of radical theory, namely its failure to develop counterfactual proposals in the light of the critiques which it presents. It is only through entering into partnership with those directly affected by injustice that workable counterfactual proposals can be systematically developed. Theories of egalitarian change need to be grounded in the lifeworld of the marginalised. Otherwise academics are likely to prescribe utopian solutions which will be duly disregarded, not only by those in power but by the very groups they claim to assist. There is a need to marry community perspective with normative prescription, scientific analysis and policy appraisal.

Yet as long as egalitarian-oriented academics remain as 'detached' intellectuals, psychologically, socially and geographically removed from those about whom they write (the 'Other', in every sense), they are clearly not in a position to develop transformative theories informed and developed by the knowledge and experience of those directly exposed to inequality.

What is being suggested here is that dialogical relationships are not only crucial for the promotion of equality within schools and classrooms (Freire, 1972a), they are crucial for the development of effective equality policies in education at regional, national or international level. And the development of effective equality policies in education means that professional educators and researchers must be working **with** rather than for marginalised groups. A dialogical relationship is essential because of the danger inherent in any equality process that the marginalised group becomes the object of charitable desire or professional career/research interest; in either case, the danger is that the interest of the professional or the philanthropist will take precedence over the interest of the specific group. If this happens (and there is plenty of evidence that it did in the disability field in the UK and Ireland), the enactment of liberal reforms which give legitimacy to the work of the professionals but which have only marginal impact in terms of equality outcomes becomes the central concern. Without power-sharing between the target equality group, policy-makers and professionals, colonisation of the marginalised is often the unforeseen by-product of policy action.

Egalitarian-oriented sociologists of education face another contradiction which has been identified already in feminist writing (Stanley, 1990; Patai, 1991; Lather, 1991). The right to speak and name the social world is granted by virtue of one's standing in what is effectively an elite institution, an established college, research institute or university. The hierarchical (and mostly patriarchal) structures which underpin research production are what give researchers the 'freedom from necessity' to write, and to have one's perspectives privileged over other voices. Without such 'prestigious' institutional affiliations, most academics would become status-less names with nothing to differentiate them from the 'crowd'. Can one maintain moral and academic integrity if one writes about equality from a privileged location in a highly unequal place? There is no easy resolution of this dilemma, although the proposal to reorder the power relations of research production and distribution has the potential to address the problem, at least in some part.

CONCLUSION

It is clear, therefore, that the structural conditions of academic writing constrain egalitarian-oriented sociologists of education from moving outside the academy to dialogue and work with the marginalised and oppressed groups about whom they write. Yet through the naming and knowing they engage in via research and theory, sociologists come to 'own' at least part of the world of these groups. There is a sense in which the researcher knows aspects of their world better than the oppressed groups themselves. If sociologists merely use this knowledge for personal career advantage, there is a very real sense in which they engage in an act of 'colonisation' — that is to say, they take data about people and use it without any guarantee of return or dividend; nor do those about whom they write have any institutional mechanism for exercising control over those who 'write their world'. Sociologists who wish to undertake truly emancipatory research have to confront moral and career dilemmas to overcome such challenges. There are, however, very real institutional options which can restructure the conditions in which research is undertaken, and which can thereby overcome at least some of these dilemmas.

What is being suggested here is that if the conditions of research production about inequality are exclusive, and do not involve the oppressed themselves as partners, then there is a very real sense in which the research process becomes part of the equality problem.

SUMMARY AND CONCLUSION

What I have attempted to do in this chapter is to review a body of work, largely within the English-speaking tradition, in the light of key questions in egalitarian theory. I have attempted to critique sociological research and theory in education within a radical egalitarian frame in particular (Tawney, 1964; Cohen, 1981, 1989, 1995; Walzer, 1983; Nielsen, 1985; Baker, 1987, 1998; Young, 1990). Notwithstanding the above, it is also recognised that there is a valuable volume of work within the liberal tradition which has much to contribute to sociology in terms of conceptual clarification and elaboration on equality (Rawls, 1971, 1985; Sen, 1980, 1985, 1992, 1997).

Sociology of education is a normatively oriented discipline with a much greater focus on educational reform than radical change. While there is a radical tradition in sociology of education, this remains quite peripheral to much of its core analysis and research. What this has meant for the understanding (and the realisation) of equality in education is that most intellectual attention is focused on amending present processes, systems and structures rather than analysing the potential for radical transformation. The dominant models of explanation are those emanating from the empiricist tradition although the development of both critical and feminist theory has moved the debate about equality from a simple concern with distribution to concerns about equality of respect and status within schools. This has made the processes and quality of schooling itself a central theme in the equality debate. The rise of 'identity' politics within postmodernist analysis has also created new concerns in sociology of education. Difference is no longer defined in class, or even race or gender, terms, but also includes sexual orientation, ethnicity, religion, colour, disability, etc. There has therefore been a move towards a concept of *equality of condition*, defined in terms of equality of respect or status, and power. With the exception of those writing within a broadly neo-Marxist tradition, most sociologists of education have not focused on the issue of equality of economic condition as a core concern in their analysis. To the extent that sociologists have ignored economic inequalities (and concentrated increasingly on status- and power-related inequalities), they have peripheralised the debate about social-class-based inequality in education (Mac an Ghaill, 1996). While it may be entirely historically justified to move the debate about equality beyond issues of distribution, the fact that those who are most economically marginalised remain the most oppressed within any given oppressed group suggests strongly that addressing economic inequality remains fundamental to the realisation of non-distributive egalitarian objectives; it is difficult to imagine having substantive equality of respect between persons without an equalisation of economic resources.

A second theme of this chapter relates to the relationship between researchers, theorists and the research subject. Despite the development of a more inclusive language within the research community in recent years, marginalised groups have not generally been involved in defining the terms and conditions under which research on themselves is undertaken. They have remained (with some notable exceptions) the subjects of sociological analysis, not the partners in its design and development. The fact that marginalised and oppressed groups have been witnesses rather than partners in the research process has meant that theories of inequality have been framed often by those who are removed from the immediate and direct experience of deep inequality. If sociologists of education are to be more than chroniclers of injustice, they need to confront the ethical dilemma posed by researching the ethically loaded subject of inequality. We need to examine the transformative potential of their analysis on a systematic basis, rather than assume its effectiveness. Moreover we also need to query the value and worth of our own work to determine whether it is, in Freire's words, a force for domestication or for freedom. The only way in which this can be systematically determined is through direct dialogue and partnership with those about whom we research and write. Without such a partnership, it would be very difficult to develop any coherent theory of egalitarian change which would have genuine transformative potential; it needs to be owned by those most directly involved.

Finally, one of the principal arguments of this paper is that sociologists of education have been working out of a liberal political philosophy in much of their work. Although few articulate their liberal political premises, they form a deep structure of much intellectual thought in education. A fundamental assumption of much equality-based research is that effective equal opportunities policies can be implemented in and through education without radical equality of political and economic condition. As suggested elsewhere (Lynch, 1995a), there are strong grounds for believing that this position is untenable, not least because it chooses to ignore the dialectical relationship which exists between political power, material property, and cultural property such as education. Economic capital is readily translatable into cultural capital (Bourdieu and Passeron, 1977). Without an equalisation of income and wealth differentials, those with superior resources can always use these to improve their control over, and access to, 'credentialised cultural capital' and thereby maintain their position of relative advantage. Equality is not only impeded in the simple distributive sense when significant income and wealth differentials exist, however; it is also impeded in terms of equality of respect or status, as vulnerable groups struggle to define their own education and identity in the face of better-endowed and/or more organised groups.

Status attainment theory is especially open to these criticisms. It endorses the notion of social mobility as a solution to the problem of inequality for marginalised peoples and groups. What it ignores is the fact that even the most radical of the espoused objectives (equality of outcome) does not address the fundamental problem of hierarchies in power, wealth and privilege. What it merely proposes is to replace or supplement the existing elite, within the economic, political, educational and other hierarchies, with new elite from hitherto disadvantaged groups. As the structural inequalities remain intact, then it is self-evident that certain people must occupy highly disadvantaged positions. All that changes is the colour, gender, etc. of those who are at the top or the bottom. What liberals ignore is the fact that inequalities do not arise from the intrinsic nature or characteristics of marginalised or excluded groups but from the way in which their unique characteristics are handled. Moreover, inequalities persist because positions are differentially rewarded or resourced in terms of wealth, power and privilege, not because of the character of the people who occupy these positions. Yet most policies treat the marginalised or excluded group as the problem when the problem lies with the structures of the institutions and systems which people occupy and the attitudes of those who control them.

Liberal equality policies have come to predominate, not simply because these are the politics which are most politically palatable to the existing power-brokers in education, but also because the marginalised peoples and groups at which these policies are supposedly directed are not an integral part of the decision-making process. Their voices, if represented at all, are mediated by professionals (such as teachers, psychologists, doctors, social workers, health care workers, etc.) and other service agencies outside their control. And mediated voices are not, by definition, organic voices. To move beyond the liberal agenda, it is essential that the oppressed groups, which have been marginalised in educational decision-making, are brought into the policy-making and research design process at all stages as equal partners, with full and adequate rights of self-representation which are resourced and supported — be these women, working-class groups, racial or other minorities.

Sociologists are not omniscient; the sociological window is but one window on the education world. If sociologists are to be effective in developing theories for equality-oriented practice, they also need to engage in collaborative research with academics (and educationalists and teachers) outside their own discipline. This applies both to those sociologists who are working with macro-systems-related equality issues, and those working with micro-processes in schools and classrooms. The credibility of critical sociology, especially, is greatly undermined when it fails to develop credible counterfactual proposals for educational change.

REFERENCES

Abraham, J. (1996). Positivism, prejudice and progress in the sociology of education: who's afraid of values? *British Journal of Sociology of Education*, 17:81–6.

Acker, S. (1987). Feminist theory and the study of gender and education. *International Review of Education*, 33:419–35.

Acker, S. (1994). *Gendered Education: Sociological Perspectives on Women, Teaching and Feminism*. Milton Keynes: Open University Press.

Alexander, K.L., Cook, M., and McDill, L. (1978). Curriculum tracking and educational stratification: some further evidence. *American Sociological Review*, 43:47–66.

Alexander, K.L., Pallas, A.M., and Holupka, S. (1987). Consistency and change in educational stratification: recent trends regarding social background and college access. In R.V. Robinson (ed.), *Research in Social Stratification and Mobility*, vol. 6. Greenwich (CT): JAI Press.

Althusser, L. (1972). Ideology and ideological state apparatuses. In B. Cosin (ed.), *Education, Structure and Society*. Harmondsworth, Middlesex: Penguin.

Anyon, J. (1980). Social class and the hidden curriculum of work. *Journal of Education*, 162 (1):67–92.

Anyon, J. (1983). Intersections of gender and class. In S. Walker and L. Barton (eds.), *Gender, Class and Education*. Lewes: Falmer Press.

Apple, M.W. (1979). *Ideology and Curriculum*. New York: Routledge.

Apple, M.W. (1982). *Education and Power*. New York: Routledge.

Apple, M.W. (1986). *Teachers and Texts: A Political Economy of Class and Gender Relations in Education*. New York: Routledge & Kegan Paul.

Apple, M.W. (1996). Power, meaning and identity: critical sociology of education in the United States. *British Journal of Sociology of Education*, 17:125–44.

Apple, M.W., and Weiss, L. (eds.) (1983). *Ideology and Practice in Schooling*. Philadelphia: Temple University Press.

Archer, M. (1984). *Social Origins of Educational Systems*. London: Sage.

Arnot, M. (1982). Male hegemony, social class and women's education. *Journal of Education*, 164 (1):64–89.

Arnot, M. (1991). Equality and democracy: a decade of struggle over education. *British Journal of Sociology of Education*, 12 (4):447–66.

Arnot, M. (1992). Feminism, education and the new right. In M. Arnot and L. Barton (eds.), *Voicing Concerns: Sociological Perspectives on Contemporary Education Reforms*. Wallingford, Oxfordshire: Triangle Books Ltd.

Arnot, M., and Barton, L. (eds.) (1992). *Voicing Concerns: Sociological Perspectives on Contemporary Education Reforms*. Wallingford, Oxfordshire: Triangle Books Ltd.

Arnot, M., and Weiler, K. (eds.) (1993). *Feminism and Social Justice in Education: International Perspectives*. Lewes: Falmer Press.

Arnot, M., and Weiner, M. (eds.) (1987). *Gender and the Politics of Schooling*. London: Hutchinson.

Aronowitz, S., and Giroux, H. (1991). *Post-Modern Education: Politics, Culture and Social Criticism*. Minneapolis: University of Minnesota Press.

Baker, J. (1987). *Arguing for Equality*. New York: Verso.

Baker, J. (1997). Studying equality. *Imprints*, 2 (1):57–71.

Baker, J. (1998). Equality. In S. Healy and B. Reynolds (eds.), *Social Policy in Ireland: Principles, Practices and Problems*. Dublin: Oak Tree Press.

Ball, S.J. (1981). *Beachside Comprehensive: A Case Study of Secondary Schooling*. Cambridge University Press.

Ball, S.J. (1987). *The Micro-Politics of the School: Towards a Theory of School Organisation*. London: Methuen.

Barton, L. (ed.) (1996). *Disability and Society: Emerging Issues and Insights*. Harlow, Essex: Addison Wesley Longman.

Barton, L., and Tomlinson, S. (eds.) (1984). *Special Education and Social Interests*. Beckenham, UK: Croom Helm.

Bernstein, B. (1971). *Class, Codes and Control: Vol. 1, Theoretical Studies towards a Sociology of Language*. London: Routledge & Kegan Paul.

Bernstein, B. (1975). *Class, Codes and Control: Vol. 3, Towards a Theory of Educational Transmissions*. London: Routledge & Kegan Paul.

Bhaskar, R. (1991). *Reclaiming Reality*. New York: Verso.

Blackledge, D., and Hunt, B. (1985). *Sociological Interpretations of Education*. London: Croom Helm.

Blossfeld, H.P., and Shavit, Y. (1993). Persisting barriers: changes in educational opportunities in thirteen countries. In Y. Shavit and H.P. Blossfeld (eds.), *Persistent Inequality: Changing Educational Attainment in Thirteen Countries*. Oxford: Westview Press.

Bourdieu, P. (1973). Cultural reproduction and social reproduction. In R. Brown (ed.), *Knowledge, Education and Cultural Change*. London: Tavistock.

Bourdieu, P. (1993). *Sociology in Question*. London: Sage.

Bourdieu, P., and Passeron, J.-C. (1977). *Reproduction in Education, Society and Culture*. London: Sage.

Bowles, S., and Gintis, H. (1976). *Schooling in Capitalist America*. New York: Basic Books.

Breen, R., Hannan, D., Rottman, D., and Whelan, C.T. (1990). *Understanding Contemporary Ireland*. Dublin: Gill & Macmillan.

Carr, W., and Kemmis, S. (eds.) (1986). *Becoming Critical: Education, Knowledge and Action Research*. Lewes: Falmer Press.

Casey, K. (1993). *I Answer with My Life*. New York: Routledge.

Chambers, R. (1983). *Rural Development: Putting the Last First*. Harlow, Essex: Longman.

Clancy, P. (1988). *Who Goes to College*. Dublin: Higher Education Authority.

Clancy, P. (1995). *Access to College: Patterns of Continuity and Change*. Dublin: Higher Education Authority.

Cohen, G.A. (1981). Freedom, justice and capitalism. *New Left Review*, 126:3–16.

Cohen, G.A. (1989). On the currency of egalitarian justice. *Ethics*, 99 (July):906–44.

Cohen, G.A. (1995). *Self-Ownership, Freedom and Equality*. Cambridge University Press.

Coleman, J., et al. (1966). *Equality of Educational Opportunity*. Washington, DC: US Department of Health, Education and Welfare.

Collins, R. (1979). *The Credential Society: An Historical Sociology of Education and Stratification*. New York: Academic Press.

Connell, R.W. (1993). *Schools and Social Justice*. Philadelphia: Temple University Press.

Coolahan, J. (ed.) (1994). *Report on the National Education Convention*. Dublin: Government Publications Office.

Cox, C., and Marks, J. (1982). What has Athens to do with Jerusalem?: teaching sociology to students on medical, nursing, education and science courses. In C. Cox and J. Marks (eds.), *The Right to Learn: Purpose, Professionalism and Accountability in State Education*. London: Centre for Policy Studies.

Cusick, P. (1973). *Inside High School: The Student's World*. New York: Holt, Rinehart and Winston.

Dale, R. (1992). Recovering from a pyrrhic victory? Quality, relevance and impact in the sociology of education. In M. Arnot and L. Barton (eds.), *Voicing Concerns: Sociological Perspectives on Contemporary Education Reforms*. Wallingford, Oxfordshire: Triangle Books Ltd.

Dawson, G. (1981). Unfitting teachers to teach: sociology in the training of teachers. In D. Anderson (ed.), *The Pied Pipers of Education*. London: Social Affairs.

Deem, R. (1980). *Schooling for Women's Work*. London: Routledge.

Delamont, S. (1983). *Interaction in the Classroom*. London: Methuen.

Denscombe, M. (1985). *Classroom Control: A Sociological Perspective*. London: Allen & Unwin.

DiMaggio, P. (1982). Cultural capital and school success. *American Sociological Review*, 47:189–201.

Donald, J., and Rattansi, A. (eds.) (1992). *Race, Culture and Difference*. London: Open University/Sage.

Dronkers, J. (1983). Have inequalities in educational opportunities changed in the Netherlands? A review of empirical evidence. *Netherlands Journal of Sociology*, 19:133–50.

Drudy, S. (1991). The sociology of education in Ireland, 1966–1991. *Irish Journal of Sociology*, 1:107–27.

Duru-Bellat, M. (1996). Social inequalities in French secondary schools: from figures to theories. *British Journal of Sociology of Education*, 17:341–50.

Duru-Bellat, M., Jarousse, J.P., and Mingat, A. (1993). Les scolarités de la maternelle au lycée: étapes et processus dans la production des inégalités sociales. *Revue Française de Sociologie*, 34:43–60.

Eckland, B.K., and Alexander, K.L. (1980). The national longtitudinal study of the high school class of 1972. In A.C. Kerckhoff (ed.), *Research in Sociology of Education*, vol. 1. Greenwich (CT): JAI Press.

Ellsworth, E. (1989). Why doesn't this feel empowering? *Harvard Educational Review*, 59:297–324.

Epstein, D. (1994). *Challenging Lesbian and Gay Inequalities in Education*. Buckingham, UK: Open University Press.

Equality Studies Centre (1995). Equality proofing issues. Paper presented to the National Economic and Social Forum, Dublin Castle, April. Dublin: Equality Studies Centre, University College Dublin.

Euriat, M., and Thelot, C. (1995). Le recrutement social de l'élite scolaire en France: l'évolution des inégalités de 1950 à 1990. *Revue Française de Sociologie*, 36:403–38.

Finch, J. (1984). *Education and Social Policy*. London: Longman.

Freire, P. (1972a). *Pedagogy of the Oppressed*. New York: Penguin.

Freire, P. (1972b). *Cultural Action for Freedom*. New York: Penguin.

Freire, P. (1973). *Education for Critical Consciousness*. New York: Continuum.

Gambetta, D. (1987). *Were They Pushed or Did They Jump?* Cambridge University Press.

Gamoran, A. (1996). Curriculum standardization and equality of opportunity in Scottish secondary education: 1984–1990. *Sociology of Education*, 69:1–21.

Ganzeboom, H.B.G., Luijkz, R., and Treiman, D.T. (1989). Intergenerational class mobility in comparative perspective. In A. Kalleberg (ed.), *Research in Social Stratification and Mobility*, 8. Greenwich (CT), JAI Press.

Giroux, H. (1983). *Theory and Resistance in Education: A Pedagogy for the Opposition*. Amherst: Bergin and Garvey.

Giroux, H. (1992). *Border Crossings*. New York: Routledge.

Goldthorpe, J.H., et al. (1980). *Social Mobility and Class Structure in Modern Britain*. Oxford: Clarendon Press.

Gouldner, A.V. (1970). *The Coming Crisis of Western Sociology*. London: Heinemann.

Hall, S. (1986). Variants of liberalism. In J. Donald and S. Hall (eds.), *Politics and Ideology*. Milton Keynes: Open University Press.

Hallinan, M.T. (1992). The organization of students for instruction in the middle school. *Sociology of Education*. 65:114–27.

Hallinan, M.T., and Sorensen, A.B. (1983). The formation and stability of instructional groups. *American Sociological Review*, 48:838–51.

Halsey, A.H., Heath, A., and Ridge, J.M. (1980). *Origins and Destinations*. Oxford: Clarendon Press.

Hammersley, M. (1995). *The Politics of Social Research*. London: Sage.

Hannan, D., and Boyle, M. (1987). *Schooling Decisions: The Origins and Consequences of Selection and Streaming in Irish Post-Primary Schools*. Dublin: Economic and Social Research Institute.

Hartman, H. (1976). Capitalism, patriarchy and job segregation by sex. Originally published as a supplement to *Signs*, 1 (3), part 2.

Heath, S.B. (1982). Questioning at home and at school: a comparative study. In G.D. Spindler (ed.), *Doing the Ethnography of Schooling*. New York: Holt, Rinehart and Winston.

Higher Education Authority (1995). *Report of the Steering Committee on the Future Development of Higher Education*. Dublin: Higher Education Authority.

hooks, b. (1982). *Ain't I a Woman: Black Women and Feminism*. London: Pluto Press.

Humphries, B. (1997). From critical thought to emancipatory action: contradictory research goals? *Sociological Research Online*, 2 (1) www.socresonline.org.uk.

Humphries, B., and Truman, C. (eds.) (1994). *Re-thinking Social Research: Anti-Discriminatory Approaches in Research Methodology*. Aldershot: Avebury.

Hurn, C. (1978). *The Limits and Possibilities of Schooling*. Boston: Allyn and Bacon.

Jonsson, J.O. (1987). Class origin, cultural origin, and educational attainment: the case of Sweden. *European Sociological Review*, 3:229–42.

Karabel, J., and Halsey, A.H. (1977). Educational research: a review and interpretation. In J. Karabel and A.H. Halsey (eds.), *Power and Ideology in Education*. New York: Oxford University Press.

Keddie, N. (1971). Classroom knowledge. In M.F.D. Young (ed.), *Knowledge and Control*. Middlesex, UK: Collier Macmillan.

Kerckhoff, A.C. (1984). The current state of mobility research. *Sociological Quarterly*, 25:139–53.

Kuhn, T. (1961). *The Structure of Scientific Revolutions*. Chicago University Press.

Lareau, A. (1987). Social class differences in family-school relationships: the importance of cultural capital. *Sociology of Education*, 60:73–85.

Lareau, A. (1989). *Home Advantage: Social Class and Parental Intervention in Elementary Education*. New York: Falmer Press.

Lather, P. (1986). Research as praxis. *Harvard Educational Review*, 56:257–77.

Lather, P. (1991). *Getting Smart: Feminist Research and Pedagogy With/In the Postmodern*. New York: Routledge.

Livingstone, D.W. (1985). *A Critical Pedagogy and Cultural Power*. New York: Bergin and Garvey.

Lynch, K. (1987). Dominant ideologies in Irish educational thought: consensualism, essentialism and meritocratic individualism. *Economic and Social Review*, 18:101–22.

Lynch, K. (1989). *The Hidden Curriculum: Reproduction in Education, A Reappraisal*. Lewes: Falmer Press.

Lynch, K. (1995a). The limits of liberalism for the promotion of equality in education. In E. Befring (ed.), *Teacher Education for Equality: Papers from the 20th Annual Conference of the Association for Teacher Education in Europe*. Norway: Oslo College.

Lynch, K. (1995b). Equality and resistance in higher education. *International Studies in Sociology of Education*, 5:93–111.

Lynch, K. (1996). Election to Dáil Éireann, the Seanad and the issue of representativeness. In Government of Ireland, *Report of the Constitution Review Group*. Dublin: Government Publications Office.

Lynch, K. (1999, forthcoming). Equality studies, the academy and the role of research in emancipatory social change. *Economic and Social Review*, 30 (1).

Lynch, K., and O'Neill, C. (1994). The colonisation of social class in education. *British Journal of Sociology of Education*, 15:307–24.

Mac an Ghaill, M. (1996). Sociology of education: state schooling and social class: beyond critiques of the New Right hegemony. *British Journal of Sociology of Education*, 17:163–76.

McLaren, P. (1995). *Critical Pedagogy and Predatory Culture*. New York: Routledge.

McPherson, A., and Willms, J.D. (1987). Equalisation and improvement: some effects of comprehensive reorganisation in Scotland. *Sociology*, 21:509–39.

McRobbie, A. (1978). Working-class girls and the culture of femininity. In Centre for Contemporary Cultural Studies Women's Studies Group, *Women Take Issue*. London: Hutchinson.

Mare, R.D. (1981). Change and stability in educational stratification. *American Sociological Review*, 46:72–87.

Mehan, H. (1992). Understanding inequality in schools: the contribution of interpretive studies. *Sociology of Education*, 65:1–20.

Mehan, H., Hetweck, A., and Lee Meihls, J. (1985). *Handicapping the Handicapped: Decision Making in Students' Careers*. Stanford University Press.

Middleton, S. (1990). Women, equality and equity in liberal educational policies, 1945–1988. In S. Middleton, J. Codd and A. Jones (eds.), *New Zealand Education Policy Today*. Wellington, New Zealand: Allen & Unwin.

Morrow, R.A., and Torres, C.A. (1995). *Social Theory and Education: A Critique of Theories of Social and Cultural Reproduction*. State University of New York Press.

Nielsen, K. (1985). *Equality and Liberty: A Defense of Radical Egalitarianism*. Totowa (NJ): Rowman and Allanheld.

Noblit, G.W., and Pink, W.T. (1995). Mapping the alternative paths. In W.T. Pink and G.W. Noblit (eds.), *Continuity and Contradiction: The Futures of the Sociology of Education*. New Jersey: Hampton Press.

Oakes, J. (1985). *Keeping Track: How Schools Structure Inequality*. New Haven (CT): Yale University Press.

Oakes, J., Gamoran, A., and Page, R. (1992). Curriculum differentiation: opportunities, outcomes and meanings. In. P.W. Jackson (ed.), *Handbook of Research on Curriculum*. Washington, DC: American Educational Research Association.

Oliver, M. (1990). *The Politics of Disablement*. Basingstoke: Macmillan.

Oliver, M. (1992). Changing the social relations of research production. *Disability, Handicap and Society*, 7:101–14.

Olson, K., and Shopes, L. (1991). Crossing boundaries: doing oral history among working-class women and men. In S.B. Gluck and D. Patai (eds.), *Women's Words: The Feminist Practice of Oral History*. New York.

O'Sullivan, D. (1989). The ideational base of Irish educational policy. In D. Mulcahy and D. O'Sullivan (eds.), *Irish Educational Policy: Process and Substance*. Dublin: Institute of Public Administration.

Patai, D. (1991). US academics and Third World women: is ethical research possible? In S.B. Gluck and D. Patai (eds.), *Women's Words: The Feminist Practice of Oral History*. New York, pp. 137–53.

Pink, W.T., and Noblit, G.W. (eds.) (1995). *Continuity and Contradiction: The Futures of the Sociology of Education*. New Jersey: Hampton Press.

Raftery, A.E., and Hout, M. (1993). Maximally maintained inequality: expansion, reform and opportunity in Irish education, 1921–75. *Sociology of Education*, 66:41–62.

Rawls, J. (1971). *A Theory of Justice*. Oxford University Press.

Rawls, J. (1985). Justice as fairness: political not metaphysical. *Philosophy and Public Affairs*, 14:223–51.

Rist, R. (1972). *Restructuring American Education*. New Brunswick (NJ): Transaction Books.

Roemer, J.E. (1996). *Theories of Distributive Justice*. Cambridge (MA): Harvard University Press.

Rosenbaum, J. (1976). *Making Inequality: The Hidden Curriculum of High School Tracking*. New York: Wiley.

Rowan, B. (1995). Part I Introduction: School effects and status attainment research in education. In W.T. Pink and G.W. Noblit (eds.), *Continuity and Contradiction: The Futures of the Sociology of Education*. New Jersey: Hampton Press.

Sarup, M. (1978). *Marxism and Education*. London: Routledge & Kegan Paul.

Sayer, A. (1994). Alternatives and counterfactuals in critical social science. Paper presented at the XIII World Congress of Sociology, Beilefeld, Germany, 18–23 July.

Sayer, A. (1995). *Radical Political Economy: A Critique*. Oxford: Basil Blackwell.

Sen, A. (1980). Equality of what? In S. McMurrin (ed.), *Tanner Lectures on Human Values*. Cambridge University Press.

Sen, A. (1985). *Commodities and Capabilities*. Amsterdam: North-Holland.

Sen, A. (1992). *Inequality Reexamined*. Oxford: Clarendon Press.

Sen, A. (1997). *On Economic Inequality* (expanded edition and with an Annex by J.E. Foster and A. Sen). Oxford: Clarendon Press.

Sewell, W., Hauser, R., and Featherman, D.L. (1976). *Schooling and Achievement in American Society*. New York: Academic Press.

Sharp, R. (1980). *Knowledge, Ideology and the Politics of Schooling: Towards a Marxist Analysis of Education*. London: Routledge & Kegan Paul.

Sharp, R., and Green, A. (1975). *Education and Social Control*. London: Routledge & Kegan Paul.

Shavit, Y., and Blossfeld, H.P. (eds.) (1993). *Persistent Inequality: Changing Educational Attainment in Thirteen Countries*. Oxford: Westview Press.

Shilling, C. (1993). The demise of the sociology of education in Britain? Extended review, *British Journal of Sociology of Education*, 14 (1):105–12.

Singh, G. (1993). *Equality and Education*. Derby, UK: Albrighton Publications.

Spender, D. (1980). *Learning to Lose: Sexism in Education*. London: Women's Press.

Spender, D. (1985). *Manmade Language*. London: Routledge & Kegan Paul.

Stanley, L. (ed.) (1990). *Feminist Praxis*. London: Routledge.

Stanworth, M. (1981). *Gender and Schooling*. London: Hutchinson.

Tawney, R.H. (1964). *Equality*. London: Allen & Unwin.

Torres, C. (1990). *The Politics of Nonformal Education in Latin America*. New York: Praeger.

Torres, C. (1991). The state, nonformal education and socialism in Cuba, Nicaragua and Grenada. *Comparative Education Review*, 35:110–30.

Torres, C.A., and Rivera, G.G. (eds.) (1994). *Sociología de la Educación: Corrientes Contemporáneas*. 3rd edition, Buenos Aires: Miño y Davila Editores.

Trent, W., Braddock, J., and Henderson, R. (1985). Sociology of education: a focus on education as an institution. In E. Gordon (ed.). *Review of Research in Education*, 12. Washington, DC: American Educational Research Association.

Troyna, B., and Williams, J. (1986). *Racism, Education and the State.* Beckenham, UK: Croom Helm.

Van Galen, J., and Eaker, D.J. (1995). Beyond settling for scholarship: on defining the beginning and ending points of postmodern research. In W.T. Pink and G.W. Noblit (eds.), *Continuity and Contradiction: The Futures of the Sociology of Education.* New Jersey: Hampton Press.

Verma, G.K. (ed.) (1989). *Education for All: A Landmark in Pluralism.* Lewes: Falmer Press.

Verma, G.K., and Ashworth, B. (1986). *Ethnicity and Educational Achievement in British Schools.* London: Macmillan.

Walker, S., and Barton, L. (eds.) (1983). *Gender, Class and Education.* Lewes: Falmer Press.

Walzer, M. (1983). *Spheres of Justice.* New York: Basic Books.

Weiler, K. (1988). *Women Teaching for Change: Gender, Class and Power.* New York: Bergin and Garvey.

Weiss, L. (1995). Qualitative research in sociology of education: reflections on the 1970s and beyond. In W.T. Pink and G.W. Noblit (eds.), *Continuity and Contradiction: The Futures of the Sociology of Education.* New Jersey: Hampton Press.

Wesselingh, A. (1996). The Dutch sociology of education: its origins, significance and future. *British Journal of Sociology of Education*, 17:212–26.

Wexler, P. (1987). *Social Analysis of Education: After the New Sociology.* London: Routledge & Kegan Paul.

Whelan, C., and Whelan, B. (1984). *Social Mobility in Ireland: A Comparative Perspective.* Dublin: Economic and Social Research Institute.

Whitty, G. (1974). Sociology and the problem of radical educational change. In M. Flude and J. Ahier (eds.), *Educability, Schools and Ideology.* London: Halstead Press.

Whitty, G. (1985). *Sociology and School Knowledge: Curriculum Theory, Research and Politics.* London: Methuen.

Willis, P. (1977). *Learning to Labour: How Working Class Kids Get Working Class Jobs.* Westmead, UK: Saxon House.

Wolpe, A.M. (1977). Education and the sexual division of labour. In A. Kuhn and A.M. Wolpe (eds.), *Feminism and Materialism: Women and Modes of Production.* London: Routledge.

Wolpe, A.M. (1988). *Within School Walls: The Role of Discipline, Sexuality and the Curriculum.* London: Routledge.

Woods, P. (ed.) (1980). *Pupil Strategies: Explorations in the Sociology of the School.* London: Croom Helm.

Woods, P. (1983). *Sociology and the School: An Interactionist Viewpoint.* London: Routledge & Kegan Paul.

Young, M.F.D. (ed.) (1971). *Knowledge and Control.* Middlesex, UK: Collier Macmillan.

Young, I.M. (1990). *Justice and the Politics of Difference.* Princeton University Press.

NOTES

1   Domain assumptions are those non-theoretical beliefs and assumptions that we hold which have been developed through biographical experience. They are sets of values and beliefs which may arise from specific cultural, political, gender, religious or other experiences; they can and do predispose us to interpret and value phenomena in very different ways. They are

separate from our intellectual or 'paradigmatic assumptions', which arise from theoretical standpoints taken on particular issues. (See Gouldner, 1970 for a discussion on this.)

2   The political canvas in Ireland, for example, never followed the radical right-wing route of the UK in the 1980s and 1990s. Consequently, critical educationalists were allowed (and even encouraged at times) to be partners in major public debates and policy analyses in education (Coolahan, 1994). Sociologists who are known critics of government policy have, for example, been appointed to important research and policy committees throughout the 1990s.

3   The term 'state' here does not refer simply to the nation state. Within Europe, most of the larger research grants are now provided by cross-European bodies (under the auspices of the European Commission for Science, Research and Development) planning research goals for Europe as a whole.

4   Equality objectives can, in some respects, be regarded as operating along a continuum. At one end of the continuum is the minimalist conception which defines equality in terms of *equal formal rights and opportunities*. Within this tradition, equality is equated with the provision of equal rights to participate in educational (and economic, social, political and cultural) life, where such rights are construed as the absence of legal and institutionalised barriers to entry and participation in a given institution or system. This view is linked to the idea of formal equality of opportunity, i.e. the idea that no one should be prevented from entry to education, employment, politics, etc., or from advancing from one level of participation to another, on the grounds of gender, sexual orientation, ethnicity, disability, or any other irrelevant characteristic, and that access to, and advancement within, these institutions should be based on merit. *Equality of participation* represents a stage beyond this where the focus is on **enabling** and **encouraging** members of different social groups to be equally able to participate in society, while *equality of success or outcome* is concerned with ensuring equal rates of success for target individuals and groups. At the opposite end of the continuum from *equal formal rights* is the concept of *equality of condition*, which aims at creating equality in the living conditions of all members of society. This refers to an ideal state where all goods, privileges and resources are distributed equally according to need. For a more detailed discussion of what is meant by equality of access, participation, outcome and condition see Equality Studies Centre (1995).

5   At the very least we need the type of counter-hegemonic curricular developments which Connell (1993) proposes. There is a need not to create curricular ghettos for the disadvantaged. Rather there is a need to '*reconstruct the mainstream* to embody the interests of the least advantaged' (p. 44).

6   A clear example of this has occurred in Ireland and Japan, both of which have highly competitive (ostensibly meritocratic, though substantively not) systems for selecting students for higher education based purely on their examination performance. The groups disadvantaged by the new system have simply circumvented the universalistic practices of the state by funding an elaborate system of 'grinds' (special privately paid tutors) to teach their children outside of school exclusively for the examination. The net result has been that the higher professionals and other upper socio-economic groups are significantly over-represented in higher education; they have maintained their comparative advantage by exercising power and resources available to them outside of the school system (Higher Education Authority, 1995: Tables 10–13).

7   In the Irish case, the teacher unions, the churches and the regionally based vocational education committees are among the most powerful mediators of the service; the central government civil service exercises major powers over all schools as well.

8   Although 44% of the population belong to the lower non-manual, the skilled and unskilled manual groups combined, only 3.6% of the members of the Dáil (Irish parliament) come from these social backgrounds. Only a meagre 12% are women. Teachers and lecturers are, in fact, the most strongly represented occupational group in the Dáil (Lynch, 1996:492–8).

9   For critical commentaries on liberal perspectives on equality see Tawney, 1964; Hall, 1986; Baker, 1987.

CHAPTER 2

RESEARCHING INEQUALITY IN EDUCATION: ISSUES TO BE ADDRESSED

Kathleen Lynch and *Cathleen O'Neill*[1]

> *We are the subject of books and papers*
> *Our lives recorded by the middle class*
> *Who steal our stories, use our oppression*
> *To serve their own needs, they won't let us pass*[2]

RESEARCH AS COLONISATION

The role that academics and researchers have to play in contributing to egalitarian change is not always self-evident. While it is clear that they contribute to ideological formation in society (through education and research), how and when their contributions can or do feed into policy and political debates is far from clear. Moreover, it is not apparent that when they do contribute to policy or politics, their work will help to challenge inequalities rather than domesticate them.

Most academics and researchers are working in universities and research institutes which are involved in elite forms of knowledge production. These institutions are heavily engaged in the practice of cultural monopoly, not only through their selection procedures for students and staff, but through the rigorous boundary maintenance procedures which they uphold within and between disciplines, and between what is defined as academic knowledge and what is not (Bourdieu, 1990). How can we develop emancipatory research procedures therefore in research contexts which are far from emancipatory? How can we work towards research methods and modes of theoretical construction which are transformative in such contexts? What is suggested here is that we need to work towards methods of research design and planning in which those who are 'named' become real partners in research and not just the subjects of research. Only when the voices of those who are named is heard at the research planning table can we begin to know how to develop emancipatory research practice. The politics of presence needs to replace the politics of absence at the research-making table (Phillips, 1995).

A central thesis of this paper is that much of what passes for research in education and in the sciences (both social and physical) generally is in fact a domesticating form of research. It names people's worlds from a distance, often in language that they do not know. By so doing, it creates communities of 'experts' who can claim ownership of other people's worlds. Such experts can and do claim superior knowledge about given communities and their problems than they possess themselves. The further removed a given group or community is from the centre of research and theoretical decision-making, the more likely it is to be named without consultation, to be 'known' in its absence.

This chapter is especially concerned about the way in which theory and research on working-class people can have colonising effects, and the need to address this in education. It is recognised that similar issues arise for other groups who are the subjects of 'expert' research. Theories are developed, and research studies undertaken, on disabled people, Travellers, children, and even women, without ever consulting with these groups about the nature or purpose of the research. Teachers are also often the subjects of research, yet they are not partners in its design, nor are they informed about the results or the interpretation of results about themselves. The fact that so many researchers are men, and so many teachers are women, further compounds the power relations of research production in education. The inevitable outcome of lack of engagement between researchers and practitioners in education is the poor dissemination of research among practitioners (Hargreaves, 1996).

Children are especially vulnerable to the gaze of experts. Their own particular concerns about schooling are rarely the subject of study. Their assumed interests, from the perspective of adults, is what is mostly investigated. Children are rarely given a say in defining the research agenda about themselves (Qvortrup, 1994). The way in which research can serve the purposes of controlling and containing particular groups is clearly not, therefore, an exclusively social-class-specific problem. However, it poses very particular problems in a class context.

It is suggested here that the inequalities experienced in the education system by working-class people[3] have been colonised by middle-class academics for their own professional purposes. Much of this colonisation has been unintentional having been greatly facilitated by the nature of the scholastic context itself.

The failure to incorporate a working-class perspective on educational inequalities has led to the impoverishment of academic analysis, as sociologists and educationalists have tended to ignore the poverty-related barriers to equality in education. The absence of a working-class perspective has resulted in policies designed to manage rather than eliminate inequality in education.

What is concluded at the end of the paper is that new institutions need to be established within universities, higher education colleges and research institutes (*Structures for Research Dialogue*), which will enable research on social class and other issues to be researched in a real partnership manner.

THE LIMITATIONS OF THE ACADEMIC PERSPECTIVE

Our starting point is a questioning of the 'positionality of the theorist' (Spivak, 1988). Researchers from many different intellectual traditions have noted the importance of recognising the social context of knowledge production (Kuhn 1961; Cicourel, 1964; Gouldner, 1970; Gould, 1981; Smith, 1988; Oliver, 1992). Yet, as Harding (1991) observes, when the scholastic context of research production is subjected to critical analysis, the focus tends to be on the limits of positivism per se. This has given rise to a new orthodoxy, namely a shift from a quantitative to a qualitative or interpretative sociology. In the search for meaning and understanding, however, the interpretations are still made by 'experts' on relatively powerless research subjects. In so far as the power relations of research production remain the same in interpretative sociology as in the positivist tradition, then it is true to say that the research process can be equally alienating for the research subjects, especially when the latter are vulnerable and powerless (Oliver, 1992). And it is true to say that the vulnerable and the relatively powerless are the ones who are most often the subject of social scientific investigation as they lack the resources to protect themselves from scrutiny.

Exploited and oppressed groups, such as women, children and working-class people, become the subjects of theory and data analysis by sociological researchers in education. Theoretical constructs and data analysis about their position/condition circulate among professional intellectuals, and those who are the subjects of the discussion are generally excluded from the dialogue about themselves.

> What little documentation there is on working-class culture has been written 'from the outside in', by middle-class writers and researchers. Inevitably, many working-class customs tend to escape middle-class attention and working-class people have failed to document the networks, language and customs central to their lives. In this sense working-class culture is neither fully understood by those outside it, nor properly documented to encourage understanding. (O'Neill, 1992:27)

Not only are working-class people unable to participate/excluded from the dialogue, but they do not own what has been written about themselves. Their oppressions become commodified in books and papers which advance the careers of their middle-class bearers. By owning data about oppressed peoples the 'experts' own part of them. The very owning and controlling of the stories of oppression adds further to the oppression as it means that there are now people who can claim to know and understand you better than you understand yourself; there are experts there to interpret your world and to speak on your behalf. They take away your voice by speaking about you and for you.

It is the very idea of the act of social investigation as neutral that is at issue here. The question is, by naming someone else's world for them are we robbing them of a voice? By speaking *for* people do we misrepresent their point of view? Can professional sociologists, no matter how well intentioned or informed, give anything but an outsider's account of a working-class world? While there is no doubt that some type of understanding is provided by academic analysis, what is provided is often a formalistic account of the reality of the 'other'. The social parameters of working-class lives are documented in empirical analysis, from a distance; the structural location of working-class groups is analysed in theory. Exploitation, urgency, struggle and necessity are lost in a sea of statistics or theoretical abstractions. Gurnah (1992), writing about these issues in the context of racism, identifies the problems in the sociology of education as being those of formalism and empiricism.

> For within sociology there are still approaches which diminish our ability to analyse, in this case black people. Formalism and empiricism in sociology are such approaches. On the one hand, formalism is preoccupied with the realm of 'race' or 'IQ', definitions of 'racism' or ethnicity or 'culture', to the exclusion of an honest look at the concrete lives and struggles of black people. Recent sociological debates tend not to be over what class action can be taken nor about how communal organisation can counter the exploitation or neglect of black people. . . . Actual subjects of struggle and their activities, if you like, are put aside in favour of the exploration of overarching 'transcendental' definitions, in the mistaken belief, I think, that they will explain and direct every aspect of concrete black life. . . . In other words, instead of studying society, they end up studying elegant 'concepts', and, via them, seek what may be expected by the theory to exist in society.
>
> Sociological empiricists, on the other hand, flood us with 'facts' about black oppression, which can become repetitive or voyeuristic. For even when they give undeniable evidence of what that oppression looks like, they simultaneously also present accounts of how black people in western societies habitually are being degraded and humiliated. What is often missing in their accounts are corresponding tales of black people's efforts to improve or reverse their condition. (pp. 90–91)

The failure of researchers within both the theoretical and empirical traditions to engage on a partnership basis with communities and groups about whom they speak is a central issue here. The problem is compounded by the fact that most of those who are leaders in educational and sociological analysis do their analysis of class from the comfort and distance of their university chairs (of all kinds). Given the structure of power relations in research production, the most eminent can afford to be the most distant from the subjects of their research.

They are not required to dialogue or interact with the people about whom they speak. The authority of their position grants them immunity from class contact. The oppressed are an object of investigation, to be understood, analysed, and, if necessary, structurally located; they are not the people with whom they live, or whose struggles they share. What Gurnah (1992:100) observes about sociologists who study black people is equally true of those educationalists who study working-class people. Many of them know very little about the people they analyse, they do not speak their language, enjoy their company, or share their sense of humour and their difficulties in everyday life.

> Academics currently argue about how poverty should be measured. They are concerned about the correct position of the line which measures poverty. This is of little comfort to a whole sub culture of families in Kilmount drawing social welfare or working in low-paid jobs. (O'Neill, 1992:22)[4]

One of the difficulties for those working in the academy is that they are rewarded for providing accounts and theories which will be recognised and appreciated by other professional academics; whether they accord with the interests and views of working-class people is not an issue, as working-class people are structurally precluded from such debates by virtue of their educational status. Generally, there is no opportunity to contest the official academic interpretation of your world or culture.

If the 'Other' of Western civilisation is the colonised subject, so the colonised 'Other' in the sociology of education must surely be the working class. It is the one about whom most has been said but who never speaks back. (Within education research generally, of course, children occupy the status of the colonised 'Other' as well; much is written about them but they rarely speak in their own voice.) It is not being suggested here that there is some pure truth that exists about social class or that there is only one voice, that of the working class itself. We are not saying that there is no role for the academic or the intellectual. We are not trying to substitute 'the lost figure of the colonised' (in this case the working class) for intellectual analysis. What we are suggesting, at the very least, is that to avoid dissociating the reality of oppression from research analysis and theory, 'researchers have to learn how to put their knowledge and skills at the disposal of their research subjects, for them to use them in whatever ways they choose' (Oliver, 1992:111). The agenda for research and theory must be set in dialogue with people themselves. It cannot be set with reference to the interests of professional educationalists or sociologists alone.

Middle-class academics are but one voice, and because they frequently do not dialogue or live with those about whom they speak, there are valid reasons for questioning the representativeness of their voice. Also, ethical questions arise. Is it not a form of abuse to use other people's oppression for one's own academic ends, when there is no return for those who are used? While it is possible and even desirable to strive for value-freedom in the methods one employs in social investigation, how can one be value-free about the issues themselves, especially when the issues under investigation are those of oppression and exploitation? Traditional research faces a fundamental dilemma here as it encourages the analysis of oppression but goes no further; whether or not the exploitative conditions change is not theoretically a researcher's concern within the strong positivist tradition.

This is not to suggest that educational or sociological data never impact on policy, nor that they do not help to reformulate political opinion on issues and concerns which are of profound importance to oppressed groups. They do undoubtedly have some impact; how and what that impact is is far from clear (Hargreaves, 1996).

Moreover, if one examines the contexts in which policy works, it is evident that the availability of the data or the theory matters only in so far as it is in line with the interests of politically mobilised groups who are in a position to press for their implementation. There is no doubt that academically produced knowledge can be used as weaponry in the fight for change. However, if there is no one who knows how to use it or who is interested and powerful enough to push it, it can be redundant. As Chambers (1983:53) points out about research on rural poverty:

> Much of the material remains unprocessed, or if processed, unanalysed, or if analysed, not written up, or if written up not read, or if read not remembered, or if remembered, not used or acted upon. Only a minuscule proportion, if any, of the findings affect policy and they are usually a few simple totals. The totals have often been identified early on through physical counting of questionnaires or coding sheets and communicated verbally, independently of the main processing.

Even when research is utilised to inform policy, it may or may not be utilised in a manner which benefits oppressed groups. There is ample evidence from surveys of the higher education sector in Ireland that those from working-class backgrounds are seriously under-represented (Clancy, 1982, 1988, 1995). Yet there have been no major improvements in the funding or grants available to students from low-income backgrounds from 1980 to the present time. In fact, the government froze the level of grant payments in 1993 despite evidence that the maintenance grants were not adequate for those who are solely dependent on them.

Before going on to examine the contexts and practices which close off working-class voices in education, we will examine some of the work which has been written about class in sociology of education. We will comment especially on the work of those who have encouraged the development of resistance in education as they have been the writers who have most clearly tried to encourage transformative class action in education.

THE ANALYSIS OF SOCIAL CLASS INEQUALITY

Unlike debates about other equality issues in education, including gender, race or disability, especially over the last ten or fifteen years, there has been no indigenous class-based analysis of educational inequalities. Working-class children, men and women have all remained dependent on middle-class sponsors (be they middle-class by origin or destination) to tell their story. In many respects a form of intellectual and cultural colonisation has continued in the social class field while it has been superseded in the race and gender areas, and to a lesser degree in other areas such as disability, by oppressed groups talking and researching for themselves about themselves. In so far as women, ethnic minorities, disabled people, or other minorities, are working-class, however, they have retained their colonised position in relation to the academy.

What Glyn Williams observes about sociology as a discipline is also true of other disciplines and discourses, including education:

> sociology is not an objective, privileged discourse but rather . . . a historical discourse developed within a Eurocentric, imperialist and statist context by members of dominant groups within dominant states and, as a consequence, it systematically fails to address social and cultural issues from the place of the minority. (Lecture given on the 'Language, Power and Equality' course at the Equality Studies Centre, University College Dublin, March 1992)

Of those who research class inequality in education, by far the most influential group are the 'equality empiricists' (Karabel and Halsey, 1977). Working out of fundamentally liberal philosophical assumptions, they defined social mobility for working-class students as the desirable educational goal. Their work is epitomised by its preoccupation with the realisation of the liberal goal of formal equality of opportunity rather than egalitarianism (Coleman et al., 1966; Blau and Duncan, 1967; Halsey et al., 1980; Goldthorpe et al., 1980; Coleman, 1990). Although neo-functionalist (Durkheimian) and neo-Weberian models are used within this tradition to analyse class inequality in education, the underlying liberal assumptions about equality of opportunity remain very similar in both cases. Certainly within Ireland, the equality empiricists have dominated debates about equality in education (Clancy, 1982, 1988, 1995; Hannan et al., 1983; Breen, 1984; Greaney and Kellaghan, 1984; Whelan and Whelan, 1984; Breen et al., 1990; Hannan and Smyth, 1996); this is partly a function of the fact that this has been the only type of research to receive substantial grant aid, although it also reflects the relative paradigmatic insulation of Irish sociology of education in particular (Drudy, 1991). In Ireland as in other countries, there has been no attempt to dialogue or link in with the voices of working-class communities in the analysis of data. The research has been written about 'the Other' from above, outside and beyond. While there is no doubt that this work has been undertaken in good faith, in terms of the social relations of research production, it has reproduced a system of unequal power relations between the researcher and the researched.

While neo-Marxists differ from the democratic liberals in that most subscribe to the more radical rather than the liberal notion of equality of opportunity, their work is still a discourse within itself, talking to itself; it generally does not liaise with working-class voices. Its language is generally remote and inaccessible to all but those who have acquired the tools of the educational, if not the sociological, trade. It has 'got entrapped by' its 'own theoretical snares' (Arnot, 1991:460). As Gurnah observes:

> education analysis, as [a] whole, has remained imprisoned within a stifling and unproductive liberal education ideology; and that includes many of the works which pass as progressive, critical or socialist. What exists as Marxist analyses are often critiques of the establishment in education and rarely focus on or offer alternatives in learning. (1992:95)

Even when it attempts to describe rather than decry working-class culture as in the case of Bourdieu, it is written from above, from the perspective of the relatively dominant. And this includes research undertaken by the middle-class co-author of this paper (Lynch, 1989)! While the work of people like Willis (1977) would have been an exception to this to some extent, it is focused solely on young men, and it is written *about* working-class 'lads' rather than *with* them. Although highly influential at the time, it has not led to any formal recognition of a working-class perspective in education, and this, in itself, shows how the structural problem of class-related knowledge stratification cannot be readily overcome.

The net effect of interpreting the world from the perspective of the 'expert' is that the viewpoint of the outsider is privileged over that of the insider who has experienced the inequality. The fact that the perspective of the expert is only one viewpoint, and one which is generally at least one step removed from the oppression, is rarely discussed. Self-reflexivity is not a requirement of the research task.

One reason why the viewpoint of the 'expert' becomes a privileged discourse is because of its greater claim to objectivity. While it is clearly necessary that objectivity should characterise the process of analysis, objectivity is always fused with subjectivity. The understanding provided by the researcher is socially situated both in terms of the researcher's own domain assumptions and in terms of her or his theoretical viewpoint (Gouldner, 1970; Gould, 1981). The values and interpretations underpinning any analysis are, inevitably, selective. Yet within the positivist tradition, researchers present what is a select view as one which is more comprehensive and epistemologically powerful than the viewpoint of either those directly affected by inequality or even other researchers (especially ethnographic researchers).

The privileging of the expert produces perspectives on inequality and injustice which are politically and emotionally detached from the experiences which generated their presentation in the first place. While academic understanding involves abstractions, the abstractions need not revisit the research subjects as 'expert opinions' which are superior to their own understanding. Yet this is often the case. As we suggest in the conclusion to this chapter, it is possible to create knowledge and understanding through partnership between the researcher and the research subject, while recognising the differences between the two positions. Knowledge created in this manner is owned by the research subject in a way that non-partnership knowledge is not. The fact that the subject is co-creator of the knowledge means that they can exercise control over definitions and interpretations of their lifeworld. They are also in a position to be enabled in research understanding through their involvement in the research process in the first place.

RESISTANCE, BORDER PEDAGOGY AND CLASS ANALYSIS

The philosophical and sociological work of Apple (1979, 1982, 1986), Giroux (1983, 1991, 1992), Aronowitz and Giroux (1991) and Fagan (1995) represents another branch of neo-Marxist thought which espouses an egalitarian perspective. Their work is rooted in critical theory and, in the case of Giroux especially, in the work of Freire. Realising that the economic and cultural accounts of working-class failure were overly deterministic, they tried to introduce the 'actor' back on to the educational and sociological stage, not so much for the purposes of explanation as for resistance. They argued for the development of a critical pedagogy as a route to working-class resistance in education (Giroux, 1983). Working out of the philosophical assumptions of 'knowledge as praxis', they have tried to produce an analysis of pedagogy and curriculum which moves away from the determinism associated with the 'economic' Marxists. In addition, they have posed the problem of social class as one to be resolved at the curriculum and pedagogical level. Giroux claims that much work in education has been only about mapping domination; he suggests that there is a need for a 'border pedagogy' which

> can also provide a valuable theoretical service by shifting the emphasis of the knowledge/power relationship away from the limited emphasis on the mapping of domination to the politically strategic issue of engaging the ways in which knowledge can be remapped, reterritorialised and decentred in the wider interests of rewriting the borders and co-ordinates of an oppositional cultural politics. (1991:511)

Giroux and Aronowitz have argued for a 'border pedagogy of post-modern resistance' (Aronowitz and Giroux, 1991:118).

In short the notion of border pedagogy presupposes not merely an acknowledgement of the shifting borders that both undermine and reterritorialize different configurations of power and knowledge; it also links the notion of pedagogy to a more substantive struggle for a democratic society. It is a pedagogy which attempts to link an emancipatory notion of modernism with a post-modernism of resistance. (Ibid.)

This perspective views teachers, and other cultural workers, as transformative intellectuals. Within education, teachers are seen as the key to social class change in education. In all of this there is the assumption that teachers, should they be converted to critical pedagogy, will inevitably use their critical skill to challenge the institutions upholding inequality in society. It implies too that teachers will act on 'behalf of' and 'for' the 'Other', whatever the oppression or exploitation of that 'Other'. Second, it assumes that once aware / converted, they will have the freedom and capacity to develop critical thought. Third, it assumes that students will be open and receptive to this perspective in formal education systems. Finally, it assumes that change will come about as a result of this approach, although it gives no indication as to how long it would be before significant change to the advantage of minorities and other oppressed groups would result from this process.

The hope which the resistance theorists bring to education is welcome and inspiring. How successful it would be in generating change is another matter; it seems seriously questionable that significant change can result from a change of pedagogical style. First there is the issue of scale and time. As Archer (1982) and others have observed, education is a contested site; the education institution operates in a context where there is a parallelogram of forces seeking to define its terms and conditions. Bringing about change involves constant political manipulation and contestation. There is no single line of influence. Given this fact, it seems foolhardy to suggest that change could occur through one arena of contestation, namely pedagogy. If the political and ethical dissent that border pedagogy requires were to become the norm in the system, an inordinately long time would seem to be required. And the outcome is far from certain.

What is also implicit in such concepts as 'border pedagogy' or 'transformative intellectuals' is the view that one group in society can or will act on behalf of the 'Other'. It is assumed that teachers will know and understand the oppressions of groups such as migrant workers, working-class people or disabled people and act on their behalf through redefining the parameters of educational discourse. Even if this is desirable (that is, that one speaks or works on behalf of the 'Other'), and this is highly debatable, it is not very likely to happen in societies where teachers are not proletarianised, or where they are incorporated into the decision-making machinery of the state itself (Lynch, 1990).

In addition, in formal state-controlled education systems, it seems highly unlikely that teachers would be given the autonomy to make 'primary the language of the political and ethical' (Giroux, 1991:510), particularly if the politics and ethics did not accord with those which are already dominant. While some countries have a written formal code prohibiting the teaching of political and ethical codes which are inimical to the state, such a code is certainly implicit in the regulations of other education systems. Furthermore, whether many teachers share the value assumptions of emancipatory education is dependent very much on their cultural and political context. While teachers and cultural workers operating in countries where there is ongoing political resistance to the state (for example as there has been in Northern Ireland or South Africa or Palestine) may well be very sensitive to the concept of 'education as conscientisation' given the level of political dissent and upheaval, it is far less likely that the same would hold true in contexts where there is no mobilisation of political resistance to the state, and where the social mobility functions of education are widely accepted.

Also, there is the question of the students themselves; students are not willing dough waiting to be kneaded into shape by their educators no matter how well intentioned the latter might be. Indeed, research shows the opposite; research on second-level students in Ireland has shown that they have a highly instrumental approach to learning and are very resistant to methodologies and curricula that are not perceived to be of immediate relevance (Raven et al., 1975; Hannan and Shorthall, 1991). There is little doubt but that this also holds true in other countries where there are close links between level of education and labour market opportunities. How students themselves, who may or may not share the politics and ethics of emancipation, may perceive border pedagogy and what their reaction to it might be, is something which needs to be explored much further.

What is often forgotten by those who adopt a Freirean approach to pedagogy is that Freire's thesis originated out of his work in the adult education field in South America. This sector of education is largely outside state control in most countries and is therefore much more autonomous both in what it teaches and in the methods that it utilises. (Although as Inglis and Bassett (1988) observe, there is evidence, even from this sector, that the oppressed are highly variable in their educational expectations, and what many want from education is individual social mobility not political empowerment/emancipation; they often see adult education as the first stage in the process of credentialism leading eventually to a well-paid job.) Freire has never fully explained how the dialogical method could be employed in a state-controlled formal school situation. He has suggested, perhaps rightly, that it is for each group in their own cultural context to explore the significance of his writing for their own system. It would seem, however, that is precisely what does not happen; authors, and Giroux and Aronowitz are among them, fail to examine the cultural and political context in which they are writing. While theories of resistance may have given back hope for change to teachers and educators depressed with the almost fatalistic determinism of economic Marxism, the only hope they give for any serious challenge to the class structure is a very long-term one, premised on the assumption that education can be used successfully to mobilise political dissent. One is left with a sense of deep frustration as the theory of 'knowledge as praxis' underpinning resistance theory seems to be divorced from both cultural and political context. As suggested previously, there are a number of conditions in which it is very difficult to see how resistance could be turned to political account. This is especially true:

> a) when credentialised knowledge plays a key role in both producing and distributing privileges as is the case in many post-colonial states; b) when large and politically mobilised groups (such as the propertyless middle classes in Ireland) are already highly successful in utilising the educational system to perpetuate their own class power and when no alternative route is readily open to them; c) when groups mediating educational services are sufficiently powerful — either independent of, or due to, their class affiliations — to become agents of counter-resistance. The strategic location of mediating groups at the centre of the educational enterprise is, we suggest, an important factor in explaining how resistances get recycled into educational products. (Lynch, 1990:17)

While this type of analysis may reflect the kind of structural determinism that those with a cultural studies perspective want to avoid, it seems to be neither sociologically sensitive nor politically astute to ignore the structural, and indeed cultural, contexts in which education systems operate. By decoding and deconstructing the agents and collectivities who create structures, it is possible to identify sites of resistance. As noted in chapter 4, a structuralist perspective need not be a deterministic perspective. Education is a highly centralised enterprise in many countries, particularly in Ireland. Within such a system, substantive political resistance cannot be effective without action at the state level. There is no mystery about the structures. The collective and individual agents, and the contexts, within and through which action can be initiated are quite visible, especially in the 'partnership' style of state management which is so strongly espoused in Ireland.

Classroom teachers are but one set of agents. Changes in pedagogical styles may be necessary but they are not sufficient for realising social change through education. The first step which is required is that oppressed and exploited groups are in a position to name their own world, and fight their own struggles, inside and outside education. They must find their own voice rather than have experts speaking 'at them', 'for them' or 'about them'. The social class experts have to hand back the voices they have territorialised; they have to let go.

THE SCHOLASTIC CONTEXT

To understand the exclusion of the working-class viewpoint in sociological analysis, it is necessary to examine the scholastic context within which academic understanding is produced. Unfortunately, the scholastic context in which we work is not one which we subject to much critical analysis:

> Thus what philosophers, sociologists, historians, and all those whose profession it is to think and/or speak about the world have most chance of overlooking are the social presuppositions that are inscribed in the scholastic point of view . . . thinkers leave in a state of unthought (*impense*, doxa) the presuppositions of their thought, that is the social conditions of possibility of the scholastic point of view and the unconscious dispositions, productive of unconscious theses, which are acquired through an academic or scholastic experience, often inscribed in prolongation of an originary (bourgeois) experience of distance from the world and from the urgency of necessity. (Bourdieu, 1990:381)

What defines the scholastic experience is the context in which it happens; it is one which is distant from 'necessity and urgency', hence the space to reflect and write. This is, of course, precisely what those who live on social welfare or on low pay lack. They lack the conditions of access to universality; they do not have the space or time to globalise their point of view.

The scholastic context is not just one which is divided along social class lines; the opportunity to be distanced from 'necessity and urgency' is more likely to be accorded to you if you are a male rather than a female, or if you work in a well-funded European or North American university rather than a poorly funded African one.

Furthermore, what one writes or publishes is interpreted not just in terms of its academic merits, but in terms of the latent intellectual identities of its authors. The whole system of knowledge creation, production and legitimisation, is one which is characterised by its own system of stratification. This applies to sociology as much as any other area of research. Those with an interest in equality are faced with a fundamental paradox:

> On the one hand, our discipline raises as a topic the social stratification of knowledge, as a problem of elites and power. On the other hand, the implicit claim of our professional practice (carrying out research which generates accounts of social milieux that add something of value to the accounts already available) depends for its legitimacy on that same stratification; our research findings (research findings which present authoritative interpretations) reproduce it. (Winter, 1991:469)

There are many layers and levels within this hierarchy, the most obvious one being that which arises from social class relations; it is reflected in the division which exists between so-called commonsense knowledge and 'objective' scientific academic knowledge (Popkewitz, 1984). But there are many others as well; there is the division of the so-called First from the so-called Third World, there is the division between the core capitalist states and the small peripheral states, and of course there are the divisions between black and white, men and women. While there has been some recognition of women's exclusion and, but to a lesser degree, that of Third World intellectuals and black minorities in white-dominated states, there is virtually no reference to the colonising intellectual relationships between core and peripheral states, or, other than in a few exceptional cases, to those of social class. Perhaps there is a fear on the part of the colonised of being seen to engage in special pleading, a fear which in itself reflects the coloniser within. And so sociologists from peripheral and poorer states (themselves an elite within their own countries of course) take the grand narratives of sociology which have been developed in highly specific historical, political and cultural contexts and try to apply them to social systems where they are only marginally appropriate. If they fail to apply the grand narratives they will not be recognised by the establishment discipline. And so they continue to wear intellectual clothes which do not fit.

In structural terms working-class people experience a similar problem; they take the diet fed to them by middle-class researchers; they call themselves, variously, disadvantaged, marginalised, socially excluded or oppressed, but they remain poor. They occupy a structural position in relation to academia in general similar to that operating between the dominated and the dominant within academia itself. However, given the nature of educational and cultural stratification, they are even less likely to be given the right of reply than other dominated groups.

Resistance to the labels or the models is construed as deviance at best, but more often as ignorance. Colonialism takes many forms; as a system of domination it involves economic, political and cultural as well as military practices. 'It is a set of relationships, not a series of battles and treaties' (O'Dowd, 1992:22). It is no coincidence therefore that there is a remarkable association between 'influential researchers and theorists' and the political/economic status of their country of origin and/or destination; just as the core capitalist states dominate the global economic order, so also do they dominate the intellectual order. Similarly within a given country, it is only those who speak in the language and voice of the established paradigm who will be heard; if one feels sufficiently empowered or emancipated to name the world differently, one will face tremendous counter-resistance.

And the inevitable question arises, who grants authority to one over another? While Hammersley (1992:197) has a point when he says that intellectuals have a claim to authority by virtue of the fact that, 'on average, their findings are less likely to be in error than information from other sources, and this stems from the operation of the research community in subjecting research findings to scrutiny and thereby detecting and correcting errors', one can think of several journals which if reviewed by subscribers to other journals would be deemed to be either of no intellectual value or even downright inaccurate in their analysis. The best example of this is the attitude of the traditional male-dominated journals to feminist journals or indeed the attitude of staunch positivists to qualitative research. The idea that there is an objective and wholly disinterested academic community out there vetting and validating all new research on universally agreed criteria is patently untrue. There is a series of research groups, many of whom never reference any work belonging to those with an opposing perspective. There is little dialogue between the dissenting voices, and there most certainly is no community, except in the most androcentric, ethnocentric and provincial sense.

The ability to put intellectual order on social events is not the prerogative of an international class of social scientists working as a cohesive community. Rather it is the prerogative of a small elite of predominantly middle-class male academics who, with a few notable exceptions, are situated in the powerful economies of the global (especially Western) capitalist order. There is a certain extent to which the writing of others, even academic writing, has a type of philosophical commonsense status similar to that held by other workers who are formally excluded from the discourse of academic analysis by virtue of their lack of education. Though the reasons for working-class exclusion are different to those for other groups, the socio-political context is very similar for both. As feminist and black writers have so eloquently observed in recent years, the language to describe oppression has, until very recent times, been exclusively in the hands of the oppressors (hooks, 1982; Smith, 1988). The latter frequently showed little interest in ending the oppression they described.

Because sociology failed to take up the full challenge of oppression in all its forms, because, as Coleman (1990:33) observed, it divorced itself (especially in its positivist tradition) from normative questions such as justice and equality, it has to some extent been superseded by other frames of intellectual reference; these intellectual traditions (Women's Studies, Equality Studies, Black Studies, Disability Studies, Development Studies) are less concerned about rigid divisions between fact and value, perhaps realising that such distinctions are ideal type models rather than rigid ontological categories. They have come to take over the space left empty by an increasingly narrowly focused sociology and indeed psychology, politics and economics.

What we are suggesting here is that the colonisation of working-class worlds by middle-class academics is greatly facilitated by the nature of the scholastic context itself. To globalise one's point of view in academic terms requires one to be relatively free from the urgency and necessity of survival demands. Those who live on welfare or low incomes are not in such a position, so no matter how great their insights or understandings, they are rarely free to document their social analysis of their world. Even on the rare occasions when they do document their world view (for example in O'Neill's (1992) *Telling It Like It Is*), however, they are automatically confronted by the reality of stratification within the knowledge system itself. To have academic (and indeed public) legitimacy one has to have academic status and by definition one lacks this status if one is working-class.

THE ABSENCE OF A WORKING-CLASS VOICE: A PROBLEM OF CONTRADICTION

The absence of a working-class perspective in education and even in sociology arises from the fundamentally contradictory position in which working-class people find themselves in relation to education, and indeed culture. To participate in the academic definition of their own class culture, working-class people must become part of the colonising/mediating group; they must become credentialised *via* higher education. While this does not mean that they abandon their class identity, the fact remains that, by virtue of the lengthy process of participating in education, they will be socialised into, if not converted to, middle-class culture.

As Aronowitz and Giroux (1991:163) point out:

> One of the crucial functions performed by schools since the turn of the century has been to erase the memory of a self-representing popular culture. . . . The objective of schooling, conscious or not, is among other things to strip away what belongs to the student, to reconstitute his or her formation in terms of the boundaries imposed by hegemonic intellectuals acting for the prevailing social order. The students who succeed in these terms must be stripped of their ethnicity, race and sex; if they are of working-class origin, their submission to the curriculum already signifies probable social mobility. Those who fail or otherwise rebel must recognise that their own subculture is not the real thing, even if they own it.

Working-class people who succeed in the education system have to abandon certain features of their background class habitus (that is, their modes of thought, perception, appreciation and action, Bourdieu and Passeron, 1977, 40–41) in a way that is not really true for other socially mobile groups. Once educated they will cease to be working-class in a way that a woman, no matter what her social position, will never cease to be a woman, a person who is black will never cease to be black, and those with a major physical disability will never be without it. Their defining identity in social class terms is automatically changed by virtue of their educational success; there is no other marginal or dominated group for whom this holds true to the same degree. This means, in effect, that working-class people exercise a structural relationship to education which is fraught with dilemmas and contradictions. As long as they remain outside of the formal credentialised system of education, they are excluded from challenging that very system. If they are to become credentialised, however, they generally cease to belong to their class of origin, at least in so far as their access to credentialised cultural capital has changed.[5] In addition, their occupational status may change due to the credential acquired. While such contradictions and dilemmas arise in education for all groups who are not male, white and middle-class, they do not arise for *all* members of any of these groups. Middle-class women, middle-class blacks and middle-class people with disabilities are not in this position. At least in their 'middle-classness' they can be at home in education at certain times and at certain stages.

This structural isolation of the working class does not occur to the same degree for any other group because no other group's culture is structurally defined in its totality as being inferior and inadmissible in education. The emergence of Women's Studies, Disability Studies, Black Feminism, etc. is an indication of how at least some women, some disabled people and some black people have begun to find a voice for themselves in education. They have begun to name their own world and to challenge the legitimacy of claims made on their behalf from within the framework of academic analysis itself. In so far as there has been a debate about what are legitimate and admissible cultural forms in education, it has been undertaken among professional educationalists and academics; working-class people have not been partners to the debate. Professional educators speak about them and for them.

From the point of view of education therefore, working-class people occupy a distinctive location in terms of their relationship to the system. Once they succeed within higher education in particular, their class identity changes. This has been insufficiently recognised even by those intellectuals most sympathetic to working-class perspectives. Class, gender, race and disability are analysed as if there were some kind of parity between them in the way that they interface with education. Yet the position of working-class people in education is structurally and substantively different from that of all other groups: if one is working-class and formally educated, especially in the sense of having obtained higher education credentials, one loses one's defining social class identity in part if not in total.

ABSENT VOICES: IGNORING ECONOMIC INEQUALITY IN EDUCATION

The absence of a working-class voice from education has been a significant factor in the theorising of inequality in education as a cultural problem to the virtual exclusion, in recent years especially, of an analysis of the direct effects of poverty and economic inequalities.[6] This is not to deny that there are very real cultural tensions between working-class children, their parents, and teachers in schools, as noted in chapter 4 and in O'Neill's (1992) study.[7] However, while the source of these tensions undoubtedly relates to the difference in habitus between the world of the school and that of the parent and the child, it is a tension that is grounded very often in the poverty which ensues from living on social welfare or low wages, a poverty which is beyond the full comprehension of those who do not live it out daily. To illustrate this point, we will draw from some of the evidence in O'Neill's study of eighty working-class families in Kilmount in Dublin.

One source of tension between schools and parents in the Kilmount study was dress. Rules about appropriate school shoes, for example, were resented, not because parents minded what shape or colour shoes were, but because most parents could not afford separate sets of shoes for school and home. As May said:

> 'It's hard enough to get them to wear sensible shoes without worrying about colour as well, especially the way kids change their mind. The same thing applies to trousers. I mean, I have been sent for over things like this and have felt like crying at being told off. It's hard enough to dress them without all this messing.' (O'Neill, 1992:97)

The principal problem which working-class people have in relation to education is that they lack adequate income to maximise the advantages that the system could offer: looked at another way, they are seriously deprived of resources relative to the middle-class people with whom they must compete for credentials. One of the two women who had borrowed money to pay school costs made this point clearly:

> 'It's not just the cost of books, which are dear enough, it's also the PE gear and runners, there's swimming, arts and crafts and photocopying costs as well. Every single day for three months I was handing over money to one or other of my four children for calculators, graph paper and so on. If I didn't have it the kids would be sent home for it. Then there's the ingredients needed for home economics, half the time I wouldn't have my dinner and I'd have to buy cookery ingredients.' (O'Neill, 1992:100)

And the tensions are not just over direct costs but over the indirect effects of poverty as it affects the learning environment at home. The expectation, especially at second level, that students will spend some hours each evening at study is a considerable cause of stress in confined spaces where the hassle of survival is paramount:

> 'Not all of us are able to help out,' says Kay, 'even if we had the time. Our house is bedlam most times because it's so small. You can hardly hear yourself think, let alone find space to study. I often think of the children

who get no help at all, do they just get behind because the teachers don't
understand the problems their parents have at home? Or do they believe
that no one cares about the kids just because they are late paying for
books and fees?' (O'Neill, 1992:97)

There is nothing 'wrong' with working-class attitudes or values. The majority
of people in working-class communities are keenly aware of the importance of
education and value it for their children (O'Brien, 1987; O'Neill, 1992; Lynch
and O'Riordan, 1996). And while Bourdieu and his French associates are correct
to say that class differences in habitus take the form of differences in manners,
tastes, styles of dress, speech, dispositions and attitudes and that there is a type
of symbolic violence being done to working-class culture in school (Bourdieu
and Passeron, 1977; Bourdieu, 1979), what alienates working-class children
from the system most of all is not only the middle-class character of the formal
and the hidden curriculum, but the absence of the financial resources to make
the system work for themselves.

It is the lack of money that underpins their sense of powerlessness and
isolation which is the most powerful excluding force (see chapter 4). How relevant
the symbolic differences would be in the absence of economic deprivation is an
open question. While there is research from Italy (Cappecchi, 1992) that cultural
indifference to education can be great in working-class communities where there
is little poverty, the Italian case of L'Emilie Romagne where multiple opportunities
for employment exist even for those without formal education is totally different
to an Irish context where there is an almost perfect correlation between one's
level of education and one's chances of getting a job (Labour Force Surveys of
School Leavers). The fact that the more secure and well-paid sector of the
working class in Ireland (skilled manual workers) have consistently high participation rates in higher education (Clancy, 1982, 1988, 1995) would certainly suggest
that working-class people can achieve well in the education system when they
have the resources to do so and when the economic conditions make education
essential for labour market participation. What is being suggested therefore is
that social class differences in style, taste and habitus generally, between working-
class children and the institution of the school, while important for understanding
inequality in education, are not as important as economic barriers. If income and
wealth differentials were eliminated, working-class 'failure' in education would
cease to be a major issue within a short time. However, as the entire social
democratic project has been built on the concept of merit, and relatedly on
differentials and relativities, reducing, never mind eliminating, income differentials initially requires a radical change in the way in which we define the
value of labour in society. Until such time as that happens, those who are
required to manage poverty within the household (and they are mostly
women) will be required to use themselves as a currency in survival. The
energy and time to facilitate one's children's education is reduced accordingly.

Because money is in short supply many women have replaced their financial budget with a time management budget. They are forced to juggle time, energy, creativity, health and patience in order to feed, clothe and educate their families. Side by side with these tasks they have to deal with the psychological effects of unemployment on their spouses and teenage children . . . Women whose families live on small incomes become the first casualties in the game of 'shift and thrift' by using themselves as currency in order to maintain a family life. Much of their 'already spread thin time' is spent in negotiation, application or communication with officials from the Department of Social Welfare or the Health Board as they seek assistance with household bills. (O'Neill, 1992:40–41)

CONCLUSION: THE NEED FOR EMANCIPATORY RESEARCH METHODOLOGIES

The failure of the social democratic project to have any significant effect on social class inequality in education is now evident in a number of countries (Breen et al., 1990; Cobalti, 1990; Halsey, 1991; Shavit and Blossfeld, 1993).[8] The failure of the project has been overshadowed to some extent by the emergence of other, and no less important, concerns for egalitarians, such as gender, race and disability. However, the fact remains that the children of low-income households, whatever their gender or colour, are still the most likely to leave school early and to perform less well within the education system.

In recent years, very little attention has been given to the direct effects of poverty and low incomes on education participation and success. In addition, dialogue with working-class people about their perspective on the education system has been remarkably absent. While we have feminist and racially informed visions of education, there is no working-class perspective. Part of the problem is that the working class occupy a structurally different relationship to the education system to other oppressed groups; being educated, in the formal sense (especially if one has undertaken higher education) is to change one's social class identity, at least in part. The same does not hold true to the same degree for women, people of different ethnic identity or people with disability. No other group changes its identity to quite the same degree by succeeding in education; no other group finds that school is about learning to be the opposite to what one is.

While the cultural difference and educational resistance models purporting to explain and challenge social class inequality in education are valuable, they must be complemented by a poverty analysis and an analysis that takes cognisance of working-class perspective and action. The absence of a poverty analysis may itself be related to the exclusion of working-class voices from the discourse of education.

DEVELOPING AN EMANCIPATORY METHODOLOGY

The solution to the dilemma posed by the colonising nature of research has been addressed systematically by feminist scholars and researchers at the theoretical and empirical level (Bowles and Duelli-Klein, 1983; Mies, 1984; Smith, 1988; Harding, 1991; Lather, 1991; Humphries and Truman, 1994). And it has also been examined extensively in the general area of the social sciences (Reason and Rowan, 1981; Bernstein, 1983; Reason, 1988; Oliver, 1992). The alternative to 'illusory value-free knowledge' is 'emancipatory knowledge'. The aim of emancipatory research is to increase 'awareness of the contradictions hidden or distorted by everyday understandings', and in so doing to direct 'attention to the possibilities for social transformation inherent in the present configuration of social processes' (Lather, 1986:259).

Emancipatory research or research as praxis involves first a recognition of the *moral right* of research subjects to exercise ownership and control over the generation of knowledge produced about them. As Heron (1981) observes, this is a human rights issue. It constitutes part of people's right to political membership of their community. Although conventional human rights thinking focuses on political rights in the more restricted political sense — that is, in the context of local, regional or national governments — there is also a need to recognise the centrality of human rights within the wide range of institutions and systems in which people participate in advanced industrial societies. People have rights to participate in decision-making that affects the fulfilment of their needs and interests; such decision-making is not confined in contemporary society to the purely political arena. It operates in the fields of health, education, planning, housing, industrial policy, family life and both national and local development. It also operates in the field of research.

> For persons, as autonomous beings, have a moral right to participate in decisions that claim to generate knowledge about them. Such a right does many things: (1) it honours the fulfilment of their need for autonomously acquired knowledge; (2) it protects them from becoming unwitting accessories to knowledge-claims that may be false and may be inappropriately or harmfully applied to others; (3) it protects them from being excluded from the formation of knowledge that purports to be about them and so from being managed and manipulated, both in the acquisition and in the application of knowledge, in ways they do not understand and so cannot assent to or dissent from. (Heron, 1981:35)

The importance of *democratising research* arises therefore because knowledge is power. The research industry is a massive one across all fields and disciplines; it takes place not only in universities or research institutes but in government departments, private companies, local and national service agencies and so on. Unless those who are directly spoken about in research, and/or directly affected by its findings, are given the opportunity to define the nature and purpose of research on themselves, research can be and often is a further instrument of oppression. This is especially the case in relation to economically, culturally and socially marginalised groups in society, as they are rarely party to research decisions or interpretations even about work which is about themselves.

Emancipatory research also involves developing a *reciprocal relationship* between the researcher and the research subject. This requires a democratisation of the research relationship through which research is used to help participants to understand and change their situation. This is especially important for research in the area of equality as research which is not oriented towards transformation effectively reinforces inequality by default. It allows inequality to persist by diverting intellectual and public attention elsewhere. Part of the requirement of reciprocal relations therefore is the enabling of participants to examine 'false consciousness', i.e. their understanding of the world which sustains their disempowerment. This presents a major challenge to researchers as it means not only negotiating understanding with research participants, but creating contexts in which people can question taken-for-granted beliefs, beliefs which may in fact be dearly held or may provide direction and meaning in life (Lather, 1986, 1991).

Knowing how or in what way the research will benefit people's empowerment is not clear. It takes time, trust and negotiation on all sides, and may not result in the research participants seeing the world in a radical egalitarian manner. Kelly's (1996) research shows how working-class community groups interpreted unemployment according to quite different socio-political frames — ranging from radical to reformist to localist — although the formal class identity of all twelve groups involved was the same.

Reciprocity also involves engaging participants in the research planning as it is only through such participation that marginalised groups can begin to control the naming of their own world. If research participation is confined to the interpretation or theoretical elaboration stage, it may be too late as issues which are not central to the group or community may have become the focus of attention in the first place.

Another feature of praxis-oriented research is its use of *dialectical theory-building* rather than theoretical imposition (Lather, 1991). Research respondents are involved therefore not only in the design of the research but in the construction and validation of meaning. To undertake theory-construction in this manner represents an enormous challenge for researchers as it imposes a substantive *educational commitment* upon them (Heron, 1981).

Systematised *reflexivity* is also a requirement for emancipatory research as it is only through the constant analysis of one's own theoretical and methodological presuppositions that one can retain an awareness of the importance of people's own definitions and understandings of their situations. Theoretical imposition is the 'natural' predisposition of most researchers given traditional academic training. Authors assume the superiority of their 'framework';

grounding frameworks in the context of lived understandings challenges this tradition and informs and enriches understanding.

There are a number of practical problems posed by the emancipatory methodology, including the fact that it does increase the cost of the research. This is not necessarily something which will be supported by research funders, although it may change over time when the importance of dialogue and its educational outcomes are appreciated. There is also very little research training in emancipatory methodology available in most educational institutions although there are exceptions to this (Reason, 1988).

DEVELOPING THE CONCEPT OF EMANCIPATORY METHODOLOGY

What is more substantively problematic about the operation of emancipatory research methods, as currently articulated, is establishing procedures whereby radical understandings can be utilised for challenging structural inequalities. Even if radical understandings emerge from research, which for example happened in Kelly's (1996) work, there is no mechanism within the emancipatory method to move this understanding into discourses and political practices which would enable it to become active in the struggle for equality. Although Mies (1984) shows how particular research led to important policy changes in Germany in relation to policies on women and violence, what is not clear is what makes it possible for this to happen. Is egalitarian development left contingent on a particular set of historical and political circumstances? Our experience within the university of using research in an emancipatory manner (to change entrance procedures) would suggest that it is essential to involve marginalised groups themselves at all stages of the research, including the policy-related implementation stage, if action is to be taken. For this to happen, organisations have to enter into new relations of dialogue and partnership with client groups which may be anathema to their organisational-cultural traditions. Certainly universities and research institutes have rarely established procedures for entering into dialogue with research participants in marginalised groups and communities. While liaisons with such groups may be permitted, they are usually kept at the periphery of the organisation where they exercise marginal power, often in adult education departments or women's studies departments.

Yet if research is to be truly emancipatory on an ongoing basis, structures and procedures have to be put in place to allow dialogue to happen. We need to have Structures for Research Dialogue (SRD). This involves a radical change in the structuring of departments in universities and research institutes. It involves 'expert' researchers entering into structured dialogue, not necessarily always on their own terms. If systems are in place whereby working-class community groups or other representatives of marginalised groups (including children and young people in education especially) are involved on an ongoing basis in planning, monitoring and commenting on research, they will play a very different and more powerful role than if they are simply research subjects being given the opportunity to participate or dialogue about research at the will of the researcher. The redefining of research power relations has implications which far exceed intervention in any given research project. A logical extension of establishing Structures for Research Dialogue would be the development of similar structures to develop dialogues on pedagogical practice, assessment, admission policy and so on. Within current emancipatory research discourses, the scope and choice of emancipatory methods are left to the researcher; there is no analysis of what kind of structural conditions are necessary to ensure that emancipatory methods are implemented on an ongoing basis. To institutionalise a truly radical approach to research, however, would require the development of new structures at both university and departmental level (and ultimately at central university and research planning level). Procedures would have to be put in place therefore whereby those who are marginalised and oppressed in society can enter into dialogue about all research undertaken in their name. They would not simply be dependent on the good will of individual researchers 'allowing *them*' to enter into dialogue, but ultimately holding a veto on *their* participation should the researchers so desire. As emancipatory research is construed at present that is what is being proposed. If Structures for Research Dialogue were in operation, all power would not rest with the researcher as they would have to explain and justify the nature of their research and theory about marginalised groups to the groups themselves. The introduction of structural procedures for dialogue for equality research is a mere recognition of the fact that the construction of knowledge is not a neutral process.

REFERENCES

Apple, M.W. (1979). *Ideology and Curriculum*. Boston: Routledge & Kegan Paul.

Apple, M.W. (ed.) (1982). *Cultural and Economic Reproduction in Education*. London: Routledge & Kegan Paul.

Apple, M.W. (1986). *Teachers and Texts: A Political Economy of Class and Gender Relations in Education*. New York: Routledge & Kegan Paul.

Archer, M.S. (1982). *The Sociology of Educational Expansion*. London: Sage.

Arnot, M. (1991). Equality and democracy: a decade of struggle over education. *British Journal of Sociology of Education*, 12 (4):447–66.

Aronowitz, S., and Giroux, H. (1991). *Post-Modern Education: Politics, Culture and Social Criticism*. Minneapolis: University of Minnesota Press.

Bernstein, R. (1983). *Beyond Objectivism and Relativism: Science, Hermeneutics and Praxis*. University of Pennsylvania Press.

Blau, P.M., and Duncan, O.D. (1967). *The American Occupational Structure*. New York: Wiley.

Bourdieu, P. (1979). *Distinction: A Social Critique of the Judgement of Taste*. London: Routledge & Kegan Paul.

Bourdieu, P. (1986). The forms of capital. In J.G. Richardson (ed.), *Handbook of Theory and Research for the Sociology of Education*. New York: Greenwood Press.

Bourdieu, P. (1990). The scholastic point of view. *Cultural Anthropology*, 5 (4):380–91.

Bourdieu, P. (1993). *Sociology in Question*. London: Sage.

Bourdieu, P., and Passeron, J.-C. (1977). *Reproduction in Education, Society and Culture*. London: Sage.

Bowles, G., and Duelli-Klein, R. (eds.) (1983). *Theories of Women's Studies*. London: Routledge & Kegan Paul.

Breen, R. (1984). *Education and the Labour Market*. Dublin: Economic and Social Research Institute, Paper No. 119.

Breen, R., et al. (1990). *Understanding Contemporary Ireland*. Dublin: Gill & Macmillan.

Callan, T., Nolan, B., et al. (1996). *Poverty in the 1990s*: Evidence from the Living in Ireland Survey. Dublin: Oak Tree Press.

Cappecchi, V. (1992). Les sorties du système éducatif et les familles désfavorisées. Paper presented at the European Symposium *Educational Systems and Disadvantaged Families*, 7–9 January, Le Touquet, France.

Chambers, R. (1983). *Rural Development: Putting the Last First*. Harlow, Essex: Longman.

Cicourel, R. (1964). *Method and Measurement in Sociology*. New York: Free Press.

Clancy, P. (1982). *Participation in Higher Education: A National Survey*. Dublin: Higher Education Authority.

Clancy, P. (1988). *Who Goes to College*. Dublin: Higher Education Authority.

Clancy, P. (1995). *Access to College: Patterns of Continuity and Change*. Dublin: Higher Education Authority.

Cobalti, A. (1990). Schooling inequalities in Italy: trends over time. *European Sociological Review*, 6 (3) (December):199–214.

Coleman, J. (1990). *Equality and Achievement in Education*. San Francisco: Westview Press.

Coleman, J., et al. (1966). *Equality of Educational Opportunity*. Washington, DC: US Department of Health, Education and Welfare.

Crompton, R. (1993). *Class and Stratification*. Cambridge: Polity Press.

Daly, M. (1992). Europe's poor women? Gender in research on poverty. *European Sociological Review*, 8 (1):1–12.

Davies, C., and McLoughlin, E. (eds.) (1991). *Women, Employment and Social Policy*. Belfast: Policy Research Institute, Queen's University.

Drudy, S. (1991). The sociology of education in Ireland, 1966–1991. *Irish Journal of Sociology*, 1:107–27.

Fagan, H. (1995). *Culture, Politics and Irish School Dropouts: Constructing Political Identities*. London: Bergin and Garvey.

Garner, C., and Raudenbush, S. (1991). Neighbourhood effects on educational attainment. *Sociology of Education*, 64 (4):251–62.

Giroux, H. (1983). *Theory and Resistance in Education*. London: Heinemann.

Giroux, H. (1991). Democracy and the discourse of cultural difference: towards a politics of border pedagogy. *British Journal of Sociology of Education*, 12 (4):501–19.

Giroux, H. (1992). *Border Crossings*. New York: Routledge.

Goldthorpe, J.H., et al. (1980). *Social Mobility and Class Structure in Modern Britain*. Oxford: Clarendon Press.

Gould, S. (1981). *The Mismeasure of Man*. New York: Penguin.

Gouldner, A.V. (1970). *The Coming Crisis of Western Sociology*. London: Heinemann.

Greaney, V., and Kellaghan, T. (1984). *Equality of Opportunity in Irish Schools*. Dublin: The Educational Company.

Gurnah, A. (1992). On the specificity of racism. In M. Arnot and L. Barton (eds.), *Voicing Concerns: Sociological Perspectives on Contemporary Education Reforms.* Wallingford, Oxfordshire: Triangle Books.

Halsey, A.H. (1991). Educational systems and the economy. *Current Sociology,* 38 (2–3, Autumn–Winter):79–101.

Halsey, A.H., et al. (1980). *Origins and Destinations: Family, Class and Education in Modern Britain.* Oxford: Clarendon Press.

Hammersley, M. (1992). On feminist methodology. *Sociology,* 26 (2):187–206.

Hannan, D., Breen, R., Murray, B., Watson, D., and Hardiman, N. (1983). *Schooling and Sex Roles.* Dublin: Economic and Social Research Institute, Paper No. 113.

Hannan, D.F., and Shorthall, S. (1991). *The Quality of Their Education, School Leavers' Views' of Their Education, of Educational Objectives and Outcomes.* Dublin: Economic and Social Research Institute, Paper No. 153.

Hannan, D.F., Smyth, E., McCullagh, J., O'Leary, R., and McMahon, D. (1996). *Coeducation and Gender Equality: Exam Performance, Stress and Personal Development.* Dublin: Oak Tree Press.

Harding, S. (1991). *Whose Science? Whose Knowledge?* Milton Keynes: Open University Press.

Hargreaves, D. (1967). *Social Relations in a Secondary School.* London: Routledge & Kegan Paul.

Hargreaves, D. (1996). Teaching as a research-based profession: possibilities and prospects. The Teacher Training Agency (UK) Annual Lecture.

Heron, J. (1981). Philosophical basis for a new paradigm. In P. Reason and J. Rowan (eds.), *Human Inquiry: A Sourcebook of New Paradigm Research.* Chichester: John Wiley and Sons.

hooks, b. (1982). *Ain't I a Woman: Black Women and Feminism.* London: Pluto Press.

Humphries, B., and Truman, C. (1994). *Re-thinking Social Research.* Aldershot: Avebury.

Inglis, T., and Bassett, M. (1988). *Live and Learn: Day-Time Adult Education in Coolock.* Dublin: AONTAS (National Association of Adult Education).

Karabel, J., and Halsey, A.H. (1977). *Power and Ideology in Education.* New York: Oxford University Press.

Kelly, M. (1996). *Educational Television: Emancipatory Education and the Right to Learn Project.* Dublin: Radio Telefís Éireann in association with the Equality Studies Centre.

Kuhn, T. (1961). *The Structure of Scientific Revolutions.* Chicago University Press.

Lather, P. (1986). Research as praxis. *Harvard Educational Review,* 56 (3):257–77.

Lather, P. (1991). *Getting Smart: Feminist Research and Pedagogy With/In the Postmodern.* New York: Routledge.

Lynch, K. (1989). *The Hidden Curriculum: Reproduction in Education, A Reappraisal.* Lewes: Falmer Press.

Lynch, K. (1990). Reproduction: the role of cultural factors and educational mediators. *British Journal of Sociology of Education,* 11 (1):3–20.

Lynch, K., and O'Neill, C. (1994). The colonisation of social class in education. *British Journal of Sociology of Education,* 15 (3):307–24.

Lynch, K., and O'Riordan, C. (1996). *Social Class, Inequality and Higher Education: Barriers to Equality of Access and Participation among School Leavers.* University College Dublin, Registrar's Office.

McLanahan, S., Sorensen, A., and Watson, D. (1989). Sex differences in poverty. *Signs: Journal of Women, Culture and Society,* 15 (1):102–22.

Mies, M. (1984). Towards a methodology for feminist research. In E. Albach (ed.), *German Feminism: Readings in Politics and Literature*, Albany: State University of New York Press.

Nolan, B. (1991). *The Wealth of Irish Households*. Dublin: Combat Poverty Agency.

Nolan, B., and Farrell, B. (1990). *Child Poverty in Ireland*. Dublin: Combat Poverty Agency.

O'Brien, M. (1987). Home school relations in inner city Dublin. University College Dublin, Education Department, unpublished MA thesis.

O'Dowd, L. (1992). Colonial dimensions. In Centre for Research and Documentation, *Is Ireland a Third World Country?* Belfast: Beyond the Pale Publications.

Oliver, M. (1992). Changing the social relations of research production. *Disability, Handicap and Society*, 7:1011–14.

O'Neill, C. (1992). *Telling It Like It Is*. Dublin: Combat Poverty Agency.

Phillips, A. (1995). *The Politics of Presence*. Oxford University Press.

Popkewitz, T. (1984). *Paradigm and Ideology in Educational Research*. Lewes: Falmer Press.

Qvortrup, J. (1991). Childhood as a social phenomenon. *Eurosocial Report, Volume 36*. Vienna: European Centre.

Qvortrup, J. (1994). *Childhood Matters: Social Theory, Practice and Politics*. Aldershot: Avebury.

Raven, J., et al. (1975). *A Summary of Attitudes of Post-Primary Teachers and Pupils*, vol. 2. Dublin: Irish Association for Curriculum Development.

Reason, P. (ed.) (1988). *Human Inquiry in Action: Developments in New Paradigm Research*. London: Sage.

Reason, P., and Rowan, J. (eds.) (1981). *Human Inquiry: A Sourcebook of New Paradigm Research*. Chichester: John Wiley and Sons.

Reinhartz, S. (1979). *On Becoming a Social Scientist*. San Francisco: Jossey Bass.

Saunders, J.M. (1991). 'New' structural poverty? *The Sociological Quarterly*, 32 (2):179–99.

Shavit, Y., and Blossfeld, H.P. (eds.) (1993). *Persistent Inequality: Changing Educational Attainment in Thirteen Countries*. Oxford: Westview Press.

Smeeding, T., Torrey, B., and Rein, M. (1990). Patterns of income and poverty: status of children and elderly in eight countries. In J.L. Palmer et al. (eds.), *The Vulnerable*. Washington: The Urban Institute.

Smith, D. (1988). *The Everyday World as Problematic: A Feminist Sociology*. Milton Keynes: Open University Press.

Spivak, G. (1988). Can the subaltern speak? In C. Nelson and L. Grossberg (eds.), *Marxism and the Interpretation of Culture*. Chicago: University of Illinois Press.

Whelan, C., and Whelan, B. (1984). *Social Mobility in the Republic of Ireland: A Comparative Perspective*. Dublin: Economic and Social Research Institute, Paper No. 116.

Willis, P. (1977). *Learning to Labour: How Working Class Kids Get Working Class Jobs*. Westmead, UK: Saxon House.

Winter, R. (1991). Post-modern sociology as a democratic educational practice? Some suggestions. *British Journal of Sociology of Education*, 12 (4):467–81.

NOTES

1 This chapter is based on a paper published by the authors in the *British Journal of Sociology of Education*, vol. 15, no. 3, 1994. It represents an attempt to develop the ideas of that paper by

exploring further the inequalities that persist in the social relations of research production. Cathleen O'Neill approaches the theme from the perspective of a community activist, while Kathleen Lynch presents a perspective from inside the academy.

2   This is a song in the play *Class Attack*, which was written in 1989/90. The play comprises a series of satirical sketches on four themes: education, the churches, the media and community work. Each sketch focuses on how middle-class institutions in society dominate working-class people and use their oppression for their own professional purposes. The play was written by a group of working-class Dublin women with some middle-class collaborators.

3   We are aware of the intellectual complexity and academic division which underpins the debate about social class (Crompton, 1993). This issue will not be addressed here although its importance is recognised. We use the term 'working class' here to refer to those who live on low incomes for most of their lives, many of whose families have lived in relative poverty and economic insecurity for generations. A significant proportion of those who are poorest in society, including women and children in particular, are primarily dependent on social welfare. Others are employed in the low-wage, casualised end of the 'secondary' labour market (increasingly in the services area of cleaning, catering, shop assisting), or they live on unrecorded earnings in the informal sector. Many do not belong therefore to the social class system in the classical Marxist sense, though they remain poor and powerless nonetheless.

4   Kilmount is a suburb of Dublin in which over 50% of the population were living on social welfare at the time the study was undertaken.

5   With education, access to embodied and social capital may also change, arising from the styles of living and learning which one engages in, and the social contacts one makes in education. (See Bourdieu, 1986 for a discussion on the different forms of cultural capital.)

6   The special edition of the *British Journal of Sociology of Education*, vol. 13, no. 4 (1992), devoted to the analysis of 'Poverty and Education' is a notable exception.

7   Cathleen O'Neill has undertaken a study of the effects of poverty on her own community, where 52% of the families live on social welfare, *Telling It Like It Is* (1992). This is a unique piece of research as it was done by a working-class woman on her own locality. Eighty families with 356 children in the Kilmount area of Dublin were interviewed and their accounts of their lives, the good and the bad, are documented in the book. The women tell their own story and we use this at times to illustrate points that we want to make about education.

8   Daly (1992) has shown that poverty differentials have grown in the UK, Italy and Portugal in the 1980s. It is estimated that forty-nine million people in the EU were affected by poverty in 1985 and that women and children are especially affected (McLanahan, Sorensen and Watson, 1989; Smeeding, Torrey and Rein, 1990; Nolan, 1991; Davies and McLoughlin, 1991; Qvortrup, 1991; Daly, 1992). Callan, Nolan et al. (1996) have identified similar trends in Ireland. We know from a whole array of social mobility studies in different European countries, including those in the North and the South of Ireland, that the social democratic project of utilising education to foster the breakdown of social class differentials has been only marginally successful. And we find in many countries in Europe that there is a great gap between those who are relatively comfortable and secure and those who are increasingly marginalised and impoverished.

CHAPTER 3

RESISTANCE IN HIGHER EDUCATION:
THE CASE OF EQUALITY STUDIES*

THE POSSIBILITIES FOR RESISTANCE AND CHANGE IN EDUCATION

The reason for including a paper on the development of Equality Studies in this book is to document the possibilities for change which exist within education. While being critical of certain resistance theorists' solutions to major social and educational inequalities, both within this volume and elsewhere, I am keenly aware nonetheless of the importance of identifying spaces and places where change is possible. Without a recognition of the role which cultural agents can play in redefining the purposes and practices of education, there is a danger of being swamped by determinism, be it of the traditional Marxist or the conservative kind.

This chapter documents some of the struggles and motivations which inspired the setting up of Equality Studies within the university system and the barriers which have to be confronted in realising change at this level. As the development of Equality Studies was a collective one involving seven key academics,[1] this paper is simply an account of the work of the group from the perspective of the author as a sociologist of education.

The chapter begins with a brief description of Equality Studies. This is followed by a brief historical account of the setting up of the Equality Studies Centre and getting the 'licence' to teach. It focuses in particular on how the Centre developed through exploiting opportunities available in University College Dublin in the mid-1980s for the presentation of new ideas on the development of the university. The second part of the paper examines the reasons why sociology, and in particular critical and neo-Marxist sociology of education, became inadequate as a way of expressing a set of feelings and ideas about equality. The final part of the paper stresses the importance of identifying and being prepared to utilise available opportunities to create constructive change in society.

* I would like to express my thanks to all my colleagues in Equality Studies whose support has made it possible to write this paper, and especially to John Baker for his helpful comments on an earlier draft. The views expressed in the paper are mine and I am aware that if my colleagues were to write a similar account of their involvement in Equality Studies it would be different.

WHAT IS EQUALITY STUDIES?

The Equality Studies Centre is a research and teaching department of University College Dublin. It offers a postgraduate diploma and master's degree programme, a non-graduate certificate programme and a Ph.D. programme. Some one hundred and fifty people have graduated from the Centre since it first opened its doors to students in 1990/91. The Centre is also actively involved in research and policy work at international, national and local levels.

The research and teaching covers four main areas of equality, with several subdivisions within each: Minorities and Discrimination, Gender Inequalities, Class Structures and Inequality, and Development and Global Inequalities.

The approach to research methodology is broadly within the emancipatory model (Lather, 1986; Lynch, 1999, forthcoming). Our goal is to work with, rather than for, marginalised groups in research and through our education programmes (which are oriented towards activists from various backgrounds). We try to maintain strong links with grass-roots organisations in teaching, research and outreach work. A multidisciplinary and interdisciplinary approach is adopted involving researchers in the fields of law, sociology, economics, political theory, feminist theory and social policy. We are the only Equality Studies Centre of our kind that we are aware of.

Despite the relative universality of 'equality' as a public value, it is a highly complex one and one which has been defined and interpreted, both politically and intellectually, in many different ways. There is an enormous difference between those who support equality only in the basic sense, those who support various liberal interpretations of equality, and those who regard radical egalitarianism as the only equality value worth pursuing in the long term (Baker, 1998). Our object is a) to work on the clarification of what is meant by equality; b) to examine patterns of inequality and their interrelationships; c) to develop explanatory paradigms for understanding inequality; d) to develop a vision of an egalitarian society and a global order; and e) to identify institutional, policy, political and strategic frameworks for achieving equality in different spheres (Baker, 1997).

HISTORICAL DEVELOPMENT

The idea of establishing a centre for the study of equality arose for a number of reasons, some of which were academic and some of which were personal. In my own case, a deep-seated understanding of the politics of knowledge was crucial. Long before the rise of postmodernism, work within the 'new sociology of education' and emancipatory education had taught me (throughout the 1970s) that the boundaries and frames of disciplines could be deconstructed and redefined (Young, 1971; Freire, 1972). It was clear that education in the context of injustice is not neutral; it is, as Freire has noted, either for domestication or for freedom. Knowing that what constitutes legitimate academic knowledge is both contested and negotiated was an important sociological insight guiding and inspiring action. The realisation that there was nothing sacred about disciplinary boundaries was a stimulus in challenging the received wisdom of the university about disciplines as non-negotiable reified entities.

THE PERSONAL AS POLITICAL

At a personal level, one of the many factors which reinforced my own interest in equality was the high visibility in both our own society and other societies, especially in majority world countries (the so-called Third World countries), of persistent economic, political, social and cultural inequalities. The persistence of human rights abuses in a wide range of countries was also a binding influence, especially when those human rights abuses were perpetrated by the so-called advanced countries of the West. The disabling and constraining effects which inequalities had on the quality of life for many millions of people, be it through hunger, torture, discrimination, lack of education, poor health care, poverty or lack of work opportunities, led to a questioning of the role of the academy in addressing these fundamental concerns. The question kept repeating itself: why do human rights abuses and inequalities persist? And what can we do to create a society and a wider global order in which injustices, inequalities and human rights abuses do not exist? A particular concern was to explore the role which the academy could play in answering these questions.

THE CHALLENGE OF THE WIDER POLITICAL CONTEXT

Equality Studies began in a particular historical context, one which recognised the importance of ideological systems as sites of resistance and as potential agents of change. Undoubtedly part of the stimulus to develop a new analysis of injustice and inequality sprang from political developments in Ireland at the time. When we formed the Equality Studies Working Group in 1986, Ireland was undergoing profound changes both economically and socially. The 1980s were a time of growing unemployment and emigration; a number of divisive constitutional campaigns around divorce and abortion were also being fought out; monetarism was being actively promoted as a guide to fiscal policy, both by Thatcherism in Britain and by Reaganism in the United States, and the winds of monetarism were beginning to blow in Ireland. These developments created a sense of urgency about developing an alternative vision for Irish society. Equality Studies seemed to offer a space to explore alternative views and to critically examine the emerging modes of thinking and policy-making.

Setting up Equality Studies involved a lot of political work (in the generic sense of that word), including the mobilisation of opinion, lobbying and strategic action. We were keenly aware that setting up Equality Studies represented a challenge to existing definitions of legitimate academic knowledge, not only in our own university, but in the wider international academic setting. Equality Studies did not exist anywhere else so its case had to be proved. Our strategy from the outset was to utilise opportunities and contradictions within the university to push for change. We also relied heavily on the support of more senior academics (professors) who either were sympathetic to our ideal, or simply believed in the liberal right to 'free speech' in a university.

In 1986 the president of the university issued an invitation to all staff to put forward new ideas for the development of teaching and research in the university. The intention was to draw up a College Development Plan and submissions were requested directly from individual staff as well as departments. A number of us with equality-related research interests organised a meeting, and a variety of staff known to have an academic interest in equality issues were invited. This led to the development of the Equality Studies Working Group, which was a loosely knit group drawn from a number of different departments and faculties, including sociology, education, law, politics, business administration, along with an economist from the environmental centre. (Members of the university's Women's Studies Forum — comprising administrative, library, secretarial, academic and other staff — were also important supporters at the time.) The Equality Studies Group prepared a proposal for the Development Plan which was submitted on 26 October 1986 and signed by Alpha Connelly from Law, Máire Nic Ghiolla Phádraig from Sociology and Kathleen Lynch from Education. The proposal put forward was the development of an inter-faculty Master's degree and postgraduate Diploma in Equality Studies.

After this began an ongoing battle for recognition, both of ourselves as serious innovators and of the academic ideals which we were proposing. And I use the language of struggle deliberately as there were numerous attempts from a variety of quarters in the university to halt the advance of Equality Studies. While left-wing and some liberal activists were our ardent supporters, certain right-wing activists of various persuasions mobilised against us. Our correspondence was not answered by the senior personnel of the college or if answered was treated lightly. One got the feeling many senior staff believed that if they ignored us for long enough we might 'go away'. Quite frankly no one seriously believed that a concept as radical as Equality Studies would ever find a home in a traditional university such as ours. Even Women's Studies, which had operated successfully as a Women's Studies Forum within the university for a number of years, had not become an established field of study or a department in UCD, and it was an established field of study in other universities while Equality Studies was not.

The first step in gaining recognition involved getting a place at a major university exhibition held in September 1987, known as 'Campus Ireland', which was designed to promote UCD. A number of influential professors within the university, and powerful groups outside, gave support. By gaining the backing of outside groups who were respected for their equality-related work, not only did we gain real political allies who could be called on for support if we were challenged, but we began to gain respect as people who had to be taken seriously. This was followed by a long period of negotiation across three faculties: arts, law, and philosophy and sociology. Our proposals were put to a vote at various faculties and academic council (the governing academic body of the university) and defeated initially. Eventually, we obtained approval (on the basis of majority votes at the various assemblies) to establish a teaching programme in 1989. Our ultimate success was related not just to the refinement and development of our proposal so that it was both intellectually and administratively unassailable, but to the effective mobilisation of support at different levels. In addition, we always worked collectively, with all planning and actions undertaken in the name of the Equality Studies Group. We thereby avoided the organisational danger of having the project identified (and possibly dismissed) as the purely personal interest of an individual. The climate of change which pervaded the university at the time and the support of key personnel among the deans and professors was also crucial to our success.[2]

In late 1989, in the context of plans for new structures in the university, we obtained approval for the setting up of the Centre. Subsequent to this, however, we experienced what could only be entitled organisational strangulation. While we (and other new centres established at the time, including Women's Studies, Drama Studies, Film Studies, etc.) were allowed to exist, we were constantly in a state of contestation with the university over resources and staffing. Only after a lengthy period of 'probation', almost six years, and numerous protests and representations were permanent staff formally allocated to the Centre. There are now three permanent staff there and several part-time staff, many of whom are based in other departments of either our own or other universities.

Establishing legitimacy was and is a major struggle for us in the university, and to a lesser degree outside of it. Our links with grass-roots organisations and with policy-makers and processes granted us a certain kind of legitimacy. It was and is more difficult to close down a centre of learning which is publicly known and respected and which has links with vocal activists than it is to close down and redeploy detached academics. Having links with outside bodies was part of a strategy for maintaining legitimacy and simultaneously a strategy for mobilising support.

In conclusion, I would tentatively suggest that the following factors were important in establishing Equality Studies in the university: 1) having a clearly articulated vision of the importance and purpose of Equality Studies; 2) developing a well-thought-out academic programme thereby foreclosing the inevitable challenge that the idea was intellectually untenable in the first place; 3) being collectively determined to persist at seeking approval over an extended period of time: 4) working collaboratively in equal partnership within the Working Group; 5) working collaboratively with other academics pursuing similar objectives across the university; 6) identifying and exploiting available opportunities and avenues open to us, including the security of being tenured staff; 7) having sponsors and supporters among senior university personnel; 8) getting the visible support of respected voluntary and other bodies with an interest in equality issues; 9) managing the inevitable conflict between careerism and idealism that new initiatives like this present.

ACADEMIC CONSIDERATIONS

At the personal level, the motivation to develop Equality Studies arose from a sense of compassion and injustice. It arose also from a desire to marry normative considerations with scientific and critical analysis, and in so doing to move beyond all three. It became increasingly clear, especially working in a field as multidisciplinary as education, that the answer to the problems of inequality was not in the hand of any single discipline. While scientific analysis offered valuable insights into the patterns and causes of inequality it did not offer alternatives; while normative political theory identified ideal 'egalitarian states', these often appeared utopian and removed from the realpolitik of public life; critical analysis identified the weaknesses and limitations of institutions and systems but failed to specify how change was to be effected within them.

My personal experience of academic life had been that much of intellectual thought is governed by fashion. When an issue was in fashion, it received intellectual attention and was supported by research funding and academic recognition. As it went out of fashion, no matter how morally compelling it might be, it became less noticeable; it became invisible. In the study of education and sociology over the years, equality themes moved in and out of intellectual discourse, as the political climate shifted. Within education, while social class inequalities were central preoccupations at times, they receded in importance as feminism problematised the position of women in Western Europe. In contexts, such as Northern Ireland, where religious discrimination and inequality was a key issue, social class or even gender inequalities did not receive the same attention that they did elsewhere. While this may seem inevitable to many, it is a practice that needs to be examined. While no one inequality is of lesser importance than another, what is questionable is the way equality issues are allowed to recede or are avoided in a relatively unproblematic way within academic discourse.[3] The politically unfashionable seems to become the intellectually marginal. While the problem of intellectual fetishisms and fads is by no means the prerogative of the social sciences, equality is too fundamental a human value to be left to fashion. It is a fundamental tenet not only of our own constitution in Ireland but of the Universal Declaration of Human Rights and of the International Convention on Civil and Political Rights. Indeed democracy itself is premised on equality.

MARXISM, IDEOLOGY, STRUGGLE AND RESISTANCE

There is no doubt that our thinking in Equality Studies has been directly influenced by Marxist theory. My own initial insights into equality issues had their intellectual origins in Marxist and neo-Marxist writing in the sociology of education. The failure of classical Marxist theory to provide a theoretical framework for the analysis of inequalities apart from social class is what made it impossible to embrace Marxism in its totality as either an analytical or a normative tool. In line with most feminists, I recognised the limitations of locating the sources of all inequality in the productive sphere of economic relations. Although the relations of production are central to any analysis of equality, classical Marxism largely ignored the relations of reproduction, and indeed of production, in the domestic arena (Delphy and Leonard, 1992). Other inequalities arising from age, race, disability, ethnicity, religion, sexual orientation or regional status were not addressed systematically in Marxist theory. Neither indeed were these inequalities addressed systematically within the Weberian tradition or within feminist theory. Equality Studies represents an attempt therefore to develop the intellectual apparatus which would both explain inequalities and offer an analysis of alternative futures both in the theoretical and the applied institutional sense. The aim is not simply to understand how to develop a classless society or a feminist one, rather how to create an egalitarian one.

One of the ways in which Marxism had a direct and positive impact on Equality Studies, however, is through its analysis of ideological institutions. Among the factors which informed the development of Equality Studies was a keen awareness of the role of ideology in the development of social change. And ideology is being used here in the positive Gramscian sense, recognising the relative autonomy of ideology, and ideology as a site of struggle. Ideology is a site of resistance, and it is one of the few sites of resistance where academics and educationalists generally exercise direct influence in terms of social change. The institutions of higher education are both definers and reproducers of dominant intellectual forms; in that sense they play a central role in the creation and development of ideologies in society. Moreover, the materialised and institutional nature of ideological practice is something that is very evident in the everyday struggles of university life. Our awareness of these sociological realities, and a realisation that Ireland is a small society, where the institutional mechanisms which can promote or resist change are both visible and relatively accessible, encouraged us to set about establishing a new intellectual agenda in academia. Gramsci's work (1976) has also inspired an awareness of the difference between the practices of organic and traditional intellectuals. Academics are not without choice; they can work either as voices of dominant forces (as traditional intellectuals) or as progressive voices (organic intellectuals) challenging the hegemonic discourses within the academy and popular culture.

The challenge of inequality demanded a move beyond the domesticating role of traditional academics; it opened up the challenge of how to develop organic voices on inequality within the academy. An awareness of the political salience of intellectual and cultural struggles, therefore, both informed and inspired the commitment to establish a new discourse on equality.

THE INFLUENCE OF SOCIOLOGY

Equality Studies like all academic discourses is both culturally and historically situated. It emerged in the context of a particular set of intellectual, cultural and political circumstances. While certain fields of sociological research offered insights and challenges which provided the impetus for Equality Studies in my own case, there were also push factors which precipitated a move outside sociological theory and research.

There were two dominant traditions in Irish sociology up to the 1980s. The first major influence on Irish sociology was what became known as 'Catholic sociology'. 'This had its origins in continental Western Europe in the social encyclicals of successive popes and the Catholic social movement of the late nineteenth and early twentieth century. It was meant to counteract the rise of socialism and secularism in Europe . . .' (Clancy et al., 1986:6–7). The second tradition was essentially an empirical, and generally atheoretical, tradition of statistical and social inquiry inspired by similar movements in Britain, in particular. The empirical tradition did not gain ground until the 1970s and the 1980s, however, with the development of funded research institutes such as the Economic and Social Research Institute (ESRI) and An Foras Talúntais (The Agricultural Institute).

The late 1960s to the 1980s saw the development of a strong empirically oriented research tradition. Yet there was a consistent normative dimension to this sociology. Inequality, especially social-class-related inequality, was a central theme in the empirical research of the ESRI and among researchers from University College Dublin, St Patrick's College Maynooth and University College Cork. This was especially true in the area of sociology of education (Drudy, 1991).

Without extensive research, it is not possible to say with certainty whether this type of orientation was due to the prior socialisation of its exponents into the secular liberal reformism emerging in post-war Europe, or socialisation into Catholic principles of justice (as defined in documents such as *Rerum Novarum*), which informed so much of Catholic social teaching, or through the influence of both traditions. O'Dowd (1992) has observed, however, that it is only in the last twenty years that secular intellectuals have dominated Irish life. Up to that time clerical intellectuals were in control. Given the central role of the Catholic church in early sociological training, in particular, it is highly likely that the Catholic concern with social justice (albeit in a weak and selective sense) exercised much influence, even if it was not always direct and visible. While Catholic social teaching was profoundly conservative around issues such as reproductive rights for women and political organisation (e.g. its entrenched opposition to communism in Europe), its concept of the ideal society was one in which market capitalism would not have free rein. It wanted to promote a social order which would be a *via media* between capitalism and socialism (Clancy et al., 1986:7). The Irish Constitution, which was directly influenced by Catholic social teaching, reflected this position, both in relation to social policy (Article 45) and in relation to private property, where it noted that the exercise of private property rights should 'be regulated by the principles of social justice' (Article 43.2.1).

Whatever the causal factors, equality was a central theme in many empirically based works throughout the 1980s and 1990s (Hannan, Breen et al., 1983; Clancy, 1988, 1995; Lynch, 1989; Breen et al., 1990; Callan, Nolan et al., 1996; Hannan, Smith et al., 1996). While equality was the central theme, the analysis was focused on understanding the inequality rather than changing it or developing models of alternative systems. Irish empirical research was strongly positivist; it assumed the mantle of 'objectivity' as the hallmark of intellectual authenticity. While theoretical interpretations were posited, the strength of the argument generally lay in the range and depth of the statistical evidence provided.

As in so much work elsewhere, equality itself was treated as an unprob-lematic good (Connell, 1993). It was never defined or disaggregated (O'Sullivan, 1989). Yet without its being named as an objective, a liberal notion of equality underpinned much of the education and related research. Success was measured in terms of the proportionate representation of working-class groups in the elite sectors of education, including upper second level and higher education. Selective social mobility for the talented working class was the implicitly espoused goal. Equality for women in education was defined in terms of equal access and participation in male-dominated fields, especially science and technology (Hannan, Breen et al., 1983). While the espousal of liberal notions of equality of opportunity was not unique to Irish sociology of education (Arnot, 1991), it was a tradition which has been largely unchallenged in Ireland.

The culturally specific experience of equality empiricism provoked the development of Equality Studies in both a positive and a negative sense. In the positive sense, it created an awareness of the importance of the equality agenda per se. It also operated as a challenge to move beyond liberalism, as much of this research within the empirical tradition did not address some of the most fundamental questions about equality, either as an intellectual concept or as a socio-political goal.

Speaking personally, there was also a distancing from theoretical sociology which represented an interrelated push factor in the development of Equality Studies. Sociological theory, as it was taught in Ireland, was founded on the intellectual concerns of the founding 'European Fathers [*sic*]', most especially

Durkheim and Weber. Its central intellectual agenda was set in the context of industrialised capitalism. Issues of colonisation or post-colonialism were not central problematics of sociological theory as it was imported into Ireland, although these were key issues within Irish society. The inequalities arising from gender, ethnicity, disability or sexual orientation also received little attention. In effect, many of the 'big public issues' which interested me as an Irish sociologist were not on the main academic menu! The problems which sociology posed for me were not unique. They were mirrored in women's detachment from the masculine bias of a male-dominated sociology (Stanley and Wise, 1983; Smith, 1987). They were also visible in the alienation of writers who were in the so-called peripheral states:

> As a New Zealander, I found myself 'marginal' — positioned both inside and outside the Anglo-American discourse which dominated the discipline . . . my reading imposed a distance between me and my natural environment. (Middleton, 1994:127)

It was no accident of history that so many of the ruling voices were themselves located in powerful capitalist states in the West, such as France, Germany and the United States. Cultural domination was a close correlate of economic supremacy. To globalise a point of view, resources were required, including access to cultural markets. Cultural markets in the form of publishing houses and journals were also centred in the colonising states, both the new and the old. And to say this is not to lay claim to some type of moral high ground. No doubt had historical circumstances been different, Irish sociology could have been ranked with the colonisers rather than the colonised.

While Irish sociologists must accept responsibility for how theoretical sociology was incorporated into intellectual and academic discourse, the experience of practising sociological theory within Ireland exposes the difficulty that any small state or society has in making sociology its own. Sociology is a historically situated discourse. It was developed in dominant states by dominant groups and consequently it is centred on dominant interests. Only through external challenges, such as those emerging from feminist theory, has it begun to make problematic the unwritten assumptions of its own origins. And most of its unwritten assumptions remain unquestioned.

Bourdieu (1993:50) has pointed out that 'the unconscious of a discipline is its history; its unconscious is made up of its social conditions of production masked and forgotten'. The problem that sociology has is that the axioms or doxas of the discipline, those intellectual assumptions which 'go without saying', which are accepted 'beyond question', are themselves problematic. They are so hidden that no one names them. And one of these axioms was, and indeed is, that those who live in smaller states and societies are expected to be interested in the sociology of large (usually colonising) states. Reciprocation of interest is not required. Indeed, to do and practise sociology is to be interested in the sociology of the big powers and their institutions. Not alone is interest expected but it is axiomatic that questions are framed in the language and theories of dominant discourses, no matter how inappropriate these might be.

So the first distancing from sociology was rooted in its theoretical distance from Irish society. The seeming inability of positivist sociology to address the issue of equality in a systematic and holistic manner created a further distance.

POSITIVIST SOCIOLOGY AND THE QUESTION OF VALUES

The limitations of the work of equality empiricists within Ireland was related to a more generalised problem with the ability of sociology to handle the issue of equality outside the liberal framework, and in a manner which was acceptable and accountable to those oppressed groups which were the subject of so many of its sociological studies. In particular, positivist sociology seemed unable to go beyond describing and explaining the level and nature of inequality in society.

Positivist sociology does not deny the existence of values. Indeed there is truth in Hammersley's claims (1992:136) that Weber has perhaps been misinterpreted in terms of value neutrality, particularly in relation to the suggestion that Weber believed that research could or should be free from the influence of values. What Weber claims, as he rightly points out, is that value judgments should not be presented as if they have been or could be scientifically validated, that researchers should seek to minimise the influence of their views about how things ought to be on their factual judgments about how they are, and that the main business of research should be the production of factual rather than value conclusions. However, this position does pose serious problems for those interested in social change and for those interested in particular value goals like equality. It eschews critique as a practice in social analysis. It denies the fact that the subject of research represents a value choice and the fact that the silence around certain themes is a value omission. It does not address the value implications of particular research methodologies and the value-laden effects of particular factual conclusions.

Knowledge does not simply have *causal* explanations and *circumstantial* correlations, it also has *consequential* implications, although these may not be self-evident at any given time. That is to say, the documentation of particular realities in the symbolic systems of academic discourse creates new realities, not least of which is the new reality of the written and spoken word itself. By defining and naming particular perspectives on selected worlds, such worlds and perspectives become more real. The way in which the worlds and stories are interpreted or defined, the perspectives on which they are based, creates particular emphases and poses certain policy options as more inevitable, feasible and desirable than others. In the field of educational research, for example, a fundamental assumption of equality empiricists has been that upward social mobility is a desirable social phenomenon (Goldthorpe et al., 1980; Breen et al., 1990; Halsey, 1991). Liberal political assumptions and values are enshrined in their research, without ever becoming explicit or articulated. It is conventionally assumed in such models that if working-class people (or disabled people, ethnic or racial minorities, women, etc.) move up the social class ladder in numbers proportionate to their representation in the population, then equality is being attained. The fact that the hierarchies of wealth, power and privilege remain in society and that the lower rungs of the hierarchy in a hierarchical system must be filled, albeit by migrant workers or ethnic minorities, is ignored or sidelined by not being incorporated into the model. The net effect of promoting selective social mobility has been to legitimate and rigidify the class structure without significantly altering the social class patterns of educational participation. Although the equality empiricists might disavow any responsibility for the policy decisions which have been implemented on the basis of their research, and while it is very obvious that research does not inform policy in any direct linear fashion, it is still a fact that certain forms of research, particularly those based on national samples and undertaken in institutions which have legitimacy with the policy establishment, are consulted, and sometimes even accepted, by policy-makers. While the conclusions may be factual, they are based on value-specific assumptions and they set the agenda for value-related policies. The research has consequential correlations which are value-driven.

The liberal political assumptions underpinning the research of the equality empiricists in education have been noted by Arnot (1991). By encouraging selective mobility, their work has implicitly and effectively reinforced deep structural inequalities. This is not to say that such an outcome was intended. Rather it is to say that the equality empiricists did not recognise that liberal equal opportunities represent a distraction from the business of equality of condition (Tawney, 1964). Such policies make unequal societies appear reasonable, as it is assumed that if only liberal policies were implemented efficiently and effectively, then inequality would not be reproduced. The reality is, however, that liberal equal opportunities will only ever have limited effects; at best they will allow only a selective amount of social mobility for the relatively advantaged within the target group (be they women, disabled people, ethnic minorities, etc.).

The severe limitations of liberal equal opportunities policies espoused within the dominant positivist traditions in the social sciences was therefore an important motivating force for establishing Equality Studies.

CRITICAL EDUCATION THEORY AND VALUES IN RESEARCH

Critical educational theory is a very real attempt to present a model of explanation which incorporates a theory of praxis-oriented action. The fundamental tension between fact and value has not been resolved even in critical theory, however; models purporting to explore the contradictions of social reality which can be exploited for action and social change are illuminating. Whether such identifications are liberatory is another matter. (For a further discussion of this point, see Questions 4 and 5, p. 4.)

In adult education circles in Ireland, for example, it is now widely recognised that *social* empowerment in the Freirean sense is not necessarily a priority value for oppressed people themselves (Inglis, 1986; O'Fathaigh and O'Sullivan, 1997). Indeed, *personal* empowerment and social mobility are, in fact, the priority for many. While the educator may define the goal as social empowerment, the outcome may very well be increased aspirations for social mobility, a feeding in to the very class structures which liberatory education itself was designed to critique.

And what this reflects is the reality of a stratified society where social mobility is a publicly lauded goal and a personal expectation among most. Also, it shows how a particular social practice will not necessarily produce a particular outcome regardless of context. While social empowerment and conscientisation may have been priority values in Recife or São Paulo, and while social and personal empowerment may be synonymous in these contexts at a given time, this is not necessarily true in other political or cultural contexts. Even if critical social theory were to address itself to alternatives, what these alternatives might be is not simply determined as the causal chain of social change is not linear, singular or predefined.

Another problem is that critical education theory has not really liaised with normative moral and political theory in any overt and direct sense. So while critical social science implies a connection between positive (explanatory / descriptive) science and normative discourses such as those of moral or political philosophy, the normative or ethical dimension is rarely acknowledged (Sayer, 1994). It is as if for researchers to 'pass' as serious, normative orientations must be concealed or slipped in without being named for what they are. To attempt to identify a vision of an alternative future was construed as utopianism, Platonic idealism, a departure from 'real' social science. The job of analysis, even critical analysis, offered no systematic opportunity to open up and explore different concepts of social systems. It certainly seemed that there was a reluctance to explore systematically the feasibility, desirability and operational rules of alternative systems. There was no serious attempt to develop 'counterfactuals', serious and systemic outlines of alternative structures and systems (Sayer, 1995).

Critical theory is excellent on critique but seems unable to offer concrete alternative models. Vague notions of justice and equality are often brought into play without any clear analysis of the policy and political implications of different types of systems. Students are taught to think critically, but not necessarily constructively, about alternatives. One area where I felt this intensely in my own teaching and research was in analysing curriculum issues and working with teachers around developing alternative views. While neo-

Marxist and critical theory presented an excellent account of how middle-class (and male, white, able-ist) hegemony operated in education, it did not offer any educationally informed concept of an alternative. The constant criticism which students made about the sociology of education was that it analysed the problems but left them bereft of a solution grounded in a theory of human as well as social development. The fields of research and theory where potential solutions and alternatives could be explored and developed were not central to the agenda of sociologists of education. As one whose primary interest was in equality, there seemed to me to be no option therefore but to work towards establishing a new field of study, one which would integrate critical, analytical and normative traditions.

CONCLUSION

What has been suggested in this paper is that Equality Studies represents a form of resistance to particular political, economic and intellectual developments in society. It represents an attempt by academics to use higher education as a site of resistance for the promotion of change. Because of the central role which higher education can, and does, play in formally articulating perspectives and visions of society, it is suggested that it is crucial for academics interested in challenging dominant paradigms and perspectives to use higher education as a site of resistance.

Much of resistance theory to date has focused on alternative pedagogies and teaching methodologies as key sites of resistance. It has focused especially on individual teachers in classrooms as agents of change. The analysis has often centred therefore on people who may have little control over the forms of knowledge that they teach. In most centralised education systems like ours, core curricula and syllabi are laid down by the state or state-controlled agencies. This is not to suggest that teachers as collective agents (be these smaller collectives such as subject associations or groups of specialised teachers, or larger bodies such as teacher unions) do not exercise power, as they do; they exercise enormous potential to realise or resist change in Irish education as they are established partners at a range of different levels within the decision-making machinery of the state. Their collective power will be reinforced with the passing of the Education (No. 2) Bill of 1997.

Those who work in higher education have not been central to analysis in resistance theory although they have a much more powerful role to play in defining and interpreting knowledge and pedagogical styles than either primary or second-level teachers. The legitimation and elaboration of new forms of knowledge and pedagogical styles is, potentially at least, much more under the control of those in higher education. The argument in this paper is that higher education is a key site for the development of resistance and counter-hegemonic struggles, and its role in the supporting of other struggles and in setting agendas for new struggles should be subjected to systematic analysis. In particular, academics are centrally positioned to become agents of counter-hegemonic struggle in contexts where they are in secure and pensionable academic positions. For those in established academic positions the price to be paid for counter-hegemonic action is relatively small, often merely lack of promotion. To say this is not to deny the very real and seemingly intractable problems that confront academics in challenging traditional intellectual frameworks and methodologies within universities and institutes of higher education and research. Equality Studies was begun by a group who were already tenured; the university has granted staff to the Centre only after intense and prolonged pressure. Indeed, it could be argued that Equality Studies may only represent a legitimation exercise within a more generalised inegalitarian higher education system. It provides a socially responsible face for the university as the need arises. From this perspective, Equality Studies could be regarded as reinforcing rather than challenging the establishment. While there is legitimacy to this claim, it is strongly deterministic.

It does not recognise the dynamism inherent in any body or institution which is proactive and strategic about its teaching, research and policy work. Neither does it recognise the generative power of such a Centre for change when it is working with activists (through teaching, research and policy work) in grass-roots and other organisations.

A central presupposition in the paper has been that, in order to ensure successful resistance, educationalists must liaise with the marginalised. Liaising with the oppressed is essential so that academic institutions can enable the voice of organic intellectuals to develop and lead from within, rather than speak in their name, rob them of a voice and thereby leave them open to manipulation and leadership from without. Dialogue with those in power is also essential for the purposes of understanding the agenda of the elites as well as changing it. To identify the points of action and the sites for intervention within the machinery of the state, for example in the field of legislation or in terms of restructuring institutions and systems, it is essential to know and understand how power operates. To be effective in identifying alternative institutions and systems to those which operate at present, it is vital to understand how the present systems function. A radical academic discourse which is articulated only at the level of academic analysis, and which is the subject of debate essentially among like-minded academics, is likely to be easily overlooked and can be readily overtaken both institutionally and intellectually.

What we are questioning in Equality Studies is the role of the academic in society, in particular the role of the radical academic interested in social change. What is being suggested here is that radical academics and educationalists need to be politically and socially engaged. The institutions of the 'new right' have not been slow to recognise the power of the higher education system to further their ends; they have directly funded research and professorial positions that will generate forms of knowledge to buttress their own particular interests. The traditional supporters of egalitarian politics, such as the trade union movement, for example, have been relatively disorganised and ineffective by comparison. They have assumed that traditional intellectuals will articulate visions and perspectives which will be available to organic intellectuals to create alternative agendas. No such alternatives have been forthcoming, not least because traditional intellectuals do not necessarily espouse radical agendas, but also because those intellectuals who do share a radical vision have lacked resources and support to develop alternative research and teaching programmes within a tightly budgeted higher education system. They have also lacked definite support systems and structures for liaising with social movements which would enable them to articulate a workable vision of the future. Given these social relations of academic production, it is not that surprising that much of intellectual attention has focused on critique rather than on change.

Equality Studies represents a challenge to the role of intellectuals but also to the role of left-wing social movements in society, including the women's movement and the disability movement. It challenges us to explore the role of critical thinkers within the churches, voluntary organisations and the trade union movement. Many egalitarian oriented groups, such as trade unions and development organisations, have not invested resources in higher education, leaving it exclusively to the state to fund critical and alternative intellectual thought. Supporters of equality need to invest in the universities and institutes of higher education if they are to be in a position to develop alternative perspectives. They need to recognise and match the type and level of funding which is being provided by powerful economic interests to support their intellectual interests in higher education. And academics need to be positioned to take on that challenge.

REFERENCES

Arnot, M. (1991). Equality and democracy: a decade of struggle over education. *British Journal of Sociology of Education*, 12 (4):447–66.

Baker, J. (1997). Studying equality. *Imprints*, 2 (1): 57–71.

Baker, J. (1998). Equality. In S. Healy and B. Reynolds (eds.), *Social Policy in Ireland: Principles, Practices and Problems*. Dublin: Oak Tree Press.

Bourdieu, P. (1993). *Sociology in Question*. Sage: London.

Breen, R., Hannan, D.F., Rottman, D., and Whelan, C. (1990). *Understanding Contemporary Ireland*. Dublin: Gill & Macmillan.

Callan, T., Nolan, B., Whelan, B., Whelan, C., and Williams, J. (1996). *Poverty in the 1990s: Evidence from the Living in Ireland Survey*. Dublin: Oak Tree Press.

Clancy, P. (1988). *Who Goes to College*. Dublin: Higher Education Authority.

Clancy, P. (1995). *Access to College: Patterns of Continuity and Change*. Dublin: Higher Education Authority.

Clancy, P., Drudy, S., Lynch, K., and O'Dowd, L. (1986). *Ireland: A Sociological Profile*. Dublin: Institute of Public Administration.

Cobalti, A. (1990). Schooling inequalities in Italy: trends over time. *European Sociological Review*, 6:199–214.

Connell, R.W. (1993). *Schools and Social Justice*. Philadelphia: Temple University Press.

Delphy, C., and Leonard, D. (1992). *Familiar Exploitation: A New Analysis of Marriage and Family Life*. London: Polity Press.

Drudy, S. (1991). The sociology of education in Ireland, 1966–1991. *Irish Journal of Sociology*, 1:107–27.

Freire, P. (1972). *Pedagogy of the Oppressed*. New York: Penguin.

Goldthorpe, J.H., et al. (1980). *Social Mobility and Class Structure in Modern Britain*. Oxford: Clarendon Press.

Gramsci, A. (1976). *Selections from Prison Notebooks*, ed. by Q. Hoare and G. Nowell-Smith. London: Lawrence and Wishart.

Halsey, A.H. (1991). Educational systems and the economy. *Current Sociology*, 38 (2/3):79–101.

Hammersley, M. (1992). The paradigm wars: reports from the front. *British Journal of Sociology of Education*, 13 (1):131–43.

Hannan, D., Breen, R., Murray, B., Watson, D., and Hardiman, N. (1983). *Schooling and Sex Roles*. Dublin: Economic and Social Research Institute, Paper No. 113.

Hannan, D.F., Smyth, E., McCullagh, J., O'Leary, R., and McMahon, D. (1996). *Coeducation and Gender Equality: Exam Performance, Stress and Personal Development*. Dublin: Oak Tree Press.

Inglis, T. (1986). *Priority Areas in Adult Education*. Dublin: AONTAS (National Association of Adult Education).

Karabel, J., and Halsey, A.H. (1977). Educational research: a review and interpretation. In J. Karabel and A.H. Halsey (eds.), *Power and Ideology in Education*. London: Oxford University Press.

Lather, P. (1986). Research as praxis. *Harvard Educational Review*, 56 (3):257–77.

Lynch, K. (1989). *The Hidden Curriculum: Reproduction in Education, A Reappraisal*. Lewes: Falmer Press.

Lynch, K. (1999, forthcoming). Equality studies, the academy and the role of research in emancipatory social change. *Economic and Social Review*, 30 (1).

Lynch, K., and O'Neill, C. (1994). The colonisation of social class in education. *British Journal of Sociology of Education*, 15 (3):307–24.

Middleton, S. (1994). A post-modern pedagogy for the sociology of women's education. In M. Arnot and K. Weiler (eds.), *Feminism and Social Justice in Education, International Perspectives*. London: Falmer Press.

O'Dowd, L. (1992). State legitimacy and nationalism in Ireland. In P. Clancy, M. Kelly, J. Wiatr and R. Zoltaniecki (eds.), *Ireland and Poland: Comparative Perspectives*. Dublin: Social Science Research Centre, University College Dublin.

O'Fathaigh, M., and O'Sullivan, D. (1997). Adult education: empowerment and access, some empirical findings. *Irish Educational Studies*, 16:184–98.

O'Sullivan, D. (1989). The ideational base of Irish educational policy. In D. Mulcahy and D. O'Sullivan (eds.), *Irish Educational Policy*. Dublin: Institute of Public Administration.

Sayer, A. (1994). Alternatives and counterfactuals in critical social science. Paper presented at the XIII World Congress of Sociology, Beilefeld, Germany, 18–23 July.

Sayer, A. (1995). *Radical Political Economy: A Critique*. Oxford: Basil Blackwell.

Shavit, Y., and Blossfeld, H.P. (eds.) (1993). *Persistent Inequality: Changing Educational Attainment in Thirteen Countries*. Oxford: Westview Press.

Smith, D. (1987). *The Everyday World as Problematic*. Boston (MA): North Eastern University Press.

Stanley, L., and Wise, S. (1983). *Breaking Out: Feminist Consciousness and Feminist Research*. London: Routledge & Kegan Paul.

Tawney, R.H. (1964). *Equality*. London: Allen & Unwin.

Young, M.F.D. (ed.) (1971). *Knowledge and Control*. Middlesex, UK: Collier Macmillan.

NOTES

1 The seven founder members of Equality Studies were John Baker (Politics), John Blackwell (Environmental Institute, an economist), Teresa Brannick (Marketing), Alpha Connelly (Law), Mary Kelly and Máire Nic Ghiolla Phádraig (Sociology), and Kathleen Lynch (Education). Sadly, John Blackwell died an untimely death in 1992. We owed a lot to him for his support as an economist in the early days of Equality Studies. Apart from those who were directly involved in establishing the Centre, there were a number of other professors and lecturers in the university who played an important role in supporting the principle of Equality Studies.

2 None of the seven proposers was either a senior lecturer or a professor at the time.

3 All the research evidence available on social class inequalities in education in the European context, for example, shows that the post-war settlement on social class, including the various initiatives introduced to promote greater equality in education, has not radically altered social class relativities in terms of educational inequality (Breen et al., 1990; Cobalti, 1990; Halsey, 1991; Shavit and Blossfeld, 1993). Yet there has been a retreat from class analysis since the 1970s. While the newly emerging equality themes of race, ethnicity, women's issues or disability are equal to social class in importance, the withdrawal of interest (and funding) from class-related research, and indeed other sociological issues of great interest to oppressed sectors of humanity (especially in so-called Third World contexts), poses serious questions about the ability of the social sciences to avoid being guided by selective political interests at a given time.

SECTION 2

INEQUALITY IN EDUCATION: ISSUES FOR PARTICULAR GROUPS

CHAPTER 4

INEQUALITY IN HIGHER EDUCATION: A STUDY OF SOCIAL CLASS BARRIERS

Kathleen Lynch and *Claire O'Riordan*

INTRODUCTION

One of the most enduring theoretical models purporting to explain social-class-related inequalities in education is structuralism. Within the structuralist paradigm there are two dominant traditions, namely Marxism and Functionalism. Traditional Marxists work from a strong model of economic determinism in which education is represented largely as a highly dependent system within capitalist societies. The role of education in reproducing class inequality is seen as one of structural inevitability (Althusser, 1972; Bowles and Gintis, 1976). Functionalists working out of a Durkheimian model of educational choice also interpret class outcomes in education in a highly deterministic manner (Davis and Moore, 1945; Parsons, 1961; Dreeben, 1968). The language of selection and allocation for a stratified labour market replaces the language of reproduction but the class outcomes are deemed to be the same. In one sense what divides the Marxists from the more conservatively oriented functionalists is their normative evaluations of particular outcomes. What functionalists deem to be inevitable, and even necessary for the maintenance of social order in society, Marxists interpret as an injustice which has to be overcome.

The economic determinists are but one strand within structuralism. Bourdieu and Passeron (1977) and Apple (1979, 1982) exemplify a different explanatory tradition within neo-Marxism, namely one which emphasises the role of culture in structural determinations. Bernstein (1971, 1975) also attempted to explore the role of culture, especially through integrating macrocosmic and microcosmic models of explanation.

Structuralists claim therefore that people are 'pushed' into certain educational positions. Whether they know that they are being pushed, or whether they are pushed without knowing who or what is doing the pushing, is an open question. In either model, the assumption is that they do not 'choose' in a free and meaningful sense of that term (Gambetta, 1987).

RESPONSES TO STRUCTURALISM: RATIONAL ACTION THEORY AND RESISTANCE THEORY

Structuralist interpretations have been challenged from a number of perspectives. One of the most persistent criticisms has been the failure of structuralists to recognise the dynamic nature of the education process itself, and the role which micro-processes play in mediating educational outcomes (Mehan, 1992). Rational action theory and resistance theory represent two contemporary, and very separate, responses to structuralism, both in terms of their intellectual origin and in terms of their political assumptions. Because of the difference in the ways in which they challenge structuralist explanations, it is worth while examining some of their basic premises about why social class inequality persists and how it should be explained.

Rational Action Theory

Working out of a liberal political perspective, Goldthorpe (1996) rejects structuralist explanations and opts instead for the use of rational action theory (RAT) to explain inequalities in education. He claims that one of the major challenges facing sociology is to explain the macro-sociological realities of persisting social class inequality in education. He calls for the use of micro-sociological analysis, and in particular for the use of rational action theory, to explain the persistence of such inequality. He suggests that 'all social phenomena can and should be explained as resulting from the action and interaction of individuals' (p. 485) and that class inequality in education persists because of the rational action of particular individuals across social classes. Working on the theoretical framework developed by Boudon (1974), he concludes that it is the 'secondary effects' of social class, based on an evaluation of the projected future costs and benefits of education, that patterns choices. The conclusion which he reaches, based on his interpretation of rational action theory, is that working-class people have lower levels of educational attainment than middle-class people because working-class families perceive the risk and opportunity costs of post-compulsory and higher education to be too high relative to their resources. They need greater assurance of success if they are to take the educational risk. Ongoing educational choices are rational responses to the opportunities and constraints operating for the different classes.

Scope and Limitations of Rational Action Theory for Explaining Class Inequalities in Education   While rational action theory is valuable as a stimulus for generating research on the micro-processes of educational life, and while such work illuminates some of the procedures whereby aggregate outcomes (inequalities) occur, rational action theory does not provide a coherent framework for understanding inequality as it does not present a convincing conceptual framework for interpreting the generative causes of differences in choices.

Rational action theory, as presented in the sociology, is a mediating explanatory model rather than a foundational one. It operates out of a weak notion of rationality which does help to explain the presenting problem as to why people behave the way they do, but does not explain what it is that conditions their choices in a particular way. Neither does it explain which options are more open and/or more acceptable to particular groups than others, and why. The model does not explore the way structures, particularly in terms of state action, might explain particular social class actions.

Rational action theory also seems to take preferences as a constant in the framing of educational choices. Yet as the work of Gambetta (1987) shows, preferences are not fixed: they can be changed by the experience of schooling itself. A good or a bad school performance can alter students' educational and occupational preferences, especially among working-class students. Evidence from Irish data, on the difference in rates of transfer to higher education for different socio-economic groups, lends support to the claim that preferences are constantly being negotiated.[1]

Class differences in education are not the result of some set of preconceived preferences therefore, rather they are the by-product of an ongoing set of negotiations between agents and structures. The neat dichotomy which is drawn between intentions and structures in RAT may serve as a useful conceptual device but it ignores the dialectical interface between intentions and institutional practices in everyday life. Intentions and social structures are presented as binary opposites without recognition of the multiple ways in which they are dialectically related.

Rational action theory is also a non-transformative explanatory paradigm. It is based on traditional positivist assumptions about the role of research in society with all the colonising and managerialist outcomes which such an approach entails. From the perspective of those working out of a transformative critical perspective on inequality, this is an important limitation, as the research itself can often reinforce the inequalities it documents by colonising the lifeworld of marginalised others and leaving them without a voice, or with a greatly weakened voice (Heron, 1981; Reason and Rowan, 1981; Lather, 1991; Oliver, 1992; Lynch, 1999, forthcoming).

Resistance Theorists

Within neo-Marxism, structuralism has been criticised for its reproductive effects on educational thought (Willis, 1977; McRobbie, 1978). Resistance theorists have noted how economic determinism can contribute to reproducing the consciousness it abhors by presenting social outcomes from education as fixed and inevitable. Working out of a praxis-oriented view of knowledge, and drawing heavily on the 'education as conscientisation' model of Paulo Freire (1972), they have challenged deterministic models of explanation through the concepts of critical pedagogy, radical democracy and transformative education (Giroux, 1983, 1992; McLaren, 1995). Resistance theorists and post-structuralists attempt to marry an analytical and transformative dimension to educational theory which will help to guide action for change. It is assumed that critical pedagogy can operate as a form of cultural politics which will facilitate class-inspired social transformation (Fagan, 1995). Teachers and 'cultural workers' are defined as agents of transformation. Feminists working out of a similar resistance model also assume a transformative role for critical education for women (Weiler, 1988; Lather, 1991).

The work of resistance theorists and post-structuralists has identified spaces and places for challenging unequal social relations through education. It has enabled people to see beyond the limits of structures and to identify modes of thinking and analysing which can facilitate change. It has offered hope for change which is important in and of itself.

Limitations of Resistance Theories   One of the limitations of resistance theory is its failure to analyse the social relations of its own theorising. Resistance theorists assume a level of political interest and engagement among working-class people which is far from proved in contemporary welfare capitalist states such as Ireland (Inglis and Bassett, 1988). Also, there is very little evidence from the research and theory in this tradition of an ongoing dialogue with working-class people themselves. Although it may be entirely inadvertent, much of the resistance theory reads as a discourse written *about* people who are margin-alised rather than with them. It reads as if it were written above and beyond those about whom it speaks. It does not appear to have taken account of the substantive critiques emanating from within numerous branches of the social sciences about the intellectual and ethical limitations of research and theory which involves neither dialogue nor co-operation with the research subjects (especially where these are marginalised groups) (Reinhartz, 1979; Reason and Rowan, 1981; Lather, 1991; Oliver, 1992; Humphries and Truman, 1994). As most of resistance theory is written by middle-class people about how to enable working-class people to resist and change class structures in an educational setting, these critiques are especially relevant.

Although the many challenges which a truly dialogical (partnership) research would present are only beginning to be addressed, what appears to be happening is that the debate about dialogue, partnership and the ethical accountability of research is taking place primarily in the empirical research field. Sociological and educational theorising does not appear to be held ethically accountable to the same degree. This has to be contested, not least because theories about inequality often frame empirical research questions in the first place.

One of the other weaknesses of resistance theory as an explanatory (as opposed to a transformative) theory is that it has failed to keep a balance between the explanatory and transformative dimension of its theorising. The work is replete with references to cultural practices which offer scope for transformative action but there are relatively few concepts which deepen our understanding of how to realise change — the precise counterfactual proposals that Sayer (1995) claims are necessary to guide action are missing in much of critical thought. Their rejection of structuralism is regrettable, as an understanding of structures as dynamic entities is necessary to guide transformative action.

EMPIRICAL RESEARCH AND POLICY PERSPECTIVES ON SOCIAL CLASS: THE INFLUENCE OF LIBERALISM

Reviews of empirical research on equality in education indicate that the equality empiricists have dominated the debate about the relationship between social class and/or socio-economic groups and educational opportunity (Karabel and Halsey, 1977; Hurn, 1978; Trent et al., 1985; Blackledge and Hunt, 1985; Arnot and Barton, 1992; Torres and Rivera, 1994; Pink and Noblit, 1995). Working within a liberal political perspective and a broadly functionalist sociological tradition, they define the solution to social-class-related inequality in terms of the promotion of greater *equality of opportunity* to move (upwards) within a class-stratified society. The work of Sewell et al. (1976), Halsey et al. (1980), Eckland and Alexander (1980), Mare (1981), Dronkers (1983), Jonsson (1987), Gambetta (1987), McPherson and Willms (1987), Clancy (1988, 1995), Blossfeld (1993) and Euriat and Thelot (1995) exemplifies this tradition in a range of different countries. The work of these equality empiricists within education is paralleled by the work of stratification theorists who documented patterns of social mobility (among white men especially) (Goldthorpe et al., 1980; Whelan and Whelan, 1984; Ganzeboom et al., 1989; Raftery and Hout, 1993).

Equality objectives are defined in basically three different ways within this literature. The minimalist conception is one where equality is defined in terms of *equalising access* to different levels of education for relatively disadvantaged groups within a stratified society and educational system. Moving from this, certain researchers focus on *equal participation*. Equality of participation is assessed not so much in terms of the quality of educational experience available to students, but rather in terms of movement up to a given stage of the educational or social ladder.

Equality empiricists have therefore implicitly endorsed the meritocratic model of education. They assume that success should be measured on the basis of achieved rather than ascribed qualities — ability and effort, rather than social class, family connections, gender, race, or other irrelevant attributes. Equality is measured in terms of how far any given disadvantaged group has progressed in accessing a hitherto inaccessible 'educational good', and in particular, by examining what proportion of the disadvantaged group have accessed a particular education sector or position relative to their proportion in the general population and/or relative to some appropriate comparator group.

Equality is deemed to be promoted if social class inequalities/advantages in education are proportionately distributed across different classes; the closer the participation or success ratio is to one, the greater the equality achieved. *The criterion for measuring equality is essentially proportionate representation for the target group* at given stages of education, or in terms of given outcomes. As lengthy participation in second-level education has become almost universal in Western countries, proportionate access to different levels and types of higher education has become the commonest measure for assessing social-class-related (more often socio-economic) inequality in education.

In so far as equality empiricists focus on differences between social groups in terms of educational *attainment*, they move from a weaker to a stronger conception of equality; from a concern with equality of access and participation to *equality of outcome*. Studies which focus on levels of performance (measured in terms of years of schooling completed, grades attained, job obtained, etc.) highlight the fact that equalising formal rights to education, or proportionate patterns of participation, does not equate with equal rates of success or outcomes for disadvantaged groups. Data documenting high drop-out rates, poor academic performance or poor employment opportunities show the limits of weaker notions of equality, in particular conceptions of equality which focus on equal access.

The liberal model of equality which informs the work of the equality empiricists has an important contribution to make to educational thought as it provides a clear map of how educationally stratified our society is in social class, socio-economic and other terms. It lays down the empirical (generally, but not always, statistical) floor on which other analyses can build. Without such work, it would be very difficult to have a clear profile of what progress (or lack of it) is taking place in educational opportunities for various groups vis-à-vis more advantaged groups.

From an equality perspective, the most serious limitation of the liberal model is that it implicitly endorses hierarchy and stratification, even though this may be unintentional. It focuses research and policy attention on mechanisms for distributing inequalities/privileges between groups; it does not challenge the institutionally and structurally grounded hierarchies and inequalities that necessitate redistribution in the first place (Lynch, 1995; Baker, 1998).

From a purely analytical perspective, one of the limitations of studies documenting patterns of association between social classes and particular educational and occupational outcomes, is that there is very little attention given to the views of the research subjects on the social mobility process itself. The perspective of the research subject on the entire process is largely ignored. Even though studies such as that by Gambetta's (1987) do attempt to explore the reasons why young people from particular social classes take different educational routes, his conclusions are based largely on correlational studies rather than on intensive investigation of individual plans and experiences.

CONCEPTUAL FRAMEWORK FOR THE STUDY

Rational choice theorists and post-structuralists in the neo-Marxist tradition are at one in their rejection of structuralist explanations of social class inequality, albeit from different standpoints. For post-structuralists, 'once the structural story is told, we have conclusions but no solutions' (Fagan, 1995:121). For liberals, the problem with structuralism is its failure to provide theoretical and intellectual frameworks which would explain 'macrosocial regularities in the class stratification systems of modern societies' (Goldthorpe, 1996:454).

What both rational action theorists and resistance theorists fail to recognise is the dynamic nature of structures themselves. This dynamism stems from the active role played by collective agents within structures. These collective actors are highly visible at the state level within the education sector and work actively to determine the form and substance of the educational institution itself (Lynch, 1990). In addition, post-structuralists fail to recognise that structure and agency are not binary opposites. Whether the actor is an individual or a collective body, it operates in a dialectical relationship within a given structure. While choices and intentions are developed in structurally loaded contexts, they nonetheless act back on these contexts and can, at times, redefine them, especially when they work through the channel of collective agency. As Gambetta has observed, it is not really possible to dissociate structure from choice:

> Educational decisions are the joint result of three main processes: of what one can do, of what one wants to do and, indirectly, of the conditions that shape one's preferences and intentions. They are the result partly of causality and partly of intentionality. (Gambetta, 1987:170–71)

In attempting to understand why only a very small number of young working-class students transfer to higher education, and why those who do transfer face difficulties in participating equally with others, we adopt a broadly structuralist approach to the analysis. It is, however, a structuralism which is oriented towards transformation of those institutions and systems which precipitate inequalities in the first place. Our hypothesis is that structures are fundamentally dynamic entities working in and through collective and individual agents. By identifying the relevant contexts and partners to educational decisions at the structural level, it is possible to locate strategies for action and change. The identification and naming of those collective agents and procedures within the decision-making machinery of the state which are responsible for particular structural outcomes focuses public attention on the actors with the capacity to alter inegalitarian practices and on the practices which must be altered. The public naming and challenging of those collective bodies which are powerful partners in education, and which thereby play a key role in the perpetuation or reduction of educational inequality, is an important procedure for the mobilisation of resistance in a small society where the agents are visible and known.[2] Ireland is a relatively small country with a highly centralised decision-making system. Over the last twenty years, a corporatist strategy to policy-making has been developed at the central government level through the Social Partnerships, and at local and regional levels. While the operation of these partnerships raises many questions about equality in power-sharing (Lynam, 1997), nonetheless the partnerships represent an important attempt to develop a more participatory democratic system of planning (Sabel, 1996). The partners to particular decisions are quite visible therefore, as indeed are the absent voices at particular tables. The visibility of the partners focuses attention on the processes which must be changed, and the role that particular groups play in either defending or challenging these practices.

The state working in and through various collective agents, both individually and corporatively, plays a central role in managing the educational relations within which inequality is produced and reproduced (see Coolahan, 1994). The state is a dynamic agent, however, which is constantly negotiating and re-creating the conditions for the operation of unequal relations in education. It operates as a mediator between students and their educational choices by specifying a range of institutional (educational and cultural) and economic conditions within which choices are framed. It creates, and redirects, polices on wealth, incomes, welfare, taxation, education, health, etc., which have a direct bearing on the opportunities and constraints operating for students in the educational site. These systems impact differentially, most notably between social classes but also within them (e.g. between welfare recipients and low-paid workers). Moreover, the state[3] controls the organisation of schooling, in terms of curricula, examinations, teacher appointments, and the relationship between schools and higher education colleges. The dynamic agents within the state have, therefore, a direct bearing on educational outcomes, including the constraints and opportunities which operate for students within the educational system.

Rather than accepting the dichotomy between agency and structure which both resistance theory and rational action theory suppose, we are arguing for a dynamic view of structures, regarding them as created and maintained by a variety of individual and collective agents acting and reacting within and through the state system. In centrally controlled education systems, such as those in Ireland, the principal site for the collective agents to influence structures in education is the state. By identifying the particularities of structural constraints (their precise economic, educational and cultural character) in particular, this research indicates clearly the areas in which transformative action is possible and necessary. It identifies spaces and places where changes can be targeted and fought for.

As a result of collective compromises, negotiations and confrontations within the state, a number of class-specific constraints operate within the educational site. We propose that there are three crucial constraints which operate for low-income working-class students in particular, while not denying sector, representatives of which we consulted about the study, that there was a need to challenge the 'cultural deficit' model of educational choice. Documenting how class-specific experiences influenced educational actions was regarded as an elementary step towards understanding transformation.

Each interviewee was invited, however, to outline the kinds of strategies that should be introduced to realise change. Although the focus of this paper is not on these per se, owing to space constraints, they did form an important part of the main report (Lynch and O'Riordan, 1996). A number of the interviewees' policy recommendations have been implemented in our own university, notably the reserving of places for socio-economically disadvantaged students, and the appointment of an Equality Officer to liaise with designated disadvantaged schools in breaking down cultural barriers between working-class communities and universities, and to work towards developing a proper information system for the communities about the university.[5]

BARRIERS TO EQUALITY OF ACCESS AND PARTICIPATION IN HIGHER EDUCATION

INTRODUCTION

This study is framed within a distributive model of social justice, while recognising the importance of a difference model (Young, 1990). We are not suggesting that the distributive model is the only, or indeed the most important, model (Connell, 1993). However, a distributive framework underpins much of the thinking within working-class communities themselves and within the wider policy arena in Ireland (O'Neill, 1992; Government of Ireland, 1997). There is a widespread belief that education is basically a social 'good' and that equality of access, participation and outcome within it are all desirable. The espousal of a distributive model does not deny the importance of the wider issues of equality of respect and status, or more fundamental questions relating to equality of condition (for a discussion on these issues see Equality Studies Centre, 1995).

The study focuses on just two distributive issues, equality of access and participation. It does not address wider and deeper equality objectives, notably equality of outcome or condition, although these are clearly higher value objectives in the sense that they are more stringent measures of equality. However, as it is impossible to have equality of outcome without equality of access and participation, it was deemed necessary at this time to focus on the more basic issues.

What is evident from the data is the remarkable level of agreement among the different participants as to the precise barriers encountered by low-income working-class students in entering and succeeding in higher education. The research shows that all four groups regarded economic barriers as the overriding obstacle to equality of opportunity, defined in terms of equality of access and participation. Social and cultural barriers were also deemed to be very important as were educational constraints. Although there are significant differences of interpretation across the four groups as to the nature of particular barriers, most notably between community activists and teachers, these will not be the primary subject of discussion here. The focus will be on the general patterns identified, rather than inter-group differences.

THE IMPACT OF ECONOMIC CONSTRAINTS ON ACCESS AND PARTICIPATION

MAKING ENDS MEET: ESTABLISHING PRIORITIES

Relative poverty was regarded as the principal barrier to equality of access and participation for low-income working-class students. This view was shared across all groups. The effects of poverty were regarded as multifarious. Even the first step of getting the money for an application form for higher education was a barrier for some:

> 'Having the money for a CAO [Central Applications Office] form can be a lot of money to ask for at home.' TLS21[6]

In low-income households, day-to-day survival, 'making ends meet', had to take precedence over optional goods, including higher education. Households with limited means regarded expenditure on higher education for one child as a 'luxury' which could be bought only at the expense of other family members. The view that *'Money is the bottom line on everything'* was widely shared among community workers, and by students and teachers.

Community workers were especially adamant about economic barriers to access and participation.

> 'Going to college is not possible financially for working-class students. . . . Because people are living where day-to-day issues are number one, college is not a primary consideration.' COMM10

> 'The cost of keeping a student [in college] is not on.' COMM8

What is notable, however, is that community activists were keenly aware of the role that structural (state-managed) conditions and systems played in perpetuating the inequalities across groups. The causes of poverty were linked closely to unemployment, especially.

It was not only teachers who noted the issue of accommodation; one in five of the forty second-level students said they lacked a proper place to work:

> 'I share a room with three girls. I cannot study there; it is too noisy.' SLS12 (DIS)

> 'I am the eldest of six. It is hard. I have to go to the library and stay back after school if I want to study.' SLS9 (DIS)

All the students in the fee-paying schools, however, had all the necessary supports for study.

PRESSURE TO LEAVE

Of the forty low-income second-level students interviewed, sixteen (40%) had seriously considered leaving school early. The financial strain of staying on in school was the main concern of six of these sixteen students:

> 'I wanted to work and get money, we haven't got it at home.' SLS20 (DIS)

> 'I've had financial setbacks, if I wanted to get grinds I have no money for them. I have an idea I won't have money to go to college.' SLS11 (DIS)

The pressure on students from low-income families to contribute financially to the budget at home was another recurring theme in the interviews with teachers from disadvantaged schools:

> 'Often students leave because they do not have the £40 for the Junior Certificate. There is pressure from home to leave school rather than be an expense.' TE1

Seven of the ten community activists also believed that pressures to contribute to the family incomes were considerable once a student reached working age:

> 'Taking part in the education system is a huge financial strain on families so the quicker the child gets out of the system the less pressure on the family budget. Books, materials, etc. are very costly. Then there is the whole social thing of buses, after-school activities . . . they all cost money.' COMM6

> 'They feel they should get a job a.s.a.p. and contribute at home thereby taking the pressure off their families.' COMM1

The pressure to leave was particularly emphasised by students in the Dublin working-class schools.

THE NEED TO WORK

Just under half of the disadvantaged second-level students worked part-time. This work was not regarded as optional. Eleven of those who worked said that their work had a negative effect on their studies for the Leaving Certificate. For some it meant missing school because they were too tired:

> 'Sometimes I have to work late on Sunday nights and I might not go to school the next day because I am too tired.' SLS33 (DIS)

Teachers also regarded participation in part-time work as an equality barrier at the Leaving Certificate stage especially.

> 'An awful lot of them have part-time jobs. It's the only way to be at school therefore they are doubly disadvantaged. The work makes them tired. They often do 22–8 hours part-time work a week.' TE6

> 'There is pressure to get a job a.s.a.p. and get out; part-time jobs in final year is a big problem here.' TE7

Participants in the fee-paying schools said money would not be a consideration for their students when thinking about going to college.

Students from low-income families who got into college often had to work to maintain themselves. Twenty-three of the forty third-level students whom we interviewed were working; three actually had full-time jobs. As one of the students put it:

> 'If I was not working, I wouldn't be able to go to college.' TLS17

Almost half of the students who worked, however, said that their work interfered with their performance in college:

> 'Part-time work affects my studies. I work as a barman and I often have to work until two in the morning so I cannot study.' TLS11

> 'If I had not got a part-time job I could not afford college. My course work suffers, however, and I honestly believe I would have got a lot better grades had I not been working.' TLS20

Almost all of the students who were not working were relying on their families to support them while in college.

BEING ABLE TO DREAM: ASPIRATIONS AND AMBITIONS

The way in which students' ambitions and aspirations for the future were influenced by the economic and social conditions in which they lived was a recurrent theme from all the interviewees. Economic and cultural constraints were regarded as highly interdependent.

> 'Good financial circumstances help you dream. For working-class kids the dream is not there . . . the working-class lifestyle does not lend itself well to [the] challenge of doing well in education. If a family is in poverty they just have to cope.' COMM10

Many of the community activists referred to the fact that the families in their areas were preoccupied with paying bills and making ends meet. They often did not have the time, money or energy to encourage educational ambitions:

> 'People think not in terms of college but rather about where their next meal is coming from.' COMM7

All but one of the school personnel reported that adverse financial circumstances of students' homes impacted negatively on students' educational expectations and performance.

> 'sights are lowered; the attitude is that you will never get there [college] anyway. One person I know got offered a course but could not afford it.' TE9

THE GRANT: 'THERE'S NO WAY YOU CAN SURVIVE ON IT' (TLS11)

The maintenance grant[8] which students got for college was not adequate to cover either the direct costs of participation, or the opportunity costs from loss of earnings. The issue of grants evoked a totally negative response from all interviewees. First, it was clear that the grant rate was so low that it denied students who got to college a chance to have equal participation with others:

> 'The grant pays for my rent and I am supposed to live on fresh air.' TLS14

> 'When I get the grant I am okay for two weeks then I have to scrounge for money.' TLS18

The grant was also perceived as being administered in a manner which exacerbated the more basic inequalities:

> 'At the start of the year you have to wait for the grant to be paid in. It's no joke. I can barely keep my head above water and I am borrowing left, right and centre.' TLS17

> 'I am often hungry and am too proud to ask for help. The grant is always late and insufficient.' TLS28

There was much criticism about the lack of consideration by grant authorities for regional variations in the cost of living.

> 'In England, your grant is allocated according to where you are going to college. In Carlow, accommodation will cost you £14/£17 [a week], here [in Dublin] accommodation costs £45 a week. Grant authorities do not take into consideration that you are living in Dublin. This is very unfair.' TLS14

Community workers regarded the low level of grant aid as a huge barrier to equal participation for those students who got to college:

> 'The grants are not satisfactory at all. As it is people cannot make ends meet never mind say extending the ends and then trying to make them meet. It is a joke.' COMM1

> 'You need an iron will to get by if relying on the grant. Some people I know on it go to VDP [Vincent de Paul, a charity] as well. It's demoralising.' COMM9

Teachers believed that poor grant provision put extra pressures on low-income families.

> 'It puts financial strain on parents already under a lot of pressure.' TE5

> 'The grant is inadequate because the books are so costly, everything is so costly in college. The grant does not equal the costs by a long shot.' TE6

CONCLUDING COMMENTS

Tight budgeting meant there was a lack of discretionary, and oftentimes necessary, spending on education. Young people were not in a position to avail of the many educational benefits which can be bought in the private market outside of the publicly funded education service. Lack of resources impacted on performance; students simply did not have the resources to achieve the 'points' (Grade Point Average in their Leaving Certificate) necessary to attain entry to higher education in an open competitive system. They were not in a position to buy the extra educational resources or services which could make a difference. These included grinds, education-related resources such as reference material and computers, and educationally relevant travel, especially in the language area. Most of these services could be purchased in the private education market by more advantaged families; this enabled them to maintain their relative advantage in the competition for places in higher education.

Poverty also affected students' study directly, firstly because they had to supplement the family income through work, thereby leaving less time for study, and secondly because they often lacked the basic accommodation and facilities for study. Community activists, teachers, and second- and third-level students each pointed out that if low-income students were to access higher education they would have to work to supplement the family income once they were beyond the compulsory school-leaving age. This limited their time for study and had the paradoxical effect of making them less educationally competitive for the very goal (access to higher education) that they were working towards in the first place.

Insecure and low incomes also impacted negatively on people's personal hopes and aspirations through creating a sense of inferiority and of social exclusion. Community activists (all but one of whom was also a parent) in working-class areas were especially vocal on this issue. It was their view that the effects of poverty on educational aspirations were direct and immediate. In particular they claimed that poverty created cultures in which people lacked 'a sense of ownership' of powerful institutions in society, including higher education. This lack of a sense of belonging lowered people's hopes and aspirations for themselves and their children.

The social exclusion emanating from poverty also created information gaps as people were often unaware of how the education itself functioned, either in terms of accessing higher education or in terms of financial entitlements if one attended.

SOCIAL AND CULTURAL BARRIERS

While the primary barriers facing low-income students in accessing and succeeding within college were economic, these were compounded by a series of interrelated obstacles which were social, cultural and educational.

THE 'CLASS DIFFERENCE' PERSPECTIVE

There was considerable variability among the participants as to how they interpreted the nature and operation of social and cultural constraints on low-income students.

There was a general belief among the community workers that one of the major barriers which working-class students confront in education is the fact that their social and cultural background is not valued in schools, or indeed elsewhere in society:

> 'The affirmations given by society to a working-class child and a middle-class child are different from the time they were born.' COMM3

Community activists believed that this devaluation of working-class ways of thinking and being was reflected in the way in which people relate to working-class people and in the way in which school curricula ignore working-class 'culture, values and mores' (COMM4). They held this institutionalised devaluation of working-class culture to be in part responsible for the lower educational self-esteem which working-class students experienced vis-à-vis their middle-class peers. They regarded this negative evaluation of working-class culture as a major contributory factor in lowering people's aspirations and expectations for higher education.

THE 'CULTURAL DEFICIT' VIEW OF TEACHERS

Most teachers believed that a major barrier to equality of access was the fact that many parents in working-class areas had a negative experience of education themselves. They claimed that working-class people did not value education like middle-class people:

> 'They do not dream of educational success for their kids as they did not have success in education.' TE11

> 'It's a cultural thing, [they] have no confidence, few role models.' TE2

Moreover, the teachers believed that class-specific cultural values permeated different schools, thereby influencing educational outcomes. A number regarded schools in low-income working-class areas as having a cultural climate which was not conducive to educational success. (Interestingly, they saw the students as the creators of that cultural climate rather than the teachers.) By contrast, the experiences of middle-class children were seen as compatible with the ethos of middle-class schools. As one teacher, who had taught in different types of schools, pointed out:

> 'Parents of students in this school [a fee-paying school] have higher expectations; they understand what is expected from their kids.' TE15

> 'Some working-class parents are not supportive of the school; [there is a] "them and us" mentality whereas middle-class parents are more supportive.' TE14

> 'Many [working-class parents] are anti-schooling or afraid of schooling or not knowing.' TE12

One teacher suggested that the barriers arose because:

> 'Working-class parents are intimidated by teachers.' TE1

Teachers believed that they and middle-class parents shared the same cultural and educational expectations. Teachers, in the Dublin schools especially, saw working-class parents and their children as being hostile or indifferent to education. Class polarisations outside school were transferred to the educational site. Whether teachers should or could be proactive in over-coming such divides was not considered by school personnel. Teachers expressed a sense of powerlessness about the dynamics of class relations and related educational expectations in the school.

INFORMATION BARRIERS

For second-level students, one of the major social and cultural barriers iden-tified was the sense of education, and particularly higher education, as being remote and alien from the lives of their families. Second-level students noted repeatedly that they knew very little about college life. Not knowing what to expect created fears and anxieties which exacerbated practical difficulties:

> 'I am worried about everything. I am worried about walking in and not being able to do the work. I am worried about getting a part-time job and having to live on my own.' SLS18 (DIS)

Two of the second-level students interviewed said they knew nothing about universities at all. The question of applying to one therefore did not arise.

> 'I do not know what universities are about.' SLS21 (DIS)

Those who had succeeded in getting in to college also spoke of their lack of information about college life at the time of entry:

> 'You do not hear much about college if you are working-class. And it is hard to get information about college and when you get there you do not know what they are talking about.' TLS33

Mature students felt that there were information barriers which were particularly problematic for them.

> 'For mature [working-class] students, how do they make a first step to even finding out about the college? You can only get CAO forms from career guidance teachers.' TLS2

ISOLATION AND THE FEAR OF ISOLATION

Second-level students expressed a range of fears and anxieties about going to college. They believed that college was a very different and unfamiliar place, and they feared isolation:

'It's so big [college]. There are so many people. I'll know nobody.' SLS31 (DIS)

'I am worried about not being able to fit in with rich, brainy and moneyed students. I would be struggling. Students might put you down and I might feel left out.' SLS16 (DIS)

'I am afraid that I won't do well in college and that I won't make friends.' SLS14 (DIS)

Seven of the forty third-level students interviewed had difficulties making friends in college. The major reasons for this, in their view, were the size of the colleges and the fact that the class background and life experiences of many students were very different to their own working-class background.

'I did not make friends in college until I was in fourth year. I could not mix. Our sense of humours were too different. We were on a different level. Everything you discuss is college, college, college!!' TLS33

'When I went to college, I was up from the country, and most of the people in my class were from Dublin and they seemed to know the college and the city. It took me a long time to form friendships.' TLS28

Fourteen (35%) of the third-level students said they were lonely while at college. This feeling was particularly acute for people when they first came to college.

'When I started college I found it difficult to make friends. I'd walk into the lecture hall and there would be a sea of faces. I did not know anybody. I had to rely on noticeboards, orientation days and trying to pick up a person to talk to.' TLS35

'I used to feel totally lonely in my first year of college. I was very shy.' TLS28

BEING AN OUTSIDER, NOT HAVING A SENSE OF OWNERSHIP

There was a perception among a minority of the second-level students that higher education, but most especially the universities, was beyond their reach, either because students did not believe in their own abilities:

'I always think that college students are so bright. I do not think that I am that bright, so college is like a dream to me.' (SLS45)

or, in a small number of cases, because they knew nothing about universities:

'I do not know anything about universities. I never even thought of it [applying to a university].' SLS21

Over one-third of the forty students who were within higher education (ten of whom were in universities) felt like outsiders because of their class origins:

'In first year I was very conscious of the fact that I spoke a lot differently to people; it was blatant, in the tutorials especially, as I am the only person from the city. It had no repercussions but I felt my differences shone. This difference can prevent you exploring ideas in a tutorial setting.' TLS33

'Sometimes I feel kind of inferior because wealthier students seem more sure of themselves. It's as if they've been here before, done it all, know everyone. It is quite intimidating.' TLS27

The fact that middle-class students had a bigger network of friends from their school and neighbourhood than working-class students further highlighted working-class students' relative social and cultural separateness from middle-class institutions, particularly its educational institutions.

'There is not a single person from my own area [in college]. I have two friends who grew up in the same area as me. They had the potential to go to college but they did not have the chance because they just could not afford it.' TLS28

Five of the forty participants said they had not settled in to college. Only one of these was in first year. The reason that these people said they had not settled was because of the culture clash they experienced between home and college. Two of those interviewed considered dropping out because they felt so different from everyone else.

'In first year I hated college. I felt everyone was different to me. I wanted to speak really well. I had to make myself be positive and stick with it.' TLS27

LIVING BETWEEN TWO WORLDS

While 70% of the second-level students in the more disadvantaged schools had friends who left school early, only a quarter of these said that this created problems for them; what they envied was the money and freedom their friends had.

'I see my friends working and they seem to be earning good money while I am slogging away at school. I would like to have the freedom their earnings give me but I do not.' SLS16 (DIS)

Only two of the forty students interviewed reported experiencing a negative response from friends who had left school, although three others said their friends had mixed reactions to their college plans. Friends who were negative about college believed the students were 'weird' going to college.

While only a small minority (five) of higher education students felt that their attendance at college alienated them from their school friends, those who expressed views on it felt the alienation strongly. For one interviewee this was one of the biggest problems she encountered.

> 'If you go down to the local for a pint, you get the impression that they are waiting to see if you are going to inflict your views on them. For example I was in the pub last week and this guy was talking to a girl about the divorce referendum. I knew this girl from school. Anyway the guy was arguing with her about the benefits of divorce, and she said he was getting as bad as me thinking he knew all the answers. I had not spoken to this girl in ten years and yet she presumed to know me and my views! When you go to college you get a label, a tag.' TLS33

Another interviewee explained how his friends from home no longer associate with him because he is a college student.

> 'Some of them think that I am snobby because I am doing law so they don't talk to me.' TLS32

A third interviewee explained how his former friends from school were uninterested in his life at college because it was a world from which they felt excluded:

> 'a lot do not go to college in poor areas so they do not want to know about a different world'. TLS24

While three of the ten community activists stated that neighbourhood influences could have a potentially damaging effect on students' ambitions, eight of the activists said that the majority of the people in their communities valued education highly:

> 'Most parents want their children to be educated even though they have had negative experiences. A lot of young parents, and single parents particularly, are enthusiastic about supporting their kids.' COMM9

> 'Education is seen as very important. The communities' attitudes are a reflection of Irish society which thinks education is important for children as a passport to a secure future and personal development.' COMM1

There was a belief, however, that there were gender differences in attitudes to education. Most of the activists stated that the male peer groups in their communities had the more negative attitude towards education.

Teachers adhered most strongly to the view that the peer group had a negative effect on educational ambitions. A 'cultural deficit' perspective informed their view of the peer group culture. Eight of the twelve teachers in the more disadvantaged schools were of this view. In their opinion:

'There would be a lot of alienation and ostracism.' TE11

'The third-level student can become "a fish out of water" in the community and at college.' TE10

EDUCATIONAL CONSTRAINTS

MIDDLE-CLASS CULTURE OF SCHOOLS AND COLLEGES: 'STAFF ARE FROM MIDDLE-CLASS BACKGROUNDS' (COMM1)

Community activists perceived educational institutions as being inflexible and unresponsive to the needs of working-class students. They claimed that the ethos of schools and colleges was predominantly middle-class, noting that the curriculum did not reflect 'working-class lifestyle, culture, values [or] mores' (COMM10) while teachers often did not understand working-class students:

'Staff are from middle-class backgrounds. They have no first-hand knowledge of the problems of students.' COMM1

There was also a belief that the culture of higher education colleges was very different to what students were familiar with, and that no real effort was made to accommodate differences:

'It goes back to the curriculum . . . there is no reflection of working-class people's lives in college other than in studies like this one.' COMM3

'You'd almost have to learn a whole new language as well as the course, and you'd have to learn a whole new way of looking [at] and analysing things.' COMM8

'The university has a sink or swim attitude.' COMM9

Community workers believed that teachers did not care enough about working-class children. The educational system was regarded as ineffectual:

'If I go into the local community school some children I see have definite remedial problems; remedial classes do not work. These kids are not picked up along the way. Kids are lost in the whole thing.' COMM9

'Education is not meeting the needs of working-class people . . . [it is] too dictatorial . . . overcrowded . . . teachers have no expectations educationally. There is no real support from the education system with confidence barriers; the teacher–pupil ratio is too high.' COMM8

CULTURAL DEFICIT VIEWS: THEM AND US

Teachers were also aware of cultural differences between themselves and students in working-class areas; the sense of difference was most acute in the larger urban areas where teachers and students were generally strangers to one another outside of school. Twelve of the sixteen teachers interviewed said that they believed there was a culture clash between themselves and working-class students. Two teachers said they did not experience such conflict; both of these were working in schools in a small town with a large rural intake. The teachers varied in how they interpreted the effects of these differences. Most interpreted differences in terms of cultural deficit:

'Children have no concept of study, of organisation. Their priorities are so different. They've no money for books yet [they have] money to socialise. They do not understand how hard they need to work; they think that three to four hours a night might kill them; they do an hour.' TE14

'Working-class parents are anxious that their kids do better than they did, but they are not realistic about how important it is to motivate kids.' TE10

Others were aware that negative views were structurally related to the limited probability of success:

'In the working-class culture there is an ethos that you will never get there; you've no chance so why make the effort?' TE6

'Working-class kids have different expectations; they've no money.' TE15

SCHOOLS MAKE A DIFFERENCE: RELATIVE ADVANTAGE AND DISADVAN-TAGE

Second-level students in disadvantaged schools felt that the quality of the schooling they experienced was not equal to that in other schools. The school was seen as a vital mediator in the education process. In students' eyes, it could make a crucial difference between getting a good grade in the Leaving Certificate and dropping out. They listed a range of areas in which they felt that their own schools were lacking compared with other schools.

Some noted the differences in subject choices and facilities.

'[In some schools] there is a better choice of subjects. If a class is full in this school you are put into another subject.' SLS28 (DIS)

'There are more facilities in other schools than there are here. People give more time to posher schools.' SLS8 (DIS)

Other students expressed the view that certain schools had a higher transfer rate to college than theirs. They believed that this created a better climate for learning compared with their own school. Students were also aware of the intensity of the competition for higher education places:

'When I went to the higher options exhibition I saw thousands there and a small number of courses. I became very worried about the competition [for college places].' SLS9 (DIS)

The learning climates were also regarded as being quite different across schools. Students in three of the five more disadvantaged schools claimed that regular disruptions in class due to disciplinary problems were an important obstacle to learning. This problem was particularly acute for students in some of the city schools:

'Discipline is a major problem in this school. Classes are taken up with correcting students and dealing with general discipline problems.' SLS13 (DIS)

'There are disruptions in at least three classes every day. It is very off-putting.' SLS15 (DIS)

The high turnover rate among teachers in the disadvantaged schools was another serious difficulty for some students.

'Teachers take regular breaks; this upsets my study.' SLS1 (DIS)

'I have had about six maths teachers in two years.' SLS14 (DIS)

TEACHER EXPECTATIONS

Eight of the ten community activists believed that middle-class teachers were either lacking in understanding of working-class students, or lacking commitment to their education:

'School staff are not aware of the problems of students. Students here come from a highly dependent social welfare community. . . . The values of the school staff are different. It is a bit of a self-fulfilling prophecy, the expectation for working-class students is lower.' COMM1 'teachers have no expectations educationally [for working-class students]'. COMM8

'The quality of teaching in working-class areas is poor. For example in one place I know there is streaming of classes into the top and low classes. The good teachers are given to the top groups. I think teachers are not committed; teacher–pupil relations are confrontational . . .' COMM10

Third-level students also stated that they felt that teacher expectations were lower for working-class students and that this was an important barrier to success, especially as the family may rely so much on the teachers' opinions.

'Teachers do not expect the working class to go on to college.' TLS7

'Teachers' attitudes display favouritism towards wealthier parents.' TLS5

The importance of the teachers was noted particularly when:

'You haven't got the money or tradition of going to college behind you.' TLS6

THE ROLE OF LECTURERS IN COLLEGE

Students who were within college also felt that support from lecturers and tutors was important. They were more reliant on this than students whose families were able to guide and support them. A minority of students believed that there were barriers to communication with lecturers in college either because they were too busy or because tutorial groups were too big:

'They do not have time to talk with the students. They are just too busy.' TLS28

'The whole purpose of having a tutor is to have someone who you can discuss things with; when there are thirty-four in a tutorial group this is very difficult.' TLS4

or because of social class differences between lecturers and students:

'One of the reasons I could not go to the lecturers when I needed help was the difference between working-class and middle-class people's problems and life experiences. If I went up to tell them that my sister had died I know the question "how" would come up. I do not want to tell them she died of a drug overdose. I wonder how they would react to this.' TLS33

RESOURCE DIFFERENCES ACROSS SCHOOLS: EXTRA-CURRICULAR ISSUES

Teachers believed that the lack of material resources in certain schools had a serious impact on the quality of education students received. They drew attention especially to the differences in the provision for extra-curricular activities. They considered involvement in extra-curricular activities to be very valuable for the students' all-round development, especially in increasing confidence:

> 'It gives them an opportunity to take on a different role, to be with teachers in a less formal situation. Extra-curricular activities also have an intrinsic value; they build up confidence and are the main reason why some people go to school.' TE2

> 'Extra-curricular activities help to develop students' confidence which, in turn, helps them to be more confident when doing their homework.' TE10

A number of students in the disadvantaged schools said that working-class students participate in extra-curricular activities inside school to a significantly lesser degree than middle-class students. (They noted, however, that they participated more in community-run activities.) One of the reasons given for the lack of involvement in extra-curricular activities was lack of resources within the schools themselves.

> 'Working-class schools do not provide extra-curricular activities as they are lacking in staff; they are lacking in facilities and lacking in the money to pay teachers.' TE16

Teachers believed, however, that the lack of involvement in extra-curricular activities was a lost opportunity as it weakened students' identification with the school, and meant that teachers and students did not have the opportunity to get to know one another in less formal and more convivial settings. When students were not identifying with the school either academically or in terms of sport, drama, music, etc., it was easier to leave.

THE QUALITY OF EDUCATIONAL FACILITIES IN COLLEGE

Working-class students from low-income families who were in college had to rely heavily on college facilities such as libraries, computers, photocopying, crèches, etc. If college facilities were overcrowded they suffered, as they could not opt to buy the services outside of college. Students believed that they could not participate in college on equal terms with other students because of the poor college facilities:

'In this college you have to queue for literally everything — phones, food, books, everything. It's exasperating.' TLS28

'The library is dreadful. I cannot get the books. It is not somewhere you can concentrate in that well, it is so packed.' TLS30

'The library facilities could be a lot better, especially nearer the exams. You would not get a seat in the library and it is very hard to get out the books you want.' TLS29

The lack of access to computers and to computer assistants was also identified as a problem for some college students, as were housing and counselling services.

'Computer access is very bad here. It is limited.' TLS11

'Computer staff are unhelpful. They cannot understand that you cannot do it [computers].' TLS30

'We had no counselling service up until last year when a guy committed suicide. [If a counselling service had been in place then] it might have made the difference.' TLS20

'The accommodation officer is not very helpful. She is focused on first years. There is not enough housing for students.' TLS35

WITHIN-CLASS DIFFERENCES: GENDER, DISABILITY, ETHNIC AND AGE ISSUES

The focus of this study was on cross-class difference. Fifty per cent of those interviewed were women. The main gender-specific barrier identified by those women was the lack of adequate childcare support in the colleges.

The other gender-related theme which emerged was related to peer group culture. Some, but not all, community workers and teachers believed that the peer group culture among working-class men was more hostile to prolonged participation in education than that among women. If anything, there was a view that women were subject to less peer pressure to leave education early.

As the study was not primarily focused on gender differences, it is possible, of course, that other gender-specific barriers may exist which did not emerge. Against that, it must be noted that girls' participation and success rates in education are better than those of boys, and that there is no significant intra-class gender difference in access rates to higher education (Clancy, 1995:56–7). On balance, it seems that gender-specific barriers to entry are not an overriding consideration at the school-leaving age, although women do experience a series of barriers at the mature student stage (Lynch, 1997).

Among the forty third-level students interviewed were a small number who were Travellers, disabled, lone parents and mature students. Each of these groups faced particular barriers which compounded class barriers.

The two women who were single parents were in different colleges; they both had difficulties with the college crèche. One of the students was in a college where the crèche was not subsidised. This created major problems for her:

> 'I cried my eyes out to think I was not entitled to anything [subsidy] for the crèche. I am a single parent and am going to college. Others the same as me with children who are working get their crèche facilities paid for but I get no support.' TLS22

The other student complained of the sexist attitudes of other students in a very male-dominated college:

> 'The majority of people in the college are males. It can be quite intimidating. Sometimes guys make snide remarks about me being a single mother. They hurt.' TLS22

One of the disabled students found the size of the university to be especially problematic owing to his mobility impairments. The lack of grant aid for specialised equipment was also an issue.

> 'I need so much equipment to get through my studies [and] there is no grant to buy specialised equipment. It costs £1,000 to buy a Braille and Speak.' TLS26

For the Traveller interviewed, the barriers to college entry were predominantly cultural. Colleges were perceived to be the preserve of settled people:

> 'The impression of what college is about is one that is associated with settled/country people only. Travelling people do not see college as an opportunity open to them.' TLS34

The mature students interviewed had a number of problems, many of these stemming from the fact that the colleges had little experience of working with mature students and accommodating their different needs. One felt he 'was treated like an idiot' (TLS2) as a mature student.

Overall, however, there was a high level of consensus about the importance of social-class-specific barriers per se.

INFORMATION IS CRUCIAL: 'I DON'T KNOW WHAT TO EXPECT' (SLS17, DIS)

The inaccessibility of information about college life led to the development of great anxieties and ungrounded fears. The anxieties and fears about the unknown world of college were barriers to access in and of themselves.

'I am worried I won't be able to handle it. I don't know what to expect in terms of study, getting to know people, passing subjects . . .' SLS17 (DIS)

Seventeen (43%) of the second-level students from low-income working-class backgrounds said they did not know how to apply for a college course. The lack of access to accurate information regarding college was particularly acute for students in one Dublin school where none of the eight senior students had heard of CAO (Central Applications Office) forms, grinds or the points system. Students in a secondary school in the west of Ireland held a number of misconceptions about college, including the belief that you had to pass first year college examinations at your first sitting. Their unfounded fear of being 'thrown out of college' at the end of one year made college appear like a daunting proposition. Other students complained about the lack of clear guidance when selecting Leaving Certificate subjects.

'I did not do the subjects I should have done for the college course I want to do because of the lack of clear career guidance in this school.' SLS36 (DIS)

All of the participants in the fee-paying schools were clear on the application process for college and knew that the option of repeating examinations existed.
Concerns about the class-based information gap as an important educational constraint were also expressed by community activists.

'In the working class there is a complete ignorance about college. Parents do not understand how they might find ways to get kids to college.' COMM2

'People do not understand the education system, the points system, methods of teaching and the inflexibility of school rules.' COMM10

'There are so many courses; ordinary people would get confused by the way the limited information was presented.' COMM6

While teachers also identified lack of guidance and information as an access barrier, they attributed more importance to the limitations of current modes of assessment and the differences in the social backgrounds of teachers and pupils. The Leaving Certificate examination with its heavy reliance on written terminal examinations was regarded as unfair on all students but especially on working-class students; moreover, teachers pointed out that 'the education system can be manipulated as people get grinds' (TE7).

CONCLUSION

The purpose of this research was to develop a deeper understanding of the barriers facing students from low-income working-class backgrounds in entering and participating successfully within higher education. The study tried to present an understanding of disadvantage from the perspective of those most directly affected by it, including second- and third-level students from low-income working-class households, community workers (who were also parents) and teachers. A small group of students and teachers in fee-paying secondary schools were also interviewed for comparative purposes. One hundred and twenty-two people were interviewed for the study.

ECONOMIC, CULTURAL AND EDUCATIONAL CONSTRAINTS

Our findings lend general support to Gambetta's (1987) thesis regarding the nature of the specific constraints operating for working-class students. Economic, social and cultural, and educational constraints were identified as the principal barriers to equality of access and participation in higher education. Our data, from each of the groups, suggest, however, that economic constraints were of greater significance than either educational or cultural constraints. While Gambetta suggests that cultural constraints[9] were of little significance, this was not our finding. Social and cultural barriers were deemed to be of considerable significance, as were education-specific constraints.

DIFFERENCES IN INTERPRETATION

Not surprisingly, perhaps, different hypotheses were presented across the groups about the way in which constraints operated. Most tension existed between teachers and the other three groups, particularly between teachers and community workers on issues of culture. Teachers drew heavily on a cultural deficit model to explain working-class alienation from schooling; community activists saw the problem as one of cultural difference. As the teachers were the only exclusively middle-class group, this is not unexpected, yet the differences between teachers and others show how particular processes and practices can be accorded different interpretations depending on the positionality of the 'theorist'. In particular, differences in class position led to differences in the interpretation of educational attitudes, values and practices. What teachers perceived as a 'choice' for parents (e.g. encouraging students to study long hours, or not to work part-time) was not construed as a 'real' choice by working-class students or community workers. Equally, while working-class students and community workers held teachers accountable for the low expectations and poor learning climates in some schools, teachers held these to be the by-products of working-class lack of interest or alienation. What was 'true' was contested from both sides. This suggests that any change-related strategy needs to address differences of interpretation as to the causes of inequality.

THE RELATIONAL NATURE OF INEQUALITY

The study also highlights the relational nature of educational inequality. It shows how class inequalities operate through a series of social, economic, political and cultural relationships. The educational disadvantage of any given person or group can really be fully understood only in terms of the advantage of others. The financial, cultural and educational experiences of working-class students need not, in and of themselves, create educational inequality; what creates the inequality is the fact that others have differential access to resources, incomes, wealth and power which enables them to avail of the opportunities presented in education in a relatively more successful manner. Moreover, relatively privileged groups are represented, either directly or indirectly, on various official bodies which make decisions about curricula and assessment, grants, etc., so they can define the nature and terms of educational opportunities in the first place.[10] In a market situation in which educational success is defined in relative terms, those with superior access to valued resources, and those whose own class are the definers of what is culturally and educationally valuable in the first instance, are strongly positioned to be the major beneficiaries of educational investment.

The data suggest that one of the principal mechanisms through which middle-class families maintained their relative educational advantage was through the private education market, notably through the use of grinds (private tuition), educationally relevant travel, summer colleges, socially exclusive schooling, and other educational supports. The extra services available to middle-class students not only boosted their examination performance, but gave a competitive confidence boost; the students in the fee-paying schools were open in admitting that they were advantaged in such a system, as were their teachers.

SCHOOLS MAKING A DIFFERENCE AND DIFFERENCES BETWEEN SCHOOLS

Differences in the quality of schooling across the communities were also deemed to be important in mediating the effects of social class on educational decisions. Many working-class students and community activists did not think that the quality of schooling in their areas was comparable to that available in 'posher' schools. Because working-class students and their families often had little or no experience or knowledge of higher education, they were heavily reliant on the guidance and supports that schools and colleges offered. They were more exclusively reliant on the public education services than middle-class students. When teacher expectations were low, when college facilities were poor, or when information was not provided through the school, working-class families often had nowhere else to turn. Middle-class parents and students, however, turned to family networks and the private education market in the event of poor schooling.

Working-class students, and community activists, were very much aware of the mediating role played by school in charting their educational future. They looked to the school for guidance and support in a way that middle-class families did not. This finding concurs to some extent with that of Gambetta (1987). He found that working-class parents were more strongly influenced in their educational decisions by the school's report of the young person's capabilities than were middle-class parents.

THE MIDDLE-CLASS CULTURE OF SCHOOLS AND COLLEGES: THEM AND US

The dominant role of middle-class personnel (teachers, inspectors, etc.) in defining the nature of the curricula and the organisation of school life was also seen as a barrier to equality. Working-class students and their parents felt excluded from decision-making about education practices and processes. They also believed that schools and colleges did not respect or reflect working-class culture and lifestyles. Some of the community workers spoke of how people felt afraid of schools and teachers. The sense of being an outsider, of being treated as inferior, created tensions around learning in schools. Teachers represented 'them', the 'Other', the dominant group.

Our data also show, however, that a number of teachers worked within a 'them and us' model in their relations with working-class students and their parents. They spoke about students and their families in terms which indicated a strong belief in the 'deficits' of working-class culture. The divisions between the lifeworlds of the students and those of their teachers led to disruptions and disharmony in the classrooms. A number of second-level students reported that disciplinary-related disruptions were a significant barrier to learning in their schools.

Cultural discontinuities were also experienced by working-class students within higher education as they felt their class backgrounds were neither reflected nor affirmed within the colleges. They experienced themselves often as outsiders in an insiders' world where other students appeared to 'have been there before, done it all, know everyone'.

The sense of discontinuity between community, home and college was exacerbated considerably by the lack of accessible, accurate information about higher education. Almost all the second- and third-level students spoke about their anticipatory anxieties and fears about going to college as a barrier in itself. The failure of the state and its educational agencies to address the information problem was noted by a number of those interviewed.

ECONOMIC BARRIERS

While cultural and educational barriers were regarded as seriously restricting educational options, economic barriers were seen as virtually insurmountable by many of those interviewed. Lack of economic security and poverty within families, combined with the failure of the state to compensate for these through an adequate maintenance grants scheme, childcare supports, disabled students supports, etc., had both a direct and an indirect effect on educational decisions.

First of all, limited economic resources dictated spending priorities in the households; day-to-day survival, 'putting food on the table', 'making ends meet', took precedence over optional goods, including higher education. For some, the costs were prohibitive. The maintenance grant was not adequate to cover either the direct costs of participation, or the opportunity costs from loss of earnings. One in four of the forty low-income third-level students interviewed said they had considered dropping out as 'trying to survive in college is unbelievable'.

Economic constraints also affected students' learning, firstly because they had to supplement the family income (or to co-fund themselves) through work, and secondly because they often lacked the basic accommodation and facilities for study. The limited time and facilities for study had the paradoxical effect of making students less educationally competitive for the very goal that they were working towards in the first place. Those who were in college who were working felt that they could not achieve as high a grade as they wished because of this. Moreover, neither second- nor third-level students were in a position to buy the extra educational resources or services which could make a difference. These included grinds, education-related resources such as reference material and computers, and educationally relevant travel, especially in the language area. Some if not all of these services could be purchased by more advantaged families, and this enabled them to maintain their relative advantage in the competition for places in higher education.

While the education effects of economic marginality were visible, some of the more indirect social and psychological effects are less so. Our research shows, however, that having a low and unpredictable income, and inadequate maintenance, actually depresses ambitions among students from low-income backgrounds, as they feel that college is not a realistic option no matter how hard they may work. Having low levels of maintenance and support therefore does not just affect those who are in college, it influences the plans and priorities of students (and their families) while they are still in second-level education.

The economic, cultural and educational practices which constrain low-income working-class students' opportunities for higher education cannot be regarded as discrete entities. They operate in a complex set of interactive ways with one another and are experienced by the students, their families and teachers as a highly integrated set of barriers to equal access and participation.

THE STATE AND THE ISSUE OF CHANGE

In a number of the comments made by students and community activists, there was an implied, and sometimes explicit, criticism of state taxation and economic policies which advantaged some groups so clearly at the cost of others. There was widespread agreement across both working- and middle-class interviewees that two major financial barriers adversely affected the access and participation of working-class students in higher education. First, in terms of equality of access, it was claimed that working-class students could not compete for 'points' (Grade Point Average in the Leaving Certificate) as they lacked the resources to gain a competitive advantage. Second, it was clear that the low level of the maintenance grant was a major disincentive to seek college entry; if one attended college, poor grant aid put pressure on students to work part-time, borrow, make demands on their families, etc., in order to survive. The strain of competing demands led to poorer performance and pressure to drop out.

When we asked the interviewees to suggest strategies for change and ways of overcoming inequalities, it was clear that the state was seen as having primary responsibility for economic inequality, while other agents within the state, such as the teachers, the universities and colleges of higher education, were regarded as having important roles to play in relation to cultural and educational barriers, both singularly and in conjunction with the state. The stories that people told indicate that policy initiatives designed to reduce economic, cultural or educational inequalities can be effective if sensitively, strategically and systematically implemented and resourced.[11]

It is clear from the data that greater financial supports had to be given (whether in welfare supports, tax provisions, realistic grant aid, etc.) to low-income families if their children were to stay and be successful in education after the compulsory school-leaving age. In particular, there was a consensus that substantial grant aid (designed to meet the economic cost of attending college) is necessary to make higher education a realistic option for low-income individuals and families. It was widely believed that such grant aid would have the anticipatory effect of raising aspirations and maybe even performance. A minority of community activists noted the importance of promoting greater economic equality in society to achieve greater educational equality. They believed that these economic barriers had to be addressed at the state level.

The data suggest strongly that making accurate information about higher education widely accessible and available in working-class communities would also significantly reduce the misconceptions and anxieties that persist about college life, while the development of a closer liaison between schools in marginalised communities and the higher education colleges could help break down information and fear barriers. The state and the higher education institutions, liaising with the local schools and education bodies, were regarded as having responsibilities in this area.

There were also a number of recommendations about ways in which colleges, curricula, texts and schools could be more inclusive of working-class students and their culture. Real partnerships between working-class communities and various organisations (state education agencies, schools, colleges, etc.) at national, regional and local level were seen as a mechanism for overcoming the information and cultural difference barriers which were so daunting for many students.

Promoting positive learning climates in predominantly working-class schools, through the better resourcing of facilities and teachers, as well as through the educational support services, was also named as an important initiative. And there were also recommendations about reviewing the selection procedures for higher education (the points system) and the introduction of reserved places for highly disadvantaged working-class students.[12]

LACK OF CLASS CONSCIOUSNESS

While students, community workers and teachers were all aware of the different social classes in society and their relative positions in terms of educational advantage, class awareness did not translate into class consciousness in the active sense of that term, except to a limited degree among community activists. When asked about the strategies and actions which should be adopted to promote equality for working-class groups, most interviewees focused on moderate reforms to offset the worst effects of class-related inequalities, such as higher grant aid, more information, and, in a small number of cases, a call for reserved places. Only among a few community activists was there any reference to the desirability of a radical restructuring and equalising of the economic relations in society. This is an important finding as it demonstrates the extent to which people accept inequality of condition in terms of wealth and income especially. The meritocratic ideology seems to have been fairly well internalised. While a few community activists did query the rights of more privileged groups in society to their wealth and incomes, this was not a dominant theme. The target of criticism was the state, the colleges, schools and teachers. The state was seen to be the agent of inequality rather than the holders of superior wealth and income. This demonstrates the extent to which people looked to the state to be a fair referee between the classes, rather than querying the class system and its endemic inequalities in itself.

CONCLUDING COMMENTS

Our data identify a number of ways in which economic, cultural and educational institutions interact to promote inequality through a series of procedures and processes in families, communities, schools and colleges. Structures do not operate as a system of abstract rules dictating behaviour in a robot-like manner; rather they are mediated by collectivities and individuals in families, peer groups, communities, classrooms, schools and colleges. Structures specify the general parameters within which decisions are made, but the latter are, in turn, negotiated and changed depending on institutional responses to particular actions. Working-class students do not 'give up' on the education system in some predetermined manner. Rather they negotiate and inhabit the education system with an eye to the opportunities which are open and those which are not. Teachers (and lecturers) are seen as agents who can open or close doors; but so too are the government, the administrative authorities in the colleges, civil servants and other mediators of education services within the state. These structural agents are not invisible; they can be named and targeted for action, especially in a state such as Ireland which has a highly centralised and corporatist system of governance. Resistance is not therefore an issue simply for committed teachers or cultural workers; rather it is a series of challenges which can be initiated at several different levels within the education and state system. It is a challenge which can be taken up by working-class community groups collectively (through such bodies as the Community Workers' Co-operative, or through political parties) or individually. The challenge to resist can be taken to, and by, teachers at trade union or professional level; and it can be taken to the state through conventional party politics, but also through the corporate decision-makers and authorities which advise the government on education matters, or which manage and plan policies at national, regional and local levels. The dialogue which has been undertaken in this research shows that there are multiple sites for action for resistance ranging from state institutional systems to individual practices in classrooms.

REFERENCES

Althusser, L. (1972). Ideology and ideological state apparatuses. In B. Cosin (ed.), *Education, Structure and Society.* Harmondsworth, Middlesex: Penguin.

Apple, M.W. (1979). *Ideology and Curriculum.* New York: Routledge.

Apple, M.W. (1982). *Education and Power.* New York: Routledge.

Archer, P., and O'Flaherty, B. (1986). A home intervention programme for pre-school disadvantaged children. *Irish Journal of Education,* 9:28–43.

Arnot, M., and Barton, L. (eds.) (1992). *Voicing Concerns: Sociological Perspectives on Contemporary Education Reforms.* Wallingford, Oxfordshire: Triangle Books Ltd.

Baker, J. (1998). Equality. In S. Healy and B. Reynolds (eds.), *Social Policy in Ireland: Principles, Practices and Problems.* Dublin: Oak Tree Press.

Beck, U. (1994). The reinvention of politics: towards a theory of reflexive modernisation. In U. Beck et al. (1994), *Reflexive Modernisation: Politics, Tradition and Aesthetics in the Modern Social Order.* Cambridge: Polity Press.

Bernstein, B. (1971). *Class, Codes and Control: Vol. 1, Theoretical Studies towards a Sociology of Language.* London: Routledge & Kegan Paul.

Bernstein, B. (1975). *Class, Codes and Control: Vol. 3, Towards a Theory of Educational Transmissions.* London: Routledge & Kegan Paul.

Blackledge, D., and Hunt, B. (1985). *Sociological Interpretations of Education*. London: Croom Helm.

Blossfeld, H.P. (1993). Changes in educational opportunity in the Federal Republic of Germany. In Y. Shavit and H.P. Blossfeld (eds.), *Persistent Inequality: Changing Educational Attainment in Thirteen Countries*. Oxford: Westview Press.

Blossfeld, H.P., and Shavit, Y. (1993). Persisting barriers: changes in educational opportunities in thirteen countries. In Y. Shavit and H.P. Blossfeld (eds.), *Persistent Inequality: Changing Educational Attainment in Thirteen Countries*. Oxford: Westview Press.

Boudon, R. (1974). *Education, Opportunity and Social Equality*. New York: Wiley.

Bourdieu, P., and Passeron, J.-C. (1977). *Reproduction in Education, Society and Culture*. London: Sage.

Bowles, S., and Gintis, H. (1976). *Schooling in Capitalist America*. London: Routledge & Kegan Paul.

Callan, T., Nolan, B., et al. (1996). *Poverty in the 1990s: Evidence from the Living in Ireland Survey*. Dublin: Oak Tree Press.

Clancy, P. (1982). *Participation in Higher Education*. Dublin: Higher Education Authority.

Clancy, P. (1988). *Who Goes to College*. Dublin: Higher Education Authority.

Clancy, P. (1995). *Access to College: Patterns of Continuity and Change*. Dublin: Higher Education Authority.

Cluskey, M.S. (1996). Parents as partners in education: an equality issue. University College Dublin, Equality Studies Centre, unpublished Master of Equality Studies thesis.

Cobalti, A. (1990). Schooling inequalities in Italy: trends over time. *European Sociological Review*, 6 (3):190–214.

Connell, R.W. (1993). *Schools and Social Justice*. Philadelphia: Temple University Press.

Coolahan, J. (ed.) (1994). *Report on the National Education Convention*. Dublin: Government Publications Office.

Council of Europe (1996). *Access to Higher Education: Access for Under-Represented Groups. Vol. II Report on Western Europe*, prepared by M. Woodrow and D. Crosier, Council of Europe, Strasbourg.

Davis, K., and Moore, W. (1945). Some principles of stratification. *American Sociological Review*, 10:242–9.

De Graaf, P., and Ganzeboom, H. (1993). Family background and educational attainment in the Netherlands for the 1891–1960 birth cohorts. In Y. Shavit and H.P. Blossfeld (eds.), *Persistent Inequality: Changing Educational Attainment in Thirteen Countries*. Oxford: Westview Press.

Department of Education (1995). *Charting Our Education Future: White Paper on Education*. Dublin: Government Publications Office.

Dreeben, R. (1968). *On What is Learned in School*. Reading (MA): Addison-Wesley.

Dronkers, J. (1983). Have inequalities in educational opportunities changed in the Netherlands? A review of empirical evidence. *Netherlands Journal of Sociology*, 19:133–50.

Eckland, B.K., and Alexander, K.L. (1980). The national longtitudinal study of the high school class of 1972. In A.C. Kerckhoff (ed.), *Research in Sociology of Education*, vol. 1. Greenwich (CT): JAI Press.

Equality Studies Centre, UCD (1995). *Equality Proofing Issues*. Paper presented to the National Economic and Social Forum, Dublin Castle, April.

Erikson, R., and Goldthorpe, J.H. (1992). *The Constant Flux: A Study of Class Mobility in Industrial Societies*. Oxford: Clarendon Press.

Euriat, M., and Thelot, C. (1995). Le recrutement social de l'élite scolaire en France: évolution des inégalités de 1950 à 1990. *Revue Française de Sociologie*, 36:403–38.

Fagan, H. (1995). *Culture, Politics and Irish School Dropouts: Constructing Political Identities*. London: Bergin and Garvey.

Fischer, C., Hout, M., et al. (1996). *Inequality by Design: Cracking the Bell Curve Myth*. Princeton University Press.

Freire, P. (1972). *Pedagogy of the Oppressed*. New York: Penguin.

Gambetta, D. (1987). *Were They Pushed or Did They Jump?* Cambridge University Press.

Ganzeboom, H.B.G., Luijkz, R., and Treiman, D.T. (1989). Intergenerational class mobility in comparative perspective. In A. Kalleberg (ed.), *Research in Social Stratification and Mobility*, 8. Greenwich (CT), JAI Press.

Giroux, H. (1983). *Theory and Resistance in Education: A Pedagogy for the Opposition*. Amherst: Bergin and Garvey.

Giroux, H. (1992). *Border Crossings*. New York: Routledge.

Goldthorpe, J. (1996). Class analysis and the re-orientation of class theory: the case of persisting differentials in educational attainment. *British Journal of Sociology*, 47 (3): 481–505.

Goldthorpe, J.H., et al. (1980). *Social Mobility and Class Structure in Modern Britain*. Oxford: Clarendon Press.

Government of Ireland (1997). *National Anti-Poverty Strategy*. Dublin: Government Publications Office.

Halsey, A.H., Heath, A., and Ridge, J.M. (1980). *Origins and Destinations*. Oxford: Clarendon Press.

Hannan, D.F., and Shorthall, S. (1991). *The Quality of Their Education, School Leavers' Views of Their Education, of Educational Objectives and Outcomes*. Dublin: Economic and Social Research Institute, Paper No. 153.

Heron, J. (1981). Philosophical basis for a new paradigm. In P. Reason and J. Rowan (eds.), *Human Inquiry: A Sourcebook of New Paradigm Research*. Chichester: John Wiley and Sons.

Higher Education Authority (1995). *Report of the Steering Committee on the Future of Higher Education*. Dublin: Higher Education Authority.

Humphries, B., and Truman, C. (eds.) (1994). *Re-thinking Social Research: Anti-Discriminatory Approaches to Research Methodology*. Aldershot: Avebury.

Hurn, C. (1978). *The Limits and Possibilities of Schooling*. Boston: Allyn and Bacon.

Inglis, T., and Bassett, M. (1988). *Live and Learn: Day-Time Adult Education in Coolock*. Dublin: AONTAS (National Association of Adult Education).

Jonsson, J.O. (1987). Class origin, cultural origin and educational attainment: the case of Sweden. *European Sociological Review*, 3: 229–42.

Jonsson, J.O. (1993). Persisting inequalities in Sweden. In Y. Shavit and H.P. Blossfeld (eds.), *Persistent Inequality: Changing Educational Attainment in Thirteen Countries*. Oxford: Westview Press.

Karabel, J., and Halsey, A.H. (1977). Educational research: a review and interpretation. In J. Karabel and A.H. Halsey (eds.), *Power and Ideology in Education*. London: Oxford University Press.

Kellaghan, T., Weir, S., O'hUallacháin, S., and Morgan, M. (1995). *Educational Disadvantage in Ireland*. Dublin: Department of Education and Combat Poverty Agency.

Kerckhoff, A.C., and Trott, J.M. (1993). Educational attainment in a changing education system: the case of England and Wales. In Y. Shavit and H.P. Blossfeld (eds.), *Persistent Inequality: Changing Educational Attainment in Thirteen Countries*. Oxford: Westview Press.

Lather, P. (1991). *Getting Smart: Feminist Research and Pedagogy With/In the Postmodern*. New York: Routledge.

Lynam, S. (1997). Democratising local development: the experience of the community sector in its attempts to advance participatory democracy. University College Dublin, Equality Studies Centre, unpublished Master of Equality Studies thesis.

Lynch, K. (1990). Reproduction in education: the role of cultural factors and educational mediators. *British Journal of Sociology of Education*, 11 (1):3–20.

Lynch, K. (1995). The limits of liberalism for the promotion of equality in education. In E. Befring (ed.), *Teacher Education for Equality: Papers from the 20th Annual Conference of the Association for Teacher Education in Europe*. Oslo College, Norway.

Lynch, K. (1997). A profile of mature students in higher education and an analysis of equality issues. In R. Morris (ed.), *Mature Students in Higher Education*. University College Cork, Higher Education Equality Unit.

Lynch, K. (1999, forthcoming). Equality studies, the academy and the role of research in emancipatory social change. *Economic and Social Review*, 30 (1).

Lynch, K., and O'Neill, C. (1994). The colonisation of social class in education. *British Journal of Sociology of Education*, 15 (3):307–24.

Lynch, K., and O'Riordan, C. (1996). *Social Class, Inequality and Higher Education: Barriers to Equality of Access and Participation among School Leavers*. University College Dublin, Registrar's Office.

Mac an Ghaill, M. (1996). Sociology of education, state schooling and social class: beyond critiques of the new right hegemony. *British Journal of Sociology of Education*, 17 (2):163–76.

McLaren, P. (1995). *Critical Pedagogy and Predatory Culture*. New York: Routledge.

McPherson, A., and Willms, J.D. (1987). Equalisation and improvement: some effects of comprehensive reorganisation in Scotland. *Sociology*, 21:509–309.

McRobbie, A. (1978). Working class girls and the culture of femininity. In Centre for Contemporary Cultural Studies Women's Studies Group, *Women Take Issue*. London: Hutchinson.

Mare, R.D. (1981). Change and stability in educational stratification. *American Sociological Review*, 46:72–87.

Mehan, H. (1992). Understanding inequality in schools: the contribution of interpretive studies. *Sociology of Education*, 65:1–20.

Mehan, H., Hetweck, A., and Lee Meihls, J. (1985). *Handicapping the Handicapped: Decision Making in Students' Careers*. Stanford University Press.

Morgan, M., Hickey, B., and Kellaghan, T. (OECD) (1997). *International Adult Literacy Survey: Results for Ireland*. Dublin: Government Publications Office.

Morgan, M., and Martin, M. (1994). *Literacy Problems among Irish Fourteen-Year-Olds, ALCE Evaluation, Vol. III*. Dublin: Educational Research Centre.

Oliver, M. (1992). Changing the social relations of research production. *Disability, Handicap and Society*, 7:1011–14.

O'Neill, C. (1992). *Telling It Like It Is*. Dublin: Combat Poverty Agency.

Parsons, T. (1961). The school class as a social system: some of its functions in American society. In A. Halsey, J. Floud and C. Anderson (eds.), *Education, Economy and Society*. New York: The Free Press of Glencoe.

Pink, W.T., and Noblit, G.W. (eds.) (1995). *Continuity and Contradiction: The Futures of the Sociology of Education*. New Jersey: Hampton Press.

Raftery, A.E., and Hout, M. (1993). Maximally maintained inequality: expansion, reform and opportunity in Irish education, 1921–75. *Sociology of Education*, 66:41–62.

Reason, P., and Rowan, J. (eds.) (1981). *Human Inquiry: A Sourcebook of New Paradigm Research*. Chichester: John Wiley and Sons.

Reinhartz, S. (1979). *On Becoming a Social Scientist*. San Francisco: Jossey Bass.

Sabel, C. (1996). *Ireland: Local Partnerships and Social Innovation*. Paris: OECD.

Sayer, A. (1995). *Radical Political Economy: A Critique*. Oxford: Basil Blackwell.

Sewell, W., Hauser, R., and Featherman, D.L. (1976). *Schooling and Achievement in American Society*. New York: Academic Press.

Shavit, Y., and Blossfeld, H.P. (eds.) (1993). *Persistent Inequality: Changing Educational Attainment in Thirteen Countries*. Oxford: Westview Press.

Szelenyi, S., and Aschaffenburg, K. (1993). Inequalities in educational opportunity in Hungary. In Y. Shavit and H.P. Blossfeld (eds.), *Persistent Inequality: Changing Educational Attainment in Thirteen Countries*. Oxford: Westview Press.

Technical Working Group to the Steering Committee on the Future of Higher Education (1995). *Interim Report to the Steering Committee on the Future of Higher Education*. Dublin: Higher Education Authority.

Torres, C.A., and Rivera, G.G. (eds.) (1994). *Sociología de la Educación: Corrientes Contemporáneas*, 3rd edition. Buenos Aires: Mino y Davila Editores.

Trent, W., Braddock, J., and Henderson, R. (1985). Sociology of education: A focus on education as an institution. In E. Gordon (ed.), *Review of Research in Education*, vol. 12. Washington, DC: American Research Association.

Weiler, K. (1988). *Women Teaching for Change: Gender, Class and Power*. New York: Bergin and Garvey.

Whelan, C., and Whelan, B. (1984). *Social Mobility in Ireland: A Comparative Perspective*. Dublin: Economic and Social Research Institute.

Willis, P. (1977). *Learning to Labour: How Working Class Kids Get Working Class Jobs*. Westmead, UK: Saxon House.

Willis, P., with Jones, S., Canaan, J., and Hurd, G. (1990). *Common Culture: Symbolic Work at Play in the Everyday Cultures of the Young*. Milton Keynes: Open University Press.

Young, I.M. (1990). *Justice and the Politics of Difference*. Princeton University Press.

NOTES

1 An analysis of the patterns of entry to higher education among school leavers (over a three-year period) shows that students from middle-class backgrounds are more likely to transfer to higher education with a modest Leaving Certificate (the Irish equivalent of A levels or baccalaureate) result than working-class students. The transfer rate to higher education

among high-performing working-class students does not vary that greatly, however, from that among high-performing middle-class students (Higher Education Authority, 1995:116). What this suggests is that middle-class students are likely to transfer to higher education even if they reach only the minimum qualification for entry. Working-class students exercise the same probability of entry only when their Leaving Certificate performance is at a high level.

2   In Ireland the powerful partners include teacher unions, university and higher education colleges, civil servants, politicians, school authorities, the churches, vocational education committees, and various official advisory and decision-making education agencies. While some of these groups play a central role in the perpetuation of the economic inequalities underpinning educational inequality, others play key roles in the cultural and educational sites per se. While parent bodies have increased power in education in recent years, due to lack of resources and mobilisation they are not yet as powerful as other named agencies. This may well change over time, and there is a likelihood that parent bodies will be middle-class-dominated, as seems to have been happening to date. (This observation has been made by a number of commentators within the parent movement; see Cluskey, 1996.)

3   There is a whole series of state maintained and controlled bodies operating as advisers and managers of the education process, such as the Higher Education Authority, the National Council for Educational Awards, the National Council for Vocational Awards, the National Council for Curriculum and Assessment, the School Inspectorate, the Teacher Registration Council, etc.

4   These represent a very small minority of Irish second-level schools (circa 5%) but most are prestigious. Apart from a small number of scholarship students, they are attended by the upper middle classes and a small upper class.

5   In late 1997 a pressure group was set up called 'The Working-Class Access Network'. It comprises working-class activists and educationalists working together to pressurise for greater class equality in education. The research contributed towards the setting up of this group with the support of the Higher Education Equality Unit (a body of the Higher Education Authority).

6   The system used for identifying respondents was as follows: COMM refers to a community worker, and the number given is their confidential ID code. TE refers to a teacher, SLS a second-level student and TLS a third-level student. DIS refers to students in more disadvantaged schools and FP to students in fee-paying schools.

7   Almost 60% of second-level schools in Ireland are owned by the churches, mostly the Roman Catholic church, but funded almost entirely by the state. Many (a recent survey by the Association of Secondary Teachers of Ireland suggests 80%) seek a voluntary financial contribution from the parents.

8   The maximum maintenance grant for a student living away from home was £1,625 in 1997/8, while the maximum rate for those living at home (defined as living within fifteen miles of college) was £647. Estimates of the full maintenance costs suggest they are two or three times the grant allocation.

9   As Gambetta's measure of culture was not especially sensitive, namely the number of years parents spent in school, his failure to establish a link between culture and educational disadvantage may be related to the nature of the measure used.

10 It is no accident that working-class community groups (or indeed women's groups or other groups representing disabled people, Travellers, etc.) are not defined as partners in education. They are not powerful agents within the education site. They are not represented on bodies such as the National Council for Curriculum and Assessment, or policy-related bodies, such as the Points Commission (appointed in 1997) set up to review access and selection procedures for higher education. They have been written out of the Education Bill No. 2 (1997) in terms of the named partners. The bill effectively endorses the following groups as partners: the patrons (notably the churches, the Vocational Education Committees and the Department of Education), national associations of parents, teacher unions, and school management organisations.

11 A complete analysis of the strategies for change identified in the study would require a paper in itself. We merely summarise here some of the key strategies identified.

12 Some of the recommendations are now being acted upon, notably the cultural and educational recommendations, although it is clear that the pressure to address these came from many sources. A commission has been set up to review the points selection system. A number of colleges are in the process of introducing a reserved places policy (including our own), or some variant of it, while university and community partnerships are being developed in a small number of colleges. On the economic side there has been no change, however.

CHAPTER 5

WOMEN AND EDUCATION

RESEARCH ON WOMEN IN EDUCATION

Just as debates about equality in education generally have been framed in terms of liberal notions of equality of opportunity, so also have debates about equality for women in education. The objective in post-war Europe (and post-1960s Ireland) has not been about the transformation of economic, social and political inequalities; it has rather been about redistributing opportunities — to acquire wealth, power and status — more fairly within an accepted stratified system (Arnot, 1991). The difficulties which a liberal equal opportunities approach to equality (premised essentially on equalising access and, but to a lesser degree, on equalising participation and outcomes) posed for women have been increasingly challenged by feminist scholars, however (Wolpe, 1976; Stanworth, 1981; David, 1985; Wickham, 1987; Arnot and Weiner, 1987; Weiner, 1989, 1994; Middleton, 1990; Arnot, 1992; Fraser, 1995). Feminists (along with other radical egalitarians) began to challenge the liberal myth that individual mobility and achievement was an attainable objective for the collective. They outed the truth that capitalist patriarchal society could deliver on its liberal promises of equality only by destabilising itself.

Within Ireland, there has, however, been relatively little academic writing about the feminist challenges to education orthodoxy. While Women's Studies has presented a challenge to the cultural orthodoxy of the male hegemonic view within the academy (Byrne, 1992; Smyth, 1992; Lentin, 1993), and while there is some emerging feminist post-structuralist work in the adult and community education field (Connelly, 1997; Ryan, 1997), there has been no substantive analysis of mainstream compulsory education in terms of its pedagogical, organisational or curriculum practices from a critical feminist standpoint. Although a body of research on women in education, both as teachers and as learners, had developed over the last fifteen years, this work is broadly within the liberal feminist tradition (Hannan, Breen et al., 1983; Kellaghan and Fontes, 1985; Murray, 1985; Slowey, 1987; Lynch, 1988, 1990; Drudy, 1990; Hannan, Smyth et al., 1996; Egan, 1996; Raftery, 1997; Warren, 1997; Drudy and Uí Chatháin, 1998; Flynn, 1998). It analyses women's position in terms of their comparative achievements, and, but to a lesser degree, experiences, vis-à-vis men either as learners or as teachers.

To suggest that much of the writing about women's experiences of education in Ireland is focused on liberal concerns regarding their relative attainments in education is not to deny the importance of this work. Up to the early 1980s, there was virtually no research at all on women's issues in Irish education; gender and women's issues in particular had a 'minority status' within Irish education research (Drudy, 1991:115). This is still true. The lack of a national Social Science Research Council until the mid-1990s meant that all forms of social scientific research were stunted by lack of funding. This was especially problematic for fields such as education, as much of the baseline data required, both as valuable material in their own right and as a springboard for other research, demanded that national studies be undertaken. These were both labour-intensive and expensive, and there was no specific source of grant aid for gender-related work apart from EU funding which supported initiatives such as the TENET project in the 1980s (Drudy, 1990). While the statistical data collected annually by the Department of Education on schools would have been a valuable source for research, this material was difficult to access. It is not surprising therefore that Irish research on women in education would focus initially on establishing basic data on women's participation and achievements vis-à-vis men. Indeed there is an ongoing need for this type of research as it provides the background for other more in-depth and challenging research on women's issues generally.

ISSUES OF DISTRIBUTION AND RECOGNITION FOR WOMEN

Not only has much of Irish research been liberal in its focus, but it has operated out of a liberal distributive model of social justice. The focus is on distributing opportunities between women and men in a fair way, not on challenging the structural conditions which create inequalities between social positions, forms of knowledge, etc. in the first place. Education is defined as an unproblematic good for women (and men) in which more means better. Gender equality has been assessed in terms of the proportionality test; the more women in senior educational positions, the more equal the society is becoming for women (Kellaghan and Fontes, 1985; Lynch, 1997; Warren, 1997); the more men or women are undertaking non-traditional 'gender' subjects, the greater the gender equality being attained (Hannan, Breen et al., 1983; Murray, 1985); the more images of women (or Travellers, or black people, or lone parents, etc.) in texts, the greater the movement to inclusion and equality (Department of Education, 1993); the more women achieve parity with men in their educational attainments, the greater the level of gender (or social class) equality in attainment (Clancy, 1988, 1995; Hannan, Smyth et al., 1996).

Irish educationalists are by no means unique in their allegiance to a distributive view of equality and justice. It has also dominated educational (and political) thinking internationally (Young, 1992; Connell, 1993; Sturman, 1997). Moreover, a concern for a fair distribution of opportunities in a visibly stratified society is a highly visible and available option for those who wish to promote gender equality. Notwithstanding the above, it is necessary to comment briefly on the limitations of the liberal distributive model of justice for women in particular.

The problem with liberal views of justice is not simply that they are premised on a paradigm of distribution, and thereby that they fail to recognise that 'the sovereignty of women, homosexuals, and people of colour involves culture as much as the distribution of goods' (Young, 1992:76, see Sturman, 1997:6), it is also that the focus within distribution is on *opportunities*, not on social positions. That is to say, there are important distributive issues which still obtain for women outside the liberal 'equal opportunities' paradigm, notably radical income, wealth and power redistributions.

Liberals do not seek the radical redistribution of wealth and power in society; rather they endorse existing social divisions by prioritising freedom over equality. As Rawls (1971:28) observed: 'Justice denies that the loss of freedom of some is made right by a greater good shared by others.' Liberalism fails, therefore, not because it is concerned with distribution, but because what it wants distributed, namely opportunities to stay or become unequal, will not promote equality for *all* women. The hierarchies which are at the centre of contemporary capitalist societies are not made problematic; the goal is to equip women to compete in the race within and between hierarchies. One of the most obvious limitations of such an approach is that it offers false promises to women. In a highly stratified society with a small number of privileged positions relative to the total number of jobs/positions available, it is patently obvious that only a few can succeed; there is less and less room on the ladder as one moves to the top. In such a 'race among women', it is the relatively advantaged in class, ethnic, racial and other terms who are positioned to 'win'. There is already ample evidence of this from research on social class in education (Raftery and Hout, 1993; Shavit and Blossfeld, 1993).

There is a need first therefore to move beyond perspectives on women which define equality in terms of having opportunities to have male standards of achievement, recognition on exclusively male terms, without any reordering of the unequal social relations which underpin women's economic, political and cultural subordination. The debate about distributive justice needs to shift from a concern for 'opportunity' to a concern for an equalising of 'rewards for social positions', so that the wealth, income and power hierarchies are radically restructured. Within the distributive frame, there is a need to recognise that substantive differences exist *between* women in terms of wealth and power both within and between societies. Power and wealth differentials are not only gendered, they are also classed, raced, dis/abled, aged, etc. in character.

Secondly, there is a need to marry a concern for substantive economic and political distribution with a recognition of difference. Independence and sovereignty for women requires a full recognition of the cultural practices, work, interests and commitments which women have made their own for thousands of years, allowing for the religious, cultural and other diversities which exist between women. In other words, there is a need to integrate policies of 'recognition' with policies of 'substantive distribution'. Without an engagement of the two sets of principles, then the politico-economic interests and cultural concerns of a relatively advantaged group of women will take precedence over those of majority women (howsoever relative advantage may be defined across cultures and countries). What is at issue here is recognising the close link between culture, politics and the economy.

The distinction which Fraser (1995) has drawn between the principles of *redistribution* and *recognition*, and the importance of both of these for promoting substantive equality for women, is central here. Like women elsewhere, women in Irish society experience a number of inequalities. Some of these are economically rooted inequalities arising within a gender/class stratified system of paid and unpaid labour markets, while others are primarily symbolic or culturally specific inequalities arising within the systems of representation and interpretation that operate in the media, the churches and education. The inequalities which women experience in society cannot be reduced to a single cause; women, like racial minorities, are 'bivalent collectivities':

> Bivalent collectivities, in sum, may suffer both socioeconomic maldistribution and cultural misrecognition in forms where neither of these injustices is an indirect effect of the other, but where both are primary and co-original. In that case, neither redistributive remedies alone nor recognition remedies alone will suffice. Bivalent collectivities need both.
> (Fraser, 1995:78)

Any solution to economic inequalities requires substantive distributive action within the political economic spheres. The basic economic subordination which many women experience arises therefore either because they are working in the *no-pay domestic sector*, or in the *low-paid sectors of the paid labour market* (such as the part-time and temporary end of the services sectors), on in the *low-graded* and low-paid jobs *within* sectors which are not comprehensively low-paid (such as health or the public service) but which are divided on income and status lines. In addition, most women working within the paid sectors also work in the domestic sector albeit not full-time. Those working exclusively in the no-pay domestic sector could be further subdivided along a range of class and status lines; many are exclusively dependent on a male partner, others are welfare-dependent, others operate within a state of male dependence and welfare dependence, while a small wealthy minority have independent financial means. A full feminist analysis of all work would need to be undertaken to determine the extent to which women occupy economically subordinate positions within these various sectors.

Whatever the range and extent of the economic inequalities which women experience, any resolution of these demands an abolition of the gender structuring of the economy on which it is based, be it the gender division between paid and unpaid labour, or the gender division between forms of low- and high-paid labour. There is, however, a significant qualitative difference between different types of economic inequalities, namely between those located in the family or domestic site, and those located in the paid labour market. Challenging the gender divisions within household labour and challenging gendered divisions of paid labour are separate tasks presenting different challenges. While dismantling patriarchal relations in the household presents a single challenge to male dominance (Delphy and Leonard, 1992), dismantling hierarchical relations of pay in the economy means challenging not only patriarchy but the global capitalist practice of stratified labour markets. To challenge and undo the practice of wage and income differentials within the paid sectors of the economy is to challenge also the 'settlement' which has been reached between capital and organised male-dominated trade union labour whereby wage and income differentials are widely accepted within an agreed set of parameters. This is not simply a gender issue as it is also a profoundly class issue (in our society, although it may be a racial, ethnic or religious issue in others), the resolution of which would be a challenge to highly paid middle-class women as well as men.

Gender is not only an economic differentiator, it is also a cultural differentiator. Women do not simply experience economic subordination, they also experience cultural exclusions and degradations arising from their sexuality. Our society is profoundly androcentric in the sense that male norms and values are persistently privileged over female norms and values; things named as 'feminine' are treated as inferior, unworthy and subordinate. These 'injustices of recognition' (Fraser, 1995) have deeply inegalitarian implications for women, not least of which is the degradation of their sexuality in the form of sexual assault, harassment, pornography and rape. In other spheres as well, that which is feminine is trivialised and ignored in terms of representations and recognition in the media, in the churches or in the curricula and syllabi of our schools and colleges.

These two bases for gender injustice are not mutually exclusive; they are closely interwoven, with one reinforcing or facilitating the other at different times. Not only can lack of recognition lead to economic subordinations as when women's demands for childcare are ignored in the political arena, forcing them back into male dependency in the family; so too can economic marginalisation inhibit recognition in fields such as literature, art or music as women have neither the resources nor the time to name their own world in the way that men are free to do. If we want to assess where women are therefore, we need to focus on *both* the politico-economic and the cultural or symbolic aspects of their subordination. The interdependency of the two makes it imperative that neither one is ignored.

CONCLUDING COMMENTS

Given the dearth of research on women in education in Ireland until recently, it is not surprising perhaps that the focus of much of intellectual thought has been on distributing opportunities between women and men, rather than on recognition issues, or on a radical restructuring of the politico-economic relations which continue to generate these various inequalities in opportunity in the first place. When beginning from a low baseline of research evidence, it is almost inevitable that much concern focuses on getting basic comparative gender data. Moreover, such research is of ongoing importance not least because it locates serious gender disparities within the education system over time. However, it is necessary to move beyond liberal distributive concerns with 'opportunities'. The research needs to examine the link between education outcomes and the underlying structural and institutional inequalities which generate differences in outcomes in the first place. In studies of curricula and pedagogy in particular, there is an urgent need to address the question of recognition from a gender (and social class, disability, ethnic and sexual) perspective. Irish researchers on education, including philosophers (Dunne, 1993; Hogan, 1995), have not yet seriously engaged with the feminist debates on these issues despite extensive writing in the field internationally.

EDUCATION AND WOMEN: PARTICIPATION AND ACHIEVEMENT

The frame within which many women still define gender equality is a liberal one. Both 'deconstructive-feminist cultural politics and socialist-feminist economic politics are far removed from the immediate interests and identities of most women' (Fraser, 1995:90). While one of the reasons for this is undoubtedly the pervasive character of liberal politics (all parties moving towards the 'centre'), it is also a function of what is visible, accessible and changeable in the short term. Most women's sense of remoteness from transformative feminist solutions is not, I suspect, because they lack empathy with these positions so much as that they feel such solutions are long-term and outside their immediate control.

In this chapter I will document some of the major changes that have occurred in education for women in recent years. Because so little work has been done on women from a critical feminist perspective which focuses on radical transformative as opposed to liberal affirmative issues,[1] the only substantive material which is available on women is that which allows us to address liberal questions. In doing this, however, I will note the silences and the absences.

WOMEN'S ACHIEVEMENTS

From a gender perspective, education is a social institution which operates according to certain universalistic principles that promote a basic equality of experience for women with men in the simple distributive sense. In terms of the allocation of staff and resources, there is no major gender difference across schools (Lynch, 1989). The curriculum, modes of assessment and pedagogical practices which are employed for women and men are fairly similar (although they are not particularly sensitive to the principles of recognition and difference). While there is a great disparity in the funding per capita across different sectors of education, to the advantage of higher education in particular, this is not an essentially gendered phenomenon, except in the case of adult and community education. As women comprise the majority of participants in adult and community education programmes, the failure to fund this field of education in a satisfactory manner disadvantages low-income women especially. And it penalises low-income women who are working at home with caring responsibilities in particular. Such women are not generally in a position to become full-time students and thereby avail of grant-aided training and higher education; as they cannot afford part-time courses in higher education, the only courses they can access often are under-resourced community and adult education programmes where they have to fund themselves (Morgan et al., 1997:96–7)!

It is clear, even from the aforesaid example, that the danger of viewing women as an undifferentiated whole is that such a classification ignores very important differences between women. It accords to all women a set of achievements, recognitions or inequalities which are particular to given sets of women. This is an especially important issue when examining women's achievements in education; yet given the way in which data are compiled in Ireland, it is difficult to make an accurate appraisal of women in different social groups. Much of what we know of women is only about women collectively; if we assess women's achievements as an undifferentiated group they can be seen to be equal to, or surpassing, men in terms of retention rates and performance across different fields.

Although women in Ireland traditionally stayed on in school longer than men (Department of Education, 1965), a trend which was directly linked to the lack of employment opportunities for women (either on the land or elsewhere),[2] the gender differential in rates of retention has been reduced in recent times. Currently women and men are fairly evenly represented in their participation levels at second level. Women's third-level participation rates have increased significantly, however, over the last twenty years. While women were under-represented in third level in 1978/9, especially in proportion to their participation in the senior cycle of second level, by 1995/6 they comprised a majority of third-level students, and over 55% of those in the HEA (mostly university sector) compared with being just 46% of such students in 1978/9 (Table 1).

Table 1

Gender Differences in Participation Rates in Second- and Third-Level Education, 1978/9 and 1995/6

Level of education	Women N		Women as % of total		Men N		Men as % of total	
	1978/9	1995/6	1978/9	1995/6	1978/9	1995/6	1978/9	1995/6
Second level	151,177	190,157	51.6	50.9	141,497	183,508	48.4	49.1
Senior cycle (general) second level	44,208	74,677	54.4	51.6	37,034	70,067	45.6	48.4
Third level	15,718	52,104	42.3	50.8	21,438	50,558	57.7	49.2
HEA designated (universities mostly) plus primary teacher education	12,732	31,249	46.4	55.4	14,729	25,194	53.6	44.6

Source: Department of Education, Statistical Report, 1978/9, Tables 1 & 3 and Department of Education, Statistical Report, 1995/6, Table 1.1.

Another way in which to assess how women are performing in second and third level is to examine their participation and success patterns in public examinations. From Table 2, it is clear that women are now excelling across a wide range of subject areas; a greater proportion of them are getting grade C or higher at both ordinary and higher level in each of the subjects listed here. Although a greater proportion of boys got A grades on higher papers in mathematics (17% compared with 13% of girls) and in chemistry (12% compared with 10% of girls) in 1996, these differentials were reversed at the B level, while girls received higher grades at A and B levels on the ordinary paper. Interestingly, there is no major difference between the proportion of girls and boys getting A and B grades in Physics at the higher level, with 9.1% of girls and 9.9% of boys getting A grades while 23.6% of girls and 22.7% of boys got B grades in 1996 (Department of Education, 1997, Tables 5.16, 5.18, 5.22, 5.24). What is notable overall is the very significant improvement in women's performance in mathematics and chemistry, while boys' performance has not altered quite as dramatically over the seventeen-year period in comparative terms. (There are also interesting and very significant differences in the pattern of awarding grades both over time and within disciplines, which could be the subject of a separate analysis.)

Table 2

Gender Differences in Performance across a Range of Leaving
Certificate Subjects,* 1979 and 1996

| | Leaving Certificate examination 1979 | | Leaving Certificate examination 1996 | |
| | Attaining Grade C or higher | | Attaining Grade C or higher | |
	% girls	% boys	% girls	% boys
Maths (higher)	35.1	44.1	82.9	79.4
Maths (ordinary)	33.5	40.4	69.3	62.1
English (higher)	50.7	49.4	68.5	61.0
English (ordinary)	37.0	34.5	64.5	49.1
Chemistry (higher)	55.6	56.3	64.2	63.9
Chemistry (ordinary)	49.5	37.9	60.7	47.2
Accounting (higher)	48.6	40.8	72.3	71.5
Accounting (ordinary)	47.6	35.9	69.8	63.2
Art (higher)	59.0	45.4	68.0	59.2
Art (ordinary)	29.6	23.9	58.6	51.4

Sources: Department of Education, Statistical Report, 1978/9, Tables 13.2 (a) and (b) and Statistical Report 1995/6, Tables 5.16, 5.18, 5.22, 5.24.

* The reason for choosing these subjects is because they are broadly representative of a range of different subject areas in the Leaving Certificate, and because there are a reasonably comparable number of *both* girls and boys taking these subjects in Leaving Certificate examination. Unfortunately subjects such as technical drawing, construction studies, physics and home economics (S&S) are still overwhelmingly taken by either boys (the first three cases) or girls (in the last case).

The pattern across different subjects is also reflected in aggregate rates of attainment in recent years. Table 3 outlines differences in performance between girls and boys in 1994, 1995 and 1996 when girls represented 51.4%, 51.5% and 51.3% of the candidates in each respective year. Whether one uses a basic low measure of attainment, such as five grade D3s at any level, or high measure, such as a minimum of six grade C3s on higher papers, of which a minimum of three were grade B3 or higher, girls' performance is better than that of boys.

As noted above, however, there are still significant differences in the types of subjects which girls and boys study in schools. These gender-differentiated patterns of choice have altered somewhat over the years with a move from women into 'male subjects' especially. Nonetheless, fields such as physics and applied mathematics are still predominantly 'male choice' subjects as are the three technologically oriented subjects of technical drawing, construction studies and engineering.

Table 3

*Gender Differences in Aggregate Leaving Certificate
Results, 1994, 1995, 1996*

	1994 %		1995 %		1996 %	
Attaining	Girls	Boys	Girls	Boys	Girls	Boys
A minimum of five D3s at any level	90.8	86.3	88.8	84.4	91.8	88.2
A minimum of six grade D3s at any level, of which a minimum of two were grade C3 or higher, on higher papers	52.1	44.6	52.4	45.7	53.4	47.2
A minimum of six grade C3s or higher, on higher papers	14.5	10.4	15.8	11.3	17.0	12.2
A minimum of six grade C3s on higher papers, of which a minimum of three were grade B3 or higher, on higher papers	11.8	8.6	12.8	9.4	14.0	10.1

Sources: Department of Education, Statistical Reports for 1993/4, 1994/5, 1995/6; Table 5.2 in each case.

WOMEN'S EXPERIENCES OF EDUCATION

We have very little research in Ireland on the nature of students' experience from a gender standpoint. Virtually nothing is known about boys in particular, especially about the way in which their masculinity is constructed in school, although this subject has begun to be investigated in the UK (Mac an Ghaill, 1994). We do know, however, that girls have a lower academic self-image than boys in spite of girls' superior academic performance (Hannan, Smyth et al., 1996). The reasons why this differential exists, and how schooling contributes to it, have yet to be investigated. Drudy and Uí Chatháin (1998) suggest that gender differentials in classroom experience may be contributing to differences in educational self-image. In a study of 136 classrooms across a wide range of subject areas, they found that girls received significantly less attention (both positive and negative) than boys in co-educational classes.

> If girls experience on a daily basis a classroom climate in which they are not being invited or encouraged to actively participate at an appropriate cognitive level, it is not so surprising that the cumulative effect of such experiences would result in 'passivity' or lack of confidence to initiate contact or discourse . . . (p. 144)

While this is a plausible hypothesis, the fact that girls in single-sex schools also seem to have a lower academic self-image than boys in single-sex schools (Hannan, Smyth et al., 1996) strongly suggests that the school or the classroom is not the only player in determining educational self-image. Hannan, Smyth et al. (p. 170) found that 'academic self-image [is] most closely related to the nature of the parental and teacher feedback given to pupils and to the set of expectations with which they are confronted'. A small study by Flynn (1998), of co-educational primary schools, suggests that the playground or extra-curricular activities are also highly gendered, and that experiences in these may contribute to the development of differences in gender identities among girls and boys. Much more research needs to be done in this field, including research on women's experience of the third-level sector, if we are to have a deeper understanding of the quality of life in schools and colleges for each gender group.

One of the most important findings in the Hannan, Smyth et al. (1996) study was that girls experience higher stress levels in second-level education than boys generally. The level of stress did not seem to be affected by whether the girls were in a co-educational or a single-sex school. The authors suggest that the school ethos may be an important factor in exacerbating or reducing stress, not whether it is single-sex or co-educational per se (p. 194). My own research in this field (Lynch, 1988) would suggest that single-sex girls' schools have a strong academic ethos, and this may be a factor which induces pressure and stress. More recent research suggests that school policy plays an important role in inducing stress, with schools and classes (such as top streams) which have a strong examination-oriented climate being regarded as especially pressurised by students (see chapter 8).

DIFFERENCES BETWEEN WOMEN

Irish women are stratified along a range of class, ethnic, age, religious, dis/ability, sexual and other lines. No major study has been undertaken to date, however, analysing differences in the experiences, and the participation and success rates, of different types of women in education. In particular there are very few data on how girls and women from different backgrounds experience education. While Fagan's (1995) study of school drop-outs does address the marginalisation of certain working-class girls and boys in second-levels, and while my own earlier research (Lynch, 1989) also examined class differences between girls in schooling, neither of these studies was especially focused on differences between women.

Given the amount of attention which has been devoted to social class differences in participation and success in education in Ireland, we still know relatively little about intra-gender differences and similarities within social groups. In particular, we know very little about such issues at the Junior or Leaving Certificate stage. Clancy's studies (1988, 1995) of higher education entrants do provide comprehensive data on higher education entry, however, and his analysis shows that rates of participation across socio-economic groups are very similar between men and women in each group. Working-class women are at the same relative disadvantage in terms of higher education as working-class men, while upper-middle-class women and men have also identical participation rates: the participation ratio for the daughters of higher professionals in higher education is 2.26 while that of sons is 2.29; the comparable rates for the daughters and sons of unskilled workers are 0.38 for both sexes. This means of course that the considerable achievements which have been documented for girls in education do not hold across social classes. Girls from working-class backgrounds are not participating at the same rate as either middle-class women or men in higher education.

Low-income working-class and other women are major participants, however, in the Adult Literacy and Community Education schemes (it is estimated that 80% of the 14,000 people participating in community education are women, Johnston, 1998), yet this is a very poorly funded sector of education in comparative terms. Older poorer women therefore are not major beneficiaries of educational investment in Ireland, something which is rarely recognised when the achievements of women in education are documented.

The only differentiator used in compiling statistics on women and men in the Department of Education Annual Statistical Reports is gender. Data about students' social class, ethnic background, disability, etc. are not available in these reports. Consequently, many differences between women remain invisible in the public domain. An example of how people with disabilities can be made invisible is available from these Annual Statistical Reports. Although the 1997 report documents the fact that 7,652 students attended special schools in 1995/6 and that a further 5,186 attended special classes in ordinary schools, no further data are provided on such students in this report; not even their gender is reported. No data are provided on Traveller children either. Given such biases, it is very difficult to make any substantive statement about the progress and experiences of minority girls and women in education.

Yet the limited research undertaken suggests that disabled women and girls are disadvantaged in a number of ways in education (Duffy, 1993). First they are disadvantaged by the way in which special schooling itself has been marginalised within the education system, especially special education for girls and boys with learning disabilities. Although there are curriculum guidelines for educating certain ('moderately handicapped') students with learning disabilities, these do not apply to all students. There is no published curriculum for students with learning disabilities, and no defined procedures for assessing the educational progress of such students (Murray and O'Carroll, 1997:501). In addition, most special schools are designated primary schools with no clearly defined procedure for examining within them, although many students with disabilities attend such schools for their entire primary and second-level education. While many students complete public examinations (notably students with physical disabilities) within special schools and classes, it is not known how girls with such impairments fare compared with boys, or what the rates of drop-out or achievement are for students with disabilities compared with mainstream students. The most basic data on differences between students with learning disabilities and those with only physical disabilities are not published.

Qualitative research by Duffy (1993) and Dalton (1996) on the experiences of students with physical impairments suggests that there is very little time or attention given to the gender-specific needs of girls and young women either in special schools or in schools which educate students with disabilities. Duffy notes in particular how disablist attitudes meant that access to basic school services such as sport were not addressed in certain schools. Lack of involvement in sport and other extra-curricular activities accentuated girls' isolation from their peers. While sexuality and relationships were a central concern to young women with physical impairments, in the context of a society with highly disablist attitudes to the sexuality of disabled women in particular, very little time or attention seemed to be given to such subjects in schools.

There is no major study of the experience of lesbian women in education in Ireland. While this may not be surprising given attitudes towards sexuality, nonetheless it is an oppressive silence; most lesbian girls and women (and gay boys and men) have to manage their sexuality by remaining quiet, fearing prejudice and discrimination (Moane, 1997). O'Fachtnáin (1992) documents a similar problem for gay men, especially in schools where fear of losing one's job as a teacher meant one had to 'pass' as heterosexual.

Neither is there any systematic documentation or research on the experiences of Traveller girls and young women in education, although there are a small number of studies documenting the alienation and prejudice which Travellers generally experience in education (Kenny, 1990/91; Ryan, 1998). The progress and experience of various other ethnic and religious minorities or refugees is also not documented. Consequently it is not possible to make any definite statement about these groups. Yet such information is of profound importance to the groups in question. It is part of the process of recognition to which I referred above. If people are not named and noted then their unique achievements, concerns and difficulties cannot be addressed. Silence and ignorance become the prevailing norms. Such silence breeds fear and anxiety and helps to fan the fires of prejudice and discrimination. It also has a negative multiplier effect; there is little incentive to undertake research in the field when the group literally cannot be located. The work of Duffy (1993), O'Reilly (1993) and Dalton (1996) documents the many difficulties facing those undertaking research in a field where there are no national data collected.

CONCLUDING COMMENTS

If one is to assess the position of women in education by defining women as an undifferentiated group, then it is true to say that there has been very significant progress by women in education over the last twenty years. Women's participation in second and third level has improved dramatically, while their rates of attainment in public examinations are consistently above those of men. Women now outnumber men in the university sector. Even in the traditional 'masculine' fields such as the sciences, women's achievements are significant in recent years. In 1962/3 for example, at the time the *Investment in Education Report* was being written, 31.7% of boys doing the Leaving Certificate were taking Chemistry, 28% were taking Physics, and 99% were taking Mathematics; the comparable figures for girls were 4.8%, 2% and 82.3% respectively (Department of Education, 1965:276). In 1996 almost 100% of girls and boys did Mathematics for the Leaving Certificate (although girls are still under-represented in higher Mathematics, comprising 44% of the candidates), while 8.5% of all women candidates, and 25.6% of boys, took Physics; 12.6% of girls and 11.3% of boys took Chemistry. Women comprised 51% of the Chemistry examination candidates and 30% of the Physics candidates (Department of Education, 1997, Tables 5.2, 5.16–5.24).

Women are not an undifferentiated social group, however. There are important social class, age, ethnic and other differences in their experiences in education. Clancy's (1995) research shows that working-class women have significantly poorer rates of participation in higher education than middle-class women and men. Older women are also under-represented among part-time mature students in higher education (Lynch, 1996). Yet women are significantly over-represented in the least prestigious and the most poorly funded sector of education, community education (Johnston, 1998). The limited research available suggests that women with disabilities experience a range of inequalities in education which are not experienced by men or women without impairments (Duffy, 1993; O'Reilly, 1993; Dalton, 1996). Numerous barriers confront Traveller girls and women in education, although there has been no major study of these (Government of Ireland, 1995). The failure to recognise these and other differences, such as those arising from sexuality or religious or ethnic status, has meant that little attention is focused on the fact that it is a particular social group of Irish women who have been successful in recent years, notably young, middle-class, white, non-disabled, settled women.

WOMEN IN MANAGEMENT: WOMEN TEACH AND MEN MANAGE

INTRODUCTION: WOMEN AND WORK

While girls' performance in second-level education would suggest that girls are primed for high levels of success in the paid labour market, such is not the case. Even a brief perusal of employment statistics shows that women are disproportionately represented at the low-wage end of particular occupations, including the professions, as well as being strongly over-represented in low-paying jobs within particular sectors, notably in the services sector, but also in manufacturing (Daly, 1985; Jackson and Barry, 1989; Blackwell and Nolan, 1990; Smyth, 1997). Before going on to comment on women's standing in education generally, it is worth noting where women are located in employment at this time.

Just under 10% of farm holders in Ireland are women (O'Hara, 1997:364). Women comprise only 18% of employers while they represent 98% of (generally unpaid) home workers (588,000) (Central Statistics Office, 1997, Tables 10, 20). Although women are significantly over-represented in professions such as teaching and nursing, these are neither the most prestigious nor the most highly paid professional occupations. Moreover, over half of all women employed in 1997 were working in three of the lower-paid sectors of the economy, namely services, shop and bar work, and clerical work, while they comprised 73% of all part-time workers (Central Statistics Office, 1997). Women's hourly rates of pay in manufacturing are estimated to be 30% below the male rate, while their average industrial earnings in 1995 were 70% those of men (National Women's Council of Ireland). Women's educational gains have not been translated into comparable employment gains; they are disproportionately represented in the lower-paid sectors of employment both within and between occupations.

WOMEN IN MANAGEMENT IN EDUCATION

Gender differences in the distribution of senior management posts in Irish education are marked at all levels of the education system (Table 4). Representation at senior management levels is best at primary level and worst in the universities and other institutes of higher education. In addition, almost all the senior administrative posts in the Department of Education are held by men although women are in the majority in the civil service and in the Department of Education. Within the inspectorate, only 9% of the posts from senior inspector upwards are held by women (Irish National Teachers' Organisation, 1995) while at the time of writing all but one of the assistant secretaries in education were men.

PRIMARY AND SECOND-LEVEL EDUCATION

Women comprise 78% of the teachers and 46% of the principals in primary schools. At second level, 29% of school principals are women, although it must be noted that over half of these (57%) are actually religious women who did not have to compete for jobs under open competition.

There are three different types of schools at second level, each with its own traditions and administrative structures. Promotional opportunities for women (and men) are quite different across the school types. Secondary schools comprise the single largest category of school with 59% of all schools being of this type. While lay women comprise 54% of the teachers in secondary schools only 14.7% of the principals are lay women. In contrast, religious women constitute about 4.3% of all teachers but they hold two-thirds of the female-held principalships. In vocational schools, where 47% of the teachers are women, 11% of the principalships are held by women; within the community and comprehensive schools, although half of the teachers are women only 6.1% of principalships are held by lay women (Table 4).

While the position of women at vice-principalship level and in other senior posts is more favourable than it is at principalship level, women are still under-represented. In primary and secondary schools, women are well represented at

Table 4

*Proportion of Women in Teaching Posts, Principalships
and Senior Management*

School type	% of teachers	% of principals	Ratio of female teachers to principals/heads
Primary (1995) (1, 2)	78.0	46.0	**1.7:1**
Second level (1995)	54.0	29.0	**1.9:1**
of whom			
Secondary (3, 4, 5)	58.2	43.2	**1.3:1 (all)**
		14.7 (lay) 28.5 (religious)	**4.0:1 (lay)**
Vocational (6)	47.0	11.0	**4.3:1**
Community/Comprehensive	49.6	8.5	**5.8:1 (all)**
		6.1 (lay) 2.4 (religious)	**8.1:1 (lay)**
Regional Technical Colleges (1995)	25.0	6.1 (Head of Department)	**4.1:1**
Dublin Institute of Technology Colleges (1996)	19.4	9.0 (Senior Lecturer Grade 2) This is the grade for heads of schools, which is a more senior post than head of department.	**2.2:1**
Universities (1995)	21.0	5.0 (Professors and Associate Professors)	**4.2:1**

Notes:
1. Almost 90% of female primary school principals are lay.
2. Just over 95% of male primary school principals are lay.
3. 34% of all female secondary school principals are lay.
4. 74.1% of all male secondary school principals are lay.
5. 42% of principals in all types of secondary schools are lay men and 14.7% are religious men or priests: i.e. 56.7% overall are men.
6. Almost all teachers and principals are lay persons in vocational schools.

Sources: Department of Education for all levels; Personnel Departments of the universities and other higher education institutions; Higher Education Authority, Irish National Teachers' Organisation, Association of Secondary Teachers, Ireland, Teachers' Union of Ireland; Egan (1996).

vice-principalship level. However, it must be remembered that within these schools such posts (and A and B promotional posts) are filled not by open competition but by seniority. Thus the favourable representation of women cannot be attributed to their success in open competition. In those schools where senior posts are filled by competition, women tend to be seriously under-represented, although not as seriously as is the case with principalships. Only one in four vice-principals in community and comprehensive schools are women, and somewhat less than one in four in vocational schools. The position with regard to A posts is also very unfavourable in these schools. While women's position in relation to B posts is slightly better than at other grades in vocational and community and comprehensive schools, these are the lowest-grade promotional posts. Moreover, women are heavily concentrated in the lowest points in the teaching scales in all types of second-level schools. While this is partly a function of the fact that second-level teaching is becoming feminised[3] (see also Warren, 1997), it is also a function of the failure of women to get promotion to more senior grades.

The fact that women are not getting promotion to middle management in proportion to their overall numbers when open competition exists, suggests that the so-called 'merit' system of promotion is far from favourable to women.

Table 5

Ireland: Gender Differences in the Distribution of Vice-Principalships and Other Promotional Posts (A Posts and B Posts)

School type	Vice-principals %		A posts %		B posts %	
	Women	Men	Women	Men	Women	Men
Primary (1995)	82.6	17.4	68.9	31.1	76.0	24.0
Secondary (1995)	41.3	58.7	47.3	52.7	54.1	45.9
Vocational (1996)	22.8	77.2	32.1	67.9	47.4	52.6
Community/ Comprehensive (1995)	26.0	74.0	34.2	65.8	50.0	50.0
Dublin Institute of Technology (1996)	**Senior Lecturer 1** 18.0					
Regional Technical Colleges (1995)	**Lecturer 2** 16.5 (data available for only six of the eleven colleges)					
Universities (1995)	**Senior/Statutory Lecturer** 12.0					

Sources: Department of Education for all levels; Personnel Departments of the universities and other higher education institutions; Higher Education Authority, Irish National Teachers' Organisation, Association of Secondary Teachers, Ireland, Teachers' Union of Ireland; Egan (1996).

It is interesting that it is only when promotional posts are given on the basis of seniority that women are likely to be adequately represented! Women's under-representation at middle-management level means that they are significantly disadvantaged when it comes to seeking principalships as they may not be seen to have the relevant experience (Kellaghan and Fontes, 1985).

THIRD-LEVEL EDUCATION

Although the majority of teachers at second level are women, women are poorly represented in teaching in higher education. Unfortunately the reasons for women's poor representation in teaching in higher education have not been researched. No more than a quarter of the lecturers in higher education colleges are women in any given sector although the proportion of junior lecturers who are women has risen significantly in recent years, particularly in the universities, where 39% of all assistant lecturers were women in 1994 compared with 24% in 1984 (Smyth, 1996, Table 2). Viewed in proportion to their representation in the teaching force, women are no better represented in senior posts in third-level education than they are overall in second level, with the representation of women in senior professorial posts in the universities being particularly poor. Within the higher education sector, women's promotional rate is best in the Dublin Institute of Technology (DIT) colleges and poorest in the universities.

The reasons why women are under-represented at senior management in higher education have not been investigated. Neither has there been any study of the management culture of the higher education institutions comparable to that undertaken by O'Connor (1996) on the Health Boards. O'Connor's work suggests that these are subjects worth researching, not least because of the evidence that the culture of public organisations is far from welcoming to women. It is, she notes:

> a hierarchical structure which is characterised by one-way communi-cation and a retentive attitude to information; where women's 'proper' place is not in management; where the 'normal' pattern of succession is along a male line; and where traditional female projects . . . become remote from the centres of resources. (O'Connor, 1996:230)

Neither job selection nor promotion practices have been researched across the colleges, although it is widely accepted within the university sector that while one's research and publications record is important at the selection stage, it is of overriding importance when it comes to promotion. Smyth and Burke's (1988) study of women academics within University College Dublin suggested that one of the reasons that women might not fare as well as men in promotion is because they often lacked the necessary research profile, often devoting more of their time to teaching and administration, both of which counted for much less than research and publications. The fact that selection and promotional boards are often overwhelmingly male-dominated is also very likely to have a depressing effect on women's applications and indeed their chances of success, as has happened in other sectors of education (Teachers' Union of Ireland, 1990; Gleeson, 1992).

APPLICATIONS AND APPOINTMENTS TO SENIOR POSTS

A study of female primary teachers in the mid-1980s found that only 16% of women who were in a position to apply for promotion intended to do so (Kellaghan and Fontes, 1985). The corresponding figure for men was 50%. A survey of second-level teachers by the Teachers' Union of Ireland a few years later indicated that there was an even lower level of interest in principalships among second-level teachers as only 3% of the women surveyed aspired to be principals. However, roughly comparable proportions of women (38%) and men (44%) were actively seeking promotion (Teachers' Union of Ireland, 1990). Research by the Association of Secondary Teachers (ASTI) confirmed earlier findings regarding women's relative lack of interest in principalships; while 16% of the men surveyed had actually applied for a principalship, only 5% of women had done so (Gleeson, 1992). More recent research by Warren (1997:76) indicates, however, that the situation may be changing in the community and comprehensive sector, with almost one in six of the applicants female between 1992 and 1994.

There is no study of the application/appointment ratio of women to men in the higher education sector. Data available to the author from UCD's Promotions Board do indicate that women are applying for promotional posts at a comparable rate to men in that university in recent years; however, they have not been as successful as men in their applications. Only 5% of associate professorships were given to women in 1997/8 although 19% of the applicants for these posts were women. A comparable pattern obtained in 1996/7.

Table 6 shows the pattern of appointments to principalships from 1991 to 1995 inclusive, although data are not available on the number and gender of applicants per place for those years. The most revealing figure from this table is

Table 6

Appointments in Secondary* Schools: 1991–5

	All-boys' schools		All-girls' schools		Co-educational schools	
	N	%	N	%	N	%
Women	0	0.0	13	62.0	6	23.0
Men	19	100.0	8	38.0	20	77.0
Total	19	100.0	21	100	26	100.0

* Secondary schools represent 59% of all 782 second-level schools.
Total number appointed = 66: total women = 19 (29%); total men = 47 (71%).
Source: Association of Secondary Teachers, Ireland (ASTI), *Report of the Equality Committee*, 1996.

that 77% of the principals appointed in co-educational secondary schools were men. While it is not clear from the data available whether women applied for posts in either co-educational or single-sex schools at the same rate as men, what is clear is that it was only in girls' schools that women were more likely to be appointed principals than men.

The application and appointment rates for women at primary level are somewhat better; female applicants outnumbered males in three out of the four years from 1989 to 1992 inclusive, and in both 1995 and 1996. However, women are still not applying in proportion to their representation in the teaching population. Overall, women's appointment ratio exceeds their application ratio within the primary sector every year since 1983 with the exception of 1987/8. This means that women who apply are more likely to be appointed than men. Although this might suggest some positive discrimination in favour of women, what is more likely true, and what the limited data available suggest, is that women are less likely to apply for posts than men if they think they lack all the necessary qualifications. Thus the pool of women applying is likely to be more qualified than the male pool, accounting for their better appointment ratio (Kellaghan and Fontes, 1985).

One of the questions which is raised in the literature about principalships, and what is clearly an issue at second level, is the proportion of women who obtain principalships in co-educational schools. From Table 7 it is clear that women are quite well represented in principalships in co-educational primary schools in Ireland: almost 44% of the principals in co-educational *primary* schools are women while 46% of *all* principals are women. The only schools in which women are really poorly represented in principalships are senior co-educational schools. These are the schools which teach senior primary classes only.

It would be interesting to see what proportion of the recent female appointments to principalships were in co-educational schools and in larger schools. Unfortunately, the data are not available on this although Warren's data (1997) suggest that it is women who are losing out as principals when small schools close down.

Table 7

Principalships in Co-educational Primary Schools, 1995/6

Type of school	Women N	Men N	Total N	% women
Junior co-ed.	86	18	104	82.6
Senior co-ed.	11	52	63	17.5
Special schools	74	49	123	60.2
Full co-ed.	992	1,394	2,386	41.6
Total	1,163	1,513	2,676	43.5

Source: Department of Education (1996).

CONCLUDING COMMENTS: WOMEN, EQUALITY AND MANAGEMENT

Liberal and voluntaristic principles underpin equality policies in Ireland to date, especially in the field of education. While the Employment Equality Agency has published guidelines for employers on promoting equality between the sexes — through such practices as appointing gender-balanced interview panels and selection boards — the guidelines are voluntary rather than mandatory. School boards and college selection panels can, and do, break the guidelines without fear of sanction. Interview boards are still strongly male-dominated (Kellaghan and Fontes, 1985; Teachers' Union of Ireland, 1990; Irish National Teachers' Organisation, 1993) and unfortunately there is still no legal mechanism to challenge this as the Employment Equality Bill (1998) does not address this issue at all; it makes no regulation regarding interview and selection boards.

Male dominance of the selection and promotion procedures makes women feel uncomfortable about seeking promotion (Teachers' Union of Ireland, 1990; Gleeson, 1992). That women know they are disadvantaged in seeking promotion is shown in an ASTI survey of second-level teachers. It found that 77% of both women and men believed it was helpful being a man when seeking promotion, while only 17% thought it would be an advantage to be a woman (Gleeson, 1992).

Although the knowledge that the entire application, selection and management process in education is male-dominated may be a disincentive for women to apply for senior posts, the limited research evidence available suggests that women's multiple role responsibilities may also have a disincentive effect. The pay and supports available to school heads in Ireland are far from adequate. Women, especially those with heavy caring and/or domestic responsibilities, often do not regard the extra rewards of a principalship or headship of a university department as being worth the extra effort and hassle required (Egan, 1996). Kellaghan and Fontes' national study of primary teachers (1985) found, for example, that there were significant differences in the types of women who intended applying for principalships: over twice as many single women without children intended to apply compared with married women. A small study of second-level principals identified a similar trend: of the nine women principals in the study, five were single with no children; one was married with no children; and while the three remaining had children, only one had a child under eighteen years of age (Daly, 1989). Although other factors may explain the differences between single and married women especially, such as the greater mobility of single women, the disproportionate responsibility which women take for caring and domestic work in households is undoubtedly a very important explanatory variable in understanding the differences between women's and men's promotional prospects.

If the position of women in teaching is to change so that they are more equitably involved in senior management, not only must promotional and selection procedures become more open and egalitarian, but also caring practices. Caring work is a fundamental part of the work of society; if women carry a disproportionate responsibility for such work, then they simply cannot compete equally with men for senior posts without seriously damaging their own health through overwork. The same issue arises with domestic work.

What is equally essential is a radical restructuring of the organisation of power and authority within work organisations. Collegial structures, power-sharing and rotating responsibility at senior levels would greatly facilitate women (and men) who may wish to manage, but who also wish to attend to equally important tasks in their personal lives. Unfortunately, certain schools, especially second-level schools, in Ireland have tended to adopt the more 'aggressive chief executive' model of management in recent years, thereby signalling to many women (and men) who do not adhere to this model that senior management is not for them. A move away from a hierarchical to a more egalitarian style of management structure is essential for the promotion of equality for women in educational management (Lynch, 1994; O'Connor, 1996).

CONCLUSION

If one utilises a simple distributive 'equal opportunities' approach to assess the position of women in education, then it would appear that *women-as-learners* have equality with men in education; they are equally represented at almost all levels of education, and surpass men in their performance in public examinations. Yet this approach to measuring equality has serious limitations, notably in ignoring differences. It does not recognise that there are still very significant social class differences, not only in the participation rates but in the performance levels of women. Low-income working-class women are much less likely to attend higher education than either middle-class women or middle-class men, while they are disproportionately represented in the poorly funded and accredited community education sector. Older women are also under-represented among mature students in higher education.

Neither does the liberal distributive model of social justice address other important differences between women arising from ethnicity, sexuality, marital status or disability, for example. It ignores important differences in the outcomes of education for Traveller, disabled or older women, as well as the differences in their experiences within education. It implicitly assumes that education itself is an unproblematic 'good'; it ignores the male-gendered nature of much of schooling, thereby reinforcing unequal gender relations within it.

The problem with the distributive model as currently construed is not simply that it fails to recognise cultural barriers to equality, it is that it is focused on opportunities, not on social positions. Women are encouraged to become socially mobile and gain a better standing in the 'hierarchy' while the hierarchy remains intact. Thus the economic and political inequalities which interface with gender and which exist in a dialectical relationship to cultural misrecognition and marginalisation, are left unexplored. Given the importance of politico-economic inequalities for women vis-à-vis men within given social classes, and for women vis-à-vis other women across social classes, especially in a society like Ireland where social class is a major social differentiator in terms of educational outcomes, this is a significant limitation of the liberal distributive model of social justice. The focus on 'mobility' for women also distracts attention, however, from the gendered character of knowledge and discourse within education itself. Debates about the androcentric biases of particular disciplines cannot become the subject of debate when the focus is on measuring women's mobility between disciplines, or between stages and levels of education, no matter how valuable this may be as a project in its own right.

When we examine the position of *women-as-educators*, even in terms of the limited criterion of 'equality of opportunity', a highly unequal set of relationships appears to exist between women and men, whereby men are significantly over-represented in management, and women are over-represented in teaching posts without senior responsibilities. This holds for all sectors of education although it is most pronounced in the universities. Debates about the androcentric culture of schools and colleges has scarcely begun, hence there is, as yet, very little research challenging the patriarchal cultures of male-dominated educational organisations.

The absence of a feminist debate about the nature of curricula and pedagogical practices in our schools (or indeed an ongoing debate about culture differences arising from differences of social class, ethnicity, etc.) is one of the most conspicuous omissions in Irish education literature. There is therefore much work to be done, not only on moving beyond simple distributive concerns about 'equalising opportunities to become unequal', but also in challenging gendered, classed and raced hegemonies which underpin pedagogical and curriculum practices within our education system.

REFERENCES

Arnot, M. (1991). Equality and democracy: a decade of struggle over education. *British Journal of Sociology of Education*, 12:447–66.

Arnot, M. (1992). Feminism, education and the new right. In M. Arnot and L. Barton (eds.), *Voicing Concerns: Sociological Perspectives on Contemporary Education Reforms*. Wallingford, Oxfordshire: Triangle Books Ltd.

Arnot, M., and Weiner, M. (eds.) (1987). *Gender and the Politics of Schooling*. London: Hutchinson.

Blackwell, J. (1989). *Women in the Labour Force*. Dublin: Employment Equality Agency.

Blackwell, J., and Nolan, B. (1990). Low pay: the Irish experience. In Combat Poverty and the Irish Congress of Trade Unions (ICTU), *Low Pay: The Irish Experience*. Dublin: Combat Poverty/ICTU.

Blossfeld, H.P., and Shavit, Y. (1993). Persisting barriers: changes in educational opportunities in thirteen countries. In Y. Shavit and H.P. Blossfeld (eds.), *Persistent Inequality: Changing Educational Attainment in Thirteen Countries*. Oxford: Westview Press.

Breen, R., Hannan, D., Rottman, D., and Whelan, C. (1990). *Understanding Contemporary Ireland*. Dublin: Gill & Macmillan.

Burke, M.R. (1996). Women staff in the RTC (Regional Technical College) sector. In O. Egan (ed.), *Women Staff in Irish Colleges*. Higher Education Equality Unit, University College Cork.

Byrne, A. (1992). Academic women's studies in the Republic of Ireland. *Women's Studies Quarterly*, 3 & 4:15–27.

Byrne, A., and Leonard, M. (eds.) (1997). *Women in Irish Society: A Sociological Reader*. Belfast: Beyond the Pale Publications.

Central Statistics Office (CSO) (1997). *Labour Force Survey 1997*. Dublin: Government Publications Office.

Clancy, P. (1988). *Who Goes to College*. Dublin: Higher Education Authority.

Clancy, P. (1995). *Access to College: Patterns of Continuity and Change*. Dublin: Higher Education Authority.

Combat Poverty and the Irish Congress of Trade Unions (ICTU) (1990). *Low Pay: The Irish Experience*. Dublin: Combat Poverty/ICTU.

Commission on the Status of Women (1993). *Report to Government of the Second Commission on the Status of Women*. Dublin: Government Publications Office.

Conference of Religious of Ireland (CORI) (Education Commission) (1995). *Women for Leadership in Education*. Dublin: CORI.

Connell, R.W. (1993). *Schools and Social Justice*. Philadelphia: Temple University Press.

Connelly, A. (ed.) (1993). *Gender and the Law in Ireland*. Dublin: Oak Tree Press.

Connelly, B. (1997). Women in community education and development — liberation and domestication? In A. Byrne and M. Leonard (eds.), *Women in Irish Society: A Sociological Reader*. Belfast: Beyond the Pale Publications.

Coolahan, J. (1981). *Irish Education: History and Structure*. Dublin: Institute of Public Administration.

Coolahan, J. (ed.) (1994). *Report on the National Education Convention*. Dublin: Government Publications Office.

Dalton, B. (1996). The provision of service for blind and visually impaired students in second- and third-level education. University College Dublin, Equality Studies Centre, unpublished Master of Equality Studies thesis.

Daly, M. (1985). *The Hidden Workers*. Dublin: Employment Equality Agency.

Daly, M. (1989). *The Under-Representation of Female Post-Primary Teachers in Promotional Posts*. University College Dublin, Education Department, M.Ed. thesis.

David, M. (1985). Motherhood and social policy — a matter of education. *Critical Social Policy*, 12 (Spring):28–43.

Delphy, C., and Leonard, D. (1992). *Familiar Exploitation: A New Analysis of Marriage and Family Life*. Oxford: Polity Press.

Department of Education (1965). *Investment in Education Report*. Dublin: Government Publications Office.

Department of Education (1980). *Tuarascáil Staitistiúil 1978/79: Statistical Report*. Dublin: Government Publications Office.

Department of Education (1993). *Report of the Working Group on the Elimination of Sexism and Sex-Stereotyping in Textbooks and Teaching Materials in Irish National Schools*. Dublin: Government Publications Office.

Department of Education (1995a). *Charting Our Education Future: White Paper on Education*. Dublin: Government Publications Office.

Department of Education (1995b). *Tuarascáil Staitistiúil 1993/94: Statistical Report*. Dublin: Government Publications Office.

Department of Education (1996). *Tuarascáil Staitistiúil 1994/95: Statistical Report*. Dublin: Government Publications Office.

Department of Education (1997). *Tuarascáil Staitistiúil 1995/96: Statistical Report*. Dublin: Government Publications Office.

Department of the Taoiseach (1987). *United Nations Convention on the Elimination of All Forms of Discrimination against Women: First Report by Ireland*. Dublin: Government Publications Office.

Drudy, S. (1990). Integrating gender equality in teacher education — the experience of an EC action project. Paper presented at the Association for Teacher Education in Europe Annual Conference, Limerick, Ireland.

Drudy, S. (1991). The sociology of education in Ireland, 1966–1991. *Irish Journal of Sociology*, 1:107–27.

Drudy, S., and Lynch, K. (1993). *Schools and Society in Ireland*. Dublin: Gill & Macmillan.

Drudy, S., and Uí Chatháin, M. (1998). Gender differences in classroom interaction in a second-level context. *Irish Educational Studies*, 17:135–47.

Duffy, M. (1993). Integration or segregation: does it make a difference? A study of equality issues relating to the education of disabled girls. University College Dublin, Equality Studies Centre, unpublished Master of Equality Studies thesis.

Dunne, J. (1993). *Back to the Rough Ground: 'Phronesis' and 'Techne' in Modern Philosophy*. University of Notre Dame Press.

Egan, O. (1996). *Women Staff in Irish Colleges*. Cork: Higher Education Equality Unit.

Employment Equality Agency (EEA) (1995). *Women in the Labour Force*. Dublin: EEA.

Fagan, H. (1995). *Culture, Politics and Irish School Dropouts: Constructing Political Identities*. London: Bergin and Garvey.

Flynn, M. (1998). A study of gender differentiation in primary school playgrounds. *Irish Educational Studies*, 17:148–60.

Fraser, H. (1995). From redistribution to recognition? Dilemmas of social justice in a 'post-socialist' age. *New Left Review*, 212:68–93.

Gleeson, J. (1992). *Gender Equality in Education in the Republic of Ireland. Second Report of the Third Joint Oireachtas Committee on Women's Rights*. Dublin: Government Publications Office.

Government of Ireland (1994). *First Report of the Monitoring Committee on the Implementation of the Recommendations of the Second Commission on the Status of Women*. Dublin: Government Publications Office.

Government of Ireland (1995). *Report of the Task Force on the Travelling Community*. Dublin: Government Publications Office.

Government of Ireland (1996). *Report of the Constitution Review Group*. Dublin: Government Publications Office.

Hannan, D.F., Breen, R., Murphy, B., Watson, D., Hardiman, N., and O'Higgins, K. (1983). *Schooling and Sex Roles*. Dublin: Economic and Social Research Institute, Paper No. 113.

Hannan, D.F., Smyth, E., McCullagh, J., O'Leary, R., and McMahon, D. (1996). *Coeducation and Gender Equality: Exam Performance, Stress and Personal Development*. Dublin: Oak Tree Press.

Hogan, P. (1995). *The Custody and Courtship of Experience: Western Education in Philosophical Perspective*. Dublin: Columba Press.

Inglis, T. et al. (1993). *Liberating Learning: A Report on Daytime Education Groups*. Dublin: AONTAS (National Association of Adult Education).

Irish Federation of University Teachers (IFUT) (1996). *Equality Issues*. Summer.

Irish National Teachers' Organisation (INTO) (1993). *Equality of Opportunity Report in Educational Management*. Belfast: INTO.

Irish National Teachers' Organisation (INTO) (1995). *Central Executive Report*. Dublin: INTO.

Jackson, P., and Barry, U. (1989). Women's employment and multinationals in the Republic of Ireland. In D. Elson and R. Pearson (eds.), *Women's Employment and Multinationals in Europe*. London: Macmillan.

Johnston, H. (1998). *Supports for Women's Education*. Paper presented to a Seminar on Promoting and Supporting Women's Education in the Six Border Counties, Monaghan, 24 March 1998.

Kellaghan, T., and Fontes, P. (1985). *Gender Inequalities in Irish Primary School Teaching*. Dublin: Educational Company.

Kenny, M. (1990/91). Integrate whom? Into what? Indigenous nomads and school. *REACH*, 4 (2).57–60.

Lentin, R. (1993). Feminist research methodologies — a separate paradigm? Notes for a debate. *Irish Journal of Sociology*, 3:119–38.

Leonard, M. (1994). *Informal Economic Activity in Belfast*. Aldershot: Avebury.

Lynch, K. (1988). The ethos of girls' schools: an analysis of differences between male and female schools. *Social Studies*, 10 (1/2):11–31.

Lynch, K. (1989). *The Hidden Curriculum: Reproduction in Education, A Reappraisal*. Lewes: Falmer Press.

Lynch, K. (1990). *Worlds Apart: Gender Inequalities in Education and Ways of Eliminating Them*. Report on the EU TENET project, Department of Education, Dublin.

Lynch, K. (1995). Women teach and men manage: why men dominate senior posts in Irish education. Conference of Religious of Ireland (CORI) (Education Commission), *Women for Leadership in Education*. Dublin: CORI.

Lynch, K. (1996). The limits of liberalism for the promotion of equality in education. In E. Befring (ed.), *Teacher Education for Equality*. Oslo: Association for Teacher Education in Europe (ATEE). Papers from the ATEE 20th Annual Conference, Oslo, September 1995.

Lynch, K. (1997). Women in educational management: Ireland. In M. Wilson (ed.), *Women in Educational Management: A European Perspective*. London: Paul Chapman.

Lynch, K., and Lodge, A. (1999, forthcoming). *Equality and the Social Climate of Schools*. Dublin.

Lynch, K., and McLaughlin, E. (1995). Caring labour and love labour. In P. Clancy, S. Drudy, K. Lynch and L. O'Dowd (eds.), *Irish Society: Sociological Perspectives*. Dublin: Institute of Public Administration.

Lynch, K., and Morgan, V. (1995). Gender and education: north and south. In P. Clancy, S. Drudy, K. Lynch and L. O'Dowd (eds.), *Irish Society: Sociological Perspectives*. Dublin: Institute of Public Administration.

Mac an Ghaill, M. (1994). *The Making of Men: Masculinities, Sexualities and Schooling.* Milton Keynes: Open University Press.

McKenna, A. (1988). *Child Care and Equal Opportunities.* Dublin: Employment Equality Agency.

Middleton, S. (1990). Women, equality and equity in liberal educational policies, 1945–1988. In S. Middleton, J. Codd and A. Jones (eds.), *New Zealand Education Policy Today.* Wellington, New Zealand: Allen & Unwin.

Moane, G. (1997). Lesbian politics and community. In A. Byrne and M. Leonard (eds.), *Women in Irish Society: A Sociological Reader.* Belfast: Beyond the Pale Publications.

Morgan, M., Hickey, B., and Kellaghan, T. (OECD) (1997). *International Adult Literacy Survey: Results for Ireland.* Dublin: Government Publications Office.

Murray, B. (1985). *Sex Differences in Education: A Comparative Study of Ireland and Switzerland.* Bern and New York: Peterlang.

Murray, B., and O'Carroll, A. (1997). Out of sight, out of mind? Women and disabilities in Ireland. In A. Byrne and M. Leonard (eds.), *Women in Irish Society: A Sociological Reader.* Belfast: Beyond the Pale Publications.

O'Connor, P. (1996). Organisational culture as a barrier to women's promotion. *Economic and Social Review*, 27 (3):205–34.

O'Fachtnáin, A. (1992). Institutionalised homophobia in the workplace: a study of gay men in Dublin. University College Dublin, Equality Studies Centre, unpublished Master of Equality Studies thesis.

O'Hara, P. (1997). Women in farm families: shedding the past and fashioning the future. In A. Byrne and M. Leonard (eds.), *Women in Irish Society: A Sociological Reader.* Belfast: Beyond the Pale Publications.

O'Reilly, J.O. (1993). The hearing impaired: equal opportunity in higher education in Ireland. University College Dublin, Equality Studies Centre, unpublished Master of Equality Studies thesis.

Organisation for Economic Co-operation and Development (OECD) (1991). *Reviews of National Policies for Education, Ireland.* Paris: OECD.

Organisation for Economic Co-operation and Development (OECD) (1996). *Education Indicators.* Paris: OECD.

Raftery, A.E., and Hout, M. (1993). Maximally maintained inequality: expansion, reform and opportunity in Irish education, 1921–75. *Sociology of Education*, 66:41–62.

Raftery, D. (1997). Teaching as a profession for first-generation women graduates: a comparison of selected sources from Ireland, England and North America. *Irish Educational Studies*, 16:99–108.

Rawls, J. (1971). *A Theory of Justice.* Oxford University Press.

Ryan, A. (1997). Gender discourses in school social relations. In A. Byrne and M. Leonard (eds.), *Women in Irish Society: A Sociological Reader.* Belfast: Beyond the Pale Publications.

Ryan, A. (1998). Teachers, travellers and education: a sociological perspective. *Irish Educational Studies*, 17:161–74.

Shavit, Y., and Blossfeld, H.P. (eds.) (1993). *Persistent Inequality: Changing Educational Attainment in Thirteen Countries.* Oxford: Westview Press.

Slowey, M. (1987). Education for domestication or liberation? Women's involvement in adult education. In M. Cullen (ed.), *Girls Don't Do Honours.* Dublin: Women's Education Bureau.

Smyth, A. (1992). Women's studies and 'the disciplines'. *Women's Studies International Forum*, 15 (5–6):615–17.

Smyth, A. (1996). Reviewing breaking the circle: a pilot project. In O. Egan, *Women Staff in Irish Colleges*. Cork: Higher Education Equality Unit.

Smyth, E. (1997). Labour market structures and women's employment in the Republic of Ireland. In A. Byrne and M. Leonard (eds.), *Women in Irish Society: A Sociological Reader*. Belfast: Beyond the Pale Publications.

Smyth, E., and Burke, H. (1988). *Distant Peaks: A Study of the Relative Staffing Levels of Women and Men in University College Dublin*. University College Dublin.

Stanworth, M. (1981). *Gender and Schooling: A Study of Sexual Divisions*. London: Hutchinson.

Sturman, A. (1997). *Social Justice in Education, Australian Education Review*, 40. Camberwell, Victoria: Australian Council for Educational Research.

Teachers' Union of Ireland (TUI) (1990). *Equality of Opportunity in Teaching*, 13. Dublin: TUI.

Warren, L. (1997). The career structure of women in education. *Irish Educational Studies*, 16:69–84.

Weiner, G. (1989). Feminism, equal opportunitites and vocationalism: the changing perspective on gender. In H. Burchell and V. Millman (eds.), *Changing Perspectives on Gender*. Milton Keynes: Open University Press.

Weiner, G. (1994), *Feminisms and Education*. Buckingham: Open University Press.

Wickham, A. (1987). *Women and Training*. Milton Keynes: Open University Press.

Wolpe, A.M. (1976). The official ideology of education for girls. In M. Flude and J. Ahier (eds.), *Educability, Schools and Ideology*. London: Croom Helm.

Young, I.M. (1990). *Justice and the Politics of Difference*. Princeton University Press.

Young, I.M. (1992). Recent theories of justice. *Social Theory and Practice*, 18 (1):63–79.

NOTES

1   Fraser (1995) makes this distinction between affirmative and transformative remedies. In education affirmative remedies are essentially liberal remedies which measure equality for women in terms of literally getting even with men, in terms of proportions of jobs and places in 'valued' education. At the cultural level, it demands respect for women without challenging the androcentric foundations of the gender code. Transformative policies are socialist in the economic sphere while being deconstructivist in the cultural sphere.

2   Within farming families, it was almost always men who inherited land; for those who could afford it, education was the woman's dowry.

3   In 1996, 75% of teachers under thirty years of age in vocational schools were women; 92.5% of those were in the secondary sector, and 95% of those in community and comprehensive schools (data received directly from the Teachers' Union of Ireland).

CHAPTER 6

THE STATUS OF CHILDREN

PERSPECTIVES ON CHILDREN AND CHILDHOOD[1]

The model of childhood which has dominated research to date is that of developmentalism. It is essentially an evolutionary model which supposes that rationality is the mark of adulthood and that childhood is basically an apprenticeship for its development. Adulthood and childhood are presented as binary opposites; being a child is presented as the antithesis of being an adult.

The developmentalist view found elaborate expression in Piaget's work. His conceptual framework dominated thinking on cognition, and granted scientific validity to the claim that children develop in predetermined stages, moving eventually to a stage where they achieve logical competence, which is the mark of adult rationality. Within sociology, socialisation theory borrowed heavily from the developmentalist view. Children were generally defined as passive subjects being socialised in schools and families into predefined social roles (Prout and James, 1990).

Underpinning this dominant discourse on children was a range of assumptions about the status and rights of children. Basically, a 'caretaking' protectionist model dominated intellectual thought (Archard, 1993). Within the caretaking perspective, children are denied the right to self-determination on the grounds of underdeveloped rationality and lack of autonomy. Children are denied rights to self-determination now, on the grounds that they will be able to exercise them in adulthood only if they are denied them in childhood. This is especially evident in arguments about education. It is assumed that going to school is necessary 'for maturation into a rational autonomous human being. Present compulsion is a precondition of subsequent choice' (p. 55).

Children are defined therefore as a homogeneous group generally incapable of exercising rational choice; no allowance is made for differences in terms of intellectual, emotional, physical or social capacity despite the empirical evidence that children (like adults) vary greatly in these abilities, not only with age, but with the vagaries of culture and individual experience. Neither is the problematic nature of children's subordinate status subjected to critical analysis within the protectionist framework. Universalistic assumptions about children's subordination underpin both theory and research. By failing to engage in a reflexive analysis of their own hierarchical assumptions, researchers have therefore contributed to the domination of children through intellectual discourse.

The last ten years, however, have witnessed the rise of a growing body of critical research and theory on children (Alanen, 1988; James and Prout, 1990; Archard, 1993; O'Neill, 1994; Qvortrup, 1994; Butler and Shaw, 1996). Just as feminist analysis has begun to uncover the unspoken word of women, and disability studies have begun to name the world from the perspective of disabled people themselves, so too there is a growing movement in the social sciences that challenges 'the politics of mutism' which silenced children's voices in the name of protecting them. The reason why it has taken the intellectual community so long to listen to children is, Ambert (1986) suggests, no different to the reason why it has taken powerful disciplines so long to listen to women (or, I would add, other marginalised groups). The lowly status of children in society made them a lowly subject of research in the academy. Moreover, children were, and are, not a mobilised political voice in most societies. There was no social movement by children demanding a place for themselves at the policy table, or challenging established perspectives in the academy.

Set in the light of recent critical work in the field, what this chapter attempts to do is to examine the position of children within a number of our public institutions in Ireland using an equality-oriented perspective. While children are different from adults, difference does not necessitate subordination or lack of respect. The economic dependency and the smaller stature of young children in particular can be recognised and accommodated without institutionalising systems of subordination and lack of respect. Granting equality of respect demands changes in the organisational practices of many of our public institutions; most conspicuously, it requires a greater democratisation of schooling for all age groups, and of other health and welfare services which care for children. It also means protecting the individual rights of children within families.

What the paper also recognises is that equality between children and adults is only part of the equation. We also need to promote equality *between* children in different social contexts. And if there is to be equality between children, this necessitates greater equality *between* adults. The health, welfare and educational rights of all children can be fully protected only in a society in which every child can exert those rights both as individuals, and in association with adults on whom they are dependent. As long as wealth and power differentials persist, between individuals and between households, both intranationally and internationally, then many children will merely experience a weak liberal, rather than a radical, form of equality of opportunity (Baker, 1998).

THE STATUS OF CHILDREN AND YOUNG PERSONS IN IRELAND

During the presidential campaign of 1997, one of the candidates (Adi Roche) made repeated proposals for the setting up of a Children's Commission to examine the many issues that affect children in our society. The proposal provoked little public debate, and was, at times, treated with derision. The level of this lack of public interest in the proposal gives some indication of how children's rights are viewed in our society. There appeared to be little public concern about the status of children (among voting adults at least, although the views of children themselves were not canvassed on the issue); children's rights were not regarded as a high political priority. The level of public indifference to issues relating to children's rights is not a temporary phenomenon, it is reflected in numerous public institutions and systems.

This chapter will address two separate but interrelated equality issues in relation to children in our society. First, it will briefly review the status of children vis-à-vis adults, and the extent to which children are accorded equality of respect with adults in our key public institutions and systems. Second, it will examine the question of inequality between children themselves. It will focus especially on the inequalities of opportunity *between* children from different social class backgrounds in the field of education.

A central claim of the chapter is that the inalienable rights which are given to the family qua institution in the Constitution (Article 41), and to parents (Article 42), have created a situation in which children's rights have been subordinated to those of the family and parents, at times of conflict. Moreover, the constitutional protection of the family has exonerated the state from intervening at times to protect children's welfare within families, and to guarantee them substantive radical equality of opportunity in education. Within the field of education, the state is obliged only to ensure that 'children receive *minimum* education, moral, intellectual and social' (Article 42.3 (2), my italic). At best, our treatment of children is welfarist and patronising; at worst, it is indifferent, condescending and lacking in respect. The patronising, and at times disrespectful, nature of Irish public policy in relation to children has been noted in the deliberations of the UN Committee on the Rights of the Child (Geneva, 12, 13, 23 January 1998).

THE CONSTITUTION AND THE STATUS OF CHILDREN

The constitutional status of children is of paramount importance in terms of understanding their position within the family, and within other public institutions such as schools, where they spend a very large part of their early working[2] lives. Articles 41 and 42 of the Irish Constitution of 1937 pertain to the family and education respectively and are the articles which have the most direct bearing on the lives of children. In line with other policy initiatives in the post-independence years, these articles were strongly influenced by Roman Catholic social teaching, in particular by the principle of subsidiarity (Duncan, 1987). The role of the state in relation to the family and children was defined in minimalist terms; the state's right to intervene in the family was largely confined to when there were 'compelling reasons' for intervention based on the welfare needs of the child (Duncan, 1996:617). The family qua family was duly accorded a range of rights in relation to children which are very strong indeed. Article 41.1 (1) endorses the view that the family is 'the natural primary and fundamental unit of Society, and a moral institution possessing inalienable and imprescriptible rights, antecedent and superior to all positive law'. Article 42.1 defines the family as the 'primary and natural educator of the child' and guarantees that the state will 'respect the inalienable right and duty of parents to provide, according to their means, for the religious and moral, intellectual, physical and social education of their children'.

The authority granted to parents over their children cannot be understood simply in terms of Catholic social teaching, however. The Constitution also reflected deeply held traditional values about the subordinate status of children. In their review of ethnographic research on children in rural Ireland, Curtin and Varley (1984:42) noted that 'Children are not wanted as an end in themselves, but always as a means of providing generational continuity on the farm, of supplying farm labour, or of acting as a hedge against old age'. Moreover, silence and passivity were highly valued qualities in young farm children (p. 43).

The Family in the Constitution

The principle of 'family autonomy' which is endorsed in the Irish Constitution has had a number of important implications for children. The granting of autonomy to the family as a social institution has meant that the most vulnerable members of the family household (most especially children, but also economically dependent women) can be and are open to manipulation, exploitation and even abuse by those who are economically and physically dominant within the family itself. Only in the more extreme cases does the state intervene to protect those who are vulnerable, and then it is required to intervene in as minimal a way as is necessary to protect the child (O'Cinneide and O'Daly, 1980). The empirical evidence available confirms that the abuse of children and women, by men especially, is taking place over a long time although much of this abuse has been publicly recognised and addressed only in the 1990s (McKeown and Gilligan, 1991; Gilligan, 1992/3; Women's Aid, 1995 a & b). One of the indirect effects of granting high autonomy to the family as a social institution is that it has resulted in a 'laissez-faire' approach to the enactment of legislation and policies in relation to the protection of children in families until very recent times. It is truly remarkable that the Child Care Act (1991) was the first piece of child welfare legislation enacted since the foundation of the state. Other European jurisdictions, including England and Wales, Finland, France and Germany, each introduced a number of legislative provisions to protect children over the same period (Gilligan, 1992/3:367).

A second question which arises in relation to the status of children under the Constitution is the protection of children's interests. While children's interests are taken into account in welfare cases in Ireland, it is generally assumed that parents know what is in the child's best interests and will act on these. The logic of this thinking is that parents' rights over children derive from their natural instinct to act always in the child's best interest. If this logic were followed, of course, it would mean that in the case of conflict, the interests of the child would prevail. This is not the case in Ireland, however, nor indeed in other jurisdictions. 'There is still a sense in which the laws in most jurisdictions confer property interests on parents in respect of their children' (Duncan, 1996:622). There is a very real sense therefore in which children in Ireland, and in many other jurisdictions, are not accorded equality of respect with adults.

This is not to suggest that children in Ireland do not have rights which are protected under the Constitution; they have all the relevant personal rights enjoyed by adults under Article 40. However, because there is no specific clause in the Constitution which guarantees the rights of children, when there is a conflict of interest between parent and/or family rights, and the individual rights of particular children, the former are most likely to prevail. Both the *Report of the Constitution Review Group* (Government of Ireland, 1996) and the *Report on the Kilkenny Incest Investigation* (Government of Ireland, 1993) recommended that a specific and overt declaration of the rights of children be inserted into the Constitution. The *Report of the Constitution Review Group* (p. 337) also recommended that the Constitution contain 'an express requirement that in all actions concerning children, whether by legislative, judicial or administrative authorities, the best interests of the child shall be the paramount consideration'.

Education and the Constitution

Not alone are the parents defined as the primary and natural educators of the child in Ireland, but the state is, as noted above, obliged only to ensure that 'children receive *minimum* education, moral, intellectual and social' (Article 42.3 (2), my italic).[3] In addition, the state is required to

> provide for free primary education and [shall] endeavour to supplement and give reasonable aid to private and corporate educational initiative, and, when the public good requires it, provide other educational facilities or institutions with due regard, however, for the rights of parents . . . (Article 42.4)

Under the Irish Constitution, parents exercise enormous control over the shaping and providing of education for their children. There is no legal requirement upon parents to take account of children's needs and interests. The child's interests are assumed to be synonymous with those of the parents; a patronising welfarism rather than a rights perspective prevails.

In theory, the freedom given to parents allows them great choice in the education of their children. The reality is, however, that choice in education is realistically open only to those with the means to exercise choice. Parents are constrained in their choices, most especially by limited means, but also by the practical exigencies of time, geographical location and the availability of accessible schools and services. One of the indirect outcomes of granting autonomy to people in a situation where little choice exists is that people must 'choose' what is currently available. Because the Catholic church controls well over 90% of the primary and second-level schools within the state, this effectively means that most people have no choice but to send their children to Catholic schools, especially at primary level.[4]

The indirect effect of 'free choice' in a strongly stratified and unequal society like Ireland (regardless of how desirable the principle of choice may be in its own right) is that only those in positions of relative privilege can exercise choice. This has become very evident in Britain in the 1990s; real choices in schools are open only to those with the means to choose (Gewirtz et al., 1994; Reay, 1996). Although this has been the situation in Ireland for a long period of time, it has never been made problematic. Many middle-class, and better-off working-class, families can and do choose to send their children to schools outside their own areas; they have access to transport and/or financial resources which allow this. Not surprisingly, however, it is families from the upper middle class who exercise greatest choice (Hannan, Smyth et al., 1996:243). Given the classed nature of school choice in a class-stratified society, it is not surprising that there is quite a strong degree of stratification *across* schools, especially in larger towns and cities where choice is possible. Children in schools serving low-income communities are especially disadvantaged in such a system as they have to attend the schools which have the least capacity for fund-raising but the greatest need.

The fact that the Constitution a) grants great autonomy to parents in relation to the education of their children; b) combines this with a minimalist approach to education provision (primary education only); and c) does not guarantee any independent *rights* to children to free education, means that children and young people are subject to the wishes and interests of their parents in matters of education. Parental resources, as well as attitudes to education, can and do determine the type and nature of education to which young people have access. The lack of any state-guaranteed right to education beyond the compulsory age means that the economic needs of the family qua family can and do take precedence over the educational needs of any given individual. While parents generally do not want their young daughters or sons to leave school early, the economic realities often force that decision in the absence of viable alternatives (Lynch and O'Riordan, 1996).

LEGISLATION AND CHILDREN

Legislative provisions and proposals indicate that there is no great advance towards a 'rights' perspective in relation to children at the public policy level.

Apart from the Education (No. 2) Bill (1997) (which will be discussed below), the two most recent pieces of legislation most directly concerned with children are the Child Care Act (1991) and the Children Bill[5] (1997). These are concerned respectively with children in care, and children involved in custody disputes. The Child Care Act (1991, Section 18 (1) (b)) does grant children negatively defined rights, such as the right to protection from abuse and other adversity 'seriously threatening to the child's health, development or welfare'. Moreover, both the Children Bill (1997, Part IV) and the Child Care Act (1991, Section 3 (2)) also give some protection to the interests of children in custody disputes, and in issues of care. The Children Bill, for example, obliges the court to 'take into account the child's wishes' in custody disputes 'as it thinks appropriate and practicable having regard to the age and understanding of the child, in the matter' (Part IV, Section 11 (25)). A similar provision exists in the Child Care Act, Section 3 (2) (b ii). These provisions, while most welcome, are far from being statements protecting children's rights. Neither piece of legislation addresses the status of children generally in our society.

The Education (No. 2) Bill (1997) and the Rights of Students

Children are accorded some consultative rights in schools in the recent Education Bill (No. 2) 1997. This is a welcome development. Section 27 (1, 2) of the bill gives students of all ages certain rights to information about school activities, and requires the Board of Management to 'facilitate the involvement of the students in the operation of the school having regard to the age and experience of the students'. The Board is also obliged, in the case of second-level schools only, to 'encourage the establishment by students of a student council and give all reasonable assistance to — (a) students who wish to set up a council, and (b) student councils when they have been established' (Section 27 (3)). In addition, Section 23 (2) (d) obliges all school principals to consult with students 'to the extent appropriate to their age and experience' in setting and monitoring school objectives.

The fact that students' democratic rights are set out on conditional terms, and that the Board of Management or the principal can determine when students are of an age, or of sufficient experience, to be consulted, has the potential to weaken the impact of these provisions considerably. The provision in Section 27 (5) which states that: 'The rules for the establishment of a student council shall be drawn up by the board and such rules *may* provide for the election of members and the dissolution of a student council' (my italic) seems to be very undemocratic, and effectively to enable the School Board to appoint a student council of its own choosing superseding the wishes of the students if it so desires. There is, regrettably, no provision for student councils at the primary level.

The rights which are granted to students in terms of appeals against teachers or staff are also very limited. The relevant section of the bill (28) does not require the Minister or the school authorities to put grievance procedures in place, it merely allows for it to happen; even then it applies only to those of eighteen years and over. As most students are in the final year of second-level education at this age, or have left school, this is a rather empty provision.

The Education Bill also gives other parties in education far more rights and control over schools, and education generally, than it gives to students. As it stands, the bill will copper-fasten the interests of a given set of corporate bodies in education at a given point in time, without any recognition of the fact that the partners in education may change or should change. The bill is replete with references to the requirement that various decision-making authorities must consult with patrons, national associations of parents, recognised teacher unions, and school management organisations. These provisions throw into sharp relief the absence of other voices, most notably those of students, but also those of community interests, be these community groups, women's representative bodies, the unemployed, disabled people, older people, etc.

Concluding Remarks

The minimal advances in the legislative sphere noted here are not accompanied by public debate about the empowerment of children. A paternalistic, care-taking ideology underpins the recent legislative proposals and provisions, and these have not been publicly contested in any systematic manner. The discourse *about* children has not changed, and there is very little public discourse *with* children. While Ireland has ratified the UN Convention on the Rights of the Child, it has not incorporated a rights-based perspective on children into its policies and procedures in the manner enshrined by the Convention. The UN Committee on the Rights of the Child, in its 'Concluding Observations and Recommendations' regarding Ireland's implementation of the Convention, has noted that 'welfare policies and practices in the State Party [Ireland] do not adequately reflect the child rights base approach enshrined in the Convention'. Regarding the implementation of Article 12 of the Convention, the Committee was 'concerned that the views of the child are not generally taken into account, including within the family, at schools and in society' (23 January 1998).

Ireland has adopted a rather fragmented approach in relation to the protection of children's rights; advances in one field run parallel with silences in others. At the root of this fragmentation and inconsistency lies a deep-rooted malaise about the rights of children.

INEQUALITIES BETWEEN CHILDREN

POLICY ISSUES: CHILDREN AND THE RISK OF POVERTY

Economic indicators show that Ireland is a relatively wealthy country (Atkinson et al., 1995). Yet, despite this, a very sizeable minority of people, especially of children, live in poverty (Callan, Nolan et al., 1996). While this is as incredible as it is unacceptable, it indicates clearly how it is impossible to separate the debate about equality for children from debates about equality between adults. Children's dependent economic status means that their welfare is tied to that of their adult parents. Inequalities between adults impinge directly on children no matter how questionable that dependency is, especially for older children and young people.

The 1994 *Living in Ireland* survey by the ESRI found children[6] to be at a higher risk of poverty than adults at each of the relevant poverty lines. While 18% of adults were at risk of being below the 50% poverty line[7] in 1994, 29% of children were living at this level; almost 8% of children were actually at risk of living on less than 40% of the average income. This pattern is not new, although the gap between children and adults has widened greatly over the twenty-one years from 1973 to 1994. In 1973 just 16% of children were at risk of being below the 50% poverty line, by 1994 the proportion had nearly doubled to 29%. By comparison, the same risk for adults increased only slightly from 15% to 18% over the period (Callan, Nolan et al., 1996:88–94). When poverty is measured in terms of deprivation indicators, rather than income lines, there is evidence from the ESRI study that the depth of poverty (how far below the average people live) has been reduced for adults at least, between 1987 and 1994. It is not possible to determine from the data presented, however, whether or not there was an improvement in the situation of children over that time.[8]

While almost 30% of Irish children have a high risk of living in poverty, the risk is not evenly spread; it is especially acute among the unemployed, and where there is a lone parent (over 90% of whom are women). Children in larger families (those with more than four children) are also at greater risk.

The ESRI study did not specifically include Traveller children living in non-permanent accommodation. People living in refuges and those who are homeless were also excluded (Callan, Nolan et al., 1996:34). While one can understand the logistical reasons for this, it does mean that the experience of children who are often most vulnerable and poor in our society is not documented in the study. As numerous reports over the years have noted, Traveller children are at a high risk of living in extreme poverty (Government of Ireland, 1995). Moreover, their poverty is exacerbated by high levels of discrimination which exaggerate the effects of poverty itself. Children of refugees and those who are homeless are also very vulnerable. If the position of all of these children was documented, and if the levels of marginalisation, powerlessness, domination and exploitation which children can experience were assessed, then the position of a significant minority of Irish children would be even worse than it appears by simply using income measures of poverty (Lynch, 1997).

While Ireland is one of the fastest-growing economies in Europe, it has the second highest level of child poverty (UN Committee on the Rights of the Child, 436th meeting, 12 January 1998). Poverty management rather than poverty elimination seems to be the guiding principle. Despite the availability of extensive evidence, for example, that certain approaches are more effective at eliminating poverty than others, governments persistently fail to base policies on these (Cantillon, 1998).[9] This is a deeply disturbing development politically as it implies a growing detachment from and indifference to those who are most vulnerable in our society, including children. It represents a move away from principles of solidarity within and between generations and social groups, and a victory for the principles of possessive individualism.[10]

POLICIES IN EDUCATION: THE PERSISTENCE OF INEQUALITY BETWEEN CHILDREN

Given the lack of state commitment to substantive equality in society generally, it is not surprising to find that there are still major inequalities between children in schools. While Ireland boasts one of the higher rates of retention to Leaving Certificate level (circa 80%) and an almost 50% transfer rate to higher education, aggregate data conceal very significant differences in patterns of achievement across social groups. While the overall level of education in the population has risen, social-class relativities in terms of achievement, especially beyond the non-compulsory level, have remained remarkably stable over time.

Literacy Issues

There are now numerous Irish studies documenting the extent of social-class- and socio-economically-related inequality in education (Clancy, 1988, 1995; O'Neill, 1992; Callan, Nolan and Whelan, 1994; Kellaghan et al., 1995) although there are far fewer studies examining the causes of inequality (Lynch and O'Riordan, 1996). One of the more recent studies which shows quite clearly the ways in which inequality is persisting is the OECD study of literacy (Morgan, Hickey and Kellaghan, 1997). Although it has received relatively little public attention, this report is a major indictment of our education system in many respects. The report shows that 17% of the sixteen to twenty-five age group are operating at the minimum level of literacy functioning (Table 3.5, p. 31). In the numeracy area, the situation is no better with 18% operating at the lowest level (Table 3.9, p. 36). Moreover, our young people are significantly less literate than those in comparator countries with the exception of Poland. The proportion of those aged between sixteen and twenty-five in Ireland who are functioning at the lowest literacy (17%) level is more than five times higher than that in Sweden (3%), more than three times that in Germany (5%), and approximately twice that in Switzerland (it varies in the two main regions from 7% to 9%) (Table 4.4, p. 48). Given the relative cultural and linguistic homogeneity of our society, this must be a matter for grave concern.

Literacy and other educational differences are not evenly spread across the population, however. Low-income working-class groups are disproportionately represented among those who have the lowest literacy levels (Table 4.6, p. 50). One longitudinal study of sixth class primary school pupils in inner-city schools found that 25% of the pupils were judged by teachers as being unlikely to be able to cope with the reading demands of post-primary schooling (Archer and O'Flaherty, 1986). This is almost twice the national average for reading difficulty at this age, which has been estimated to be between 12.5% and 16% (Morgan and Martin, 1994).

Early Drop-Out, Retention Rates and Attainment Levels

Literacy levels are one measure of differences in educational opportunities. Early drop-out and lower rates of educational attainment are also indicators of the level of inequality in education. There is clear evidence that early school leaving is disproportionately high among the low-income working-class groups (National Economic and Social Council, 1993; European Social Fund, 1996). Research on public examinations at second level gives even clearer indications of the social class differences in educational retention rates and attainment. Analysis of school-leaver surveys shows that while over 90% of students from upper socio-economic groups reach the Leaving Certificate level, only a little over half (53%) of the children of unskilled backgrounds reach this stage. Moreover, of those who stay on to complete the Leaving Certificate, just 29% and 28% of the unskilled and semi-skilled respectively attain at least two Cs in higher level papers, while between 62% and 80% of the four higher socio-economic groups attain these grades (Technical Working Group to the Steering Committee on the Future of Higher Education, 1995: Table 8.2).

Despite the increased participation by all social groups in education over the last thirty years, therefore, there are still major differences in both access to education and participation within it, based on social class. Clancy's study *Access to College: Patterns of Continuity and Change* (1995) shows that while there has been an increase in the rate of participation in higher education by all social groups in the last twelve years, disparities in participation based on social class are still considerable: 38% of all higher education entrants come from the four highest socio-economic groups although these constitute only 21% of the relevant population, while just 35% of entrants come from the five lowest socio-economic groups although these constitute almost 56% of the relevant age cohort. The contrast in participation rates at the upper and lower end of the class continuum are, however, much greater, with 89% of the children of higher professional parents going on to higher education compared with just 14% of those from unskilled and semi-skilled manual backgrounds (Clancy, 1995:154–5).

The failure to provide adequate grants and income supports for students from low-income families who stay in school beyond the compulsory age (including adequate maintenance grants for higher education) has been identified as one of the major barriers to equality of participation in higher education in particular (Clancy, 1995; Lynch and O'Riordan, 1996). Moreover, there are no real supports to meet the opportunity costs of staying on in education beyond the compulsory age for second-level students from low-income families (ibid.). The push to leave is much greater than the pull to stay, and successive governments have ignored this problem.

While there has been a serious attempt to equalise *access* to education (in the sense of giving people the right to benefit from all levels of education by eliminating fees for second-level and higher education, for example), what we have lacked is a coherent national plan to equalise *participation* rates and *benefits* from education for all social groups. Having equal rights to access without ensuring equal rights to participation and benefits guarantees the perpetuation of inequality. Programmes such as 'Early Start', 'Breaking the Cycle' and 'Youthreach' are welcome developments, and such programmes and others[11] do make an important contribution within the resources available to them. However, given the depth of inequality in our society, such programmes alone can do no more than ameliorate the worst effects of inequality for a relatively small group of children and young people. They are too small in scale and lacking in scope to address the root causes of inequality in education, much of which emanates from the serious economic inequalities which are allowed to persist in our society. Any policy to promote equality in education *between social classes* can succeed only if it is accompanied by economic policies aimed at eliminating the income and wealth differentials which perpetuate educational inequality in the first place.

INEQUALITY IN EDUCATION: SUBSIDIARITY, VOLUNTARY SCHOOLS, PRIVATE MARKETS AND THE PERPETUATION OF INEQUALITY BETWEEN CHILDREN

The Implications of Subsidiarity

There is a very real sense in which the constitutional principle of subsidiarity underwrites inequalities of various kinds, most especially by the way in which it allows essential services to be offered in the private market, often making it impossible for those without sufficient means to access them and use them on equal terms with others. Education is one sphere where the voluntarism emanating from the principle of subsidiarity is especially problematic.

Even if the political will to eliminate poverty between children prevailed, one of the difficulties of overcoming educational inequalities in Ireland is that most primary and second-level schools are privately controlled: almost all national schools and some 60% of second-level schools are church-controlled. Because of this, the state is often exonerated from having full responsibility for promoting equality both between schools and within them. It can and does present itself as being just one of the 'partners' in education (Government of Ireland, 1995:7); it thereby absolves itself from having complete responsibility for education matters.

It is widely known that there are serious inequalities in the quality of educational services available to different children within the state, especially in terms of access to sports and other extra-curricular facilities (Lynch, 1989), but also in terms of school buildings and extra-educational supports such as grinds and education-related resources (Lynch and O'Riordan, 1996; Lynch and Lodge, 1997). Inequalities in the quality of the education service provided are effectively permitted by Article 42, which enshrines the principle of subsidiarity in terms of state aid for private and corporate educational institutions. While this principle, in itself, does not promote inequality, what it does do is to exonerate the state from having the defining responsibility for the quality of the educational service offered to all classes of students. The state is required to act only 'when the public good requires it'.

What happens, in effect, with education is that the widely agreed principle of equality of educational opportunity for all (and there have been numerous statements by various Ministers for Education since the late 1960s declaring their support for greater equality in education) is neither constitutionally nor legislatively grounded. There is no compulsion on successive governments, from a constitutional point of view, to ensure that there is equality of provision in the educational service and supports offered to all students.

One of the indirect outcomes of the ongoing 'symbiotic' relationship between church and state in education[12] is that voluntary contributions play an increasingly important role in influencing the kind of educational services and facilities (beyond the common core) which are available in many schools. A survey by the Association of Secondary Teachers, Ireland (1996) of 365 secondary schools in 1996 found that 80% of these were involved in fund-raising. Moreover, the clear majority of both parents and teachers in the schools were involved in contributing in some way to the process. Where parental incomes are such that they can sustain a consistent level of voluntary contributions, the quality of the education service in schools can be improved accordingly, and this is true at both primary and secondary level. Where parents are poor and cannot sustain significant contributions, the quality of the service is adversely affected. Although it is clear that parents' 'voluntary contributions' are a relatively small element in the funding of schools, they are a significant contribution if not only the direct but the indirect contributions are counted, such as fund-raising events for new buildings. Moreover, state support for private fee-paying schools in the secondary sector, which is effectively endorsed in the Constitution in the subsidiarity principle, ensures that inequalities in provision arising from differential access to resources in particular communities are compounded by inequalities arising from differentials in the resources of individual families.

Although the voluntarism which underpins some of the funding in Irish education is not intended to operate as a mechanism for the perpetuation of inequalities between schools, one of the unintended consequences of voluntarism is the development of inequalities in the quality of the educational environments in which students are educated. At one end of the continuum stand the fee-paying schools where fees are often more than twenty times the modal (typical) voluntary contribution in most other secondary schools (reported as being between £25 and £50 in 264 of the schools surveyed by the ASTI in 1996). A stage below these stand those free scheme secondary schools which can raise substantial moneys through voluntary contributions and fund-raising, although these are in the minority. While the community/comprehensive and vocational sector receives grant aid which compensates the schools for the fee/voluntary contribution element in secondary school income, they cannot solicit voluntary contributions. There is public provision for basic facilities in these schools, but it is far from adequate in many cases. Schools which are free to raise funds through fees and voluntary subscriptions, and which service a clientele which can contribute to these, are clearly advantaged in this situation. Schools which cannot raise voluntary contributions locally, on the other hand, are distinctly disadvantaged.[13] The indirect effect of the subsidiarity principle in education, and the voluntarism flowing from it, is therefore the development of significant difference in the quality and range of resources and facilities across schools (Lynch and Lodge, 1997). Schools serving low-income working-class or small farm communities are increasingly disadvantaged as they simply cannot compete in the 'voluntary market' for funds. The inequities arising from reliance on local (voluntary) funding for schools has also been noted by the UN Committee on the Rights of the Child, who asked the Irish government to address it (436th meeting of the Committee, Geneva, 13 January 1998).

While the merits of the principle of subsidiarity are self-evident in a pluralist society, whether it should be the defining constitutional principle governing the provision of such basic services as education (and indeed health) is most questionable. We are in the midst of what can truly be called a 'knowledge revolution', as historically important as the industrial revolution. The Irish economy itself is heavily dependent on such knowledge-based industries, and the central role which education can play in our economic development is recognised in a number of policy documents in recent years, including *Charting Our Education Future: White Paper on Education* (Department of Education, 1995) and *Science, Technology and Innovation: The White Paper* (Department of Enterprise and Employment, 1996). Education is not an optional extra in such a society. It is both a fundamental individual right and a public necessity.

Private Markets in Education

What is compounding the differences between schools is the ongoing development of a parallel system of private education which is being funded outside public institutions by parents and students themselves. The most conspicuous examples of this parallel system of private education are the so-called 'grind schools', the primary purpose of which is to offer an educational advantage to those who can pay for the service (Dowling, 1991). These private institutions are, however, but one element in the private education market. It is not unreasonable to suggest (although it has not been systematically researched) that there are thousands of second-level students who also pay for private tuition (grinds) on a one-to-one basis. In addition, there is a growing private extra-curricular education market in Ireland in music, art, elocution, drama, certain sports, summer camps, etc., all of which are offered outside of school for those who can afford to pay. What the development of private markets in education indicates is that those with access to higher incomes have the resources to subvert attempts by the state to equalise opportunities in the publicly controlled sector of education. As long as people own and control significantly different levels of wealth and income, then it is almost inevitable that they will be advantaged in education. They have the freedom to use their excess resources to buy extra educational services on the market as required. The under-resourcing of public education greatly exaggerates the impact of the private market not least because more and more expenditure is required by any given individual to make good the deficit in the publicly controlled sectors of education.

INEQUALITY BETWEEN CHILDREN: WILL THE EDUCATION BILL (NO. 2) 1997 MAKE A DIFFERENCE?

One of the objects of the Education Bill is 'to promote equality of access to and participation in education and to promote the means whereby students may benefit from education' (Section 6 (g)). The Minister for Education is responsible for ensuring that this principle is enacted.

While this is a welcome provision, it is largely aspirational in character. There are no guidelines outlining how it is to be interpreted (for example in terms of budgetary allocations); there are no procedures specified for monitoring or sanctioning the Minister if she/he fails to comply with the provision. Given that it is a vague provision in the first instance, monitoring and sanctioning would probably be impossible anyhow.

The bill does make a number of references to various forms of disadvantage, however, and to equality issues. Section 15 (2) (g) requires the School Board, 'within the resources provided to the school', to 'make reasonable provision and accommodation for students with special educational needs'.[14] Section 15 (2) (d) requires the Board to publish its policy 'concerning admission to and participation in the school and ensure that as regards that policy principles of equality . . . are respected'. Section 32 deals specifically with educational disadvantage. This section states that

> The Minister *may* by order, following consultation with patrons, national associations of parents, recognised school management organisations, recognised trade unions and staff associations representing teachers and such other persons as the Minister considers appropriate, establish and maintain a committee to advise him or her on policies and strategies to be adopted to identify and to correct impediments to education arising from social and economic disadvantage which prevent students from deriving appropriate benefit from education in schools. (Section 32 (1), my italic)

Finally, the National Council for Curriculum and Assessment (NCCA) in carrying out its functions is to 'have regard to the desirability of achieving equality of access to and participation in education' (Section 40 (3) (b)).

It is clear from the above that the Education Bill is not designed to promote equality in education in any substantive sense between advantaged and disadvantaged students. Calling on school boards and the NCCA to 'respect' or 'have regard to' equality principles is welcome. But it raises the question as to which equality principle they will adopt. If they adopt a basic, or even a liberal, approach to equality, then very little will change in terms of the relative advantage of particular students (Baker, 1998). Moreover, many educational inequalities occur *between* schools, and between students across different schools. These cannot be addressed by a provision which is addressed only to the Board of Management of a single school, or even by the NCCA, whose sole remit is curriculum and assessment.

The provision for students with physical and learning disabilities is made conditional on having resources available; it does not guarantee extra moneys for them, hence it is difficult to see how it could promote equality. Any school is free to say it lacks resources, if it decides that special-needs students are not a priority in the first place.

Although students with disabilities are named as target groups covered by the legislation, the bill makes no reference at all to the promotion of gender equality as an objective, or to racial, religious, ethnic (Traveller) or other equality. While it is assumed that these groups are covered under the general provisions of the bill, it is far from certain that all provisions apply to all of them at all times.

The bill gives the Minister permission to set up a committee to examine and correct disadvantage, but this is not mandatory (although there is a suggestion that this may change and be made mandatory); neither is there any guarantee that funds will be made available to the committee to achieve its goals. This contrasts with the position taken in relation to the body which is to be set up to plan and research the teaching of Irish (a welcome development in its own right). Section 31 (4) of the bill specifies that the Minister *shall* set up a body for this purpose. She or he may use part of the annual budget to grant-aid the latter. No provision is made for funding the committee on disadvantage should it be set up. (Quite amazingly, also, there is no requirement in the bill for the Minister to fund research on education; research is mentioned in only two places: where it is stated to be one of the functions of inspectors (Section 13 (3) (c)), and where it is stated to be one of the functions of the body overseeing the teaching of Irish. It is hoped that this will change before the bill is enacted, otherwise there will be no requirement on the Minister to fund broadly based independent research on education which is needed for policy planning on an ongoing basis.)

Inequality in Education as a Relational Phenomenon

As long as there are huge income and wealth differentials in our society (and the *Living in Ireland* survey of 1994 has shown that the number of children and adults living in poverty increased between 1987 and 1994 (Callan, Nolan et al., 1996), then it will not really be possible for the socially and economically disadvantaged to avail of education services on equal terms with more advantaged groups. While the question of income and wealth differentials is not strictly speaking an educational concern, it is a simple fact that it has a direct bearing on educational outcomes. If there is a serious intent to eliminate social and economic inequalities, as opposed to managing them, then our economic policies must not be such that they offset the positive gains of educational initiatives designed to overcome inequalities. Economic policies also need to be gender-proofed to take account of the very particular wealth and income differentials which exist between men and women.

Much of the discussion on educational inequality tends to focus on what are defined as 'the problems' of the so-called 'disadvantaged' (mostly working-class students). There has been a tendency in educational research to explain social class differences in education by pathologising working-class culture and lifestyle. A cultural deficit model of educational inequality has been normalised in much of educational thinking. This implies that the reason low-income working-class groups (school leavers and adults) are not well represented in the non-compulsory education sector is because they have socially and culturally problematic backgrounds. In a very real sense the cause of class inequality is located in the subject of that inequality.

This is both a damaging and an inaccurate representation of social reality as it pathologises and stereotypes whole social groups, while depressing expectations among educators, and among the groups themselves when they are exposed to such images. Moreover, it misrepresents the nature of social causality as disadvantage can be understood only in the context of advantage. What creates inequality in education is not simply the financial, educational and social and cultural experiences of any particular group in and of itself. What creates the disadvantage is the fact that upper socio-economic groups have superior access to resources, incomes, wealth and power which enables them to avail of the opportunities presented in education in a relatively more successful manner than other groups. This holds true for younger and older students. In a market situation in which educational success is defined in relative terms, those with superior access to valued resources and culture are inevitably positioned to be the major beneficiaries of educational investment.

It is not only at the level of ideology that inequalities have become legitimated, it is also happening through a host of institutional practices, including wage, wealth and welfare bargaining. Various 'Programmes for Government' and national agreements (and Partnership 2000 is no exception, while it is not quite as inegalitarian as other agreements) reinforce rather than challenge structural inequality. Change is permitted, but only on the fringes. The core differentials of power, wealth and income are not altered. Undoubtedly one of the major reasons for this is the political marginality of the groups most affected by poverty (Hardiman, 1998).

As the superordinate-subordinate relations are built into the structures of institutions and systems, they become normalised and habitualised. The relational character of inequality becomes invisible as it is experienced and presented as inevitable. One of the problems faced in challenging the inequality experienced by disadvantaged children and students therefore is the widespread cultural acceptance of inequality itself. That cultural acceptance is learned both through the habitual practice and experience of inequality, and through the formal articulation of inegalitarian ideologies in opinion formation institutions. Unfortunately, we also have learned to accept inequality because of the public silence of so many people with knowledge and understanding of inequality. Many of those who know of injustice and poverty do not speak out to challenge it in a public fashion as much as they could. What comes to mind is a piece by Bertrand Russell, 'The Harm that Good Men [*sic*] Do', written in the context of World War II. He notes that silence is dangerous in the face of injustice; by wanting to remain pure, 'above controversy' or 'above politics', many of us contribute to the very injustices and inequalities which we may abhor in private. This is especially problematic for intellectuals and academics who have the training and the tools to speak, or who can assist and support others to speak in their own voice.

CONCLUSION

LISTENING TO CHILDREN

It has been relatively easy to ignore children in the documentation of inequality; and researchers have been as 'child-blind' as others. We rarely collect data on issues such as poverty directly from children themselves. Adults are allowed to speak for children and to name their world. We see nothing wrong with organising conferences, meetings and conventions about children without involving them as partners. The National Education Convention (1994) is perhaps one of the best examples of a democratic forum on education from which most of the principal education players, namely children, were excluded. While we have learned not to discuss or plan for other groups, including women, Travellers or people with disabilities, without at least consulting with them, we have not yet begun to take children sufficiently seriously to establish structures whereby they can exercise control and influence over institutions which affect them directly. Although our failure to establish structures for listening to children is not unique to Ireland, our institutions are, in several regards, less respectful of children than those in other countries (Nic Ghiolla Phádràig, 1991; Qvortrup, 1994).

Children's structurally generated political powerlessness has guaranteed that they are neither organised nor resourced to be heard in the first place. Moreover, children cannot influence the political process directly as they lack the franchise. Even at the more basic level of consultation, children are not counted as partners in most institutions that affect them directly, such as schools and welfare institutions (although, as I have noted above, the principle of partnership has received some limited support in the Education Bill (No. 2) 1997). If children are to be heard, and if their voices are to be taken seriously, then the institutions for consultation with children need to be established (including some forum in the research field), and children themselves need to be trained and educated as to how to use the democratic system in their own interests. We must not assume, as has often happened with women and other groups which were structurally excluded from the exercise of public power, that they know how to use power effectively without education and training.

If we are to give children equality of respect, we need to begin with our Constitution. We must take up the recommendations of both the *Report of the Constitution Review Group* (Government of Ireland, 1996) and the *Report on the Kilkenny Incest Investigation* (Government of Ireland, 1993) that a specific and overt declaration of the rights of children be inserted into the Constitution. The recommendation of the *Report of the Constitution Review Group* (p. 337) that the Constitution should contain a provision guaranteeing that 'the best interests of the child shall be the paramount consideration' in all actions concerning children, also needs to be implemented.

We need to review many of our current policies and practices in relation to children and young people, not least of which is the age at which young people can exercise their vote. We need to examine options such as having a Children's Ombudsperson (which has worked quite satisfactorily in the Nordic countries), a Charter of Children's Rights or a Children's Parliament where views can be heard. Setting up a Commission on the Status of Children is one of the most effective ways in which to explore all of these issues, and to arrive at effective and acceptable proposals for action.

The democratisation of structures for children is not only a rights issue, for the children themselves, it is also an educational issue. As Archard (1993:164) observes, 'Active democratic citizens are not born overnight when a certain age is reached.' If we want young people to know, appreciate and involve themselves in the democratic institutions of our society, we cannot forestall democratic engagement until they are past their most formative years. Yet this is effectively what has happened to date (apart from some minimal education about civic society through texts alone), with the attendant evidence that many young people are deeply disillusioned with the political institutions of our society. One of the most effective ways in which to learn the value and purpose of democratic participation is through practice. By participating in democratic processes at home, in schools and in other public places, children can learn the principles of democratic engagement at a young age. The self-confidence and sense of responsibility that comes from real democratic involvement is of benefit to young people both as private individuals and as citizens.

EDUCATION AS A KEY TO WORK AND FULL PARTICIPATION IN SOCIETY

For a variety of historical and other reasons, the creation of wealth in Irish society is heavily dependent for the foreseeable future on the quality of education provided across all sectors of the economy. Moreover, knowledge, and increasingly the *credentialised knowledge* provided by formal education, is a major form of capital in its own right. Because of the central role which knowledge plays in determining the generation of wealth, it is extremely important that all people have access to education, and can participate and benefit from it on equal terms, so that they are not excluded from the process of wealth generation in society. As the *Annual School Leavers Surveys* show that there is a positive correlation between the level of education attained and employment opportunities (the higher the level of education attained, the higher one's chances of getting employment), people who leave school without any formal credentials are severely disadvantaged in the labour market. Equality of educational opportunity is important from an individual labour market standpoint therefore, as access to paid employment is increasingly tied to level of education attained (Breen, 1991).

Education is also of crucial importance for both personal development and the development of civil society. It is essential for the development of all the social, cultural and political institutions which contribute to the creation of an inclusive, dynamic and integrated democratic state. Also, the failure to equalise access to, participation in and benefit from education means that much of the talent and ability available in society is underutilised and alienation and detachment develops among those who are excluded from participation.

LEGISLATING FOR EQUALITY IN EDUCATION

In view of both the importance of education in determining access to the labour market, and its crucial importance for the personal development of the individual and the social, cultural and political development of society, there is a need for a provision promoting equality in education both in the Constitution and in legislation. The absence of a strong equality provision in legislation means that there is no clear requirement on the government to disburse funds in a manner which will promote substantive equality of opportunity in education.

At present those who have most private resources can benefit most from all forms of education because their families can bear both the direct and indirect costs that prolonged participation in education demands. What this means in effect is that those with most private resources benefit most from state education investment as both the direct costs and opportunity costs of education provision rise as one moves from first to third level (Tussing, 1981). In addition, those with greater financial resources can also avail of the wide range of services in the *private education market* outside of schools and colleges themselves. The economic inequalities which allow such differences in opportunities to develop, especially at extreme ends of the wealth and incomes spectrum, must be addressed.

We also need to recognise, however, that childhood is *part of* life not a preparation for life. Young people in Ireland spend approximately fourteen years of their lives in school, and almost half continue in education for a further two to three years. The quality of the educational experience matters, not simply in terms of career or economic outcomes, but as an experience in and of itself. Given its lengthy duration, schooling must be meaningful for young people and respectful of their rights and interests at that time in their life. When we think of equality in education, we must not view schooling as some type of unproblematic good, where more is better (Connell, 1993). There is much that needs to be changed in terms of curricula and assessment in our schools, but time and space does not allow for a discussion of these issues here. No matter what the content of schooling, it must not be simply evaluated in terms of some long distant, and often uncertain, future job goals. What is offered in the name of education in schools must be meaningful to young people, and the way school life and other institutions are organised and administered must be respectful of them, regardless of age.

REFERENCES

Alanen, L. (1988). Rethinking childhood. *Acta Sociologica*, 31 (1): 53–67.

Ambert, A.M. (1986). The place of children in North American sociology. In P. Alder and P. Alder (eds.), *Sociological Studies in Child Development*. Greenwich (CT): JAI Press.

Archard, D. (1993). *Children: Rights and Childhood*. London: Routledge.

Archer, P., and O'Flaherty, B. (1986). A home intervention programme for pre-school disadvantaged children. *Irish Journal of Education*, 9:28–43.

Association of Secondary Teachers, Ireland (ASTI) (1996). *Staffing, Funding and Facilities in Irish Second Level Schools: Survey Commissioned by the ASTI*. Dublin: ASTI.

Atkinson, A., Rainwater, L., and Smeeding, T. (1995). *Income Distribution in OECD Countries: The Evidence from the Luxembourg Study (LIS)*. Paris: OECD.

Baker, J. (1998). Equality. In S. Healy and B. Reynolds (eds.), *Social Policy in Ireland: Principles, Practices and Problems*. Dublin: Oak Tree Press.

Breen, R. (1991). *Education, Employment and Training in the Youth Labour Market*. Dublin: Economic and Social Research Institute, Paper No. 152.

Butler, I., and Shaw, I. (1996). *A Case of Neglect: Children's Experiences and the Sociology of Childhood*. Aldershot: Avebury.

Callan, T., Nolan, B., and Whelan, C. (1994). Who are the poor? In B. Nolan and T. Callan (eds.), *Poverty and Policy in Ireland*. Dublin: Gill & Macmillan.

Callan, T., Nolan, B., Whelan, B., Whelan, C., and Williams, J. (1996). *Poverty in the 1990s: Evidence from the Living in Ireland Survey*. Dublin: Oak Tree Press.

Cantillon, S. (1998). Research and policy-making. In S. Healy and B. Reynolds (eds.), *Social Policy in Ireland: Principles, Practices and Problems*. Dublin: Oak Tree Press.

Clancy, P. (1988). *Who Goes to College*. Dublin: Higher Education Authority.

Clancy, P. (1995). *Access to College: Patterns of Continuity and Change*. Dublin: Higher Education Authority.

Connell, R.W. (1993). *Schools and Social Justice*. Philadelphia: Temple University Press.

Curtin, C., and Varley, T. (1984). Children and childhood in rural Ireland: a consideration of the ethnographic literature. In C. Curtin et al. (eds.), *Culture and Ideology in Ireland*. Galway University Press.

Department of Education (1995). *Charting Our Education Future: White Paper on Education*. Dublin: Government Publications Office.

Department of Enterprise and Employment (1996). *Science, Technology and Innovation: The White Paper*. Dublin: Government Publications Office.

Dowling, T. (1991). Inequalities in preparation for university entrance: an examination of the educational histories of entrants to University College Cork. *Irish Journal of Sociology*, 1:18–30.

Drudy, S., and Lynch, K. (1993). *Schools and Society in Ireland*. Dublin: Gill & Macmillan.

Duncan, W. (1987). Child, parent and state: balance of power. In W. Duncan (ed.), *Law and Social Policy: Some Current Problems in Irish Law*. Dublin University Law Journal.

Duncan, W. (1996). The constitutional protection of parental rights. In Government of Ireland, *Report of the Constitution Review Group*. Dublin: Government Publications Office.

European Social Fund (ESF) (1996). *Evaluation Report: Early School Leavers Provision*. Dublin: ESF Programme Evaluation Unit, Davitt House.

European Social Fund (ESF) (1997). *Preliminary Evaluation: Preventive Actions in Education*. Dublin: ESF Programme Evaluation Unit, Davitt House.

Fischer, C., Hout, M., Janowski, M.S., Lucas, S.R., Swidler, A., and Voss, K. (1996). *Inequality by Design: Cracking the Bell Curve Myth*. Princeton University Press.

Gewirtz, S., Ball, S., and Bowe, R. (1994). Parents, privilege and the education market place. *Research Papers in Education*, 9:3–29.

Gilligan, R. (1992/3). The Child Care Act 1991: an examination of its scope and resource implications. *Administration*, 40 (4):347–70.

Government of Ireland (1993). *Report on the Kilkenny Incest Investigation.* Dublin: Government Publications Office.

Government of Ireland (1995). *Report of the Task Force on the Travelling Community.* Dublin: Government Publications Office.

Government of Ireland (1996). *Report of the Constitution Review Group.* Dublin: Government Publications Office.

Hannan, D.F., Smyth, E., McCullagh, J., O'Leary, R., and McMahon, D. (1996). *Coeducation and Gender Equality: Exam Performance, Stress and Personal Development.* Dublin: Oak Tree Press.

Hardiman, N. (1998). Inequality and the representation of interests. In W.F. Crotty and D. Schmitt (eds.), *Ireland and the Politics of Change.* Harlow, Essex: Addison Wesley Longman.

Higher Education Authority (1995). *Report of the Steering Committee on the Future of Higher Education.* Dublin: Higher Education Authority.

Irish National Teachers' Organisation (INTO) (1994). *Poverty and Educational Disadvantage: Breaking the Cycle.* Dublin: INTO.

James, A., and Prout, A. (eds.) (1990). *Constructing and Reconstructing Childhood: Contemporary Issues in the Sociological Study of Childhood.* Lewes: Falmer Press.

Kellaghan, T., Weir, S., O'hUallacháin, S., and Morgan, M. (1995). *Educational Disadvantage in Ireland.* Dublin: Department of Education and Combat Poverty Agency.

Lynch, K. (1989). *The Hidden Curriculum: Reproduction in Education, A Reappraisal.* Lewes: Falmer Press.

Lynch, K. (1997). Inequality, social exclusion and poverty. In Combat Poverty Agency, *A Selection of Papers from the Combat Poverty Agency Policy and Research Conference 'Prioritising Poverty'.* Dublin, April.

Lynch, K., and Lodge, A. (1997). *Equality and the Social Climate of Schools: Report of Findings from Student Essays and Focus Groups.* Research report submitted to the Research and Development Committee, Department of Education, Spring.

Lynch, K., and O'Riordan, C. (1996). *Social Class, Inequality and Higher Education: Barriers to Equality of Access and Participation among School Leavers.* University College Dublin, Registrar's Office.

McDonnell, A. (1995). The ethos of Catholic voluntary schools. University College Dublin, Education Department, unpublished Ph.D. thesis.

McKeown, K., and Gilligan, R. (1991). Child sexual abuse in the Eastern Health Board region of Ireland in 1988: an analysis of 512 confirmed cases. *Economic and Social Review*, 22 (2):101–34.

Morgan, M., Hickey, B., and Kellaghan, T. (OECD) (1997). *International Adult Literacy Survey: Results for Ireland.* Dublin: Government Publications Office.

Morgan, M., and Martin, M. (1994). *Literacy Problems among Irish Fourteen-Year-Olds. ALCE Evaluation, Vol. III.* Dublin: Educational Research Centre.

National Economic and Social Council (NESC) (1993). *Education and Training Policies for Economic and Social Development.* Dublin: National Economic and Social Council.

Nic Ghiolla Phádraig, M. (1991). *Childhood as a Social Phenomenon: National Report, IRELAND.* Vienna: European Centre.

Ó Cinnéide, S., and O'Daly, N. (1980). *Supplementary Report to the First Report of the Task Force on Child Care Services*. Dublin: Government Publications Office.

O'Neill, C. (1992). *Telling It Like It Is*. Dublin: Combat Poverty Agency.

O'Neill, J. (1994). *The Missing Child in Liberal Theory: Towards a Covenant Theory of Family, Community, Welfare and the Civic State*. University of Toronto Press.

Prout, A., and James, A. (1990). A new paradigm for the sociology of childhood? In A. James and A. Prout (eds.), *Constructing and Reconstructing Childhood: Contemporary Issues in the Sociological Study of Childhood*. Lewes: Falmer Press.

Qvortrup, J. (1994). *Childhood Matters: Social Theory, Practice and Politics*. Aldershot: Avebury.

Reay, D. (1996). Contextualising choice: social power and parental involvement. *British Educational Research Journal*, 22 (5):581–96.

Technical Working Group to the Steering Committee on the Future of Higher Education (1995). *Interim Report to the Steering Committee on the Future of Higher Education*. Dublin: Higher Education Authority.

Tussing, D. (1981). Equity in the financing of education 2. In S. Kennedy (ed.), *One Million Poor*. Dublin: Turoe Press.

Women's Aid (1995a). *Domestic Violence: The Social Context*. Dublin: Women's Aid.

Women's Aid (1995b). *The Effects of Violence in the Home on Children*. Dublin: Women's Aid.

NOTES

1 I would like to express my appreciation to my colleagues Dympna Devine, Niamh Hardiman and Máire Nic Ghiolla Phádraig of University College Dublin for helpful advice and comments on an earlier draft of this paper. I would also like to thank the Children's Alliance for materials they sent me which were helpful in preparing the chapter.

2 I use the term 'working' here deliberately to denote the fact that schooling is work for children. It involves application, effort and engagement that is no different in substance to what is required of adults at work. The principal differences between children's school work and adults' work is that children do not get paid for theirs!

3 Interestingly, and regrettably, there is no obligation on the state to ensure that children receive any physical education.

4 It would be wrong to assume, however, that there is a simple causal relationship between ownership of schools and influence on children. The reality of life in schools is such that no simple causal relationship can be assumed between administrative control and influence, especially in highly mobile, literate and culturally diverse societies. The curricula, the examination systems and much of the organisation of learning is under the control of the state and its agents, directly or indirectly; in this sense, young people are subjected to a range of ideological influences in schools other than the influence of the churches (Drudy and Lynch, 1993). Indeed the hidden curriculum of school life would suggest that the dominant norm in second-level schools is that of competitive individualism (Lynch, 1989) and there is scant evidence of strong religiosity among young people in Catholic-run schools at the present time (McDonnell, 1995). There is a whole confluence of influences determining the values of young people in our society, including the media, cultural institutions such as music, and of course the peer group.

5 This bill was passed by both houses of the Oireachtas at the time of writing (November 1998), although it was not yet enacted.

6 A child is defined in the study as a person under eighteen years of age, as in the Children Bill (1997) and in the Child Care Act (1991).

7 This means living on 50% or less of the income of the average person. Average income is measured in terms of average disposable income (Callan, Nolan, et al., 1996:67–8).

8 In this, as in most poverty studies, children are not studied separately from their parents. This is unacceptable, especially if one wishes to understand fully the position of children. It means that we lack basic data on children's lives (Qvortrup, 1994).

9 The December 1997 Budget is a particular case in point. Policies were openly enacted (and vehemently defended) in that Budget which would benefit the better-off in society to a disproportionate degree — most notably the 50% reduction in capital gains tax, the reduction in corporation profit tax, and the lowering of the top tax rate for high earners — while only minor concessions were made to the most vulnerable, including children.

10 The way in which budgetary allocations are made does give a clear indication of how wealth and income differentials are perpetuated in our society. Those who are central to the executive and legislative decision-making machinery of the state, and those who have the corporate and/or legal or collective power to influence the elected and appointed State Managers (namely the government of the day and the civil servants), are strategically located to direct the course of major public decisions about investment, production, taxation, employment, interest rates and wages, even though their political constituency may be relatively small. Major structural inequalities are not accidental therefore; neither are they the outcome of some hidden market forces which are outside public control (Fischer, Hout et al., 1996). The so-called free market does not operate according to some hidden rules of economic rationality. The market is embedded in a set of laws, policies and practices which are extensively regulated and managed by the state. Major structural inequalities between groups are the outcome of legal, financial and strategic decisions taken over many years. Such inequalities are not inevitable; they can be reversed by different policies and legislative provisions.

11 The initiatives include increased financial aid and extra teachers in both primary and second-level schools in need; free books and meals; the Home–School–Community Liaison programme; curriculum changes such as the introduction of the Vocational Preparation and Training Programme (VPT) and the Leaving Certificate Applied Programme (LCAP). The preventative actions in relation to disadvantage are reviewed in the report of the European Evaluation Unit (European Social Fund, 1997).

12 This is a relationship which is mutually beneficial in several respects. The churches have provided the original premises and some small proportion of ongoing expenditure in return for the control of 'ethos'; the state benefits not only from the churches' investment and free labour (up to now) but from the legitimating role which the churches bring to the entire educational process. The state controls curricula to a large degree, however, and lays down regulations in relation to the appointment of teachers. (See Drudy and Lynch, 1993:73–89 for further discussion of this point.)

13 The inequalities arising from differences in local capacity to pay voluntary contributions and engage in fund-raising also applies at primary level.

14 Special educational need is defined in Part 1 (2) as applying to students with mental and physical disability and exceptionally able students.

CHAPTER 7

MATURE STUDENTS AND DISADVANTAGE IN EDUCATION

INTRODUCTION

There are compelling reasons why all adults, and in particular socially and economically disadvantaged adults, should be enabled to participate in further and higher education. First there are compelling economic reasons. The creation of wealth is no longer solely dependent on land, labour and capital as traditionally defined. A crucial role is played by *knowledge-based capital* as distinct from financial or material capital. In a post-industrial era, knowledge, and increasingly credentialised knowledge, is a major form of capital in its own right. The Irish economy is, for a variety of historical and political reasons, even more reliant on knowledge-based capital than other economies. It lacks the industrial infrastructure that underpins the powerful economies of core capitalist states. Consequently it needs to develop a form of capital for which it has a sound infrastructure, namely education.

It is especially important that it develop the educational potential of adults as well as school leavers because adults are already fully integrated into both society and the economy. As the Culliton Report (Culliton, 1992) observed, Irish industry (and indeed agriculture, services, etc.) can be successful only to the extent that it meets the standards of international best practice in a given field. The Report claims there is little evidence that firms in Ireland are providing systematic in-house re-education and training for their employees (for a variety of reasons) at a desirable level. The White Paper on *Science, Technology and Innovation* (Department of Enterprise and Employment, 1996) echoed these sentiments in relation to science and technology education and research. In the light of this, provision must be made in the higher and further education sectors for the recurrent education of adults.

While adults from upper socio-economic groups are likely to have availed of higher education opportunities as school leavers or are in a financial position to re-enter higher education to update their knowledge in particular fields, often neither opportunity is available to those from lower socio-economic groups. Working-class adults in Ireland have not had equal access to either initial or recurrent higher education; they are doubly disadvantaged. Their contribution to society and the economy has been greatly circumscribed by the lack of opportunity to develop their knowledge-based capital. For those who are not in employment, further education is generally the only way in which they can re-enter the economy on an equal footing with participating citizens.

Enabling adults, particularly socially and economically disadvantaged adults, to benefit from higher education contributes not only to the economy but to the quality of life of each individual, and to the social and cultural life of society. While the personal, social and cultural benefits of education impact back, over time, on the economy, the improved quality of life which education can offer is, in itself, a benefit to all social groups. Education can and does contribute to a fuller experience of citizenship among all members of society.

Participation in higher education is especially important for socially and economically disadvantaged groups, however, as it enables them to participate in both the economic and the social life of society in a way which has hitherto been denied to them. In the process it helps demystify what is for many an alien institution, namely higher education. And when it is critical and reflexive, it gives people more knowledge and control over their own lives, and over the social and cultural institutions in society. This, in itself, can be personally and socially empowering and fulfilling.

The demand for 'a second chance' in higher education from disadvantaged groups, such as working-class people, people with physical impairments and women, can be justified therefore in so far as jobs, at both entry and promotional stages, increasingly require evidence of credentialised knowledge, and in so far as higher education improves personal quality of life and enriches the social and cultural life of society. Higher education is less and less of a luxury and more of a necessity; in this context it can be seen as a right rather than a privilege.

Before examining the precise barriers and inequalities facing adults, particularly low-income adults, in higher education, it is necessary to present a profile first of those who are currently mature students.

A PROFILE OF UNDERGRADUATE MATURE STUDENTS IN IRELAND[1]

A series of studies by the Higher Education Authority over the past fifteen years shows that there has been a dramatic increase in the rate of retention to higher education among school leavers; yet there has not been a comparable rise in the participation rates of full-time mature students (Clancy, 1995:41–2). In fact, the participation rate of full-time mature student entrants to higher education via the Central Applications Office (CAO/CAS) system has remained relatively static over the period. In 1980, just over 3.5% of CAO/CAS entrants were mature, while the comparable figure for 1993/4 was 3.4%. If all full-time mature entrants are included, as opposed to those who applied through the CAO system,[2] the proportion of mature entrants to all full-time entrants rises to 5.4% for 1993/4.

When compared with participation rates for either Northern Ireland or the United Kingdom as a whole, these rates are very low (Table 1). Even allowing for the fact that mature students in Britain and Northern Ireland are calculated as mature at twenty-one years as opposed to twenty-three, and that the demographic profile of the Republic is different to that of Britain in particular, with a larger concentration in the younger age cohorts, Table 1 shows that there are great disparities between the participation rates of mature students in the Republic of Ireland and in the UK. Mature students are over five times better represented in UK colleges compared with those in the Republic of Ireland. The differential rates of participation between the Republic of Ireland and Northern Ireland are especially noticeable as the demographic profile is not that dissimilar. Furthermore, as distance education entrants are included in the Republic of Ireland data but Open University data are not included in the UK calculations, this means the differentials may be even greater than Table 1 suggests.

Table 1

Mature Entrants in Northern Ireland, the Republic of Ireland and England, Scotland and Wales

	Republic of Ireland 1993/4	Northern Ireland 1992/3	England/Wales/Scotland 1992/3
	%	%	%
Full-time	5.4	29.0	33.0
Part-time	85.0	85.0 (estimate)	85.0
Total mature entrants	6,665	5,458 (estimate)	251,300

1. Age twenty-three or over is the cut-off point for mature students in the Republic of Ireland while age twenty-one or over is the cut-off point in Northern Ireland and Britain.
2. The figures for Northern Ireland include only mature entrants to Higher Education Colleges within Northern Ireland.

Sources: (1) Department of Education and Science (UK), *Statistical Bulletin*, Issue No. 16/94, Table 5 (1994) and data obtained from the Department of Education in Northern Ireland.
(2) The data for the Republic of Ireland are based on the statistics on mature student entrants for 1993/4 provided by the colleges to the Technical Working Group to the Steering Committee on the Future of Higher Education.

While there has been a substantial increase in the number of mature students in part-time programmes in recent years (Technical Working Group (TWG) Report, HEA, 1995), socially and economically disadvantaged mature students have not been the major beneficiaries of this educational expansion. The fact that greater mature student participation fails to give rise to any significant increase in the representation of socially and economically disadvantaged groups in higher education is not exclusive to Ireland. It has also been identified as an issue in Britain and the OECD generally (OECD Centre for Educational Research and Innovation, 1987; Gallagher et al., 1993).

STATUS, GENDER AND COLLEGES ATTENDED

There were 6,665 mature entrants to higher education courses in 1993/4, 75% of whom were part-time students, while 43% were women.[3] Of those who are part-time, 41% were women, while half of all full-time students were women. Overall, men are better represented among mature entrants than among school-leaver entrants: 57% of the former are men, compared with 51% of the latter.

All the sectors of education had a reasonable proportion of mature students, with 35% entering the university sector, 25% the Dublin Institute of Technology colleges and 21% the Regional Technical Colleges (now the Institutes of Technology). The remaining 19% of entrants are in other institutes of higher education, including the private colleges. Research on part-time mature students shows them to be even more strongly concentrated outside the university sector than full-time students (Technical Working Group Report, TWG, HEA, 1995).

The pattern of representation of mature students across the colleges is not dissimilar to that in Britain, although the concentration of mature students outside the university sector is greater in Britain: in 1992, 80% of all first degree mature students in Britain were studying at polytechnics (new universities) and other colleges, as were 98% of all other undergraduate mature students (Department of Education and Science, 1994, Table 6). While only 5.4% of Irish full-time entrants are mature, the comparable figure in Britain is 33% (based on twenty-one years and over as opposed to twenty-three years or over in Ireland); the proportion of part-time students who are mature is the same (85%) in both jurisdictions.

SUBJECT AREAS

Table 2 gives an indication of the areas of study undertaken by mature students. Arts/Humanities were by far the most popular single areas of study with 32% of entrants in these fields; the other popular areas were Commerce/Business Studies (14%), Computer Science/Information Studies (11%), Engineering (10%) and Health Science (10%). There were some gender differences in areas of study especially in engineering and health science: 17% of men were taking engineering programmes and only 4% of women; 15% of women were in health science compared with 5% of men. Overall, the strong concentration of mature students in the Arts/Commerce area is the most notable finding. Healy's (1998) study of students on the Third Level Allowance Scheme (TLA)[4] also found that Arts/Commerce subjects were extremely popular fields of study.

Table 2

Subject Choices among Mature Entrants, 1993/4

Agriculture	0.2
Architecture	0.4
Art/Design	1.4
Arts	31.5
Commerce/Business	14.3
Communication	0.4
Computer Science	11.4
Dairy Science	0.2
Dentistry	0.0
Economic/Social Studies	9.5
Education	0.8
Engineering	9.8
European Studies	0.2
Health Science	10.0
Interdisciplinary	2.7
Law	2.1
Medicine	0.1
Music	0.6
Science	1.6
Social Science	1.2
Social Work	0.7
Veterinary	0.1
Women's Studies	0.8
Total	**100.0**

Source: K. Lynch, Technical Working Group to the Steering Committee on the Future of Higher Education: national data from colleges.

AGE

Over half of mature entrants in 1993/4 were under thirty years of age. Only 15% were over forty years of age (Table 3). Two more recent but smaller studies, by Healy (1998) on higher education students on Third Level Allowances, and Fleming and Murphy (1997) on mature students in the National University of Ireland, Maynooth, identified similar age patterns among mature students. Moreover, both also found that a majority of students were single and without children.

Because of the lack of analogous cross-national data, it is not possible to make a direct comparison between the age profile of mature students in Ireland and elsewhere. However, the data from Britain do indicate that one-third of mature students entering higher education in Britain in 1992 were between the ages of twenty-one and twenty-four years. The breakdown for the over-twenty-five age group is not available. Earlier data from the OECD (OECD Centre for

Table 3

Age Profile of Mature Student Entrants, 1993/4

Age	%
23–26	30.8
27–30	20.9
31–35	22.1
36–40	11.1
41–50	9.7
50+	5.4
Total	100.0

Source: K. Lynch, Technical Working Group to the Steering Committee on the Future of Higher Education: national data from colleges.

Educational Research and Innovation, 1987:35) also show that 'the typical mature student is relatively young' (i.e. between the age of twenty-five and thirty-five). The OECD study did not count those under twenty-five as mature students.

GENDER

The majority (57%) of mature student entrants in 1993/4 were men, as were the majority of mature students attending higher education colleges in 1992/3. The gender differential is most evident among part-time students, where 59% of mature entrants and two-thirds of all mature attendees were men. Gender parity appears to be approached only among full-time mature entrants. While Fleming and Murphy's study (1997) found that women comprised 55% of mature students in Maynooth, this study was based almost entirely on Arts students (95% were in Arts) so it is not representative of the entire student body nationally. Healy (1998) found that 66% of those on the TLA were men, which is not surprising given that the scheme was designed originally for those unemployed for twelve months or more; men are significantly more likely to be registered as unemployed than women given the bias in the welfare codes which has prohibited many married women from claiming unemployment assistance in their own right.

The gender profile of mature students in Ireland is quite similar to that in Britain although the differentials in favour of men are more pronounced in Ireland overall: 52% of all British entrants in 1992 were men as were 57% of Irish entrants in 1993/4. The overall gender differential is accounted for by the more favourable representation of women among part-time entrants in Britain, where 49% of all part-time entrants are women by comparison with 41% in Ireland. Women are especially well represented in the Open University 'associated students' group, of whom two-thirds were women in 1992.

Table 4

*Gender Profile of Undergraduate Mature Students
in the Republic of Ireland*

	Mature entrants 1993/4		Mature students attending 1992/3	
	Female	Male	Female	Male
Full-time	50.0	50.0	46.0	54.0
Part time	41.0	59.0	34.0	66.0
Total	43.0	57.0	38.0	62.0

Source: K. Lynch, Technical Working Group to the Steering Committee on the Future of Higher Education: national data from colleges.

However, while there is gender parity among full-time entrants in Ireland with 50% of all such entrants being women, in Britain just 47% of full-time undergraduate entrants were women in 1992 (Department of Education and Science (UK), *Statistical Bulletin*, Issue No. 16/94, September 1994, Table 3).

Data from OECD countries show that in most countries on which data is available, women are under-represented among mature students (for example in France, Germany, Austria and Australia). The exceptions to this are Sweden, Finland and the United States. There is some evidence to suggest that female participation is greatest where women's participation in paid employment is highest (OECD Centre for Educational Research and Innovation, 1987:39).

ROUTE OF ENTRY

Data on selection criteria for entry to higher education were available only for full-time students. The data obtained from the colleges on the 1993/4 entrants show that while 43% were accepted on the basis of mature years, a sizeable minority, 29%, entered on the basis of the Leaving Certificate.

In interpreting the findings it needs to be noted that the route of entry reported here is based on how the colleges defined student mode of entry. For example, students accepted on the basis of mature years could have (and a number did have) a Leaving Certificate. However, they were accepted by the colleges on the basis of mature years not on the basis of their Leaving Certificate grades. Others were accepted on the basis of Leaving Certificate grades even though they were mature. The latter group tended to be those who had higher Leaving Certificate grades. Healy (1998) also found that a high proportion (55%) of mature students (on the Third Level Allowance Scheme) had a Leaving Certificate, albeit not necessarily at matriculation level, while a further 16% had either an undergraduate diploma or a degree.

Table 5

Route of Entry as Defined by the Colleges:
Mature Student Entrants, 1993/4

Mature years	43.0
Leaving Cert. only	29.0
Leaving Cert. & Post-Leaving Cert.	2.0
Transfers from other higher education courses	4.0
Other accredited	18.0
Other including non-Irish qualifications	4.0
Total	**100.0**

Source: K. Lynch, Technical Working Group to the Steering Committee on the Future of Higher Education: national data from colleges.

SOCIO-ECONOMIC STATUS

Only a little over one-fifth of mature student entrants to higher education (22%) are drawn from the four lowest socio-economic groups although the latter comprise 44% of the general adult population (Table 6). Whether socio-economic status is measured in terms of the students' or the parents' background, it is clear that mature students are more likely to come from the intermediate non-manual group rather than any other single socio-economic group. This is especially the case if socio-economic status is measured in terms of the students' own occupational background. The other principal groups from which current mature students are drawn heavily are lower professionals and employers/managers. While the participation ratio for salaried employees (3.6) shows that this is the group which is most over-represented in the mature student population relative to the national population, they still comprise just under 10% of mature student entrants. The strong concentration of mature students in the intermediate non-manual and the lower professional groups suggests that the socio-economic profile of mature students is somewhat different to that of school-leaver entrants. There is a stronger concentration of lower-middle-class groups in the mature student population and a weaker concentration of higher professionals, farmers and skilled manual workers in particular.

The research conducted by the Technical Working Group (TWG) on part-time students provides corroborative evidence for these findings. It found that 32% of part-time students (85% of whom are mature) were from intermediate non-manual backgrounds while 23% were from lower professional back-grounds (TWG, HEA, 1995, chapter 10).

It is useful at this point to make some comparisons between the findings of the HEA study of CAO/CAS entrants in 1992 (Clancy, 1995) and the TWG findings on 1993/4 mature entrants (Table 6). There are, however, a number of cautionary points to bear in mind in doing this. First, while the HEA data cover all entrants and are based on parents' socio-economic status, the TWG data on mature entrants are based on data provided by the colleges on the students' own socio-economic status. Data were available on the socio-economic status of 1,359 mature entrants in 1993/4.

What is evident from the available data is that farmers and higher professionals are much better represented among the general entrant body than among mature students: their respective participation ratios are 1.35 and 2.47 for all entrants and 0.12 and 0.96 among mature entrants. Salaried employees are the group with the highest participation ratio among mature students (3.6 compared with 1.48 among all entrants), followed by employers and managers (2.4 compared with 1.86 among all entrants), lower professionals (2.13 compared with 1.47 among all entrants) and intermediate non-manual workers (1.44 compared with 0.91 among all entrants).

Lower socio-economic groups are only marginally better represented among mature entrants than among school-leaver entrants, although their rate of representation did not reach parity (1:1) for any of the four lowest socio-economic groups (Table 6). Perhaps what distinguishes the mature students from school-leaver entrants most therefore is their stronger lower-middle-class profile; the representation of working-class groups among mature students is generally not any better than it is among school-leaver entrants and this holds for both part-

Table 6

Comparing Rates of Participation for Mature Entrants and All Entrants on the Basis of Socio-economic Status (SES)

	SES of population in paid employment age 25–64 1986 Census	SES distribution of mature entrants 1993/4	Participation ratio for mature entrants 1993/4	SES distribution of all entrants 1992/3	Participation ratio for all entrants 1992/3
	%	%			
Farmers	11.7	1.5	0.12	16.7	1.35
Agricultural workers	2.7	0.4	0.15	1.8	0.6
Higher professionals	5.4	5.2	0.96	10.4	2.47
Lower professionals	9.2	19.6	2.13	7.2	1.47
Employers and managers	7.3	17.2	2.4	16.4	1.86
Salaried employees	2.6	9.3	3.6	4.0	1.48
Intermediate non-manual	17.2	24.7	1.44	10.2	0.91
Other non-manual	12.3	4.8	0.39	9.3	0.72
Skilled manual	18.7	6.2	0.33	18.3	0.71
Semi-skilled manual	6.6	6.0	0.91	2.6	0.44
Unskilled manual	6.3	5.1	0.81	3.0	0.37

1. *Source*: K. Lynch, Technical Working Group to the Steering Committee on the Future of Higher Education: national data from colleges.
2. Source of data on 1992/3 entrants: Clancy, 1995, Table 13.

time and full-time students (TWG, HEA, 1995, chapter 10). The findings of both Healy (1998) and Fleming and Murphy (1997) confirm that lower professionals and intermediate non-manual workers, such as clerical workers, are the two most strongly represented socio-economic groups among mature students.

PRINCIPAL ECONOMIC STATUS OF FULL-TIME STUDENTS

A small survey of individual full-time mature students was undertaken by the Technical Working Group for the HEA Committee on the Future of Higher Education. A random sample of 370 mature students were surveyed by postal questionnaire in seven different colleges; 52% responded.

Bearing in mind that the sample was small, what the study does indicate is that while the mature students are predominantly middle-class, especially lower-middle-class, the majority of *full-time* students are without secure employment; only 31% of students reported their principal economic status as being in employment while 19% were signing on as unemployed. Of those in first year in college who were registered unemployed (signing on), 80% had been unemployed for at least two years, while 27% of those in first year who were without work but not registered as unemployed had also been unemployed for at least two years.

What these findings suggest is that many full-time mature students are people who are in the margins of the paid labour market. They may have a lower-middle-class designation, as defined by current or previous employment, but this does not mean they have any security of employment. The study of mature students in NUI Maynooth also found that only a small minority (20%) were in secure employment.

EDUCATIONAL BACKGROUND

All the available data on mature students indicate that a clear majority of them have a Leaving Certificate, albeit at a lower Grade Point Average than school-leaver entrants. An analysis of mature student applicants through the CAO system in 1993/4 found that 63% of those who accepted places had a Leaving Certificate, mostly a full Leaving Certificate. The study conducted by the TWG of full-time mature students also found that a majority of those attending college (78%) had a Leaving Certificate while the TWG survey of part-time students found that the highest level of qualification attained by 84% of these students was a Leaving Certificate or some higher-level qualification.

Not only do a large proportion of mature students have a Leaving Certificate, a significant minority have post-secondary qualifications as well. The findings of the small survey of full-time students and the larger survey of part-time students undertaken by the Technical Working Group both confirm this.

From Table 7 it is evident that 44% of the full-time students surveyed had some professional or post-secondary qualification already. The survey of part-time students (85% of whom were mature) undertaken by the TWG identified a similar pattern with 37% of those surveyed having either a professional qualification, a certificate, diploma or degree already (TWG, HEA, 1995, chapter 10). Healy (1998) also found that a significant number (31%) of those on Third Level Allowances had a post-school certificate, undergraduate diploma or degree already (in addition to the 55% who had a Leaving Certificate). This indicates that the scheme is serving the relatively advantaged among the disadvantaged.

Table 7

Survey of Full-Time Mature Students
Educational Background

Highest Level of Education Attained	%
Professional course (includes nursing)	10.4
Degree course	3.1
Diplomas (includes NCEA)	16.6
Certificates (includes NCEA)	14.0
Foundation / access courses	8.7
Short-term courses (includes FÁS)	2.1
Secretarial / business courses	5.2
Other post-second-level courses	2.6
Full Leaving Certificate only	21.2
Other second-level/lower qualifications	16.1
Total N = 193	100.0

Source: K. Lynch, Technical Working Group to the Steering Committee on the Future of Higher Education: survey of individual mature students.

MOTIVATIONS FOR ENTRY TO HIGHER EDUCATION

Mature students are a more diverse group than traditional school-leaver entrants to higher education. Not only do they vary more in age, and on certain social background variables such as education, but they vary considerably in their motivation for attending higher education (OECD Centre for Educational Research and Innovation, 1987). While no major study has been conducted in Ireland on the motivations of mature entrants, the small study of full-time mature students conducted by the TWG for the Committee on the Future of Higher Education did inquire about student motivations. When asked to state their *primary* reason for entering (or re-entering) higher education, work-related reasons emerged as the major motivating factor (Table 8). Half of the students gave specific work-related reasons for attending higher education. Work also featured as the principal reason for returning to education in Fleming and Murphy's (1997) and Healy's (1998) studies of mature students.

Even those who stated that their principal reason for entering higher education was to avail of the opportunity which was denied to them when they were young (24%) or that it was fulfilling a lifelong personal ambition (23%) did not rule out the importance of third-level education for improving work opportunities. In most cases, work-related reasons were stated as secondary motivations.

Table 8

Survey of Mature Students, 1993/4
Reasons for Return to Study

	%
Work-related: to further employment prospects	23.8
Work-related: wanted change in career	15.6
Work-related: needed qualification for job	9.9
Personal fulfilment: lifelong ambition	23.3
Second chance: lacked the opportunity when young	23.8
Other reasons	3.6
N = 193	100.0

On the other hand, those who presented work-specific reasons as their primary motivation for entering higher education also mentioned other motivating factors, albeit not so strongly. There were no major gender differences in the reasons given for returning to study, with both women and men placing a strong emphasis on the job-related importance of qualifications.

Career-related reasons were also the principal motivations cited by part-time mature students for entering higher education (TWG, HEA, 1995, chapter 10).

MATURE STUDENTS AND DISADVANTAGE

The typical mature student therefore is a person under thirty-five years of age who is single and has no children. She/he has completed the Leaving Certificate, is living in an urban area, and has not yet obtained a third-level qualification. She/he tends to be participating in higher education to improve career prospects. There is a reasonable probability, however, that the person may have some professional or post-secondary qualification already.

She/he is most likely to come from a lower-middle-class background and is slightly more likely to be male than female. The person is most likely to be a part-time student, and to be studying outside the university sector. While there is almost a 50% chance the person will be on a degree programme, there is an equal chance that they will be on other undergraduate programmes.

There is a difference, however, between the mature student who is part-time and the one who is full-time. The part-time mature student is slightly more likely to be a man than the full-time student. While the part-time student is usually in employment,[5] the typical full-time mature student defines her/ himself as not being in employment. And a considerable number of those registered as unemployed have been unemployed for at least two years.

The data available suggest that lower-income and/or marginalised groups are poorly represented in the mature student sector, especially among part-time students. Yet there is evidence that relative to school-leaver entrants, mature students are more likely to come from lower-middle-class backgrounds. An analysis of the principal economic status of *full-time* mature students shows that full-time higher education may be catering for relatively disadvantaged lower-middle-class groups, namely those who did have some post-secondary education already but who are not in secure employment. In the last five years particularly, the Third Level Allowance Scheme has increased opportunities for unemployed people (mostly men and people with good educational backgrounds), disabled people, and lone parents (mostly women), to attend higher education on a full-time basis.[6]

One of the difficulties about recording the extent and nature of disadvantage among mature students is the fact that data are not collected systematically on this group; there appears to be no system in the colleges for tracking mature students beyond their first year. Nor is there a clear procedure for identifying other groups such as the unemployed,[7] disabled students, lone parents or ethnic minorities. The lack of accurate data makes it impossible to develop a detailed understanding of the nuances of inequality and disadvantage across different sectors of the potential mature student population. This is a phenomenon which was adverted to in the OECD report on *Adults in Higher Education* (OECD, Centre for Educational Research and Innovation, 1987).

The OECD research shows that the socio-economic profile of mature students internationally is quite similar to that in Ireland: only a minority of mature students use higher education as a means of achieving radical upward social mobility, transgressing class boundaries. A review of research on mature students in Britain confirms this trend; it found that there is no evidence that increased provision for mature students per se has provided extra places for the socially and economically disadvantaged (Gallagher et al., 1993:9). It is clear therefore that if mature students from socially and economically disadvantaged backgrounds are to avail of higher education, then specific supports and targets need to be put in place to achieve this.

The next section will examine the kind of strategies which need to be pursued, and the issues which need to be addressed, if adults who were unable to avail themselves of higher education when they were young are to get a 'first chance' in higher education.

THE POLICY CONTEXT: ISSUES TO BE ADDRESSED

It is not surprising to find that mature students from socially and economically disadvantaged backgrounds are not adequately represented in higher education. Notwithstanding the work of bodies such as AONTAS (the National Association of Adult Education) in promoting greater equality for low-income groups in adult and further education, and the development of recent initiatives such as the Vocational and Technical Opportunities Scheme, and Community Education Programmes at a national level (see Dolphin and Mulvey, 1997), there has been a rather laissez-faire approach towards the promotion of mature student participation in further and higher education, especially among socially and economically disadvantaged groups. While the extension of the Higher Education grants scheme to mature students, the development of the Third Level Allowance Scheme, and the provision of limited supports for part-time students, are recent advances in this field, the reality remains that access and participation for mature students in higher education remain difficult. The fact that lower socio-economic groups are very poorly represented in higher education at present is proof of this.

The absence of proactive policies — such as the provision of adequate financial support for adults in further and higher education, the development of flexible modes of delivery and assessment procedures, and the provision of childcare and guidance services within colleges — has made it extremely difficult for the economically and socially disadvantaged mature student to enter and succeed within the system. In a competitive context where there is no equality of condition (that is where differentials in wealth, income, power and privilege remain substantial), the relatively advantaged, both within and between socio-economic groups, win out over the relatively disadvantaged. This holds true for adult learners as much as school leavers.

This section of the paper therefore will examine some of the barriers to equality of access and participation facing mature students from socially and economically disadvantaged backgrounds in Ireland.

SOCIAL CLASS INEQUALITY AND EDUCATIONAL DISADVANTAGE

In recent years numerous reports and studies have been published which highlight the pervasive character of social class inequality in education in Ireland (Conference of Major Religious Superiors, 1992; Coolahan, 1994; Irish National Teachers' Organisation, 1994; Higher Education Authority, 1995; Department of Education, 1995; Clancy, 1995; Kellaghan et al., 1995; Lynch and O'Riordan, 1996). While the educational system itself has expanded and developed, and while enrolments in higher education have increased elevenfold between 1950 and 1990, the fact remains that the social class profile of participants within higher education has not changed to any radical extent (Clancy, 1995). The same holds true in a wide variety of other countries (Shavit and Blossfeld, 1993; Council of Europe, 1996). Mature students are part of this trend rather than exceptions to it.

The reasons why such class differences persist can be understood only in the context of what happens at all other levels within the education system, and in terms of the socio-economic conditions of different classes in Irish society as a whole. In terms of academic attainment, what is clear is that there are significant social class differences in educational attainment at both primary and second level. Although there are no national examinations at primary level, surveys of reading literacy indicate that literacy difficulties are more concentrated among lower socio-economic groups than others (Archer and O'Flaherty, 1986; Morgan and Martin, 1994; Morgan et al., 1997).

Research on public examinations at second level gives even clearer indications of the social class differences in educational attainment. As noted above in chapter 6, the analysis of school-leaver surveys shows that while over 90% of students from upper socio-economic groups reach the Leaving Certificate level, only a little over half (53%) of the children of unskilled backgrounds reach this stage. Moreover, of those who stay on to complete the Leaving Certificate, just 29% and 28% of the unskilled and semi-skilled respectively attain at least two Cs in higher level papers, while between 62% and 80% of the four higher socio-economic groups attain these grades (Technical Working Group Report, TWG, HEA, 1995).

SOCIAL AND EDUCATIONAL BARRIERS TO EQUAL PARTICIPATION: REPORT OF A SURVEY[8]

Pre-application Stage

Social class differences in rates of retention and attainment help explain why participation rates among mature students in particular are social-class-differentiated. When it comes to higher education entry, those mature applicants who have successfully completed the Leaving Certificate are automatically more advantaged. Proof of this is presented above, as over 60% of mature student entrants through the CAO have a Leaving Certificate while even higher proportions of part-time students have been awarded Leaving Certificates. Those without a Leaving Certificate therefore are automatically disadvantaged vis-à-vis others when applying for entry as mature students. The development of alternative access routes for mature entrants to further and higher education is a conspicuous and urgent requirement in Irish education and has been noted in a number of reports (Higher Education Authority, 1995; Fleming and Murphy, 1997; Healy, 1998).

Our research (see endnote 8) on mature students' perceptions of the barriers to higher education entry and participation confirms the importance of the qualifications barriers. In a study of mature students, lacking qualifications was stated as a major barrier to higher education entry: 45% of the full-time mature students surveyed identified lack of adequate qualifications as the first major obstacle that many mature students had to overcome. When account is taken of the fact that the students surveyed were already within higher education, and were not from the lowest socio-economic groups, it is clear that the issue of qualifying for entry is even more problematic for other groups. Both the survey and the interview data obtained from unsuccessful mature applicants also strongly suggest that lacking the necessary entry qualifications is a major barrier at the pre-application stage.

The fact that mature applicants from low-income working-class backgrounds have not attained comparable school leaving qualifications to more middle-class students is, however, a mediate or proximate cause of inequality rather than a foundational one. It reflects the differences in resources and opportunities available to different social groups within our society. Differential access to resources enables certain social groups to maintain their advantage in an openly competitive system such as education. Differential rates of retention (and indeed of performance) at Leaving Certificate level are therefore a symptom rather than a cause of inequality.

Application Stage

Once students have overcome the qualifications barriers, and this may take some time for those who have to return to do a Leaving Certificate or undertake an equivalent access programme, there are a number of other barriers which they have to confront. First, there is an information deficit about higher education, especially among people who live outside the established information networks of schools and colleges (Healy, 1998). The difficulty for adults of getting complete and accurate access to information about higher education was raised in the study undertaken with individual mature students. While the Department of Education's *Information Booklet for Mature Students* was welcomed, it was pointed out that adults need guidance in making their choices. No national system of guidance exists for adults at present. This is especially problematic for working-class students and for women working at home without an income, as both groups have few means of accessing guidance and information of a generalised nature about the higher education options open to them.

Research internationally indicates that among the most important barriers facing adults entering higher education are the psychological ones, a fear of the unknown and a fear of failure within the unknown (Gallagher et al., 1993). This is especially the case for adults from lower socio-economic backgrounds among whose friends and associates there may be no tradition of or support for entering higher education. Lack of social and family supports can be exacerbated by a lack of finance (Fleming and Murphy, 1997).

Our survey and interview data suggest that the fear of entering higher education for the first time ('entering the unknown', as a number of people named it) is a barrier, in and of itself. These fears and anxieties are exacerbated by anticipatory 'worries about money', and by concerns that the application and selection processes were not entirely clear or fair in all cases. Fleming and Murphy (1997) also found that a whole series of constraints and difficulties faced those adults who wished to enter higher education, and among these were a lack of 'college knowledge' (knowledge about how the whole system works).

Participation Stage

Once students enter college the nature of their problems changes. The most important single source of difficulty reported by full-time mature students in our study was lack of adequate finance: 40% said lack of adequate financial resources was their major problem. A further 24% cited their major difficulties as being psychological, such as feeling alienated within the institution and juggling time around different commitments. Exam pressures were the only other named source of anxiety (13%).

When asked if they had enough time for study, 55% said they had, but 45% had not. The principal reason people did not have enough study time is because of family and/or work commitments. Of those who reported having difficulties, 45% cited this as their biggest problem, while 26% said the workload was too heavy; a further 17% reported the loss of time spent travelling as a problem. Time pressures were a special problem for women with dependants, for whom the juggling of different commitments was a significant source of stress. The fact that female mature students have particular difficulties in participating in higher education has now been well documented in a wide range of countries and in Ireland (Edwards, 1990; Cochrane, 1991; Council of Europe, 1996; Scott et al., 1996; Fleming and Murphy, 1997).

FINANCIAL BARRIERS TO EQUALITY OF ACCESS AND PARTICIPATION

As noted above, financial barriers are regarded as the single most important obstacle to equality of participation in higher education by mature students.

Financial barriers operate at both distal and proximate levels. At the distal level, it is self-evident that students from low-income backgrounds have relatively low disposable incomes. Lack of access to a reasonable and secure income (in a society which prizes wealth and security) can have a profound influence on people's self-image and on their expectations, both of themselves and of education. People learn, through a whole array of social processes, that they occupy a subordinate position in society and this impacts negatively on self-image and expectations. In addition, subjective aspirations are strongly conditioned by the objective (financially permissible) opportunities available (Bourdieu and Passeron, 1977). People lower their educational sights, not because they lack ability, interest or motivation but because they know that the higher education option is financially inaccessible. Finally, access to the social and cultural artefacts and experiences which build confidence and supplement learning — such as travel, extra-curricular involvements, holidays and cultural events — is generally costly in our society. The inevitable outcome therefore is income-related access to valued educational and cultural resources and the lowering/raising of expectations, self-image and ambitions accordingly.

And there is evidence from both at home and abroad that people from lower socio-economic backgrounds often lack ambitions and expectations for higher education arising from their sense of being strangers and outsiders in cultural institutions such as education (Bourdieu and Passeron, 1977; O'Neill, 1992). Irish research suggests that both young people and adults in working-class communities often perceive higher education, especially universities, as belonging to others, but not to themselves (Lynch and O'Riordan, 1996). This sense of being an outsider and not 'owning' higher education is not simply a function of education-related experiences, it is also the by-product of more general social-class-related exclusions from the social and cultural life of society (ibid.).

Financial barriers also impact directly on educational experience. Those who own and control superior financial resources exercise a freedom of choice within education which is not open to others. They are in a position to maximise their educational advantage in the private education markets outside of schools. Superior income allows students to have access to valuable educational resources such as books, computers, travel, special interest courses, and, when necessary, extra tuition. This both improves performance and raises expectations. Not only are higher-income households better positioned to pay for the direct costs involved in 'out-competing others' in education, however, they are also in a better position to manage the indirect costs. The opportunity cost of returning to education impacts differentially across households with those on lowest incomes bearing the greatest burden. In the absence of a comprehensive grants system for mature students, it is self-evident, therefore, that those who lack the resources to maintain themselves in college cannot attend. Adults with dependants and without any independent income (and these are mostly women) are especially disadvantaged in this situation.

ACCESS, PARTICIPATION AND GENDER EQUALITY[9]

Specific Barriers for Women: Dependency

The representation of women among mature students in Ireland is noticeably lower than that of men. This is particularly the case among part-time students. While this pattern holds internationally, the gender differential in Ireland is greater than in many European countries. Although the reasons for this are many and varied, there is no doubt that the lower participation of women in the paid labour force is a contributory factor (OECD Centre for Educational Research and Innovation, 1987). Women who are financially dependent lack independent means to avail of higher education. Scott et al. (1996) found that lack of money was one of the principal reasons why women with children drop out of higher education.

In our study, we found that this dependency took class-specific forms. Working-class women who were in low-income or welfare-dependent households often simply lacked the means to enter higher education. Even if they were to have their fees paid, the direct costs of participation in higher education (books, travel, etc.) were deemed too high relative to disposable income. The indirect costs, in terms of time and childcare, and the opportunity costs in terms of lost opportunity for casual work, were also deemed too high.

A separate problem identified by married women of all classes, but especially by better-off middle-class and working-class women, related to their direct dependency on their spouses. At present eligibility for a mature student fees grant is determined by the level of spouses' earnings. There was a strong feeling among married women of all classes that this was unjust as it meant that a husband could, and did, veto the woman's return to higher education. It was recognised that this could also happen to men who were dependent on spouses, although this is a far rarer occurrence.

Specific Barriers for Women: Childcare and the Care of Other Dependants

There are 588,000 women in Ireland who are defined in the Labour Force Survey as working at home; they represent 98% of home workers (Central Statistics Office Labour Force Survey, 1997, Table 10). Many of these women exercise a caring role for either children or other dependants. The absence of adequate support services for carers means that many such women are not in a position to enter higher education if the opportunity arose. The cost of providing alternative care is often prohibitive relative to disposable income and was identified as such by the women in both the survey and the interviews. Knowing that there is not an adequate support system of childcare, in particular, is known to be a barrier to higher education entry for women in other countries as well (OECD Centre for Educational Research and Innovation, 1987; Council of Europe, 1996).

Specific Barriers for Women: Conflict over Time

While almost half of the mature students surveyed stated that they did not have enough time for study, time problems were particularly acute for women with care commitments. These women felt under considerable pressure trying to balance their caring and other domestic commitments with study. While men and women experience similar time conflicts, such as the conflict between work and/or travel and study, the care pressures were felt more keenly by women. Fleming and Murphy's (1997) findings confirm this as well.

Specific Barriers for Women: Access to Transport

Access to transport was identified as a barrier for women in rural areas especially, many of whom lacked any affordable or accessible transport. While the lack of public transport affected both women and men, a number of women pointed out that even if there was a car in the household, it generally belonged to the husband as he was the principal earner. Lack of access to transport reflected women's dependent status, and meant that they could not travel to college even if the opportunity arose. It is indicative of the wider problem of intra-household differences in access to resources between women and men (Cantillon, 1997).

It is clear therefore that while women and men from low-income backgrounds experience similar difficulties in entering and successfully participating in higher education as mature students, women face barriers which are exclusive to themselves. Gender-specific barriers take different forms depending on class background, regional location and age.

CONCLUSIONS: MECHANISMS FOR PROMOTING EQUALITY OF ACCESS AND PARTICIPATION FOR MATURE STUDENTS

RESERVING PLACES FOR DISADVANTAGED MATURE STUDENTS

As the rate of representation of mature students in higher education in the Republic of Ireland is significantly lower than in other countries, and is also much lower than in Northern Ireland, there is clearly a need to redress the balance. The problem is particularly acute for socially and economically disadvantaged adults. While it is recognised that there are great pressures on higher education places from school leavers, and that there is a clear need in the interests of social justice to reserve places in higher education for the socially and economically disadvantaged among these, this need not preclude the development of a more proactive policy in relation to disadvantaged mature students as well. As noted above, most mature students are quite young: 52% are under thirty years of age and more than 70% are under thirty-five years. The cohort from which mature students are drawn is not that many years older than the school-leaver cohort, and as with school leavers a very sizeable proportion of mature students is also disadvantaged.

Reserving places for mature students is principally an issue in full-time day programmes, however. (While a small number of colleges have a quota of places for mature students, the data available indicate that the quota rarely exceeds 10% except where evening programmes are on offer. As these courses are generally designed for mature students, the question of reserving places does not arise.) Moreover, if extra places are targeted for mature students, they should apply in all fields of study within the colleges. To date mature students have been concentrated in a narrow range of fields, mostly in the arts, humanities, social science and business areas: there is a need to provide openings across all disciplines.

If there is to be any change in the participation rate of mature students, however, colleges need to set targets. Some system for monitoring and reporting on progress should also be put in place.

PRE-ACCESS COURSES: ENABLING ADULTS TO QUALIFY FOR ENTRY

One of the points raised repeatedly throughout the literature is that equality of access to higher education for mature students cannot be successfully promoted if policies to broaden access are brought to bear only, or even mainly, at the point of entry to higher education. Many disadvantaged mature students have a number of barriers to overcome before they even reach a point where they are eligible to apply for higher education. Acquiring the qualifications and resources, and developing the confidence to apply for entry in the first place, are monumental tasks for many. The first step in this process for those without prior qualifications is generally a return to learning in their own community. A precondition for improving the participation of disadvantaged groups in higher education therefore is the development of well funded and resourced community, adult and further education. Without such, disadvantaged groups cannot even reach the stage where they can qualify for entry to an access course or a Leaving Certificate programme (Dolphin and Mulvey, 1997; Healy, 1998).

ACCESS, FOUNDATION AND PREPARATORY COURSES

After they have completed the preparatory work there is also a need for more access and/or foundation courses for adults. While there is provision in this area at present, access provision is very uneven and has developed on an ad hoc rather than a planned basis (Lynch and O'Riordan, 1996; Healy, 1998). Developing systems for accrediting prior learning, and establishing the relationship between these, new access/foundation programmes and traditional qualifications, such as the Leaving Certificate, also needs to be part of any future access provision for adults.

Even for mature students who may have the required points for entry to a given course, there is need for a preparatory course prior to commencing full-time study. Ideally all mature students entering higher education should be given a preparatory course on study skills, essay writing, project writing and research skills, note taking, library research, examination systems, time management and any other skills required in higher education. They would need continued support throughout their first year as well. This is especially true for students who may be entering higher education through non-traditional routes. And there is evidence from experience in Scotland

(University of Dundee) that this type of programme not only is effective for non-traditional entrants but also reduces the failure rate among standard entrants (Lynch and O'Riordan, 1996).

FINANCIAL SUPPORTS FOR MATURE STUDENTS

Financial barriers are a major obstacle for many aspiring mature students. Even for those who qualify for supports such as the Third Level Allowance Scheme, the strain can be considerable. The problems are especially acute for mature students with dependants (Fleming and Murphy, 1997). While many young students can rely on family supports, especially those from financially secure households, mature students with dependants are rarely in a position to seek assistance from their own families, especially if they are from low-income backgrounds (Redpath and Robus, 1989). This needs to be taken into account in any form of grant provision or financial support system.

ADDRESSING THE FUNDAMENTAL ECONOMIC INEQUALITIES WHICH UNDERPIN DISADVANTAGE

Although increased grant aid would greatly assist low-income mature students in the short term, it does not resolve the underlying causes of disadvantage. As long as there are huge income and wealth differentials in our society, then it will not be really possible for socially and economically disadvantaged adults to avail of higher education on equal terms with more advantaged groups. Put simply, the same team will always tend to lose if the rules are written against them. Income, wealth and power differentials are inextricably linked to educational differentials.

ADDRESSING THE DEPENDENT STATUS OF MARRIED WOMEN

Married women's dependent status, in terms of both welfare and taxation, has been identified as a major source of inequality between women and men in the Report of the Second Commission on the Status of Women (1993). It is not strictly speaking an educational problem although it does have serious implications for married women students in terms of their entitlements to grant aid. In view of this, the necessary changes in welfare, taxation and other social insurance systems recommended by the Commission should be implemented to allow women to have independent rights and entitlements. Without these, women are effectively beholden to their spouses if they want to return to higher education.

SELECTION PROCEDURES: FLEXIBILITY AND OPENNESS

At present, entry requirements for mature students across the colleges are far from clear and there is no systematic procedure for explaining to unsuccessful candidates across the colleges why they were not successful. This is something which needs to be rectified as there is considerable confusion and disquiet among applicants about the criteria that are utilised in selection. In the course of our research we held meetings and discussions with over fifty mature students in three different colleges and with twenty unsuccessful candidates. There was a widespread belief expressed that colleges ultimately relied on Leaving Certificate results to select mature students. Although this may not be correct, the fact that so many mature students who attend higher education do have a Leaving Certificate and/or a post-Leaving Certificate qualification lends credence to the view.

While it is inevitable that flexibility in the entry requirements and procedures for mature students would mean that application procedures would be more complex than those which obtain for school leavers, complexity does not preclude clarity and openness. If the colleges are to be open to second chance students, in particular to students who do not have conventional academic backgrounds, then it is essential that they make their criteria for selection clear to such students.

Furthermore there needs to be consistency across departments and faculties in the approach to mature students. A persistent cause of disquiet among mature students generally is that there does not appear to be any centralised college policy in relation to mature students which operates in all faculties and departments. Individual departments and faculties appear to have considerable autonomy in deciding to select or reject mature students, while the reason for the difference across departments within a given college are often far from clear. This issue was raised at interview in the Irish research for the TWG and is regarded as a problem to be addressed in the UK as well (Gallagher et al., 1993).

ALTERNATIVE ENTRY ROUTES

While there are certain alternative entry routes to higher education in Ireland, apart from the Leaving Certificate (including access courses such as the Vocational and Technical Opportunities Scheme, Return to Learning and Foundation Courses), not all are developed on a national basis, and many are neither widely publicised nor clearly understood. While recognising that there is work in progress in this area, it is essential that any alternative entry procedures which are developed are tied to some system of equivalencies, both with the Leaving Certificate and with one another.

A mature student should be able to know at any given time where they stand in terms of meeting the criteria for entry to a given course. To guarantee this, weightings or credits must be given to various tests, interviews, portfolios, non-accredited but relevant prior learning, and all other mechanisms used for selection at entry. And there is a need to establish a national agency to manage the entire access procedures and programmes operating outside of the Leaving Certificate system.

STAFF DEVELOPMENT AND TRAINING

Academic, and administrative, staff who liaise with mature students need to be fully briefed on the needs of mature students. There is no doubt that the education of older adults is not the same as that of school leavers and staff development programmes need to take account of this. The role of non-academic staff in answering queries, supplying information and administering admissions should be recognised as crucial and training provided when necessary. The central importance of such staff development has been noted in the UK research as well (Gallagher et al., 1993).

INFORMATION

One of the barriers to equality of access is lack of information. While there is a general information booklet available for mature students, ideally every college should have its own information booklet and/or video for mature students which would include practical information covering all the relevant issues for students, including precise information on selection criteria, times of classes, library hours, crèche facilities, restaurant facilities, etc. This would enable mature students to make an informed judgment and to plan well in advance.

APPROPRIATE COURSE STRUCTURES: PEDAGOGICAL STYLE AND ASSESSMENT

Adults entering higher education are not school leavers. Colleges must not assume therefore that the policies and practices which work with school leavers are also appropriate for mature students. More flexibility in both the mode of delivery of education and the modes of assessment are essential if colleges are to facilitate the disadvantaged mature students. Modularised courses, with the option of taking both daytime and evening courses at degree, diploma, certificate, level, etc. over an extended period of time is essential if mature students are to be facilitated (Council of Europe, 1996).

A move away from a heavy reliance on written terminal examinations (on which there is usually no feedback except for a grade or mark) to course work and project work with feedback as part of the assessment would not only suit mature students better, but might also be of great educational benefit to all students.

Finally there is a need to set up systems for communicating with adult students which respects both their experience and their knowledge. Mature students expect to be treated as adults and to have their views on curricula, modes of assessment, teaching, etc., respected (Weil, 1986; Edwards, 1990). Developing systems to allow for two-way communication between teachers and students seems essential for all students, but especially for mature students.

CHILDCARE, GUIDANCE AND OTHER SUPPORT SERVICES FOR MATURE STUDENTS

The importance of support services for disadvantaged mature students in higher education is emphasised throughout the research literature. Their need for career counselling and guidance has been particularly strongly emphasised.

It would seem desirable therefore for colleges to establish a support office for all types of non-traditional entrants which is properly resourced. This could be a place where students with equality concerns could meet, as well as being a place for information and guidance. Without targeted resources, the needs of disadvantaged students will not be met.

While crèche facilities and childcare supports are essential for all students, they are especially important for mature socially and economically disadvantaged students who are women. Mature students are more likely to have children and those who are disadvantaged will not be in a position to afford private childcare. Without some kind of childcare support, higher education is not a real option for low-income women or men with dependants (Council of Europe, 1996). The fact that most mature students in Ireland are single and have no children indicates how essential care-support services are for those wanting to return to education.

RECORDING STUDENTS' STATUS

One of the major barriers faced when conducting the research on mature students was actually identifying them in the colleges after they had completed their first year. Colleges had considerable difficulty identifying mature students (and indeed other special category students such as disabled students). Given this problem, it seems desirable that there would be a standard form introduced across all colleges in higher education to collect data on students. Students who enter as mature students should be capable of being identified in college records at any given time in their educational career.

TRACKING STUDENT PERFORMANCE

Although Fleming and Murphy's (1997) study in Maynooth found that mature students performed slightly better than mainstream students in their first year, we know little about the progress of mature students generally within college. Tracking students' progress within higher education is not standard practice in Ireland. This can disadvantage mature students (and other non-traditional entrants) in two ways. First, because stereotypical, and frequently negative, assertions made about them (especially about their academic capabilities) cannot be challenged systematically due to lack of evidence. Even if such students were having difficulties (although there is no evidence to suggest that mature students perform any differently to school-leaver entrants) there is no procedure for identifying the nature and scope of their problems and delivering assistance. The need to have accurate data on the entry and performance of higher education students seems self-evidently important, not only for mature students but for all students.

REFERENCES

Archer, P., and O'Flaherty, B. (1986). A home intervention programme for pre-school disadvantaged children. *Irish Journal of Education*, IX:28–43.

Bourdieu, P. (1989). *Distinction*. London: Sage.

Bourdieu, P., and Passeron, J.-C. (1977). *Reproduction in Education, Society and Culture*. London: Sage.

Cantillon, S. (1997). Women in poverty: differences in living standards within households. In A. Byrne and M. Leonard (eds.), *Women in Irish Society: A Sociological Reader*. Belfast: Beyond the Pale Publications.

Central Statistics Office (1997). *Labour Force Survey, 1997*. Dublin: Central Statistics Office.

Clancy, P. (1995). *Access to College: Patterns of Continuity and Change*. Dublin: Higher Education Authority.

Cochrane, C. (1991). First year at university: a study of mature female students. *Irish Journal of Education*, XXV, pp. 42–51.

Commission on the Status of Women (1993). *Report to Government of the Second Commission on the Status of Women*. Dublin: Government Publications Office.

Conference of Major Religious Superiors (CMRS) (1992). *Education and Poverty*. Dublin: CMRS.

Coolahan, J. (ed.) (1994). *Report on the National Education Convention*. Dublin: Government Publications Office.

Council of Europe (1996). *Access to Higher Education: Access for Under-Represented Groups. Vol. II Report on Western Europe*. Prepared by M. Woodrow and D. Crosier, Council of Europe, Strasbourg.

Culliton, J. (1992). *A Time for Change: Industrial Policy for the 1990s*. Dublin: Government Publications Office.

Department of Education and Science (UK) (1994). *Statistical Bulletin Issue No. 16/94*. London: HMSO.

Department of Education (1995). *Charting Our Education Future: White Paper on Education*. Dublin: Government Publications Office.

Department of Enterprise and Employment (1996). *Science, Technology and Innovation: The White Paper*. Dublin: Government Publications Office.

Dolphin, E., and Mulvey, C. (1997). *Review of Scheme of Grants to Locally-Based Women's Groups*. Dublin: Department of Social, Community and Family Affairs.

Edwards, R. (1990). Access and assets: the experience of mature mother-students in higher education. *Journal of Access Studies*, 5 (2), Autumn.

Fleming, T., and Murphy, M. (1997). *College Knowledge: Power, Policy and Mature Student Experience at University*. NUI Maynooth, Maynooth Adult and Community Education Series.

Gallagher, A., Richards, N., and Locke, N. (1993). *Mature Students in Higher Education: How Institutions Can Learn from Experience*. University of East London, Centre for Institutional Studies.

Healy, M. (1998). *Everything to Gain: A Study of the Third Level Allowance Scheme.* Dublin: AONTAS (National Association of Adult Education).

Higher Education Authority (1995). *Report of the Steering Committee on the Future of Higher Education*. Dublin: Higher Education Authority.

Irish National Teachers' Organisation (INTO) (1994). *Poverty and Educational Disadvantage: Breaking the Cycle*. Dublin: INTO.

Kellaghan, T., Weir, S., O'hUallacháin, S., and Morgan, M. (1995). *Educational Disadvantage in Ireland*. Dublin: Department of Education and Combat Poverty Agency.

Lynch, K., and O'Riordan, C. (1996). *Social Class, Inequality and Higher Education: Barriers to Equality of Access and Participation among School Leavers*. University College Dublin, Registrar's Office.

Morgan, M., Hickey, B., and Kellaghan, T. (OECD) (1997). *International Adult Literacy Survey: Results for Ireland*. Dublin: Government Publications Office.

Morgan, M., and Martin, M. (1994). *Literacy Problems among Irish Fourteen-Year-Olds. ALCE Evaluation, Vol. III*. Dublin: Educational Research Centre.

OECD Centre for Educational Research and Innovation (1987). *Adults in Higher Education*. Paris: OECD.

O'Neill, C. (1992). *Telling It Like It Is*. Dublin: Combat Poverty Agency.

Redpath, B., and Robus, N. (1989). *Mature Students' Incomings and Outgoings*. London: HMSO.

Scott, C., Burns, A., and Cooney, G. (1996). Reasons for discontinuing study: the case of mature age female students with children. *Higher Education*, 31:233–53.

Shavit, Y., and Blossfeld, H.P. (eds.) (1993). *Persistent Inequality: Changing Educational Attainment in Thirteen Countries*. Oxford: Westview Press.

Technical Working Group (TWG, HEA) to the Steering Committee on the Future of Higher Education (1995). *Interim Report to the Steering Committee on the Future of Higher Education*. Dublin: Higher Education Authority.

Weil, S.W. (1986). Non-traditional learners within traditional higher education institutions: discovery and disappointment. *Studies in Higher Education*, 11:219–35.

NOTES

1   The national data on which this chapter is based were compiled for the Technical Working Group to the Steering Committee on the Future of Higher Education. Most of the data are based on mature student applicants for 1993/4 although some data were also collected on the general mature student population in the colleges for the previous year, 1992/3. The chapter

also reports on a study of mature students (N = 370) (chosen randomly across seven colleges) which was undertaken in 1993 / 4; this involved survey work, group interviews and individual interviews with mature students.

2   At the time the study was undertaken a number of colleges did not require all mature applicants to apply through the CAO system, hence the difference between the overall figure and the CAO figure.

3   This figure includés only those students who were undertaking recognised third-level courses in the colleges, ranging from certificates to diplomas and degrees. It does not include those on access courses to higher education.

4   This scheme allows people to receive their social welfare payments while attending college. It covers fees as well. The scheme was first introduced for unemployed persons only in 1990; since 1993 it has been extended to lone parents and, more recently, to people on disability maintenance allowances.

5   The Technical Working Group survey of part-time students in 1993 / 4 found that almost 90% were employed. This is not surprising, however, as there is no grant support for mature part-time students, although there is some provision for tax relief. The latter provision is of value only to those who are in employment.

6   There is a substantial body of people with post-secondary education and qualifications who are returning to full-time higher education. Their employment profile indicates that a large number of these are effectively unemployed (although not always registered as such) and / or that they are in insecure or low-paid employment. Mature students who are part-time are generally employed.

7   The standard research procedure for classifying those who are unemployed is on the basis of their previous occupation. Given the extent and nature of long-term unemployment in our society, this gives a very misleading representation of social trends. It also prevents any systematic tracking and analysis of the unique problems of those who are long-term unemployed. Their concerns and problems are by no means synonymous with people in employment from comparable socio-economic backgrounds.

8   The data presented here are based on a survey of full-time mature students which I conducted for the Technical Working Group to the Steering Committee on the Future of Higher Education. The work was undertaken with the assistance of Marjorie Fitzpatrick and Eileen O'Reilly. There were 370 students surveyed, of whom 52% responded. Focus group discussions were also undertaken with mature students in three different colleges; in all, fifty people attended these. A number of these students were also interviewed individually. A comparable survey of unsuccessful mature student applicants was also undertaken in the colleges (five of the seven agreed to be involved). A total of 310 applicants were surveyed but the response rate was low, 23%. A further twenty interviews were undertaken with unsuccessful mature applicants.

9   The data on gender issues emerged from the survey of individual mature students reported above. Many of the gender-specific issues were raised in the group interviews in the different colleges.

10 And indeed gender differences and inequalities are often attributed to some kind of deficit on women's part in particular. In certain research literature (for example that which focuses on women's ambitions and aspirations) it is implicitly assumed that women are the problem rather than the institutions and structures which ensure their subordination in the first place.

SECTION 3

INSTITUTIONAL ISSUES

CHAPTER 8

ESSAYS ON SCHOOL

Kathleen Lynch and *Anne Lodge*

Section 1: Introduction

THE RESEARCH CONTEXT

As noted in chapter 1, there is a large corpus of research undertaken on the equality theme in education. In terms of theoretical perspective, the pendulum swings from the functionalist analysis of the equality empiricists, operating largely out of a liberal political tradition, to the work of critical theorists and feminists which challenges core assumptions about the inevitability of inequality in education, and the possibilities for resistance. The latter group work out of a radical egalitarian perspective informed by neo-Marxism and, more recently, by critical feminist and postmodernist analysis.

While much of the early equality-focused research, in both the structural-functionalist and the neo-Marxist tradition, worked out of a *distributive model* of justice (where the solution to inequality for a given target group was defined in terms of equalising their access, participation and success within the system, getting more of the 'good' which is education), more recent work, especially in the critical tradition, has moved the equality debate on to focus on *equality of respect*, particularly respect for difference. As educationalists began to address complex issues of gender, ethnicity, sexual orientation and disability, it became clear that what was assumed to be educationally 'good' was itself problematic (Connell, 1993). The focus moved from just getting more education for all at all levels, to questioning the value of particular forms of education, including pedagogical practice, curriculum choices, organisational procedures and policy prescriptions.

In defining the groups who are to be respected, and whose lifeworlds should be accommodated in schools, there has, however, been very little problema-tising of the core relationship of schooling, that between teacher and pupil. While Freire's work (1972, 1973) has presented an alternative model for analysing the dynamic of educational relationships, there is a widespread view that his concept of 'education as dialogue' is difficult to operationalise outside of an adult education context. While Giroux (1983, 1992) and McLaren (1995)

have explored the possibility of utilising a Freirean methodology in school settings, their work is essentially a philosophical exposition on the role of teachers
as transformative intellectuals. The students are defined as partners in this
process, but there is little analysis of what students may or may not want from
a transformative teacher. The fact that students may resist critical pedagogical
practices is not seriously entertained. Giroux's work is written from the
perspective of the radical educator with the explicit ambition of linking radical
pedagogy to transformative democratic politics. Oppression is equated with
sexism, racism and class inequality but not with age per se. How young people
might become agents in the struggle for a transformative politics that would
alter their own status as subordinates in an adult world is not examined.

Within the empirical tradition, researching students' perspective on schools
is not new. However, when interpreting and classifying what students say,
researchers have interpreted students' concerns within models and disciplines
within which young people have no voice. The paradigms and concerns of the
disciplines, and the research frames used to interpret data, while important in
their own right, may not be sufficiently sensitive to the views of young persons.
People such as Cusick (1973) did study life in schools from a student's perspective. However, the analysis focused unproblematically on the school system
as it structured and ordered students' lives. The 'batch processing' of pupils was
defined as a type of 'educational inevitable'; its anti-egalitarian implications for
young people were not problematised. Willis (1977), McRobbie (1978) and
Everhart (1983) also listened to students and documented their world view,
within neo-Marxist and feminist paradigms. They did not examine the world
view of students in terms of their position vis-à-vis adults. The gender/class
axis was the one which dictated the frame of the analysis.

What this chapter attempts to do is to prioritise the 'voices' of young people
themselves in naming equality agendas in school. (We will be presenting the
teachers' views on equality in schools in a later publication.) Using the essays
written by young people, it identifies their equality priorities in school. Rather
than treating views about teachers and peers as a set of predictable 'complaints'
about schooling, it analyses these concerns in the light of current debates about
equality and difference. In taking their perspectives seriously, it identifies a more
varied set of equality concerns among young people on schooling than that
which is found in much of the literature. What young people define as equality
issues are not synonymous with those of adults. The unequal power relations
between schoolchildren and adults, and the ordering of educational relations
through ability-related grouping and signification practices, leads to the
development of equality concerns among young persons which are different to
those identified in much of the literature.

Research based on a distributive model of social justice, and this includes
much of the work on social class issues, and those working out of the
'difference models', has not really engaged with the issue of age, and the adult-

centredness of so much thinking in the equality field. Within the distributive tradition, education is defined as a 'good'. Young people's concerns with its mode of organisation and its purposes have not been taken especially seriously. A paternalistic, caretaking ideology informs most of educational theory. Children's and young adults' criticisms of schooling generally experience the fate of trivialisation; at best they are listened to with benign indifference. The researcher takes the parent or teacher perspective and assumes that the parent is the trustee of the child's interest. As the trustee has judged that a lengthy period of schooling is in the young person's interest, the case is closed for listening. Young people's critical views of education cannot be taken seriously within this paternalistic frame of reference (Archard, 1993).

Those for whom equality involves respect for difference rather than simply distribution have, however, created a space in which the voices of young persons can be heard. Even though they did not create these spaces to hear young people especially, the spaces and cracks which are open allow their voices to be heard.

THE STUDY

This chapter presents findings from an ongoing research project on 'Equality and the Social Climate of Schools'. One of the goals of this study is to take the equality agenda in schools as it is defined by young persons themselves. A number of research techniques were employed to listen to young persons, including focus groups, informal meetings and discussions, and essays. In addition, a more structured questionnaire was devised for measuring attitudes to schooling. The questions included in the questionnaire were informed by an earlier pilot study (involving one whole school population) which explored the equality issues concerning young people, based on a range of research methodologies. This chapter reports on our findings from the essays alone.

Twelve schools representing all different school types were chosen in six different counties for the study. To ensure anonymity, all the schools were given fictitious names. A deliberate sample of five or six classes (depending on whether the school had a five- or six-year cycle) across different year groups were chosen in each of the twelve schools. The classes were representative of all ability types within the school. Students within these classes were asked to write an essay on whether or not they had ever been unequally or unfairly treated in the school, and what kinds of changes they would like to see in schools to make them more just and equal places. The essay question was as follows:

> We would like you to write here about any time or place when you think you've been unfairly or unequally treated since you came to this school, either by other pupils or by teachers.

> To make school a fairer and more equal place, what kind of changes would you like to see in it?

A total of 1,202 students, 77% of the total sample population, completed essays about school. Their views about the most pressing equality issues in their schools are presented here.

Emancipatory research principles have guided the research process with schools being invited to comment on the research goals and instruments at the design stage. In addition, each school was visited prior to the study and teacher comments and views on the research were taken into account. Unfortunately it was not possible to consult with students about the research design prior to the study due to lack of resources. Ideally they should have been consulted as they were central to the research process. However, students were consulted about the research process and design at the pilot stage, and consultations with the students did take place in the main study while the research was ongoing through informal discussions and focus groups. The students were keen that their views would be presented to teachers and this happened in all the schools. Brief individual reports were prepared for all the participating schools and the findings presented in summary form at a staff meeting.

SECTION 2: EQUALITY THEMES IN THE STUDENT ESSAYS

EQUALITY AND THE EXERCISE OF AUTHORITY AND POWER

The equality theme which emerged most strongly from student essays and interviews was concern about the operation of authority and power within schools. While it is inevitable, to some degree, that the theme of teacher authority and power would emerge in a school setting, the fact that the issue emerged spontaneously and strongly suggests that this is a major concern for young people in school.

Students' principal equality concerns related to perceived unfair treatment by teachers. The inequality which arose from differences in age and status between students and teachers was the dominant theme in the essays. Just under 48% of the students stated in their essays that unequal or unfair treatment by teachers was an equality issue for them (Table 1). Moreover, their sense of unequal treatment centred on questions of power and its perceived misuse. While one-third of the students in two schools mentioned 'unjust or unfair treatment by teachers' as their primary equality concern, there were six other schools where over 50% of the students stated this to be their major concern; in one of these schools, 56% of the students named unfair or unequal treatment by teachers in their essays as a priority concern.

The solutions which students presented to the inequalities they experienced in relation to adults were centred on organisational practice and attitudinal change. A minority of students (approximately 10% in four of the schools) made specific proposals for increased democratic input by students in their school; while 47% called for greater equality of respect and improved democracy (Table 1). The themes of the essay material were also confirmed in focus group discussions, observations and student questionnaires.

Democratic Structures: Lack of Truly Participatory Democratic Structures in Schools

Pupils in all schools, especially seniors, were interested in having greater democratic involvement in issues directly affecting them at school.

> 'I am eighteen years old. I am an adult, able to vote, work independently, yet I am taught and punished like an eight-year-old. I have no responsibility, [I am] unable to mature as a person. Some people lack confidence because of teachers. [It] should change very soon.' (A sixth year student in St David's) (As noted already, all school names are fictitious.)

Students wanted to have their opinions taken seriously; they wanted to be involved in decisions that affected them.

> 'I think that students are not asked for their opinions on most things — everything is decided for them.' (A fourth year student in St Peter's)

Many were interested either in having a Student Council established or in the existing Council being given real authority, rather than just being allowed to carry out activities (such as running discos) which they regarded as unimportant. They wanted to have some genuine input into the way in which school rules were drawn up.

> '[What] we need in this school [is] a Student Council, where students' rights will be held up. At the moment it is what the teacher says goes. But I think we need student representatives.' (A fifth year student in St Patrick's)

> 'I would like a student board set up especially for our fifth, sixth and RLC [Repeat Leaving Certificate] students so we can have our say.' (A sixth year student in St Dominic's)

When these views were put to teachers in schools (at our research feedback sessions) where no Council currently exists, some staff members feared that such a development would lead to 'anarchy'. In those schools where Councils already existed, concerns were raised separately by pupils, and some teachers, about how the students could be encouraged to take these bodies more seriously, and also how the Councils could be given more realistic democratic involvement by the school institution.

In general, there appeared to be a communication gap between students and teachers about the nature and purpose of democratic structures. Pupils who had no involvement in exercising authority in the schools seemed to be genuinely interested in being a part of the institution, and in having the opportunity to dialogue with the teachers on a partnership basis about these issues. They did not wish to take complete control or 'wreak havoc', yet teachers expressed great fears, and appeared to lack a clear understanding about how such participatory democracy would work in schools. The problem which seemed to exist in schools which had Student Councils was that students in many cases saw them as having no real control or influence so they did not take them seriously. In one of the schools (Dunely) students effectively boycotted an attempt by staff to set up a Students' Council (by voting for the most unsuitable candidates) as they had not been consulted about either the setting up of the Council or its functions. They believed it would have had no real impact on the way the school was run so they did not see much point in supporting it.

Overall, there was greater interest expressed by girls in both single-sex and co-educational schools in having an involvement with the school institution than was expressed by boys in either co-educational or boys' schools. However, boys in single-sex schools had more interest in being involved with democratic structures than did their counterparts in co-educational schools.

Equality of Respect

The demand for greater democratic control and involvement in decision-making was complemented by a concern for greater respect. Students were keenly aware not only of the power differential which exists between teachers and students in schools but of the respect differential.

> '[I would like] for teachers to act as they [do] with other adults. For them to show respect.' (A third year student in St Peter's)

> 'More respect for the students because in order for teachers to gain respect from students, the teachers must first give respect.' (A fifth year male student in Ballydara Community College)

Several students expressed concern in their essays about the importance of having a 'right of reply' when accused of wrongdoing. Students pointed out that if one was respected, then one should be given the chance to defend oneself in the face of accusations rather than being punished without consultation. This was especially resented when punishments meted out were humiliating. And there were complaints about the humiliating nature of sanctions among pupils in all the schools.

> 'A teacher in our school if you do the smallest thing wrong in [subject], she makes you feel about two inches tall. She humiliates you in front of the whole class and sometimes makes people cry.' (A third year student in St Cecilia's)

> 'They [teachers] bully many students with unnecessary punishments for innocent enough things and some extremely hurtful comments.' (A fifth year male student in St Ita's)

Concerns were also expressed about perceived inequalities in the punishments meted out for various misdemeanours. Individual pupils complained, in all schools, that a minority of teachers were unfair in how they assigned blame, and in the way that they sanctioned pupils. Public humiliation of pupils, or, in a small minority of cases, punishments involving physical contact such as pushing, was considered to be particularly unjust. It was noted in all schools as well that where pupils had problems or negative interaction with either one individual teacher or a small group of teachers, this coloured their attitude to the school as a whole, making negative their whole experience of the school.

> 'She [the teacher] made us stand for the whole class and embarrassed us in front of the whole class. She told us we were pathetic little children and that we made her feel sick. She made me feel like shit.' (A fifth year student in St Peter's)

> 'the punishments which [the teacher] had given us, e.g. standing with our faces against the door, are unjust'. (A third year student in St Cecilia's)

> 'I would like if they were nicer. This school is not that nice. I would like if people were nicer, some of the teachers are very hard.' (A first year female student in Ollan Community College)

Confidentiality and Labelling

Students in all schools expressed concern about being labelled by teachers, or by the peer group, as a 'troublemaker'. Such a label could result from poor behaviour as a junior pupil; being perceived as a part of an undesirable friendship group; or having older siblings or relations whose behaviour had been poorly regarded. This last category was considered to be particularly unfair and was deeply resented by students.

Concern was also expressed by students in the essays about the lack of respect for confidential information. A number of students complained that any interactions they had with teachers, particularly of a negative nature, or any confidential information about their health or family background which became known to one teacher would be discussed with the rest of the staff. This issue emerged in all of the single-sex girls' schools in particular, although it was by no means confined solely to them.

> 'Teachers should keep out of students' personal lives.' (A second year student in Our Lady's)

> 'Records of pupils shouldn't be made available to new teachers because this could give them a prejudiced opinion of students with a bad reputation.' (A third year student in St Peter's)

> 'I know that one of the teachers who did not teach me was going around talking about me. She lives in the same neighbourhood and therefore I heard about it.' (A sixth year female student in Ballycorish Community School)

> 'The teachers not talking about what happens in class and sub/new teachers not told to watch out for certain people, etc.' (A fifth year student in Ballinroe secondary school)

Girls also complained in co-educational and single-sex schools about male teachers and other school employees having access to their private spaces such as their lockers, diaries and the toilets.

Pupil–Teacher Relations: The Phenomenon of 'Us and Them'

A strong sense of social distance between teachers and students existed in certain schools and there were a number of different reasons for this. One factor was the extent to which teachers operated as a socially exclusive group apart from students. In one of the disadvantaged schools, staff operated as a mutually supportive tight-knit community, and although there was no overt antagonism between staff and students, students felt very excluded from the school institution. Interestingly, where a school staff was less intensely cohesive, this did not happen to the same degree. One school was found to have a strongly differentiated staff environment, yet this did not appear to impinge upon pupil happiness with their lives in school. In fact, students in this school (which had a predominantly lower-middle-class and working-class intake) identified quite strongly with the school as an institution.

A second factor which seemed to play a part in creating a sense of alienation between teachers and pupils was the presence of high levels of control and very high attainment expectations. Pupils reported a strong sense of surveillance and of stress in such an environment. A third factor was the social class of pupils. Schools which had a high intake of pupils from working-class backgrounds were more likely to regard the peer group as separate from the teacher authority figures. This sense of detachment was expressed mainly as a lack of trust, although it also found expression in the unwillingness to report problems like bullying to teachers.

The sense of alienation from the school and its rules was expressed in strong language by a number of individual students in different schools.

'This school is like a jail because they even lock the classrooms at lunch.' (A first year student in Our Lady's)

'[The school] should change its prison image.' (A fifth year student in St Patrick's)

'The teachers are all really moany. I get so fucking pissed off with it and you can't shout back at them no matter how much they shout at you. I think we should be treated like normal fucking human beings.' (A second year female student in Ballydara Community College)

Conclusion

The exercise of power and authority in the school was the greatest single equality concern expressed by students in essays. While gender or social class inequalities may exercise the minds of adult educators as important equality concerns, in terms of the operation and outcomes of the education system, what is interesting is that young people themselves defined the use of authority and power as equality issues as well.

Relative to the number of concerns about unequal and unfair treatment by teachers, there were relatively few comments on unequal or unfair treatment by one's peers. While it is obvious that any question about unfair or unequal treatment in school will elicit comments on teachers, and in that sense the essay titles did focus students' minds, nonetheless there was a groundswell of opinion in favour of the democratisation of structures in schools with 48% of essays overall expressing some concern about unfairness, and 47% of students each calling for more democracy in schools and more respect for students (Table 1). These views were borne out in the focus groups and also seem to be confirmed by the preliminary analysis of the statistical data undertaken to date.

ACADEMIC DIFFERENTIATION AND ABILITY GROUPING

Next to the question of authority, ability grouping and differential treatment on the basis of one's perceived abilities were the themes to emerge most strongly from the essays. One-fifth of all students raised equality concerns about the ways in which pupils were treated in different ability groups, or within mixed groups, because of their perceived abilities.

Attitudes towards Ability Differentiation and Grouping

Pupils in high-stream or banded classes stated a preference for a hierarchical system of ability grouping. They equated lower-stream classes with poor behaviour and low academic attainment. They felt that their own learning would suffer in a mixed ability setting.

> 'They should sort out classes more fairly. . . . Some classes are very mixed intellectually, which results in people not doing as well as they could.' (A fifth year student in Ballydara Community College in a higher band)

On the other hand, students in lower-streamed or banded classes felt inferior due to the fact that they were not in the top academic group. This was a persistent theme in the groups classified as low-ability in different schools.

> 'There shouldn't be any separate classes for students of different intelligence.' (A fourth year student in Dunely)

> 'All the classes getting treated fairly and not all the brainy people in one class. All [top-stream classes] think they're so brainy and everyone else and teachers are always comparing us to [them] and it's unfair.' (A first year girl in Ollan Community College)

All types of students claimed that teachers had a preference for the higher-stream groups or individuals. This perceived inequality of teacher respect was reported in schools which were mixed-ability classes as well as those with streamed or banded structures.

> 'My [subject] teacher can be nice to me but there's a girl in my class who is very clever. He is always praising her, and the rest of the class he thinks aren't any good. He is always comparing us to this clever girl.' (A second year student in St Cecilia's)

> 'The students who are not as academically gifted should be treated equally to those who are academically talented. I think that teachers are more sympathetic and patient with the higher grade classes. I am in a higher grade class . . . The lower level classes are often referred to as "weak students" which I think is extremely unfair. I would like to see these students being treated with more respect and patience.' (A third year student in St Patrick's)

'When I was doing my junior cert. I was in an honours [subject] class but I was doing pass. My teacher never spent any time with me doing work. There were five pass pupils and we were all intelligent because we were in the top 60 out of 120 in our year. But the highest anyone got was a B in pass. I got a C. I struggled through my work because five minutes out of every forty minutes was spent on us. This has almost ruined my career ambitions of being a teacher.' (A fourth year student in Ballinroe secondary school)

'I think all students should be treated equally by teachers. If you're not very clever, the teachers shouldn't embarrass you in front of your class-mates; they should help you with your problem and not make you feel stupid in class.' (A sixth year female student in Ballycorish Community School)

High academic achievers were perceived to be allowed greater involvement with the school institution as well.

'There are people in this school who would make very good prefects but are not academically inclined therefore do not receive badges!! It is usually "bright" students who become prefects.' (A sixth year student in St Cecilia's)

'I would like to see equal responsibility to each student, not just to good students. Stupid students don't have as much.' (A second year student in Ballinroe secondary school)

'Teachers favour other students because they are in the top class or whatever. This really annoys me as they are considered the best. All the debating team are from the top class just because they are more intelligent than others.' (A fourth year student in St Patrick's)

'On school trips it is always the brainy students that are picked to go.' (A fifth year student in St Dominic's)

In some schools this lack of respect was internalised by pupils.

'Teachers look down their noses at some pupils and make remarks about them. Some pupils think they are better than everyone else and make little of the people who are not as clever as themselves.' (A second year student in Our Lady's)

'People don't treat me right because I'm not as intelligent as the other pupils in the year.' (A second year student in St David's)

'Sometimes students can be condescending and snobby towards others. That's totally wrong and they should be told sharply when they do this, e.g. grades, fashion, looks, size and behaviour. Everyone does their best but when others flash "As" and honours to gloat about it is quite agitating and down-putting.' (A fifth year student in St Patrick's)

In schools with a large cohort of students from low-income working-class households, labelling by teachers as a high academic achiever was sometimes a source of embarrassment.

'Students calling you a lick because you are in a high class [is a problem for me] but I don't know how I got there. And if there was a person more clever than you the teachers will treat him better than you and they [teachers] will always pick on you.' (A first year student in St Dominic's)

'And the teachers respect me like I'm a brainbox.' (A second year student in a high-stream class in Ballinroe secondary school)

Some pupils in lower-streamed classes felt that the dominant ethos of their class was one in which work was negatively valued. They claimed that disruption and having fun were an important part of their class identity and that this adversely affected work.

Where a mixed-ability situation existed in the first year, and pupils were subsequently banded or streamed, first years expressed fears and anxieties at the prospect of their class groups being changed. Part of their worry related to losing friends, but they also felt that there was competitive pressure to do well in examinations in order to attain a place in a higher-stream group. Overall it was clear that streaming and banding created anxieties and worries among the junior classes in particular.

Just over 18% of students expressed concerns about ability differentiation and grouping in schools. Further analysis of these and other results by ability-group type will be necessary to determine more precisely the sources and causes of concern.

Examination Pressure and Stress

Pupils in examination classes (Junior Certificate and Leaving Certificate) complained of examination stress and pressure. They blamed this mainly on the national system of assessment rather than on their own particular schools.

'I think there shouldn't be as much emphasis on junior cert. and leaving cert. as there is. I think they should rule out junior cert. and leaving if in any way possible. I think there is too much stress put on the students due to these tests.' (A third year student in St Peter's)

'[They should] make a fairer points system for leaving cert.' (A first year student in St David's)

Leaving Certificate pupils expressed concern about competition for college places and/or the need to attain a reasonable Leaving Certificate in order to have any possibility of getting a job when they finished school. Pupils felt that some kind of continuous assessment system, or a mechanism which allowed them to sit more than one set of examinations, would reduce some of the stress and potential unfairness of the current situation. In schools where pupils were assigned to high-streamed classes after first year, these junior pupils complained of examination pressure from the outset because they were very conscious of the necessity of gaining and maintaining a place in a higher-streamed class. Particularly high levels of examination- and achievement-related stress were reported in single-sex girls' schools. In three of the girls' schools, between a quarter and one-third of the students complained of pressure. While 16% of those surveyed in one of the boys' schools also complained, the sample in that school contained a disproportionately high number of high-stream and Leaving Certificate pupils compared with others. In five of the remaining seven schools, between 7% and 15% expressed concerns about examination pressure, while just 5% and 3% expressed concerns in Ballyborris Community School and St David's respectively.

'They don't care what's happening to us. All they care about is the grades.' (A fifth year student in Our Lady's)

A number of individual pupils complained of pressure due to parental expectations.

'Sometimes after doing badly in exams, I feel like committing suicide as my parents expect me to get straight As in my exams.' (A third year student in Ballinroe secondary school)

Instrumental View of Schooling

Students' definition of the successful, admired teacher is reasonably standard across age groups and across schools. They emphasised both the instrumental and affective role of the teacher. It was important that the person have a sense of humour, and be able to maintain control without being aggressive or humiliating pupils. An attitude of respect for the pupils as individuals was also deemed essential, and it was expected that the person would be in command of their subject and an effective communicator. Young people were interested in learning and at the same time developing a warm, humorous and mutually respectful relationship with the teacher. They described actual teachers who fitted this definition within their schools.

'I wish all the teachers were like Mrs . . . All she cares about is for the students and not for her reputation. Just for us. She may seem tough, but that is only because she cares.' (A fourth year student in Our Lady's)

Students were upset by bad teaching because this lessened their chances of achieving good results in examinations.

'I am in [subject] and I cannot give my best because my teacher is not good. I feel hard done by.' (A fifth year student in St David's)

Individual students described having to take extra classes in a specific Leaving Certificate subject because their own teacher was not completing the course. Some of the students from low-income families had to take up a part-time job to be able to pay for these grinds.

'Outside of school I have to get . . . grinds because I feel that I am not achieving my best in her class.' (A third year student in St Cecilia's)

'I have a useless teacher for the past two years who teaches me two subjects. I am aiming to do well in my [subject] but because he is so useless it means that I have to do extra grinds and courses which are expensive and I have to pay for them myself.' (A sixth year student in Ballycorish Community School)

Conclusion

Next to the issue of authority, ability differentiation and academic pressure emerged from the essays as the most important equality theme (Table 2). Students perceived the ability-differentiated treatment of pupils in class to be a particular cause of inequality. Those allocated to low streams or bands voiced an especially strong sense of unequal treatment in such classes, while others complained of unfair treatment of academically less able students in mixed classes. Not surprisingly perhaps, high-stream/band pupils were supportive of an ability-differentiated grouping system.

That students identified ability grouping and ability differentiation as equality concerns highlights the extent to which one's academic identity is a defining element in one's educational experience. Unfair treatment in these areas is regarded as having serious consequences for students in school socially, personally and academically. Hence the widespread concern.

What is more surprising perhaps is the sense of injustice which students expressed about academic pressures in schools. What emerged here from the essays and focus groups (and this occurred in relation to ability grouping as well) is a sense of resentment about a system over which students had little control but to which they were subject nonetheless. The issue of authority and power also arose here. Many students seemed to be caught between two sets of equally high expectations, those of their school and those of their parents. While some had internalised parents' and teachers' ambitions, others had not. There was a sense of resentment and resistance to parent and school expectations among a number of those interviewed. They expressed concerns about being controlled and managed by adults, often without much regard for their personal cares or ambitions. This sense of frustration that emerged from being the focus of both parental and school ambitions found expression in the strong critique of the authority structures of schools in particular. As the study was not concerned with parents per se, we cannot determine what students' views were on the exercise of authority in families.

GENDER AND EQUALITY

A number of themes emerged from the student essays about gender issues in schools; these included general concerns about unequal treatment on the basis of gender, criticism of gender-related controls and sanctions and interest/concerns about co-education. While gender was identified as a source of inequality by 22% of the students in St Ita's (a co-educational fee-paying school), there were only two other schools, St Patrick's (a girl's school) and Ollan Community College, where concerns about gender inequality emerged spontaneously in more than 10% of the essays. Gender-related inequalities were scarcely mentioned at all in the four boys' schools. Interestingly, these were the schools in which there was the greatest interest in having co-education introduced (Table 3).

Given the nature of the essays, however, one must exercise care in interpreting this relatively low level of concern with gender issues; gender-related inequalities emerged as an important issue in a number of the focus groups, which are not the subject of this chapter. What is evident is that there is considerable variability in attitudes and concerns about gender issues across schools.

GIRLS' SCHOOLS

Academic Achievement and Stress

There were a number of notable differences between single-sex girls' and boys' schools. Stress and control were prominent issues in the essays from girls' schools but not in the boys' essays. Achievement, in terms of examination results and the attainment of college places, was perceived by female pupils to be very important in their schools. This ambition was not always internalised by the pupils; but in cases where they perceived themselves to be unambitious, girls reported feeling that they were not liked by teachers because they lacked academic ambition. These concerns did not emerge to any great extent in the boys' schools.

> 'They don't care what's happening to us. All they care about is the grades. They compare everyone's leaving cert. grades. They have compared this year's leaving cert. grades to last year's. They put a lot of pressure on us. [They don't] care about us, they just care about the school's name.' (A fifth year student in Our Lady's)

Surveillance and Control

Competitive individualism was therefore a strongly approved value in girls' schools, while it was complemented by an equally strong focus on the development of the traditional feminine characteristics of nurture and artistic expression. Subject choices, as well as extra-curricular activities, provided in girls' schools were largely in the traditional mode (music, drama, debating/ public speaking, girl-specific sports). Observation during our visits to the schools showed that assertive or challenging behaviour was sanctioned in all of the girls' schools, while nurturing and traditional feminine behaviour (defined unspecifically as being 'ladylike') was identified as the school's ideal. In each of the girls' schools, girls claimed (at focus group interviews) that the traditional nurturing role of women (as the primary carers in society) was represented as an ideal one for women in their school.

Perceived high levels of control of appearance and behaviour were also reported by pupils in single-sex girls' schools. Uniform regulations were regarded as intrusive and fastidious. Many girls felt that their personal lives and their bodies were being 'policed' in the school. None of these themes emerged in the boys' schools.

> 'And girls shouldn't have to wear a skirt. It's sexist, in school especially where we should be learning that we are equal to fellows. . . . It's also unfair how girls' schools have to do choir and singing. . . . And I hate when we hear how we should act like young ladies and tie back our hair.' (A third year student in Our Lady's)

> 'Two of the rules should be changed, that we can only wear one ring and we should only wear our school coats. (1) Our school coats are too cold and don't keep you warm. (2) We are not going to wear about five rings on each finger — about three small ones would do.' (A second year student in St Cecilia's)

There was also reporting that the school was attempting to control students' behaviour and appearance outside of school.

'I was unfairly treated when my principal called me up to the office, telling me that the crowd I am hanging around with outside of school are taking drugs. She also told me that I shouldn't be hanging around with them, even outside of school.' (A third year student in St Cecilia's)

In one school, rumours circulated among pupils about attempts by the school principal to control girls' social lives. Whether these claims were valid or not is another matter; nonetheless they were widely believed by the students:

'She [the principal] tells our parents that we shouldn't be allowed out to discos and she said that when the disco is on she will drive around town and pick up any girls from this school and bring them home.' (A second year student in a girls' school)

Yet some girls internalised the rules and approved of the controls:

'I think that this school is fair and equal. If you work well and put effort in and abide by the rules, life is easy. You are treated by the way you behave which I think is fair.' (A sixth year student in St Peter's)

'I think everyone in this school is given the same opportunities. It is whether or not they avail of them. It could not be made more fair and equal in my opinion.' (A sixth year student in St Cecilia's)

BOYS' SCHOOLS

Masculinity and Sport

Physical strength and sporting ability were highly prized in the four boys' schools. The equation of superior masculinity with physical prowess and sport was particularly evident in the schools where sporting success was central to the school's sense of identity, namely St David's (rugby) and Dunely (hurling). Many students in these schools believed that there was an institutional bias in favour of pupils who excel on the sports field.

'There is one person [a rugby-playing peer] here who thinks he is hard and everybody thinks the sun shines out of his hole. Nobody can touch him even though he is as thick as a brick and unfunny. He beat me up and I couldn't do anything about it.' (A third year student in St David's)

'I get on well in my school, although when I came here first and to this day, teachers and principals discriminate against students who are not interested in sport especially HURLING.' (A fifth year student in Dunely)

'I hate this school. Nobody likes you (adults, teachers, school management) unless you are on the rugby squad. The adults think that you haven't got a hope and you're a slacker unless you are a super-clever person or you're on a rugby team. This is wrong and it should be changed.' (A third year student in St David's)

Peer Policing of the Body

The boys' schools generally gave their students latitude to manage their appearance and behaviour as they saw fit. They did not attempt to control and sanction students' appearance or behaviour to the same extent as girls' schools. However, the peer group took a strong sanctioning and controlling role in a way that was not evident in girls' schools.

> '[I'm] not really accepted by everyone because I'm not that good at sports. For some reason, people often say derogatory comments to my face. I don't know why. But I still get on with my life.' (A fourth year student in St David's)

> 'Because of my thin build, I have been bullied in the past which led to low self-confidence and often being looked down on by other physically bigger students.' (A sixth year student in Ballinroe secondary school)

> 'I have been teased since I came to the school about my size. I am generally small for my age and comments such as "a speck of dust is like a mountain to you" have been made. I have never actually been bullied physically but the teasing has sometimes gotten to me.' (A third year student in Dunely)

> 'When I came to this school some pupils started calling me fat. But I have got on with some of the pupils but still other pupils are pushing me around and still calling me fat.' (A first year student in St Dominic's)

Toughness was highly prized (and expected) in the boys' school with a predominantly working-class intake.

> '. . . I am a blue belt in Tae Kwon Do, that is a sort of self-defence. Sometimes I don't want to defend myself in case it ends up in a fight [with a peer in the school yard]. But the thing that is not fair is because if I am in a fight the teacher takes the two of us into a classroom.' (A first year student in St Dominic's)

CO-EDUCATIONAL SCHOOLS

Awareness of Gender Differentiation in Co-educational Schools

Co-educational second-level schools in Ireland tend to be very diverse in character. The vocational schools and community colleges have traditionally catered for a relatively large proportion of lower-middle-class and working-class students; these schools are radically different from the fee-paying co-educational schools which are predominantly upper-middle-class in intake; community/comprehensive schools, and co-educational free scheme secondary schools, tend to have a more heterogeneous social class intake than the other two. The four co-educational schools chosen for this study represent these different traditions and were therefore quite distinctive. Attitudes to gender issues varied considerably across these school types.

Awareness of gender equality issues and perceptions of gender bias were highest in the fee-paying school (St Ita's), particularly among the girls. Here, the main focus of concern was sport and many female students were indignant at the perceived institutional bias in favour of traditional male sports.

> 'Girls are treated as less important in this school, and [named teacher] here doesn't seem to care. The girls' . . . team won the whole tournament, and a huge big trophy and all, but the principal just said one small thing about that but when the boys' . . . team win one match it's headline news for weeks.' (A first year girl in St Ita's)

Physical education was gender-segregated in this school. Female students viewed the activities provided for the girls as boring and inferior.

> 'Girls and boys should have p.e. together maybe every two weeks. This is a co-ed school. The boys always play [field games] while the girls do gymnastics, which isn't fair.' (A second year girl in St Ita's)

Individual boys in this school were also aware of gender equality issues as they affected them.

> 'Girls are often seen as having to play a very feminine role, boys are often seen as having to play a very masculine role. I don't like this.' (A second year boy in St Ita's)

> [Following a row with a teacher] 'I felt like crying so I stormed out of the classroom and tried to get up to the principal's office. But I was told by Mr . . . to be a man and not to cry.' (A second year boy in St Ita's)

In other co-educational schools, there was not the same level of awareness of gender issues. Although individual pupils raised issues, such as perceived harsher punishments for male than female students, these were not major themes.

> 'I came in about two minutes late for . . . [male teacher's] class and he gave out to me and he made me stand up for the whole class. Then two

girls came in about five minutes after me and he said to them "hurry up".'
(A first year boy in Ollan Community College)

Individual senior girls were aware of traditional, stereotypical views held by
teachers, but once again, this was the exception rather than the rule.

'The principal only asks the boys to help in carrying chairs for example.
What really gets me fuming is when we're having a debate or a quiz, the
teacher usually asks the boys all the sports questions and the girls the
gossip questions.' (A fifth year female student in Ballydara Community
College)

'We have a male teacher who is very sexist towards girls in the class. He
told us we were useless and that the boys should have more chance to
develop their skills than us (even though we've never done that subject
before). He hardly ever calls us by our names (he says 'Girl' or 'Woman').
He says he is only messing with us and he probably is but I still find it very
downgrading.' (A fourth year student in Ollan Community College)

'While picking subjects to take at junior cert level, I wanted to do
Mechanical Drawing. However, some boys decided they also wanted to
do this but there wasn't enough places in the class. Myself and three other
girls were then discouraged from doing the subject by our guidance
counsellor. We then had to pick another subject. I had to do Art which I
wasn't very interested in and the boys got to do Mechanical Drawing.' (A
sixth year student in Ballycorish Community School)

One of the interesting findings from the essays (and focus groups) was the
extent to which what could clearly be defined as sexist practices and procedures
went largely unnoticed or disregarded by students. Gender inequality was not
part of most students' daily vocabulary-of-analysis. Students often seemed to
lack both the language and the general awareness to articulate concerns about
gender issues. There was also a sense, in some of the co-educational schools for
example, in which sexist behaviour was considered 'normal'.

In one school, for instance, senior boys regularly lined narrow school
corridors while waiting for their next class and touched passing female pupils
and younger female teachers. What was evidently a form of sexual harassment
for both female students and teachers was not noticed, or if noticed condoned.
The researcher both witnessed and experienced this. Yet no female students at
this school raised the issue in their essays. When the researcher brought up the
issue with senior pupils at focus group interviews, the girls did not make any
comment about it. Senior male students saw it as a 'bit of fun', something
'harmless'. However, for both less established female teachers and female and
junior students, the experience was described by one person as 'running the
gauntlet'.

In Ballycorish Community School one of the researchers attended the school prize-giving. It was noted that prizes went disproportionately to male students, and this was a pattern over a number of years. While staff were already aware of this and had concerns about it, students did not comment on it at all in essays or interviews.[1]

What might be regarded as standard educational practice in a co-educational school was seen by some students as something of a breakthrough in gender relations:

> 'Students are treated equally in some cases. In this school, it's great that teachers encourage you to do a subject that you like such as a girl doing metalwork and a boy doing Home Economics, despite their sex!' (A sixth year girl in Ballycorish Community School)

SILENCE ON SEXISM

In two of the schools in the study the attitudes expressed by some junior and senior male students towards female teachers and female peers were overtly sexist. The behaviour of certain male students reflected these attitudes. In both schools, there were complaints to the researcher from female members of staff about the negative, sexist behaviour of male pupils and also of some male colleagues. The following is an example of the type of comment which was made by certain male students in their essays:

> 'Get rid of women teachers who look like Demi Moore and go around with mini-skirts up to their ass and big breasts which would knock Mike Tyson out. These women teachers come down to our desk and throw themselves across you. Rubbing against you. The next time she comes down to me and does that again I will get up and pin her to the wall and . . . It is extremely difficult to concentrate and do your study. Please don't take offence at this but it is true. Don't even think of coming looking for me because I would find it very embarrassing. Thank you.' (A fifth year student in a secondary boys' school)

There was no evidence of sanctioning of overt sexist behaviour by male pupils in these two schools. In fact, female teachers claimed that certain male teachers were overtly sexist in their behaviour towards female colleagues as well.[2] In one co-educational school, female students complained that certain male teachers' behaviour was sufficiently unpleasant and antagonistic to women to either prevent them choosing traditional male subjects, or to cause them to transfer from those subjects.

Unsolicited attention by male teachers to female colleagues, such as 'eyeing them up and down', making comments about clothing, legs, sexual appearance, and a feeling by a female vice-principal of 'being shunned' by a clique of male teachers, which included the school principal, were all reported in one of the co-educational schools. Interestingly, the only written complaint about unfair gender-related treatment in the school in question came from a junior male student in the school who noted that he got bullied by some of the older boys on the corridor.

Conclusion

The gender equality themes which emerged in the essays varied between school types. Although the boys' schools in the study were selected to match the girls' schools as closely as possible in social and academic profile, regional location and size, the high level of emphasis on academic achievement which was present in each of the girls' schools (and especially in Our Lady's) was unparalleled in the boys' schools. The net outcome of this concentration of effort and energy was the development of a reportedly high-stress school environment. This is a finding which confirms the research findings of Hannan, Smyth et al. (1996).

Not only were girls in all-girls' schools experiencing strong organisational expectations[3] to achieve well, these were the schools in which the highest level of sanctioning and control of social and dress behaviour was reported. In one school, girls referred to the fact that they were 'under surveillance' all the time, while in another all-girls' school, visiting students from Germany who had been on exchange there, said the system of control in operation reminded them of a prison. The girls who reported their concerns about surveillance and control in essays and focus groups regarded these as gender equality issues because they felt that such controls were imposed on them primarily because they were girls; they felt that boys were not subjected to the same levels of control. It is interesting that the girls reported concerns about stress and control as an equality issue in their essays. They believed that parents and teachers collaborated in this system, which was designed to ensure their educational and social conformity and obedience.

It should be noted, however, that many girls in the all-girls' schools had internalised norms of achievement, self-control and self-discipline. If they were in a position to achieve and conform at the expected level to the prevailing norms, they were quite happy in school.

Strict obedience, and conformity to codes of dress and behaviour, were not expected to the same degree in the boys' schools. Boys were not being socialised to be self-policing about their dress and personal behaviour in the same way that girls were. Neither were the same high levels of academically related stress reported in the boys' schools. In fact, as can be seen from Table 3, very few boys (none at all in two schools) reported in essays that they were treated unequally by the school because of their gender. This is not to say that boys are not socialised into certain stereotypical roles in boys' schools, however; it is merely to say that boys do not *perceive* themselves to be treated unfairly or unequally on gender grounds.

What was present in the boys' schools, however, was a strong *peer* code about height, body size and sporting prowess. Being physically strong and fit was a mark of status. Boys who were thin and/or small were negatively sanctioned by their peers through jokes, and even bullying. Masculinity was strongly equated in each of the boys' schools (by the boys themselves) with various forms of physical prowess. While there were some exceptions to this, both within and between schools, the equation of masculinity with physical strength, height and sporting ability was the dominant theme.

It should be noted, however, that the teaching staff in at least two of the boys' schools were proactively involved in counteracting the hegemony of the 'masculinity = strength' peer group code, through educational and personal programmes. These adult-initiated programmes did not appear to have altered the dominant peer group code to any significant degree.

The findings here in relation to the core peer norms in boys' schools and the organisational culture of girls' schools confirm earlier findings by Lynch (1989) on the hidden curriculum of schools. They suggest that the organisational culture of girls' single-sex schools may not have changed much in recent years, although now there appears to be an even stronger emphasis on academic achievement. Neither have the peer group values of boys changed in terms of how they define masculinity.

There was considerable variability across the four co-educational schools in terms of the manner in which gender issues emerged. While girls in the fee-paying school expressed concerns about their lack of equal status with boys in the school, this theme did not emerge spontaneously in the essays from the other three schools to the same degree. Less than 16% of the students in the other three schools actually complained of specific gender inequalities in their schools. This is in spite of the fact that quite overtly sexist practices occurred in one of these schools. The fact that senior school staff were not aware of this as an issue until our findings were presented also indicates how limited the awareness of gender issues is in some schools.

SOCIAL CLASS AND INEQUALITY

Irish second-level schools are largely socially self-stratifying. Parents with access to sufficient income can, and do, send their children to schools of their choice. Those with access to private transport can take their children to a school outside their own area. Those without private transport and money must rely on local provision, or on what is accessible via the public transport system. Families in the upper income bracket can avail of either fee-paying day schools (especially in Dublin) or boarding schools. In a society in which there are still major differences in wealth and incomes (Callan, Nolan et al., 1996), what this means, in effect, is that those who have resources can exercise choices and those without resources generally cannot, or have relatively restricted choices depending on the area they live in. If society lacked major differences in levels of income and wealth, then equality of choice would exist for all; when it does not, then choice truly exists only for those with the resources to exercise it.

It is not only the resources of parents which affect entry patterns but the tradition, and the social and academic identity, of the school. Secondary schools which had traditionally been selective, either in terms of academic ability or in terms of fees (prior to the free scheme), retain an image in many towns and cities of being socially exclusive. People lack a sense of ownership of such educational institutions even though they have the formal right to attend them (Lynch and O'Riordan, 1996).

Three of the schools in the study had been involved at different times in selecting on the basis of academic attainment. Both staff and students in these schools noted that although they were now non-selective free scheme secondary schools, the perception among many local people was that they were still designed to cater for a more socially select and academically oriented intake. The perceived identity of the school would, they believed, discourage certain low-income parents from applying to them. One of the community colleges in the study had the opposite identity problem. It had been the only non-selective school in a medium-sized town for over thirty years; it was therefore identified in the public mind as being neither socially nor academically select. The principal and staff here claimed that many people (from middle- and upper-income groups especially) would not send their children there because of its historical identity. This was the case despite the massive expansion of the school in terms of both student intake and its academic and extra-curricular achievements.

A third factor which affected school choice was the presence/absence of the voluntary contribution. This was an issue in the 'free scheme' secondary schools only.[4] While payment of the voluntary contribution is obviously not a requirement for entry to the free scheme sector, teachers pointed out that it operated as an indirect access barrier for some parents who felt they may not be able to meet the request. Certain parents would feel that their child would be disadvantaged in a school if they could not pay the voluntary contribution; they would opt instead to send them to schools where no voluntary contribution was required. The net outcome of this is greater social selectivity *between* schools even in the non-fee-paying sector.

While it is self-evident that fee-paying schools are socially and (in some cases) academically selective, the latent historical identity of other schools also affects their intake. Not only did parents exercise choice on the basis of available resources therefore, but they exercised it on the basis of the perceived identity of the school. Teachers pointed out in interviews that many parents wanted children to 'feel at home' in the school; when they had a choice, they chose schools which were not only educationally suitable but perceived to be socially suitable. The net effect of this rather complicated process of educational choice was that there was a relatively high level of social class homogeneity *within* schools. Our statistical data on the social class background of pupils will provide more information on this issue, but it is evident that social class differences between schools were more distinctive than differences within schools, especially at the more extreme ends of the social class continuum.

Given the way in which students were selected into schools, it is not very surprising therefore that there was relatively little evidence of articulated social class tension within schools. Where complaints were made, they related mainly to perceived better treatment of pupils from higher social class backgrounds, or of those whose parents were known to be of higher social status. The term 'social class' was not part of their vocabulary-of-analysis, however. Students from low-income and working-class backgrounds generally named social class differences in terms of others who 'were posh', or who had 'rich' parents, or 'snobs'. Middle-class students (in towns and cities), on the other hand, referred to the fact that they lived in a 'good area' and that others were 'rough'. In one of the fee-paying schools, students referred to students from a community college (with whom they happened to be debating) as 'knackers'; a student in a private housing estate referred to her neighbourhood as a 'good area'. They did not go so far as to say that the public housing estate was a 'bad area' but that was clearly the implication.

> '[A] lot of students get treated better if their parents are richer or have more important jobs. Like some students get treated better because they have teachers as parents.' (A fifth year student in Ballycorish Community School)

> 'I think that students should be treated equally regardless of their family or social background. In my school, students whose parents are teachers in the school are given more attention and encouragement. In class, when the teacher is explaining something he/she looks directly at them as if there was no one else present. They never seem to get anything wrong and when they occasionally do the teacher tries to cover it up and makes excuses for them. Students who come from a poor social background are not treated with as much respect.' (A sixth year student in Ballycorish Community School)

Some students from low-income backgrounds felt that they had to prove themselves before they were accepted as being equal to others:

'I am now in fifth year and from first year I have made a bad name for myself and I think this is because I'm not as posh as my school mates. Every time something happens teachers seem to point the finger. I am working hard but still I am feeling left out with some teachers.' (A fifth year student from a relatively low-income background in St Ita's)

'One girl accused me of bullying her and because she was very rich, they believed her and they wouldn't believe me and I hadn't actually done anything so that all went on my records.' (A second year girl from a relatively low-income background in St Cecilia's)

One of the schools in which there was most awareness of relative social class difference was St Peter's (a girls' school designated disadvantaged). This school had a sizeable minority of students bussed in from an outlying suburb which had high unemployment. The local students, who were slightly better off, and the bussed-in students had not gelled into a unit.

'Some of the students are prejudiced against others. Say one person from our class who lives in . . . [local area] thinks she is brilliant and that people from . . . [outlying suburb] are poor. Which is not true. She is a snobby cow. She is always telling people they are poor because they don't have a new school jumper, etc.' (A third year student bussed in to St Peter's)

'I feel that other pupils are jealous of me because I'm very good at school and come from a good area. They sometimes take it out on me maybe because they're bored or bitter.' (A third year student in St Peter's from a nearby middle-class area)

Social distinctions within and between schools, arising from differences of income and status, are often very subtle. While it is obviously impolite to refer to others as one's social inferiors, many students in the study had a clear perception of themselves as socially superior to others. This was especially evident in the fee-paying schools where students displayed keen awareness of their own privileged social class position. A number saw their schools as exclusionary social devices which enabled their parents to select socially acceptable peers for them.[5] These students were more likely than others to view their teachers in a servicing role.

'Teachers should really obey pupils especially in a fee-paying school.' (A third year student in St David's)

'This school needs a lot of updating. The teachers treat us all right but they still are quite above us. They need to treat us as young ladies, not little girls.' (A fourth year student in St Cecilia's)

'You should not have to pay so much for an education where the teachers do nothing at all — they talk and talk but they do not describe what they're doing and frankly they do not deserve a salary.' (A second year student in St David's)

Students in free scheme schools and in community schools and colleges were less class-conscious than those in fee-paying schools. There was less discussion of class difference in the focus groups. There were some exceptions to this, however. One of the schools (St Dominic's) was based in an inner-city area where there was a high level of social exclusion and unemployment. Another (St Peter's) drew most of its students from large public housing estates in the city suburbs where there was high unemployment. The school itself was located in a mixed neighbourhood of public and private housing. In the focus groups, students in these schools expressed concern about the potential prejudices people from outside their areas might hold against them because of their address. They also noted how their relative social class disadvantage was evident when they had direct contact with more socially selective schools in sport or debating.

'In debates with other schools no matter how good or how much effort you put in, the other school will always win if they have a certain name or accent. Especially the private schools. They are expected to be of a higher standard, so naturally they come out on top.' (A sixth year student in St Peter's)

Students in schools which had a predominantly lower-middle-class and working-class intake also commented on the confidence differential between themselves and their opponents from predominantly middle-class schools, when they met for debates and sporting competitions. They felt they lacked the confidence (but not the competence) of their fee-paying competitors in particular.[6] Some students also felt that students from 'wealthier schools' were biased against them because of their less privileged social backgrounds.

Conclusion

The fact that parents can send their children to a school of their choice, provided they have the resources or the transport to exercise that choice, means that social-class-related stratification between Irish second-level schools is more evident than social stratification within schools. While there were relatively few reports of social-class-related tensions within schools, there were tensions arising from relatively minor class differences. A content analysis of student essays across the twelve schools, for example, found that just 4% of students spontaneously mentioned social-class-related issues as causes or contexts for unfair or unequal treatment within any given school (Table 4). Caution must be exercised, however, in interpreting these findings. Irish second-level students would have relatively little experience of reporting on social-class-related inequalities in schools (there has never been a major study, for example, or major debates on class biases in the curriculum; or on how social class impacts on classroom interactions; or on whether teacher attitudes to working-class and middle-class students differ, etc., as have occurred in other countries) so there has been no context in which a public debate about in-school inequalities arising from social class could take place. Many students would lack the vocabulary-of-analysis to explore social class issues in schooling.

However, from the focus group discussions, it was clear that students in disadvantaged schools and in fee-paying schools (especially the latter) were aware of social class differences between themselves and others, and could articulate these clearly. Students in the fee-paying sector were especially direct in naming themselves and their schools as socially superior to others.

SEXUAL ORIENTATION

The issue of sexual orientation was raised spontaneously in only nine of the twelve hundred essays as a cause of unequal treatment in schools. This is not to suggest that sexual orientation is not a sensitive or important subject in schools, but merely to point out that it was a subject on which there was great silence.

When the subject emerged in the focus groups, it caused a lot of discomfort and unease among both junior and senior pupils in general. There was very limited awareness among students about sexual differences, although high levels of hostility and fear were reported by boys towards gay males in particular.

> 'Set all fags on fire.' (A second year student in Ballinroe secondary school)

> 'Gays should not be allowed to be educated. They have a perverted problem.' (A third year student in St David's)

> 'Mr . . . has a problem with me but maybe that's because I have a problem with him, he is GAY! He is always poking me and I think he is bent.' (A third year student in Ballinroe secondary school)

Being gay was also perceived as a disorder by some:

> 'I think this school should be made a co-education [school] for the sake of the students already attending. For I'd say of the students that don't really mix outside they probably end up *gay*.' (A third year student in St David's)

And teasing and bullying among boys sometimes centred on labelling as gay.

'Sometimes out in the yard, I don't like it when people call me names or say I'm gay.' (A first year student in St Dominic's)

In single-sex girls' schools, there were varying levels of unease and nervousness around the issue of lesbianism. Articulated hostility towards lesbian women was not as great, however, among female students as was hostility towards gay men among male students. Within co-educational schools, the gender differences in attitudes notable between single-sex schools also prevailed.

Students were generally not accustomed to addressing the subject of sexual orientation, so they literally did not know what to say or how to say what they did feel or know. It was notable, however, that where an individual teacher or a specific school programme had addressed the issue, as had occurred in St Peter's and St David's, students in focus groups were better able to examine their own ambiguous feelings and fears. A proactive approach by their school or teacher was judged by them to have helped to create a space in which this aspect of sexuality could be explored. This same approach was regarded by a senior male student in St Ita's as vital to encourage understanding in all schools.

'[There is a need for] mass education about the normality and accept-ability of homosexuality. There is a huge lack in sex education in school [on this subject].' (A sixth year student in St Ita's)

Conclusion

Sexual orientation was a subject on which there was great silence in the schools. While at least one boys' and one girls' school had addressed the theme specifically in their personal development programmes, most students displayed visible discomfort and unease if the subject arose in the focus groups. Many students seemed to lack a vocabulary to name their feelings and views on the subject of sexual differences. The only views which boys especially felt comfortable expressing were those of hostility and derision.

DISABILITY ISSUES

Most pupils had very little direct contact with anyone who had a disability. Where there was a disabled pupil in the school, that individual tended to be either the only person or one of a very small number in that institution with a disability. Most disabilities reported by school principals were either mobility- or sight-related. There were, however, a small number of individuals who reported having learning difficulties to the researcher in the course of filling out the questionnaire. These pupils did not consider themselves to have a disability.

Pupils did not express direct negative attitudes towards persons with disabilities. However, those who had little previous contact with disabled students defined them as deserving 'sympathy' and being 'in need of care'. Attitudes to disability therefore reflected assumptions about the 'dependency' of disabled people, combined with a view that having an impairment was some type of 'tragedy' deserving sympathy. The normality of impairments was not visibly part of students' awareness.

Where students had had some opportunity to mix on equal terms with disabled students in their school, there was some evidence of a basic rights perspective on disability issues. Students expressed concern about the unsuitability of their school buildings (and in one case of the pushing on crowded corridors and stairs) for a person with a mobility-related impairment. Where pupils had direct contact with a person with a disability in their class, or as a member of their friendship group, they did not describe that individual in terms of their 'helplessness', or with a sense of pity.

> 'There could be better facilities for the handicapped pupil such as a lift so he can get upstairs instead of being stuck downstairs all the time.' (A fourth year student in St David's)

> 'More facilities should be provided for the disabled people and extra time between classes so they can get to class on time.' (A sixth year student in St Cecilia's)

Conclusion

Overall, disability was a very minor equality theme in essays with only ten students naming it as an issue spontaneously. This does not suggest that disability-related inequalities are not important in and of themselves; rather it suggests that disability issues had not arisen for the students. The fact that there were so few disabled students in the schools ensured that there was little awareness of disability-related inequalities in schools.

The dominant attitude to disabled students, expressed in both the discussions and the essays, was one of ignorance combined with pity. Of those who expressed a view, most felt that disabled students would be dependent and in need of care. There were only a few individual students who were aware of the educational rights of disabled students.

RACE, ETHNICITY AND TRAVELLERS

Only a small number of students (N = 20) raised the issue of race or ethnicity as a source of inequality in schools. Given the fact that Irish schools are so homogeneous in ethnic and racial terms, this is not surprising. The largest ethnic minority are the Travellers, and as most Travellers do not transfer to mainstream second-level education it is not possible to examine their experiences in schools in a general study of this nature. What did emerge, however, particularly in discussion groups, was a clear expression of settled students' views on Travellers.

Attitudes to Travellers

High levels of prejudice towards Travellers were encountered across most of the schools in discussions following on from the essays. Pupils expressed fear, resentment and mockery. In some cases, mockery of a particular area or location was related to the fact that some of the people who lived there were Travellers. In general, Travellers were regarded as 'undeserving' and unacceptable to the majority.

> 'Travellers should not be allowed to collect dole because they abuse it and they are not really Travellers, they stay in the same place.' (A third year student in St David's)

> 'I think because this school is quite snobbish there are inequalities, which are a result of students' attitudes. . . . For example, although I myself wouldn't have anything against a Traveller coming to this school, I think she would get a hard time due to a large number of snobs in the school.' (A sixth year student in St Cecilia's)

Where positive attitudes were expressed, these tended to be held by individuals who had previous or ongoing positive contact with Travellers (as neighbours or as school friends in their primary schools). Some of the most noticeably positive attitudes expressed by individuals were in towns or places where a proactive approach had been taken in a locality to increase understanding and acceptance between Travellers and settled people.

Other Ethnic Minorities

In most of the schools involved in the project, students had negligible contact with ethnic minorities. One rural school was involved in a cultural exchange with two African teachers at the time the research was taking place there. This was the first contact the majority of those pupils had ever had with people from other cultures. In a number of other schools there were a tiny minority of pupils whose families had come to Ireland as refugees.

Most students therefore had only limited contact with the odd individual who was ethnically different, consequently it was difficult to assess their attitudes to people who were racially different. Cultural homogeneity also meant that there were relatively few students in the study who came from minority groups. Of those who did, however, a number found Irish students to be quite racist.

'I am originally English so when I arrived in this country I got some abuse because of my accent. I am also quite dark-skinned, so in this country it pertains to being a "nigger".' (A fifth year student in Ballinroe secondary school)

Conclusion

The lack of any sizeable ethnic minority in most schools meant that there was no real test of students' behaviour and attitudes towards racial and ethnic minorities. Attitudes towards Travellers were often negative although there were not sufficient Travellers in any of the schools (and unfortunately none in the classes studied) to determine if they experienced inequality of treatment in schools.

RELIGIOUS DIFFERENTIATION

Most Irish schools are relatively homogeneous in religious terms, so it is difficult to determine whether or not students would experience religious prejudice or discrimination if they were from a minority religion. The limited evidence available from the study, however, is not that encouraging.

In one school, with a large rural intake, junior pupils expressed worry about their ability to understand or be 'close to' a peer with a different religious affiliation. When probed, this appeared to be based on complete lack of contact with members of other religious denominations. They simply said they did not know if they could cope with difference as they had no experience of it.

In another school, some students felt isolated by their peers because of their religious beliefs and morals.

'The students are very cold to you if you are smart and you don't do drugs or smoke or drink when you go out. They have problems with you if you have ANY morals or religion about your life.' (A fifth year student in St Ita's)

A predominantly Roman Catholic school had a small minority of students from a minority Protestant religion. Although there was no overt tension or division between pupils in the school based on religion, students were aware of the family religious affiliation of their peers because it was a close-knit rural area. There was silence about the issue of religion and religious differences, although everyone recognised that they existed. There were no complaints about religious discrimination in this school, but there was in another one.

'I am a Protestant and I am in a Catholic school. The other pupils do not understand me and give me a hard time. My last year's religion teacher nearly had a heart attack when she/he discovered my religion, she/he began to treat me more like I was above the class. I received a lot more attention than other class members and the class naturally assumed I was a lick. They threatened me with threats like I'll send the IRA to your gaff. Now they are only slightly better.' (A third year student in Ballinroe secondary school)

SECTION 3: SUMMARY AND CONCLUSION

Theme 1: The Exercise of Authority and the Demand for Greater Democracy by Young People in Schools

The perceived misuse of power and authority by adults in schools was the equality theme which emerged most strongly from student essays and interviews. When one takes account of the fact that the student essays were spontaneously composed, this is an important finding.

Students' principal equality concerns related to perceived or unequal treatment by school staff: 48% identified specific incidents and contexts in which they felt they had been unfairly or unequally treated. Students attributed this unfairness and unequal treatment to the way in which power and authority was exercised in schools and the lack of respect for young people by adults. There were strong complaints in all schools about the lack of democratic procedures, particularly those of a participatory and consultative nature, which would forestall some of the conflicts about authority in schools. Almost half of the 1,200 students called for more democracy and greater equality of respect for students in the ways that schools are organised. When we examined the material from the focus groups in conjunction with the essay material, the concern about authority emerged even more strongly.

What is clear is that there is a groundswell of opinion among students in second-level schools in favour of the democratisation of school structures. Many students currently feel that the exercise of power and authority in schools has failed to keep pace with the democratisation of structures in families, and in other public institutions where participation by, and consultation with, 'client groups' has become common practice. They feel that they are treated with limited respect simply because they are young.

Theme 2: Academic Differentiation and Ability Grouping

Next to the question of authority, the theme of ability and ability grouping was the most frequently cited equality concern among the students. Students were keenly aware of the academic labels and their implications for their educational future, as well as their social and personal identity in schools. They monitored any changes in grouping with a keen eye, and were highly sensitive to any designations or changes in grouping practices which signified a demotion or negative labelling. Not surprisingly, it was those in the lowest streams and bands, and those who felt they were labelled as 'weak' in mixed situations, who deemed the grouping and grading system to be most unfair. In all, just under one-fifth of all students raised equality concerns about the ways in which students were treated in different ability groups or within mixed groups because of their perceived abilities.

The spontaneous identification of ability grouping and/or ability labelling as an equality issue shows how students' equality concerns are not synonymous with those of adult educationalists or academic researchers. Students were aware that schools mediate privilege/disadvantage by stratifying them for a hierarchically organised labour market. They were conscious of the inequalities in opportunity which arose from ability classification, and they wanted a right to intervene or challenge these at times.

Theme 3: Gender Equality Issues

A number of themes emerged from the student essays about gender issues in schools; these included general concerns about unequal treatment on the basis of gender, criticism of gender-related controls and sanctions, and interest/concerns about co-education. By comparison with the interest in issues of authority and ability grouping and labelling, interest in gender was low, especially among boys. However, it is clear that girls, especially in all-girls' schools, regard the levels of control and surveillance which are sometimes imposed on them in some schools as being gender-specific. They felt that the controls were imposed on them primarily because they were girls. They believed that parents and teachers collaborated in this system which was designed to ensure their educational and social conformity and obedience. The higher levels of surveillance and control in girls' schools was also associated with reports of stress and tension over work (Hannan, Smyth et al., 1996). It should be noted, however, that many girls in the all-girls' schools had internalised norms of achievement, self-control and self-discipline, so for these there was no sense of being imposed upon by others.

Strong conformity to codes of dress and behaviour was not expected to the same degree in the boys' schools. Neither were the same high levels of academically related stress reported. This is not to say that boys are not socialised into certain stereotypical roles in these schools, however; it is merely to say that boys do not *perceive* themselves to be treated unfairly or unequally on gender grounds.

Our own observations, and other data collected from the schools, indicate that gender is a very important equality issue, yet many students lack both an awareness of the issues and the vocabulary to articulate their concerns and their feelings. This was especially true in the co-educational schools, where gender emerged as a strong equality theme only in the essays written in the fee-paying school. Gender-related social exclusions, and overt sexual behaviour, were observed, yet these practices were not always named as issues in essays. The ability and willingness to name gender (and other) inequalities is undoubtedly a function of having the language to do so, and being in an environment that allows/encourages it.

Theme 4: Social Class and Inequality

Social class differences in Irish second-level schools are more evident between schools than within schools. The fact that parents can choose to send their children to a school of their choice, provided they have the resources or the transport to exercise that choice, means that social-class-related stratification *between* schools is more evident than social stratification *within* schools. We found relatively little evidence therefore of social-class-related tensions within schools, although there were tensions arising from relatively minor class differences. Students were aware, however, of social stratifications within and between schools and 4% of students in all complained of experiencing inequality in school because of their social class background.

As with the question of gender, caution must be exercised in interpreting this finding. Even more so perhaps than gender, social class is not a dominant theme in either popular public discourse or, more particularly, school discourse. In fact, there has never been a study focusing on social class differences in the treatment of students in classrooms per se in Ireland so there has been no context in which a debate could take place. Student silence on class issues, no less than their silence on other issues, may indicate as much the lack of an appropriate language as it does a lack of concern about social class.

What was clear from the focus groups, however, is that students at extreme ends of the social class spectrum (in disadvantaged and in fee-paying schools, especially in the latter) were aware of social class differences between schools, and between particular neighbourhoods. Students in the fee-paying sector were quite direct in naming themselves and their schools as socially superior to others.

Theme 5: Equality Issues Arising in Relation to Sexual Orientation, Disability, Race, Ethnicity and Religion

The fact that Irish schools are relatively homogeneous in terms of race, ethnicity, religion and disability means that there were only a very small number of students from these minority backgrounds in the study. It was difficult to determine therefore if being part of a particular minority group in terms of ethnicity, religion, etc. resulted in unequal treatment in schools. What limited evidence is available suggests that Irish students may not be that tolerant of differences especially when a minority *group* is involved, as opposed to just isolated individuals.

While students felt quite comfortable discussing issues such as disability or religion, they were very ill at ease with the subject of sexual orientation. Only nine students reported concerns regarding inequality on the basis of sexual orientation, yet when the subject was raised in discussion groups, it was clear that this was a very sensitive issue for students. It was also a subject on which there was great silence. There was very limited awareness among students as to whether any member of their peer group was lesbian, bisexual or gay, yet high levels of hostility and fear were reported by boys towards gay males in particular.

Hostility towards Travellers was also quite overt even though most of the students in the study had never attended schools with Travellers.

Overall there were high levels of ignorance among the students about peoples and groups who were different from themselves — be these differences related to disability, race, religion or sexual orientation. Where schools had introduced an education programme about different minorities, however, students displayed the most understanding and tolerance. This was especially noticeable in the attitudes towards Travellers and people who are lesbian or gay.

CONCLUDING COMMENTS

Research on equality in education has been based for many years on a 'distributive' model of social justice. It has been assumed that if a given group got greater access to different forms of education, and participated successfully within each level, then equality in education was being achieved. This was certainly the model which informed research on social-class-related disadvantage in education.

What has become clearer in recent years, however, is that working out of a distributive model of justice for the promotion of equality in education is necessary but not sufficient. While distributing more education to those groups who want it is crucial, it may also be necessary to change the education system itself to take account of the differences which various groups bring to that system. Schooling needs to recognise and respect difference if it is to treat all people with equality of respect. It cannot assume that all people will fit the one mould.

One of the most visible 'differences' in schools is the age and power difference between teachers and students. Yet this is a 'difference' which is not subjected to critical analysis as an equality issue in education. This is especially true in the empirical literature, where gender, social class, racial or ethnic differences are prioritised over age. This paper attempts to redress the balance.

It examines equality issues in schooling from the perspective of young people themselves. It shows how the view from below (young persons) is not the same as the view from outside (researchers) or the view from on top (adult teachers) in terms of equality priorities.

Most young people in Ireland spend fourteen years of their entire life in school. Almost half continue on their education for two or more years in higher education. This is a lengthy sojourn by any standards. The quality of the experience of schooling, *qua schooling*, matters, not just in terms of young people's future, but in terms of their present life. If schooling and education is an alienating and disrespectful experience, this is not only undesirable in terms of a lost opportunity for experiential democratic learning, it is undesirable because it is a negative experience in a formative period of a young person's life for a prolonged period of time. It shows a profound lack of respect for young people which passes on to the next generation. What is clear from this research is that young people are above all calling for the introduction of democratic institutions and systems in schools which show greater respect for them as individuals with views, wishes and ambitions which are not synonymous with those of adults.

REFERENCES

Archard, D. (1993). *Children: Rights and Childhood*. London: Routledge.

Callan, T., Nolan, B., et al. (1996). *Poverty in the 1990s: Evidence from the Living in Ireland Survey*. Dublin: Oak Tree Press.

Connell, R.W. (1993). *Schools and Social Justice*. Philadelphia: Temple University Press.

Cusick, P. (1973). *Inside High School: The Student's World*. New York: Holt, Rinehart and Winston.

Everhart, R.B. (1983). *Reading, Writing and Resistance: Adolescence and Labour in a Junior High School*. London: Routledge & Kegan Paul.

Freire, P. (1972). *Pedagogy of the Oppressed*. New York: Penguin.

Freire, P. (1973). *Education for Critical Consciousness*. New York: Continuum.

Giroux, H. (1983). *Theory and Resistance in Education: A Pedagogy for the Opposition*. Amherst: Bergin and Garvey Press.

Giroux, H. (1992). *Border Crossings*. New York: Routledge.

Hannan, D.F., Smyth, E., McCullagh, J., O'Leary, R., and McMahon, D. (1996). *Coeducation and Gender Equality: Exam Performance, Stress and Personal Development*. Dublin: Oak Tree Press.

Lynch, K. (1989). *The Hidden Curriculum: Reproduction in Education, A Reappraisal*. Lewes: Falmer Press.

Lynch, K., and O'Riordan, C. (1996). *Social Class, Inequality and Higher Education: Barriers to Equality of Access and Participation among School Leavers*. University College Dublin, Registrar's Office.

McLaren, P. (1995). *Critical Pedagogy and Predatory Culture*. New York: Routledge.

McRobbie, A. (1978). Working class girls and the culture of femininity. In Centre for Contemporary Cultural Studies Women's Studies Group, *Women Take Issue*. London: Hutchinson.

Willis, P. (1977). *Learning to Labour: How Working Class Kids Get Working Class Jobs*. Westmead, UK: Saxon House.

Notes

1 As certain prizes in this school such as 'best all-round student of the year' were largely based on popular vote, it was clear from the voting practices that girls were voting for boys for this prize ahead of girls. The reverse was not true of the boys.

2 This issue will be dealt with in more detail in a later publication.

3 They also received high levels of support from teachers, however. Indeed the teachers in these schools also reported themselves to be stressed and 'killing themselves to get good results'. The pressure for 'results' was not confined to the students.

4 Vocational, community and comprehensive schools and colleges cannot ask for such a contribution while the payment of fees precludes the need for a voluntary contribution in the fee-paying sector.

5 This was evident in the attitudes part of the study, which will be presented later in the analysis of quantitative data.

6 We had direct experience of this in the study as Ballydara Community College was involved during the study in a debating competition with St Ita's. The students in Ballydara spoke after the debate about the high level of confidence which St Ita's students displayed.

TABLES 1 TO 5: EQUALITY ISSUES EMERGING SPONTANEOUSLY IN ESSAYS

Table 1

Equality and the Exercise of
Authority and Power in Schools

School*	Description	Complaints of unfair treatment by teachers/ school authorities Calls for fair treatment	Criticism of lack of respect and democratic involvement Calls for greater respect and democracy	Specific suggestions for increased democratic participation	Total essays written
		%	%	%	N
St Peter's	ssg, fr (disadv)	52.6	66.7	11.4	114
St Patrick's	ssg, fr	51.7	53.4	10.2	118
St Cecilia's	ssg, fp	55.9	63.8	4.7	127
Our Lady's	ssg, fr	43.6	76.6	6.4	94
Ballinroe	ssb, fr	50.5	38.5	7.3	109
St David's	ssb, fp	38.8	30.2	12.1	116
Dunely	ssb, fr	52.9	29.8	3.8	104
St Dominic's	ssb, fr (disadv)	41.0	27.9	3.3	61
Ballydara	co-ed, Comm Coll	52.4	35.9	2.9	103
St Ita's	co-ed, fp	31.7	41.6	9.9	101
Ballycorish	co-ed, Comm Sch (disadv)	46.3	52.2	0	67
Ollan	co-ed, Comm Coll	48.9	35.2	4.5	88
Total N		573	562	82	1,202
% of all essays		47.7	46.8	6.8	

KEY: **ssg** = single sex girls' secondary school
ssb = single sex boys' secondary school
co-ed = co-educational school
fp = fee-paying
fr = free scheme secondary school
Comm Coll = Community College
Comm Sch = Community School

* All schools named are fictitious.

Table 2

*Equality, Academic Differentiation
and Ability Grouping*

School	Description	Complaints of unequal treatment due to ability group allocation or due to label as not 'academically able'	Students stating that the level of exam pressure was unjust and unfair	Total essays written
		%	%	N
St Peter's	ssg, fr (disadv)	12.3	28.1	114
St Patrick's	ssg, fr	26.3	14.4	118
St Cecilia's	ssg, fp	34.6	29.9	127
Our Lady's	ssg, fr	33.0	25.5	94
Ballinroe	ssb, fr	11.0	11.9	109
St David's	ssb, fp	19.0	3.4	116
Dunely	ssb, fr	5.8	10.6	104
St Dominic's	ssb, fr (disadv)	9.8	16.4	61
Ballydara	co-ed, Comm Coll	12.6	10.7	103
St Ita's	co-ed, fp	6.9	6.9	101
Ballycorish	co-ed, Comm Sch (disadv)	14.9	4.5	67
Ollan	co-ed, Comm Coll	22.7	14.8	88
Total N		216	183	1,202
% of all essays		18.0	15.2	

Table 3

Gender Equality Issues

School	Type	Complaint about specific inequality	Control/ surveillance of image, demeanour and behaviour	Issues relating to school sport	Comments on co-education	Sexist/ violent comments made in essays about peers or staff	Total essays written
		%	%	%	%	%	N
St Peter's	ssg, fr (disadv)	0.9	11.4	0	4.4	1.8	114
St Patrick's	ssg, fr	14.4	26.2	2.5	4.2	0	118
St Cecilia's	ssg, fp	9.4	14.1	6.3	3.9	0	127
Our Lady's	ssg, fr	2.1	27.6	2.1	16.0	0	94
Ballinroe	ssb, fr	0	3.7	0.9	10.1	5.5	109
St David's	ssb, fp	0.9	5.2	31.0	23.3	8.6	116
Dunely	ssb, fr	0	3.8	17.3	18.3	4.8	104
St Dominic's	ssb, fr (disadv)	0	3.3	0	13.1	1.6	61
Ballydara	co-ed, Comm Coll	8.7	10.7	1.9	1.0	2.9	103
St Ita's	co-ed, fp	21.8	28.8	18.8	0	4.0	101
Ballycorish	co-ed, Comm Sch (disadv)	6.0	6.0	1.5	0	1.5	67
Ollan	co-ed, Comm Coll	15.9	11.3	2.3	0	0	88
Total N		82	158	92	96	32	1,202
% of all essays		6.8	18.1	7.7	8.0	2.7	

Table 4

Social Class and Equality

School	Description	Reported differential and unequal treatment on the basis of social class in school	Perception of improved school facility requirements Awareness of different facility provision between schools	Total essays written
		%	%	N
St Peter's	ssg, fr (disadv)	7.9	7.0	114
St Patrick's	ssg, fr	2.5	27.1	118
St Cecilia's	ssg, fp	2.4	27.6	127
Our Lady's	ssg, fr	7.4	26.6	94
Ballinroe	ssb, fr	0.9	10.1	109
St David's	ssb, fp	2.6	12.9	116
Dunely	ssb, fr	2.9	13.5	104
St Dominic's	ssb, fr (disadv)	0	57.4	61
Ballydara	co-ed, Comm Coll	5.8	7.8	103
St Ita's	co-ed, fp	4.0	17.8	101
Ballycorish	co-ed, Comm Sch (disadv)	11.9	9.0	67
Ollan	co-ed, Comm Coll	3.4	17.0	88
Total N		50	222	1,202
% of all essays		4.2	18.5	

Table 5

Equality Issues in Relation to Minority Groups

School	Type	Race/ethnicity	Disability	Religious identity	Sexual orientation	Total essays written
		%	%	%	%	N
St Peter's	ssg, fr (disadv)	0	0	2.6	0	114
St Patrick's	ssg, fr	0.8	0.8	0.8	0	118
St Cecilia's	ssg, fp	0.8	0.8	3.9	0	127
Our Lady's	ssg, fr	1.1	0	0	0	94
Ballinroe	ssb, fr	1.8	4.6	0.9	2.8	109
St David's	ssb, fp	1.7	0.9	0	1.7	116
Dunely	ssb, fr	1.0	0	1.0	0	104
St Dominic's	ssb, fr (disadv)	0	0	0	1.6	61
Ballydara	co-ed, Comm Coll	1.0	1.0	2.9	1.0	103
St Ita's	co-ed, fp	9.9	1.0	1.0	2.0	101
Ballycorish	co-ed, Comm Sch (disadv)	0	0	1.5	0	67
Ollan	co-ed, Comm Coll	1.1	0	1.1	0	88
Total N		20	10	17	9	1,202
% of all essays		1.7	0.8	1.4	0.7	

CHAPTER 9

STRATIFICATION IN SCHOOL: KNOWLEDGE AND 'ABILITY' GROUPING

Education in Ireland is big business; almost one million people attend education full-time; several thousand others attend adult, community and higher education on a part-time basis. Within the OECD, Ireland has one of the highest rates of retention within second level, and a high transfer rate from second-level to higher education. The retention rate at second level is almost 80% and the aim is for 90% completion by the year 2000. In addition, almost 50% of the relevant age cohort transfer from second-level to higher education (Department of Education, 1997:ix–xii). Educational expansion is especially visible in the higher education sector, where enrolments increased elevenfold between 1950 and 1990, ahead of all other EU countries with the exception of Germany and Greece (Clancy, 1994).[1]

'ABILITY GROUPING' AS PART OF THE EQUALITY DEBATE

Although education is big business, there is relatively little research and debate about the organisational life of schools in Ireland. While grouping pupils within schools and classes is common practice, there has been only one major study on grouping per se, and this was focused exclusively on second level (Hannan and Boyle, 1987). There has been no national research on grouping in the primary sector. Yet grouping is the subject of several major studies in other countries. There is widespread recognition internationally that tracking students into different streams, either within or between schools, or grouping them within classes, has serious consequences for learning (Barker Lunn, 1970; Rist, 1970; Sharp and Green, 1975; Rosenbaum, 1976; Eder, 1981; Hallinan and Sorensen, 1983; Oakes, 1985; Kerckhoff, 1986; Gamoran, 1989, 1992, 1996; Hallinan, 1992, 1994; Oakes et al., 1992).

Before undertaking any discussion of grouping, however, it is necessary to comment briefly on the concept of ability itself. Ability is not a singular entity which is fixed and measurable on some linear scale, although this is a view which is widely adhered to among educationalists in Ireland and elsewhere (Fontes and Kellaghan, 1983). There are multiple abilities and intelligences, many of which are much more highly prized and developed in particular cultures and societies than in others (Gardner, 1983, 1991; Sternberg, 1990; Gardner et al., 1996).

Once one recognises the multiple forms of human ability, this presents an automatic challenge to the language of 'ability grouping'. When educationalists speak of ability grouping, they tend to define ability in singular rather than plural terms; the very idea of 'ability grouping' stems from a culture which supposes a generic, singular and hierarchical view of ability (reflected in the popular educational parlance of 'bright' and 'weak' pupils). It is a culture which does not recognise differences or give equal status to abilities of different kinds. Yet contemporary research suggests that there is no one simple 'ability line' on which all children can be grouped for all subjects; there is no singular generic entity called ability or intelligence. There are multiple forms of ability and people vary greatly in their interests and competencies across these. Moreover, while all people have the capacity to develop all their human abilities, the extent to which people can or will develop these is contingent on a host of contextual influences including personal preferences, family interests, social class position as well as cultural preferences and priorities. Tests which purport to measure human ability or intelligence in absolute reified terms are profoundly misleading therefore; at the very most what tests measure is a student's prior attainments in a particular sphere. Tests of mathematical or verbal reasoning ability are too often given a credence and a standing in education which is untenable given the limited skills they measure. All such tests measure is the competencies which students have attained in particular spheres at a particular time.

There are two sets of equality-related questions to be addressed about grouping therefore. The first questions relate to the known outcomes of 'ability grouping' as currently practised in schools: namely, does ability grouping produce unequal outcomes? In other words, do students from low and middle bands or streams have the same educational chances as those in higher streams? The related question arises, are students distributed across streams and bands in a fair and equal manner across social groups?

These are questions, however, which do not problematise the very premises on which 'ability grouping' is based. To pose questions in the purely distributive sense of 'who gets what from different groups' is to deny the fact that the way in which ability is tested and measured is itself profoundly problematic. The second set of questions to be addressed therefore are about the institutionalised bias which is inherent in the way in which ability is both defined and tested in schools, a bias which consigns many students to a life of educational failure, and many others to a life of relative failure. While streaming, banding or tracking may exacerbate the biases arising from ability differentiation along singular lines (most commonly based on linguistic and mathematical-based tests), biases occur regardless of whether or not schools track or stream when teachers have a highly stratified view of human ability (Barker Lunn, 1970). The problem stems from the fact that only particular forms of knowledge have been legitimated within education as being of high standing — the linguistic and mathematically based disciplines primarily (Gardner, 1983). Other forms of understanding, no matter how culturally important or significant, are deemed to be inferior and those who excel in the 'delegitimised' forms of intelligence are generally classified as 'weak' students. The problem stems from a lack of acknowledgment that people learn, represent and utilise knowledge in different ways.

> [The] educational system . . . assumes that everyone can learn the same materials in the same way and that a uniform universal measure suffices to test student learning. Indeed as currently institutionalised, our educational system is heavily biased toward linguistic modes of instruction and assessment and, to a somewhat lesser degree, toward logical-mathematical-quantitative modes as well. (Gardner, 1991:12)

What is absurd about this, especially in contemporary society, is that educational credentials are used to select people for a diverse range of occupations, many of which never require extensive knowledge of the type which schools value. The cognitive competencies which are tested in schools are only one of a range of competencies required in people's personal and occupational lives. The educational institution has, in certain respects, become cut off from many of the lifeworlds and labour markets which it serves at the very time that educational credentials are being used more than ever to select and stratify people within the labour market.

This raises the question of the hegemonic power of the academy within the education sector as it is the higher education institutions, especially the universities, which play a key role in controlling definitions of valid knowledge and assessment in education. Until the received wisdoms of the academy are challenged, it is difficult to see how schools alone can redefine or revalue different forms of knowledge and understanding.

PART I
GROUPING PRACTICES IN SCHOOLS

BACKGROUND ISSUES

Teaching practice in Irish primary schools is based on the principle of child-centredness (*Teacher's Handbook* (Department of Education, 1971); *Report of the Review Body on the Primary Curriculum* (Department of Education, 1990a); *Report of the Primary Education Review Body* (Department of Education, 1990b); *White Paper on Education* (Department of Education, 1995)). The use of project work, guided discovery activities and group teaching are recommended for the implementation of the primary curriculum. It is a formal policy of the Department of Education to group students for teaching within primary classes and the architecture of primary classes is designed to facilitate this with pupils being placed in small groups around tables for teaching purposes. The precise procedures which are used for allocating students to groups in any given case is far from clear, although it is known that a range of procedures are used overall, including observation, homework, standardised tests and classroom discussions (Department of Education, 1995:28). That highly subjective judgments determine pupils' class placement at times is quite likely; one study undertaken in north-west Ireland (Carr, 1988) found that standardised tests were not used to allocate pupils, rather the teacher's personal assessment of student ability was the criterion. In common with international research in this field, Carr also found little evidence that students moved groups within the school year, no matter how they progressed, a finding confirmed in Devine's (1991) research. Devine also documented young primary children's views and feelings about being grouped within classes. She found that children were keenly aware of the significance of the grouping process and its status distinctions.

Unfortunately there is no national research on the outcomes of group-based teaching and learning at primary level, although there is extensive research in this field in the United States. Gamoran and Hallinan's (1995) review of research in the field notes that the results of studies are fairly consistent:

> They show that students in high-ability groups attain higher achievement and learn at a faster pace than their peers in low ability groups . . . Further . . . student growth in achievement is faster in high groups than in low groups. (p. 115)

Given the international evidence on within-class grouping, it is highly likely that grouping practices in Irish primary schools place particular students at an ongoing educational disadvantage. There is an urgent need for research on this issue.

The debate about 'ability grouping', in so far as it has happened in Ireland, has tended to focus on second-level education. By international standards, second-level schools in Ireland are relatively small in size. Almost 55% have less than 500 students. Although the majority of schools (76%) have over 300 students, there are a number of schools, 8%, which have only one class in each school year (Department of Education, 1997:42). The first factor which must be borne in mind when discussing streaming or tracking in second-level schools in Ireland therefore is the size of the school. A minority of schools are too small to stream or band so the question does not arise. Even in larger schools, class groups in different subjects may be too small to stream or set, especially at senior level.

A second consideration when examining issues of streaming and banding is the long-standing tracking between schools which operated in Ireland for some forty years.

Under the Vocational Education Act (1930) the remit of vocational schools was to focus on vocational ('continuation') education per se, and to prepare students for immediate employment and for the examinations which were vocationally oriented at the time, namely the Group Certificate and the City and Guild examinations. Many vocational schools did not prepare students for the Leaving Certificate therefore until the 1970s. This meant that their public identity was firmly established as being less academically oriented when they went into open competition with secondary schools. Moreover, although vocational schools can, and do, offer a full range of subjects for public examinations, they still have a more technologically oriented curriculum than most secondary schools. This is especially true of smaller vocational schools which cannot afford to expand their subject options outside their traditional range. Although all Leaving Certificate subjects are now accorded equal status in terms of 'points' by the colleges (with the exception of home economics (general)), this was not the case up to the early 1980s, when common level papers in construction studies, technical drawing and engineering were not recognised by the universities. This reinforced stratification between vocational and secondary schools.

There is also a social class issue at stake here. Vocational schools were traditionally the schools which served the children from working-class and small farm families (Hannan et al., 1983, 1996). Middle-class parents are still reluctant to send their children, especially girls, to vocational schools even where it is known that they have a strong academic orientation. While there are exceptions to this, for example when vocational schools are 'stand-alone' schools (i.e. they are the only second-level schools within an area and there is no major competing secondary school in the vicinity), this is not the norm. Middle-class parents tend to send their children to secondary schools more than to any other school type (Hannan et al., 1996:243).

Community and comprehensive schools were all established since the late 1960s. They represented an attempt by the state to overcome the limitations of the binary system which had existed up to that time. In terms of social class intake, they occupy a median position between vocational and secondary schools (ibid.). They tend to be larger in size than other schools (almost three-quarters have 500 or more pupils) and are more likely therefore to have banding than other school types.[2]

COMPETITION BETWEEN SCHOOLS AND ITS IMPLICATIONS FOR GROUPING

Ireland operates according to free market principles in relation to school choice. Under the Irish Constitution (Article 42) parents are recognised as the primary and natural educators of their children. They are free to send their child to the school of their choice or to educate them at home (provided they meet certain requirements) if they so wish. This does not mean that the state is obliged to pay for the education of children far away from home, rather that parents can 'choose' it if they wish.[3] The effect of 'free parental choice' on schools is that they are often in competition with one another for pupils. In the mid-1990s, almost two-thirds of second-level schools reported that they were competing for pupils with other schools (Hannan et al., 1996:79). Vocational schools were particularly affected by this, with 77% of vocational school principals claiming that they were adversely affected by 'creaming off', while only about one-quarter of secondary schools were in this position (ibid.).

Although there is evidence that parents from all social classes exercise choice between schools, it is those with the greatest resources who have the greatest choice. This is reflected in the findings from Hannan et al. (1996:243) that it is students from upper-middle-class families who are least likely to be attending their nearest school. Research from the UK also confirms that substantial choice exists only for those who can afford to exercise choice (Gewirtz et al., 1994; Ball et al., 1995; Reay, 1996).[4]

Up to 1995, secondary schools could select pupils on the basis of academic ability (although not all did) by using entrance tests. A ruling by the Minister for Education prohibited this practice in all schools receiving public funds. However, the fact that schools do not or cannot select by examination does not mean that selection does not occur. Schools control entry by many means; these include required attendance at an attached primary school (a common selection mechanism in fee-paying schools with primary departments); attending a local feeder school; having older siblings in the school; being within a defined catchment area; or 'first come, first served' (Lynch, 1989; Hannan et al., 1996). Moreover, many schools still undertake pre-entrance tests even though these cannot now be used directly for selection.

While many of the above procedures may appear socially neutral in their effect, this is not the case. The principle of 'first come, first served' means that parents who are most organised and informed about the operation of the system (middle-class parents generally) are most likely to 'come first'. The 'first come, first served' principle also discriminates indirectly against Travellers, whose nomadic lifestyle does not facilitate advance planning of this type. The use of pre-entrance tests is also problematic. Many students may not be aware that they need to do such tests, and may disqualify themselves inadvertently. Knowledge is crucial here too: those who do not know that tests exist cannot do them; or pupils and parents may find the prospect of doing tests intimidating so they opt for schools which do not do such tests. The fact that many secondary (free scheme) schools ask for a 'voluntary contribution' can also have a disincentive effect on low-income families, especially if there are a number of children involved. Finally, because secondary schools are legally defined private institutions offering an educational service, this gives them rights in relation to the control of pupil entry and expulsion which would not be permitted in more democratically controlled education systems.

The net outcome of the competition between schools is that secondary schools have, on the whole, won out in terms of attracting a larger cohort of academically interested students. This occurred not least because they have been competing with unfair advantage for many years, having a virtual monopoly on academic education up to the early 1970s, and latterly because of their selection practices, which were condoned if not supported by the state.

When we analyse the patterns of ability grouping in schools, we find that the fact that secondary schools could and did 'cream off' the more academically interested students had implications for how students were grouped in vocational schools in particular, and in community and comprehensive schools, especially if the latter were in competition with secondary schools for pupils, which most are. More than 70% of vocational and community/comprehensive schools operated streaming or banding at the Junior Certificate classes compared with just 49% of secondary schools in 1993/4 (Hannan et al., 1996:93). It now seems that if vocational or community or comprehensive schools are to compete on equal terms with secondary schools, in terms of attracting the more academically oriented students, they are under pressure to stream or band. Having top streams or bands is a guarantee that academically interested students will not be disadvantaged in non-selective schools.

However, while secondary schools are far less likely to stream than vocational or community/comprehensive schools, there are very significant variations between schools within the secondary sector in their streaming practices. Streaming, the most rigid form of 'ability' grouping, is much more prevalent in boys' secondary schools than in girls' or co-educational schools: 44% of boys' schools stream at Junior Certificate level compared with only 17% of girls' schools and 29% of co-educational schools. This greater adherence to streaming, in Junior Certificate grades especially in boys' schools, is an ongoing phenomenon (Hannan and Boyle, 1987; Lynch, 1989) although there has been some reduction in the proportion of all school types which are streaming or banding in first year of second level, and also at the Leaving Certificate stage. One cannot explain grouping by so-called ability simply in terms of intake therefore. It is also a policy decision within schools.

Given the evidence from international research on the self-fulfilling effects of grouping, what is especially questionable is the relatively high proportion of second-level schools which group students by some 'ability' measure in their first year of second-level education: 45% (of those schools large enough to group) operate either streaming or banding for all subjects in first year (Hannan et al., 1996:247). As banding is effectively a form of streaming in large schools, albeit not as polarised, it is clear that many young students entering second-level schools are effectively tracked from an early stage. As students move towards their first major public examination in their junior years, 60% of schools stream or band on 'ability' (p. 93) while 35% do it at the Leaving Certificate stage (p. 247).

Ireland does not have a well-developed system of evaluating students at entry to second level. A study by MacNamara (1987) (on the use of standardised tests in a sample of 100 second-level schools) found that schools used a wide variety of tests and procedures to group pupils, a number of which were quite subjective. Moreover, many of the standardised tests used at that time were not standardised on an Irish population. Given the difficulty of measuring 'ability' accurately at any time, but particularly when there are only relatively crude mechanisms for assessing ability, it is clearly quite arbitrary to allocate children to banded or streamed classes simply on the basis of such tests, especially when there is evidence that prior group assignment is a significant determinant of later group placement (Gamoran, 1992; Hallinan, 1992). It is a matter of some concern therefore that although it is known to be difficult to move across stream or band once allocated (Barker Lunn, 1970; Oakes, 1985), and that streaming has a negative effect on the performance of students in low streams (Hannan et al., 1996:198), a substantial number of Irish schools stream or band at some or all stages of second-level education.

While streaming and banding is strongest in the public schools which are least selective, namely vocational schools, it is, not surprisingly, rather weak in the most socially selective schools, namely those which are fee-paying secondary (Hannan and Boyle, 1987; Lynch, 1989). While there are a number of factors which contribute to this, not least of which is the selective nature of entry on social class terms, one important factor is the influence of the parents within such schools. Parents who pay fees to ensure educational advantages for their children are not willing to accept rigid streaming or banding if their individual child is to be subject to it (Lynch, 1989). Parents exercise power over grouping policy in fee-paying schools in a way which is not as evident in public schools.

VALUES, POLICIES AND GROUPING

There are a number of structural factors which precipitate the use of streaming or banding at Junior Certificate level. Because there is a core curriculum for the Junior Certificate, this makes grouping feasible as classes are large enough to track or stream. In addition, all Junior Certificate subjects are offered at both higher and ordinary level and the three core subjects (Irish, English and Mathematics) are offered at three levels (higher, ordinary and foundation). While ordinary and higher papers share basic course elements, the foundation courses in the three subjects would be significantly different to the higher papers in particular. Thus, at the Junior Certificate level, the fact that knowledge itself is stratified within subject areas means that student stratification is readily accepted. This also happens at Leaving Certificate level, although the wider range of options, and higher student drop-out at this stage, reduce the options to stream and band in any rigid sense.[5]

While the intake into a school, the level of competition between schools and the stratification within subjects play an important part in determining what type of grouping takes place, grouping policy is also a function of the values and aspirations of the schools themselves. There has been an intense debate in many schools about the issue of ability grouping and it is an issue on which many staffs are deeply divided. There is evidence, from both past and recent studies, that girls' schools, almost all of which are run by women's religious orders, are significantly less likely to stream than boys' schools, almost all of which are run by male religious bodies with male principals (Hannan and Boyle, 1987; Lynch, 1989, 1997). Given that girls' schools cater for a significantly larger cohort of the student female population than boys' schools do, and that they are in fact more socially heterogeneous as well, if streaming and banding was purely a function of intake then girls' schools should stream more than boys'. Yet they do not. This strongly suggests that there are policy differences between girls' and boys' schools about grouping. While Hannan and Boyle (1987:170) attribute the difference to the higher instrumental-achievement orientation in boys' schools and the stronger 'expressive-moral' orientation in girls' schools, other research evidence suggests the reasons are more complex. Research undertaken in the 1980s found that there was a stronger achievement orientation in girls' schools than in boys' (as measured in terms of number of in-house assessments set, checking of assessments, feedback to students, awards for academic achievement, etc.) (Lynch, 1989). What made the schools different was the fact that girls' schools *combined* a strong achievement orientation with a strong 'expressive-moral' orientation. The fact that girls in all-girls' schools perform better in public examinations than boys in single-sex schools (Hannan et al., 1996:111) lends credence to the claim that girls' schools, despite their lack of streaming, have a strong achievement ethos. It also seriously challenges the claim that streaming or banding are educationally beneficial for all students, one of the stated purposes of such grouping practices in the first place.

The difference in policy between girls' and boys' schools may well arise therefore from differences in expectations and in perceptions about what are the desirable outcomes of schooling. There is evidence, for example, that while girls' schools have a strong academic climate, they also have a reasonably strong caring ethos, measured in terms of time and attention to personal development, and stated school goals (Lynch, 1989:65; McDonnell, 1995). Could it be that girls' schools are less stratified because managers and principals in these schools have made a proactive decision to avoid the known negative outcomes of rigid streaming and banding, and have developed other mechanisms for managing differences? Given that there is much international evidence that women manage schools in a less hierarchical and more collegial fashion to men, and that they have a more interventionist approach to management (Shakeshaft, 1989; Ozga, 1993), this is a subject which needs to be further researched in Ireland.

THE EFFECTS OF DIFFERENT FORMS OF ABILITY GROUPING ON EDUCATIONAL OUTCOMES

There have been two national studies over the last fifteen years which have examined the impact of grouping practices on educational attainment in public examinations using national samples (Hannan and Boyle, 1987; Hannan et al., 1996).

Both studies confirm that rigid streaming has a net negative effect on average academic performance when all the relevant factors are controlled for. In the earlier study, it was found that strong streaming had a slight negative effect on overall academic performance in the school (as measured by a range of measures including retention rates, Leaving Certificate performance and the proportion achieving university places). In addition, rigid streaming and curricular differentiation practices were associated with a slight, albeit statistically insignificant, increase in junior and senior cycle drop-out rates, and with slightly lower entrance rates to universities (Hannan and Boyle, 1987:139–45). In sum, therefore, strong differentiation had a slightly negative effect on educational outcome. Moreover, there was very little evidence of movement between classes or categories for the first three years of second-level schooling, the period when streaming is strongest (p. 73).

Finally and not surprisingly, strong stratification between classes was asso ciated with greater differentiation in academic performance between classes. Streaming had therefore a definite polarisation effect on academic performance between upper and lower streams (p. 149). This is in line with international research findings in the field (Kerckhoff, 1986; Hallinan, 1994).

The Hannan and Boyle (1987) study did report a case study of one school which operated a traditional streaming system but where the performance of students with lower measured ability improved with streaming; this school also had lower drop-out and failure rates after five years. These changes arose in the context of substantially increased resourcing of lower streams (teaching them in classes which were half the size of ordinary classes and giving extra remedial classes), altered pedagogical styles, the allocation of committed and effective teachers to the classes, and increased home support (pp. 173–4). Hannan and Boyle note therefore that the effects of grouping are mediated through the processes of teacher allocation, quality of instruction, etc., which come to be associated with different grouping methods, and that it is not the function of the grouping process in and of itself. They found, for example, that there was nearly as much difference in achievement means and variances *within* each schooling differentiation category as there was between them (ibid.). What their data show therefore is that the way in which particular forms of grouping are managed has an effect on attainment outcomes.

While Hallinan (1998) has also noted the potentially neutral character of different grouping practices, empirical research data suggest that what is theoretically possible is rarely institutionally realised. Schools for a whole host of reasons do not differentially allocate resources to the lower streams in a streamed situation, not least because of competing demands on resources. To suggest therefore that streaming or banding are neutral in their outcomes is to ignore the wealth of empirical evidence which shows that this is not the case in practice for the great majority of schools.

More recent research on the effects of streaming and banding generally confirms earlier findings. At Junior Certificate level, streaming has been found to have a negative, albeit statistically insignificant, effect on average academic performance across schools. That is to say, controlling for all the relevant variables, students in streamed schools scored, on average, just under half a grade lower in the Junior Certificate than those in mixed classes. However, there was no evidence of any such effect at the Leaving Certificate level (Hannan et al., 1996:127–55) although this may be due, at least in part, to the fact that streaming at the Leaving Certificate level is far less cohesive and rigid.

Hannan et al. (1996) also found there were significant variations in the academic performance of the upper and lower streams, and between upper streams and those in mixed classes. Controlling for all the relevant variables, those in the top stream got an average of one grade higher than those in mixed classes with those in the lowest stream getting over a grade and a quarter lower than those in mixed classes (ibid.). The negative effect of being in a low stream (and the positive effect of being in a higher one) was found to persist when measured ability was controlled for.

One of the reasons why students who enter low streams or bands do not perform as well as others in examinations is because they are sitting lower grade or 'ordinary' papers which lower their Grade Point Average (GPA). This happens because those allocated to a lower stream or band are often not allowed to take higher papers in a given subject. Being in a low stream and band can also mean that one is not allowed to take optional subjects which are regarded as being 'too academic' for low streams. In certain schools, students are not allowed take a European language or, in some cases, science (Lynch, 1989). The net effect of this is that students in low streams or bands have their higher education options seriously curtailed at a very young age. As all the universities require students to have a Leaving Certificate in at least one European language (other than Irish or English), and as a very large number of higher education courses have a scientific requirement, students in low streams or bands can be seriously curtailed in their post-school options very early on in their educational careers.

SOCIAL AND PSYCHOLOGICAL EFFECTS OF GROUPING

Research undertaken on the social and psychological effects of grouping suggests that strong tracking (or grouping by 'ability') has a negative effect on the self-image of those in the lower streams (Rosenbaum, 1976, 1980; Patchen,

1982; Oakes, 1985). Teachers have also been found to have low expectations of students in 'low-ability' groups (Oakes et al., 1992). There is, as yet, little known about the social and psychological effects of grouping in second-level schools in Ireland. Hannan, Smyth et al. (1996) found that academic self-image was not really affected by the grouping process in operation in the school. In fact, those in the top streams in streamed/banded schools had, on average, lower self-images than others (p. 168). One possible explanation for this is the interactive effect between the strong competitive ethos in top streams, academic expectations, and status in class vis-à-vis others. Clearly only a small number of students can top the class; those who hold an average or bottom position in a top stream may feel relatively deprived compared with the successful minority and this may have an adverse effect on their academic self-image. Students in less competitive classes, by contrast, may have lower expectations, or may not invest so much of their identity in being academically successful, with the result that their self-image may not be as adversely affected by relatively lower academic performance.

Body image was not found to be strongly associated with grouping systems either, although it was found that Leaving Certificate students in bottom/ remedial classes had lower body image than those in mixed-ability or higher classes (p. 173). Nor did the type of grouping in the school have any obvious effect on pupils' stress levels. As there has not been any study in Ireland which set out to examine the relationship between grouping practice and social and psychological outcomes of schooling per se, the conclusions here must be taken as very tentative.

Concluding Comments

Within-class grouping is widespread in Irish primary schools, yet little is known about the implications of grouping at this level. Given international evidence on the effects of early grouping practices, particularly the known negative implications of being placed in 'low reading or mathematics groups' over time, there is an urgent need to examine the nature of grouping practices, and to appraise their effects on primary school pupils. This is especially imperative in the light of the OECD literacy survey (Morgan et al., 1997) which indicates that a very large number (in comparative terms) of young Irish people are functioning with only minimal literacy and numerical skills: in terms of reading documents, for example, 17% of those aged between sixteen and twenty-five were at the lowest level of functioning, while 18% of this age group were at the lowest level of functioning on numerical tasks (pp. 31, 36). There are many questions to ask about primary (and second-level) education in relation to this data; and one question is, what, if any, effect do current grouping procedures have on outcomes? They are known to have an effect in other countries.

What is clear from the data available is that there is considerable variability both between and within schools as to the nature of grouping which exists at second level. Most schools use a mixture of systems although they may operate one predominant system. At present, mixed grouping is the most widely used practice at school entry (used by 58% of all schools, including the 5% which are too small to stream or band, in first year). Streaming or banding is the modal type of grouping at Junior Certificate level (in almost 50% of schools), while at Leaving Certificate level, mixed ability is again the modal form of operation being practised by 65% of all schools. It is common, however, in schools which have mixed ability as an operating principle to find that there are certain subjects which are taught exclusively in higher and ordinary classes. Students may be in a higher class for one subject and an ordinary class for another. This system is quite common with popular subjects such as English, Mathematics, French, etc., at Leaving Certificate level where there is scope to create two or more classes due to the numbers taking the subject.

Given that rigid streaming and banding is most likely to occur in those schools with the highest intake of working-class and/or low-income students, and there is some evidence (O'Kelly, 1986) that those from working-class backgrounds are most likely to be allocated to the lowest stream or band, then it is clear that the practice of grouping by rigid systems of streaming or banding raises serious equality issues relating to social class. Moreover, all students who are grouped by ability into lower streams or bands are disadvantaged in terms of the curriculum choices which are open to them, the level at which they can study particular subjects, and the institutionalised low status accorded to them within schools. Grouping by 'ability' is therefore an important equality issue in education.

PART II
EQUALITY ISSUES ARISING

There are at least two ways in which one can assess the equality implications of streaming and banding in Irish schools. First, one can examine it, as has been done traditionally, in terms of its implications for particular streams or bands (further disaggregated by social class, gender ethnicity, etc.). It is possible to assess the effects of grouping on both pupil experience of schooling and educational performance. The limited research in Ireland confirms international trends showing that rigid tracking or streaming disadvantages those in lowest streams or bands, depresses aggregate school performance and exaggerates drop-out rates. As students from socially and economically disadvantaged backgrounds are those most likely to have reading difficulties entering second-level education (Kellaghan et al., 1995) and as streaming and banding is generally done on the basis of tests with a strong emphasis on written linguistic ability, it is quite likely that students from low-income working-class backgrounds are disproportionately represented in the lowest stream ceteris paribus. Further research is necessary on this issue.

To assess equality in terms of the proportionality test for different streams or bands, and/or different social groups, is to operate out of the classical liberal model of equality of opportunity. First, it is to assume that the criteria and procedures for grouping students in schools are reasonable and fair. It is also to accept that the forms of knowledge which are legitimated in education, through their inclusion and accreditation in school texts, are in fact inclusive of all relevant cultural knowledge forms and understandings in a given society. These are all highly questionable assumptions. While there is undoubtedly inequality in the simple proportionate sense of 'unequal opportunity for those allocated to lower streams or bands', this is only one part of the equality problem in relation to 'ability' grouping in schools. There are a number of other fundamental questions to be addressed, including questions about the procedures for assessing ability; the criteria for grouping students in schools 'by ability'; the developmental nature of human ability; and the relatively unproblematic manner in which certain forms of knowledge are regarded as central to education while others are treated as peripheral, regardless of students' interests and predispositions, or indeed society's needs.

HOW 'ABILITY' IS DEFINED AND ASSESSED IN SCHOOLS: A QUESTION OF EQUALITY OF RESPECT

Child-centredness is a fundamental principle underpinning the curriculum in Irish primary schools. The *White Paper* (Department of Education, 1995:19) states that 'Primary education now emphasises the central position of the individual child and promotes a curriculum related to the child's interests and needs.' While second-level education does not claim to be child- or person-centred in the same way, it does aim at junior level to ensure that students 'complete a broad, balanced and coherent course of study in a variety of curricular areas relevant to their own personal development and to allow them to achieve a level of competence in these which will enable them to proceed to senior cycle education' (p. 47). And at senior level the aim is to encourage and facilitate students to continue in full-time education during the post-compulsory by providing a stimulating range of programmes suited to their abilities, aptitudes and interests. The objectives are 'to develop each student's potential to the full, and equip them for work or further education' (p. 50).

Regardless of the rhetoric of child-centredness which pervades primary education, and of the ideology of developing all students' abilities which pervades both levels of education, the practice in schooling, especially as measured in terms of what is assessed and the procedures for assessment, presents a rather different picture. Both the way in which 'ability' is defined and the ways in which it is then assessed in mainstream education are seriously problematic. The inadequacy of the assessment system was noted in the *Report on the National Education Convention* (Coolahan, 1994).

There are twenty-six subjects on the junior curriculum although a number of these are offered in only a small number of schools and are taken for examination in a given year by only a few hundred students out of a student cohort of approximately 60,000 (for example Latin, Greek, Hebrew, typewriting, Italian, environmental and social studies, and classical studies). In addition, there is no formal appraisal of students' performance in physical education, civics, computer studies or religion (Department of Education, 1997). The actual subjects taken with any degree of popularity number eighteen. Of these, five are languages; three others are heavily linguistically based (history, geography and business studies); and two are mathematics-based (science and mathematics). There is only one art-based subject (art, craft and design) and one music subject (music), while the remaining six are technologically oriented (home economics, metalwork, materials technology, technical graphics, typewriting and technology). Although the arts, music and technical subjects are not primarily assessed in terms of written linguistic ability, it remains an important part of the medium of assessment for all subjects, especially at the higher levels.

The use of written terminal examinations also prevails although there is provision for 'alternative assessment techniques' to be used in at least thirteen of the Junior Certificate subjects (Hanafin and Leonard, 1996).

At Leaving Certificate level, the pattern in terms of curriculum provision and take-up is not dissimilar, although there is a slightly wider range of subjects on offer (and there is a much wider range of science subjects and business subjects on offer). Technological subjects occupy a similar position to that which obtains at junior levels, while art and music are still effectively one-subject options (Department of Education, 1997).[6]

Successful completion of second-level education in Ireland is measured in terms of one's performance in public examinations, most especially the Leaving Certificate as increasing credentialism has greatly reduced the value of the Junior Certificate. Regardless of the rhetoric of educating the whole person therefore, students are appraised at the end of their schooling in terms of examination performance by further and higher education institutions, and by employers (European Social Fund Programme Evaluation Unit, 1996). Research has shown that students are well aware of this (Hannan and Shorthall, 1991).

The fact that the curriculum, especially at the Leaving Certificate level, is heavily linguistically oriented in both cognitive content and mode of assessment[7] means that most students must be highly proficient in written linguistic self-expression if they are to perform well in the examination. The only other option is to gain high grades in mathematically oriented subjects. Students whose primary intellectual orientation may be in the visual spatial, bodily kinaesthetic, musical or interpersonal spheres are seriously disadvantaged in the public examinations. Not only do they lack a cognitively relevant set of options from which to choose, but they lack a medium of self-expression which is sympathetic to their intelligence. In addition, over 80% of the work in most subjects is assessed in one terminal examination. Performance on a single occasion becomes the measure of a student's future worth for higher education institutions and among employers.

Not alone are the knowledge forms limited and the modes of assessment heavily oriented to linguistic and to a lesser degree mathematical forms, they are also strongly academic within each of these forms, especially in the higher papers at both junior and senior levels.

The role of the universities, and more recently the other higher education institutions, is crucial in this entire process. Universities have traditionally played a central role in granting legitimacy only to linguistically and mathematically based forms of assessment. Up to the early 1980s they refused to recognise those subjects which did not ensure a high linguistic and mathematical component in their assessment procedures (e.g. technical drawing and construction studies). They still do not recognise home economics (general). In effect, the universities exercise a controlling influence on the curricula, syllabi and modes of assessment utilised in second-level schools. Only the forms of knowledge which have high status in the 'academy', and modes of assessment recognised by the academy, are granted legitimacy. The two dominant historical traditions in education, the classical literary tradition and the scientific-technical tradition, effectively dominate the classrooms of the late twentieth century. The irony of this is that schools are now much more closely integrated with other social institutions in our society than they were in the past, yet the procedures for assessment, and the subjects they assess, remain remote from the very institutions which they claim to serve. As Gardner (1991) points out:

> academic knowledge is typically assessed with arbitrary problems that a student has little intrinsic interest in or motivation to answer, and performances on such instruments have little predictive power for performances outside of a scholastic environment. (p. 133)

There is much which passes as education therefore which is of marginal relevance for life outside school, especially when viewed in terms of the wide range of skills and predispositions which are necessary in contemporary society. Moreover, schooling downgrades and marginalises many human intelligences by not giving them equal respect. Once we step outside schools and the academy, the irrelevance of text-based learning and assessment in decontextualised settings becomes evident. While this would not matter much if education credentials were used only in the field within which they have some currency, namely the educational world, it matters greatly when they are used to select for different occupations and employments. It matters especially when educational credentials are major determinants of life chances.

An analysis of different trends in the economy shows that the services sector is the most rapidly expanding sector. Within this sector, and even in manufacturing, the nature of employment is changing with a strong emphasis on personal service-type industries requiring a wide range of communication and interpersonal skills. There is a greater demand for innovativeness at all levels, and there is also an increasing demand for persons who are adaptable and multi-skilled (Culliton Report, *The Future Needs of Irish Industry*, 1992; *Science, Technology and Innovation: The White Paper* (Department of Enterprise and Employment, 1996)). Yet schools have tended to teach the same curricula and syllabi with only slight modifications from what was presented a quarter of a century ago. Written terminal examinations with a strong abstract theoretical bias are still the norm. Unlike places of work, schools are remarkably similar in organisational structure to what they were in the nineteenth century. Despite the greater humanisation of pedagogical style and forms of discipline, authority is still hierarchically stratified; pupils are age-stratified and subject-stratified; public examinations still dominate the system in practice if not in theory. The social, economic and cultural revolutions which have occurred outside of schools have impacted only on the margins of the educational system.

That the educational system has become, in part, a self-perpetuating system responding to a considerable degree to the dynamic of its own reproduction has been evident for some time (Archer, 1982). Those who are at the pinnacle of authority in this massive industry, the universities, and, increasingly, other higher education institutions, exercise an enormous degree of power over the nature of educational experience for those at other levels, indirectly if not directly (Coolahan, 1981). And this system of control creates great injustices and frustrations for those who cannot find a sense of achievement within it. The high rates of retention in second-level education therefore and the development of so-called 'mixed ability' belies the fact that different forms of knowledge and relatedly different forms of ability do not have parity of esteem within schools.

To identify 'mixed ability' therefore as the solution to the 'ability' question is to ignore one of the most serious problems with contemporary education, namely that different abilities are not formally recognised. Even in its own terms, there are many questions which need to be addressed regarding the nature of the learning that takes place in schools and colleges. Only one appraisal of the cognitive skills assessed in the Leaving Certificate has been undertaken (Madaus and Macnamara, 1970) and this raised many questions about the level of cognitive skills required to succeed in the examination. Unfortunately there has been no similar study undertaken in higher education. Yet as Gardner (1991) has noted, even in higher education, many students do not have real understanding of the subject matter as they are never asked to apply it in real situations. He argues that 'formal testing has moved much too far in the direction of assessing knowledge of questionable importance in ways that show little transportability' (p. 134).

What is being suggested here is that the debate about tracking, streaming and grouping in schools cannot be divorced from the debate about the nature of ability itself; nor can it be separated from the debate about what constitutes culturally important forms of understanding and how these are to be assessed educationally.

Because schooling played only a minor role in determining life chances fifty years ago, at least in Ireland, what one learned in school and how one was assessed was less problematic than it is now. Nowadays, the nature of the credential one obtains in school strongly determines one's life chances (see *School Leaver Surveys* for various years, Department of Enterprise and Employment). If schooling is accrediting and recognising only a narrow range of talents and abilities (most especially those which academics regard as important), then there is a serious injustice being done to those whose talents and abilities are not assessed in school.

While there are welcome developments in education — such as the introduction of the Leaving Certificate Applied, Transition Year and the introduction of the Civic, Social and Political Education Course — which provide opportunities for developing different abilities, these programmes are still in their infancy. It is not at all clear at the time of writing, for example, what recognition employers, and especially higher education institutions, will grant to the Leaving Certificate Applied programme.

THE MARGINALISATION OF PERSONAL INTELLIGENCES: A FEMINIST ISSUE?

Although musical, spatial and bodily kinaesthetic intelligence have some place in schooling, certain intelligences have almost none at all, notably personal intelligences (Gardner, 1983). This is a very interesting phenomenon as both intrapersonal (the ability to know oneself, and to be able to appraise one's own feelings, motivation and behaviour) and interpersonal intelligences (the ability to read, understand and respond to the desires and interests of others) are not only crucial in a service-sector-dominated society, but are of profound importance for people's personal relationships. The ability to form and develop satisfactory personal relationships is crucially dependent on advanced personal intelligences. These kinds of intelligences have been traditionally developed outside of education settings, notably in the home, and will undoubtedly always continue to be so. However, they are also capable of being greatly advanced through formal educational development and understanding. Yet there has never been any serious consideration given to their development, except through ad hoc personal development courses, or through some modules within the home economics programmes. While there is now a relationships and sexuality programme, the primary focus of this is sexual relationships rather than the more generic task of developing all-round personal intelligences.

One question which must be addressed by educationalists is why the knowledge base of caring and love labour (Lynch, 1989; Lynch and McLaughlin, 1995) is being ignored in this manner. Is it possible that the indifference to personal intelligence arises because of the patriarchal split between the public and the private domains? Is it because caring and love labour are not paid forms of work, because they have a use value but not an exchange value, that the knowledge associated with them is so easily marginalised? For it is undoubtedly the case that caring has been hidden behind capital, and the resources, skills and capacities needed to care have not been seriously examined, nor has there been a serious attempt to develop them through schooling, which is after all the major culture-legitimating institution in our society.

Certainly those who have framed and designed our curricula over the last 100 years have been predominantly class men, middle-class men for the most part, who had wives to care for them and their children. Given the domain assumptions[8] of their existence, it is not surprising that they would define the labour of caring and loving as private and ignore the knowledge and skills associated with it. Yet we know increasingly that knowledge, understanding and capacity to love and care require deep understanding not only of ourselves but of others, and that they are crucial for the emotional stability of the human person. The development of personal intelligences is crucial for the development of the caring aspects of culture.

This is, at least in part, a feminist issue. Schooling has been increasingly driven by the perceived needs of the economy, the demands of the public sphere (although in my view, the demands of even this sphere are now being misread by educationalists; the personal is as relevant to the public as the public is to the private and the personal). The knowledge and understanding required for successful personal relationships has not been deemed to be of sufficient importance to be formally advanced through analysis and development in education. It is considered a private affair managed by women with so-called intuitive understanding of such matters! Such a perspective not only demeans the tasks involved in care but misrepresents the sophistication of the understanding required for deep personal relationships.

Further, personal intelligences are required in virtually every occupation in life; the issue of their development is not simply to do with the private personal sphere. In an economy in which the services sector is rapidly expanding, and in which success in the manufacturing and the agricultural sectors relies increasingly on developing relationships both within companies in terms of collegiality, and without in terms of successful marketing etc., the development of inter-personal and intrapersonal intelligences is of central importance.

Concluding Remarks

Equality in education must begin with equality of respect for different forms of knowledge and understanding. One of the forms of knowledge which has been most neglected in education is that associated with personal intelligences. This has meant that the knowledge and understanding which we need to develop satisfactory personal relationships is, in many senses, still in a primitive state. Yet there is virtually nobody in the world who does not actively seek out meaningful personal relationships as a core element in their human existence. The needs of the 'love and care economy' which preoccupies so much of our time, especially women's time, have not been prepared for except in a rudimentary fashion.

The cultural hegemonies in education are not only class hegemonies as Bourdieu and Passeron (1977) suggested, there are also gender and racial hegemonies, not just within disciplines but between them (hooks, 1982; Harding, 1991; Said, 1991; Weiner, 1994). The gendered (and indeed classist, racist and ethnocentric) nature of knowledge is not simply evident therefore *within* subjects, that is in the invisibility of feminine-oriented themes and interests within traditional 'subjects', rather it is evident in what is omitted from schooling in its entirety, in the forms of knowledge and understanding that are left outside of formal education. There is a cultural imperialism[9] going on in schooling which is not only class-biased and racially biased but also gender-biased. And one of the most significant biases is that which ignores the development of personal intelligences.[10]

CONCLUSION

There is no national research data on the effects of grouping students within primary classes. This is a major deficit in Irish educational research as there is considerable evidence from other countries that the effects of within-class grouping are far from neutral (Hallinan, 1987, 1994). Findings regarding the effects of ability grouping within Irish second-level schools are broadly in line with international trends, although streaming has been found to have a negative effect on average educational outcomes, measured in terms of examination grades, as opposed to a neutral effect. Streaming is also associated with higher drop-out rates, fewer transfers to universities and increased variance in performance within the streamed schools. Thus, in terms of distributive justice, grouping by stream or band has a negative effect on the opportunities of those allocated to the lowest stream or bands.

However, a change to 'mixed ability' will not guarantee equality of treatment in the way that is often supposed. Mixing pupils by 'ability' will not end stratification in the minds of teachers unless teachers have learned to appreciate differences in abilities; teachers can and do play a key role in mediating institutional practices in classrooms. In addition, mixing students will not promote substantive equality in schools unless schools give formal recognition to students' diverse talents. The real problem in education for many students who are now designated as 'weak' or 'low ability', etc. is not that they are 'weak' or 'lacking in ability' in some generic sense, but rather that they possess abilities and intelligences which are not recognised in a formal and systematic way in education. Until such time as educational institutions (and the universities have a key role to play here as the most powerful definers and legitimators of credentialised knowledge) actually begin to recognise different forms of intelligence, and give each type equal respect with the other, the problem of stratification in schools will be merely relocated from one site to another, from between classes to within classes.

A 'mixed-ability' perspective is still fundamentally a hierarchical perspective. It generally equates ability with linguistic or mathematical abilities (as measured in standardised tests), and ranks students within these as 'high, average or low'. While moving to 'mixed ability' does help reduce the grosser structural injustices arising from rigid grouping (provided teachers are supported and educated in how to utilise it, and have a non-streaming attitude) this cannot promote equality *between abilities* as it fails to deal with the fundamental dilemma at the heart of contemporary education, namely its failure to recognise different forms of human intelligence rather than to stratify all people within one or two fields.

REFERENCES

Archer, M.S. (1982). *The Sociology of Educational Expansion*. Beverly Hills: Sage.

Ball, S.J., Bowe, R., and Gewirtz, S. (1995). Circuits of schooling: a sociological exploration of parental choice in social class contexts. *Sociological Review*, 43:52–78.

Barker Lunn, J. (1970). *Streaming in the Primary School*. Slough: National Foundation for Educational Research (NFER).

Bourdieu, P., and Passeron, J.-C. (1977). *Reproduction in Education, Society and Culture*. London: Sage.

Carr, M. (1988). The practice of within-class ability grouping: a study of teachers and pupils in the Stranorlar INTO branch in Co. Donegal. University College Dublin, Education Department, unpublished M.Ed. thesis.

Clancy, P. (1988). *Who Goes to College*. Dublin: Higher Education Authority.

Clancy, P. (1994). Expanding enrolments in higher education — some trends and implications. In *The Role of the University in Society*. Dublin: National University of Ireland.

Clancy, P. (1995). *Access to College: Patterns of Continuity and Change*. Dublin: Higher Education Authority.

Coolahan, J. (1981). *Irish Education: History and Structure*. Dublin: Institute of Public Administration.

Coolahan, J. (ed.) (1994). *Report on the National Education Convention*. Dublin: Government Publications Office.

Culliton, J. (1992). *A Time for Change: Industrial Policy for the 1990s*. Dublin: Government Publications Office.

Department of Education (1971). *Primary School Curriculum: Teacher's Handbook*. Dublin: Government Publications Office.

Department of Education (1990a). *Report of the Review Body on the Primary Curriculum*. Dublin: Government Publications Office.

Department of Education (1990b). *Report of the Primary Education Review Body*. Dublin: Government Publications Office.

Department of Education (1995). *Charting Our Education Future: White Paper on Education*. Dublin: Government Publications Office.

Department of Education (1997). *Tuarascáil Staitistiúil 1995/96: Statistical Report*. Dublin: Government Publications Office.

Department of Enterprise and Employment (1996). *Science, Technology and Innovation: The White Paper*. Dublin: Government Publications Office.

Devine, D. (1991). A study of reading ability groups: primary school children's experiences and views. University College Dublin, Education Department, unpublished M.Ed. thesis.

Eder, D. (1981). Ability grouping as self-fulfilling prophecy: a micro analysis of teacher–student interaction. *Sociology of Education*, 54 (3).

European Social Fund Programme Evaluation Unit (1996). *Evaluation Report: Early School Leavers Provision*. Dublin: European Social Fund Programme Evaluation Unit.

Fontes, P., and Kellaghan, T. (1983). Opinions of the Irish public on intelligence. *Irish Journal of Education*, XVII (2):55–67.

Gamoran, A. (1989). Rank, performance and mobility in elementary school grouping. *Sociological Quarterly*, 30:1009–123.

Gamoran, A. (1992). The variable effects of high school tracking. *American Sociological Review*, 57:812–28.

Gamoran, A. (1996). Curriculum standardisation and equality of opportunity in Scottish secondary education: 1984–1990. *Sociology of Education*, 69:1–21.

Gamoran, A., and Hallinan, M.T. (1995). Tracking students for instruction: consequences and implications for school restructuring. In M.T. Hallinan (ed.), *Restructuring Schools: Promising Practices and Policies*. New York: Plenum Press.

Gardner, H. (1983). *Frames of Mind: The Theory of Multiple Intelligences*. London: Paladin.

Gardner, H. (1991). *The Unschooled Mind: How Children Think and How Schools Should Teach*. New York: Basic Books.

Gardner, H., Kornhaber, M.L., and Wake, W.K. (1996). *Intelligence: Multiple Perspectives*. Fort Worth: Harcourt Brace.

Gewirtz, S., Ball, S., and Bowe, R. (1994). Parents, privilege and the education market place. *Research Papers in Education*, 9:3–29.

Hallinan, M. (1987). *The Social Organisation of Schools*. New York: Plenum Press.

Hallinan, M. (1992). The organisation of students for instruction in the middle school. *Sociology of Education*, 65:114–27.

Hallinan, M. (1994). Tracking: from theory to practice. *Sociology of Education*, 67 (2):79–91.

Hallinan, M. (1998). Educational reform and the organisation of schools. Lecture at University College Dublin, Equality Studies Centre, 5 January.

Hallinan, M., and Sorensen, A.B. (1983). The formation and stability of instructional groups. *American Sociological Review*, 48:838–51.

Hanafin, J., and Leonard, D. (1996). Conceptualising and implementing quality: assessment and the Junior Certificate. *Irish Educational Studies*, 15.

Hannan, D., Breen, R., Murray, B., Watson, D., and Hardiman, N. (1983). *Schooling and Sex Roles*. Dublin: Economic and Social Research Institute.

Hannan, D., and Boyle, M. (1987). *Schooling Decisions: The Origins and Consequences of Selection and Streaming in Irish Post-Primary Schools*. Dublin: Economic and Social Research Institute.

Hannan, D.F., and Shorthall, S. (1991). *The Quality of Their Education: School Leavers' Views of Their Education, of Educational Objectives and Outcomes*. Dublin: Economic and Social Research Institute, Paper No. 153.

Hannan, D.F., Smyth, E., McCullagh, J., O'Leary, R., and McMahon, D. (1996). *Coeducation and Gender Equality: Exam Performance, Stress and Personal Development*. Dublin: Oak Tree Press.

Harding, S. (1991). *Whose Science? Whose Knowledge?* Milton Keynes: Open University Press.

hooks, b. (1982). *Ain't I a Woman: Black Women and Feminism*. London: Pluto Press.

Kellaghan, T., Weir, S., O'hUallachain, S., and Morgan, M. (1995). *Educational Disadvantage in Ireland*. Dublin: Department of Education and Combat Poverty Agency.

Kerckhoff, A.C. (1986). Effects of ability grouping in British secondary schools. *American Sociological Review*, 51:842–58.

Lynch, K. (1989). *The Hidden Curriculum: Reproduction in Education, A Reappraisal*. Lewes: Falmer Press.

Lynch, K. (1997). Women in educational management: Ireland. In M. Wilson (ed.), *Women in Educational Management: A European Perspective*. London: Paul Chapman.

Lynch, K., and McLaughlin, E. (1995). Caring labour and love labour. In P. Clancy et al. (eds.), *Irish Society: Sociological Perspectives*. Dublin: Institute of Public Administration.

McDonnell, A. (1995). The ethos of Catholic voluntary secondary schools. University College Dublin, Education Department, unpublished Ph.D thesis.

MacNamara, J. (1987). Standardised tests in second-level education. University College Dublin, Education Department, unpublished MA thesis.

Madaus, G.F., and Macnamara, J. (1970). *Public Examinations: A Study of the Irish Leaving Certificate*. Dublin: Educational Research Centre, St Patrick's College.

Morgan, M., Hickey, B., and Kellaghan, T. (OECD) (1997). *International Adult Literacy Survey: Results for Ireland*. Dublin: Government Publications Office.

Oakes, J. (1985). *Keeping Track: How Schools Structure Inequality*. New Haven (CT): Yale University Press.

Oakes, J., Gamoran, A., and Page, R.N. (1992). Curriculum differentiation: opportunities, outcomes and meanings. In P.W. Jackson (ed.), *Handbook of Research on Curriculum*. New York: Macmillan.

O'Kelly, A. (1986). A case study in a community school: an analysis of streaming and its effects. University College Dublin, Education Department, unpublished M.Ed. thesis.

Ozga, J. (1993). *Women in Educational Management*. Buckingham: Open University Press.

Patchen, M. (1982). *Black–White Contact in Schools: Its Social and Academic Effects*. West Lafayette, Indiana: Purdue University Press.

Reay, D. (1996). Contextualising choice: social power and parental involvement. *British Educational Research Journal*, 22 (5):581–96.

Rist, R. (1970). Social class and teacher expectations: the self-fulfilling prophecy in ghetto education. *Harvard Education Review*, 40:411–51.

Rosenbaum, J. (1976). *Making Inequality: The Hidden Curriculum of High School Tracking*. New York: Wiley.

Rosenbaum, J. (1980). Social implications of educational grouping. In D.C. Benlinger (ed.), *Review of Research in Education*, vol. 7. Washington DC: American Educational Research Association.

Said, E. (1991). *Orientalism: Western Conceptions of the Orient.* Harmondsworth, Middlesex: Penguin (originally published 1978).

Shakeshaft, C. (1989). *Women in Educational Administration.* California: Sage.

Sharp, R., and Green, A. (1975). *Education and Social Control.* London: Routledge & Kegan Paul.

Sternberg, R.J. (1990). *Metaphors of the Mind: Conceptions of the Nature of Intelligence.* Canada: Cambridge University Press.

Technical Working Group to the Steering Committee on the Future of Higher Education (1995). *Interim Report to the Steering Committee on the Future of Higher Education.* Dublin: Higher Education Authority.

Weiner, G. (1994). *Feminisms and Education.* Milton Keynes: Open University Press.

Young, I.M. (1990). *Justice and the Politics of Difference.* Princeton University Press.

NOTES

1 Educational expansion has not been paralleled by a comparable increase in educational equality for working-class groups. At both primary and secondary levels, there is evidence that educational disadvantage, as measured in terms of reading attainment, is disproportionately concentrated in low-income working-class communities (Kellaghan et al., 1995). Literacy difficulties are also disproportionately concentrated in lower socio-economic groups (Morgan et al., 1997). There is also ongoing evidence that students from unskilled and semi-skilled manual backgrounds are more likely to drop out of school early, to attain lower grades in the Leaving Certificate examination and to have lower transfer rates to higher education (Clancy, 1988, 1995; Technical Working Group to the Steering Committee on the Future of Higher Education, 1995). Entrance to higher education, especially into the more elite sectors of higher education, is still dominated disproportionately by students from upper socio-economic groups; even where working-class students have increased their absolute level of educational attainment, they still remain relatively disadvantaged. Within higher education, they are over-represented in diploma and certificate courses run outside the university sector (Clancy, 1995).

2 While almost all vocational, community and comprehensive schools are mixed-gender, 64% of secondary schools are single-sex. In all, 36% of secondary schools are mixed, 36% are single-sex female and 28% are single-sex male (Department of Education, 1997:43).

3 The state does provide support for boarding for religious minorities in particular (mostly Protestants who have no Protestant school nearby) and for those living in remote island communities.

4 The 'free choice' ideology is an appealing one but it masks the deep structural reality that there can be little choice of school for those on very low incomes in a stratified society. Those without resources cannot move between schools at will especially if travel is involved. Moreover, they cannot move neighbourhoods to be strategically placed near sought-after schools, unlike those on higher incomes.

5 It is ironic that at the very time that universities in Ireland have moved away from the stratification of degree courses (into general/pass or honours) towards common papers, second-level education has become more stratified. There has been no debate about this but it does indicate how deep-rooted assumptions are about stratification in education.

6 There is a major gender difference in access to the technically oriented subjects at both senior and junior levels as nearly all single-sex girls' schools do not offer any of the three principal subjects in this field (engineering, technical drawing and construction studies). Nor are they available in most single-sex boys' schools although provision in these is somewhat better. These subjects have traditionally been offered only in vocational and community/comprehensive schools.

7   Nine of the thirty-three Leaving Certificate options are languages while six other subjects —
    classical studies, history, geography, economic history, business organisation and economics
    — are either wholly or totally dependent on linguistic forms of self-expression in
    examination and mode of assessment.

8   See note 1, chapter 1.

9   Young (1990:59) defines this as 'the universalising of one group's experience and its
    establishment as the norm'.

10 There can be no complete internal settlement to the problem of differentiation and stratifi-
    cation between people, and between forms of knowledge, in schools. While the relationship
    between the labour market (both paid and unpaid) and schooling is not a simple mechanistic
    one, in which labour market values are transported undiluted to the education site, schools
    are porous institutions where the values of society are constantly being filtered and
    negotiated (McDonnell, 1995). Students know both the market value of particular subjects
    and the level at which a given subject is taught (Hannan and Shorthall, 1991). The fact that
    certain forms of labour are differentially rewarded on the labour market means that the
    forms of knowledge which are differentially valued outside of schools tend to be differen-
    tially regarded within, especially when schooling is directly tied to labour market entry. So
    physics is generally more highly valued than home economics, as engineering is more highly
    valued than domestic work; higher mathematics tends to have higher status than higher art
    as excelling in the former gives access to more lucrative occupational opportunities than the
    latter. External market-related valuations, institutionalised in terms of pay and rewards for
    different occupations, infiltrate the perceptions and valuations placed on particular forms of
    knowledge and understanding.

SECTION 4

CONCLUSION

CHAPTER 10

EDUCATION AND SOCIAL JUSTICE: LIBERALISM, RADICALISM AND THE PROMOTION OF EQUALITY IN EDUCATION

Liberal equal opportunities policies have dominated public policy-making in the field of education (Arnot, 1991; Connell, 1993). While critical theorists, neo-Marxists, feminists and postmodernists have challenged the liberal agenda in education, and public policy generally, they have not eroded the influence of liberalism on policy-making.

A central theme in this chapter is that the pursuit of liberal equality policies can be a mere distraction from the business of equality in a more substantive sense. Promoting equal opportunities policies in a highly unequal society makes systems of inequality seem reasonable and acceptable; it moves the debate away from inequalities of wealth, power and prestige to the question of how to distribute inequalities more fairly (Baker, 1987:46).

CONCEPTIONS OF EQUALITY

Before examining the reasons why liberal policies cannot promote equality in any substantive sense, it is necessary to outline briefly different strands of political thought in relation to equality, and to locate liberalism within these. Baker (1998) suggests that there are essentially three strands of political thought in relation to equality: basic, liberal and radical. While it is not possible to examine these in detail here, the fundamental differences between the positions are outlined in order to clarify the position of liberalism.

BASIC EQUALITY

Basic equality upholds the view that all people are equal in dignity and worth; the belief that everyone is equally deserving of respect as a human person. This is the principle underpinning the Universal Declaration of Human Rights; it is a principle which is presupposed by other, more robust models of equality.

The basic view can and does accommodate widely different definitions of equality. Many of those peoples and countries which subscribe to the principle of 'equal dignity and worth' adopt a minimalist approach to equality. They would recognise that all human beings have basic needs for food, clothing, shelter and a right to bodily integrity, but would not go much further than this. In certain respects, basic equality is a principle which prohibits fundamental human rights abuses, rather than one which promotes a robust interpretation of equality. Basic equality does challenge racial, ethnic, sexual or social supremacism, however. It challenges the belief that certain people are 'superior to others' and deserving of greater respect because of some social, religious, ethnic or other designation. The principle of basic equality is important in and of itself, not least in a world order in which torture, rape and genocide are widely practised. While there are many obvious weaknesses with the principle of basic equality, not least the fact that it can be interpreted in widely differing ways, without it, it is impossible to justify giving each person an equal right to an equal life with other people.

LIBERAL EQUALITY

Liberal thinking presupposes basic equality and is centrally concerned with distribution; it is focused on distributing burdens and benefits, including inequalities, fairly in society.

What comprises the liberal view of equality is not simple. There are strong (radical) forms of liberalism, which espouse legislative and other policy provisions to promote equality of participation, and even equality of outcome in certain cases. There are also weaker forms of liberalism which do not go far beyond equal formal rights. One of the defining features of liberalism is the assumption that major inequalities, in terms of income and wealth especially, but also in terms of power and status, will always exist. The variations in the liberal approach to equality are discussed in more detail below.

RADICAL PERSPECTIVES

Radical egalitarian thought has its origins in Marxism, and in more recent times in radical feminism. It challenges the view that inequality is inevitable, believing it to be the outcome of collective decisions, made at state, corporate, political and other levels. In this century, R.H. Tawney (1964) launched a scathing attack on liberal views of equality. The core part of this critique focused on the failure of liberals to address economic and political inequalities. He argued that 'equality of condition', i.e. equality in the distribution of wealth, income and power, was central to any truly egalitarian society. He regarded equality of opportunity as a distraction from the more substantive issue of equality of condition. Radical theorists tend to be structuralists, although they hold a critical rather than a deterministic view of structures (Nielsen, 1985; Baker, 1987; Young, 1990; Delphy and Leonard, 1992; Cohen, 1995). They believe that political and economic structures are socially constructed and can be socially dismantled.

Unlike liberal and basic egalitarian theory, radical egalitarian theory defines economic equality as a central component of equality of condition. It also focuses on the issue of production in a way that liberal egalitarians do not. It specifies the type of ownership of the means of production which is necessary to promote equality in society: for Cohen it is joint world ownership of external goods; for Nielsen it is 'co-operative, democratically-controlled workers' social ownership and control of the means of production'; Baker also emphasises the importance of democratic forms of social ownership, while Tawney stresses the importance of a 'widely diffuse' ownership system of land and capital. Delphy and Leonard take a radical feminist (and anti-Marxist) perspective on ownership. They argue that the household is a unit of production and that control of services within the family is a key equality issue for women and children.

DEGREES OF LIBERALISM: EQUALITY OBJECTIVES AND THE LIBERAL FRAMEWORK

Equality objectives can, in some respects, be regarded as operating along a continuum. At one end of the continuum is the minimalist conception of equality which defines equality in terms of *equal formal rights and opportunities* and is a central component of equality of access. *Equality of participation* represents a stage beyond this where the focus is on enabling and encouraging members of different social groups to be equally able to participate in society, while *equality of success or outcome* is concerned with ensuring equal rates of success for these groups. At the opposite end of the continuum is the concept of *equality of condition* which aims at creating equality in the living conditions of all members of society. This refers to an ideal state where all goods, privileges and resources are distributed equally according to need (Equality Studies Centre, 1995).[1]

In policy terms, basic equality is focused only on minimal equal formal rights, while radical equality stands at the other end of the continuum supporting equality of condition. Liberalism occupies an interim position, with the weak interpretations focusing on equal formal rights and equality of access, while the stronger versions would support equal participation, and even procedures such as affirmative action, to promote equality of outcome.

Although they place a higher value on equality than conservatives, liberals prioritise general prosperity, or even security, above other goods. They value the freedom of the individual over and beyond the general realisation of equality objectives (Dworkin, 1984). Justice as fairness is a central tenet of contemporary liberalism, and within this perspective, 'Justice denies that the loss of freedom for some is made right by a greater good shared by others' (Rawls, 1971:28). Because of the prioritisation of freedom over equality, the focus of interest within liberalism has been on promoting equality of opportunity for individuals rather than equality of condition.

Before going on to examine the origins and limitations of liberalism, it is necessary first to review the scope and limitations of different conceptions of equality, a number of which are central to the liberal tradition.

EQUAL FORMAL RIGHTS AND OPPORTUNITIES, AND EQUALITY OF ACCESS: SCOPE AND LIMITATIONS

The minimalist conception of equality is that which defines equality in terms of the provision of equal rights to participate in education and in economic, social, political and cultural life, where such rights are construed as the absence of legal and institutionalised barriers to entry and participation. This view is linked to the idea of formal equality of opportunity, i.e. the idea that no one should be prevented from entry to education, employment, politics, etc., or in advancing from one level of participation to another, on the grounds of gender, sexual orientation, ethnicity, disability, or any other irrelevant characteristic, and that access to and advancement within these institutions should be based on merit.

To a large extent, formal and quasi-legal barriers to equal access and participation in education have been removed in Europe, although there are exceptions such as the requirement for entry to primary teaching in Ireland, where disabled people have experienced direct discrimination which is not yet outlawed under law.[2] Indirect discrimination has not been prohibited in Irish education, however, nor is it addressed in the draft Education Bill (No. 2) 1997. Its relative invisibility and indeterminacy makes it difficult to address. An example of a non-formal barrier would be the fact that schools and colleges have no facilities to cater for deaf or blind students and no provisions in their budget to address their needs (for example for an interpreter or a Brailling service). This means in effect that a rule exists that all people must be able to hear or read print to attend the school or college in question. Clearly, deaf and blind people respectively cannot meet these regulations and thereby experience indirect discrimination.[3] Ethnic minorities can experience similar indirect discrimination when schools fail to take any account of their culture and lifestyle. Travellers are indirectly discriminated against in many schools which operate a 'first come, first served' selection policy, for example. Being nomadic, most Travellers do not and cannot plan where they will be years in advance. As they do not 'get their names down' on school waiting lists, they are effectively excluded indirectly from attending schools with such a policy. The rule favours people who can plan their lives, and where they will live, many years in advance. Not only does such a rule indirectly discriminate against Travellers but it excludes other groups such as refugees, migrant workers or those living in marginalised communities, many of whom may lack either the knowledge or the resources to plan in advance.

EQUALITY OF PARTICIPATION: SCOPE AND LIMITATIONS

It is now widely recognised that equality of formal rights and opportunities has little impact on the promotion of equality in any substantive sense. Substantive equality depends not simply on having the formal right to participate but on having the actual ability and resources to exercise that right, that is by being able to participate.

The second way in which equality can be conceptualised therefore is in terms of equality of participation. This comes close to what Rawls terms 'fair' equality of opportunity. It involves both **enabling** a designated disadvantaged or minority group, or an individual member of the group, to participate and **encouraging** them to participate.

Enabling participation means ensuring that the basic material needs and the basic psychological, educational and other needs of the target group are met so that they are in a position to participate on equal terms. For example, if working-class children are to participate on equal terms with middle-class children in public examinations, they must have access to the same quality and level of resources. If women who have worked full-time in the home as carers and domestic workers for many years are to return to the paid labour market and participate equally with others, they need to be prepared educationally and psychologically for such a return.

To have equal participation, it is also necessary to encourage participation. **Encouraging participation** means ensuring that the members of the target group are motivated to participate and are accepted by others as full participants. This means going beyond provision for basic or other needs. It could mean the development of a proactive policy in a given school such as equality training for teachers and equality work with students which would create a climate encouraging practices promoting equal participation. Or it could mean affirmative action through direct advertising for marginalised groups to enter a given programme, or devising special support services so that they will be able to participate fully and effectively if they do enter.

Equal participation assumes the pre-existence of equal formal rights and opportunities and equality of access. Policies based on the equal participation principle go beyond the protection of formal rights and the prevention of discrimination as they actively intervene to enable and encourage equal participation. However, enabling and encouraging equal participation does not ensure it. While interventions such as improved education and training about equality issues within a given school may make the environment for women, Travellers or disabled people more favourable, or while developing access programmes for various types of disadvantaged students to enable them to enter higher education will undoubtedly improve their rates of participation, such policies do not guarantee equal participation as the interventions work on the principles of facilitating equality rather than ensuring it. Voluntarism and selectivity are at the heart of the equal participation objective. The agency or body that sets out to promote equal participation is required to enable or encourage participation, it does not have to ensure it. Schools and colleges can effectively lay claim to promoting the equal participation objective by engaging in a selective range of activities although the scope and level of the interventions may be far from comprehensive. (A frequent example is the development of an equality policy without allocating the resources to achieve it, or without specifying targets or deadlines for achieving objectives etc.) Such procedures give public legitimacy to an organisation, although their interventions have limited impact. Moreover, as noted above already, policies promoting equal participation will favour the relatively advantaged among the disadvantaged as they will be in the strongest position to avail of whatever services and supports are offered.

EQUALITY OF OUTCOME: SCOPE AND LIMITATIONS

The degree of success people experience in the course of their participation in a given context is the primary determinant of status in contemporary society. If society was not hierarchically stratified in terms of wealth, power and privilege, then the question of equality of success or outcome would not be so significant. However, since society is so stratified, then it follows that achieving equal rates of success or outcomes for particular groups or individuals is one way in which to define equality.

Equality of outcome represents a stage beyond the objective of equal participation and refers to policies which promote equality in the outcome of social processes. In particular, equality of outcome between marginalised or excluded groups and those not marginalised means achieving overall equality between these groups in terms of access to, and the distribution of, educational, economic, cultural, political and other benefits. In so far as it is adopted by liberals, equality of outcome is at the radical end of the liberal perspective.

Mechanisms for promoting equal outcomes include 'affirmative action', 'preferential treatment' or 'reverse discrimination', and 'quotas'. It should be noted, moreover, that a number of these strategies could also be employed to achieve equality of participation. For example, affirmative action could include the running of a special third-level access programme for disabled students to enable them to participate on equal terms with able-bodied students when in the third-level education system.

There are, however, a number of difficulties associated with the realisation of this objective. The most obvious one is the fact that groups which are dominant in the present system, and/or who are already beneficiaries, will resist any strategy for their displacement. And equality of outcome policies would effectively demand displacement, for example, in sensitive areas such as entry to higher education. Another difficulty is the complexity of managing quota systems, for example, especially with groups where definitional problems arise in relation to their identification, such as with disabled people. Also, positive discrimination or quota systems are likely to be most effective for easily identifiable large groups such as women, and where the quota set is at a substantial level. Given the fact that women represent more than half the population, the promotion of policies of equality of success or outcome would clearly have a considerable advantage for them. The principle would also have a positive and visible effect on large groups such as working-class people, while its impact on smaller groups, albeit significant, would be less visible. Their low representation in the population (e.g. less than 1% of the population in Ireland belong to the Traveller ethnic minority group) would mean that the quota could be met by appointing or selecting very small numbers of people. Furthermore, even if equality of outcome policies are successful, and equal rates of success for marginalised groups are achieved, the mobility out of these marginalised groups by the successful minority can indirectly peripheralise groups further as the most advantaged are selected out.

A further challenge presented by the 'equality of outcome' approach to equality is that if it is operated singly for one group, without being simultaneously implemented for all other groups, this would result in substantial inequalities within the group itself. For example, if equality of outcome was pursued as an objective for women but not for disabled people or working-class people, it would not address inequalities among women arising from social class or disability. If equality of outcome is to be fully effective therefore, it needs to be operationalised for all groups simultaneously.

Notwithstanding these difficulties, equality of outcome represents a radical challenge to existing policies.

Although equality of outcome would represent a major advance in the promotion of equality in society, it does not address the fundamental problems of hierarchies of power, wealth and other privileges. What it does is replace or supplement the existing elites within the economic, political, educational and other hierarchies with new elites from hitherto disadvantaged groups. While this would represent a significant shift in the balance of power and privilege, it must be noted that privileged positions are by definition scarce and only a small number of any given group will ever enter these positions.

Also, regardless of which disadvantaged group is in question, it is likely to be the relatively advantaged from within that group who will become upwardly socially mobile in any system which promotes equality of success or outcome. (The same issue arises with equal participation policies.) It is the relatively privileged who will be best positioned to take advantage of the new opportunities for participation or success.

The Philosophical Origins of Liberalism and Its Failure to Address Economic Inequalities

To appreciate fully the limitations of liberalism as a framework for developing equality policies in education, it is necessary to comment briefly on its origins in political philosophy.

Liberalism, like all political philosophies, is of its time and place, and is profoundly shaped by the historical context of its existence (Hall, 1986:47). Although liberalism is a fractured philosophy with both conservative and radical tendencies (with Adam Smith and John Locke on one side and Thomas Paine on the other) in the analysis of equality, liberals have generally weighed in on the conservative side. The reasons why this happens arise from the sociological roots of liberalism. It emerged in the seventeenth and eighteenth centuries *in opposition* to the old feudal order and *aligned with* the emerging bourgeois order (p. 39). The antagonism which led to the emergence of liberalism was essentially one *within* the elites of society: an antagonism between the old feudal lords and the champions of free trade, the merchant classes. Up to the eighteenth century, privileges and powers had been legally defined in the interests of the feudal estates.

> The *roturier* was not merely a social inferior, but the victim of economic disabilities imposed by law. The noble by inheritance or purchase did not merely possess a title; he was the owner of profitable immunities. The special characteristic of the class system in France and Germany had been, in fact, that inequality was not primarily economic, but juristic, and that, in spite of gross disparities of wealth, it rested on difference, not merely of income, but of legal status. (Tawney, 1964:92–3)

Since the major inequalities which the bourgeoisie experienced were legal rather than economic the focus of their interest was juristic rather than economic.

> A distinction was drawn between *égalité de droit* and *égalité de fait*, between formal or legal equality and practical or economic equality. The primary aim of reformers was the achievement of the first, since, once the first was established, the second, in so far as it was desirable, would, it was thought, establish itself. (pp. 94–5)

And the logic of liberalism was correct. If legal barriers were removed between those elites in society who had similar resources in terms of wealth and power, then equal opportunities were realisable for the disadvantaged group (the new bourgeoisie). Once legal and quasi-legal barriers were removed, groups could then compete equally as they had access to equal resources. The problem is, however, that the conditions which operated for the bourgeoisie vis-à-vis the feudal lords do not operate in the relations between most dominant and subordinate groups in contemporary European society. Juristic inequalities are generally of far less significance than economic inequalities or power inequalities. While recognising that there are groups for whom formal equality before the law is still a problem, groups such as the unemployed, women or disabled people are often more disadvantaged in Western European societies by their lack of resources than by the formal legal barriers to their advancement.

Liberal reformers have been centrally concerned, therefore, with ensuring that people are equal in both legal and quasi-legal terms. The interest is in formal, juristic equality in the civil and political realm, rather than substantive, economic equality. The dominant traditions within liberalism are primarily concerned with protecting equal formal rights and ensuring equality of access: 'once the rules governing admissions to places of education, appointments to jobs and promotions are fair, a society is an equal opportunity society' (O'Neill, 1977:179). Unequal results are justified if everyone has an equal opportunity to succeed.

Liberals also believe that equality of opportunity is to be achieved by maximising the economic and political liberty of the citizen. They have espoused the cause of an open meritocratic society where those with intelligence and ambition (IQ + Effort) can rise to the top. Liberty is defined therefore in a negative way — it is defined as freedom from constraint so that one can be free to compete. The law is there to regulate between competing contenders 'without questioning or interfering with the basic dispositions of wealth and power in society' (Hall, 1986:42).

In the post-Rawlsian period, liberal educationalists have, however, moved beyond a simple preoccupation with equality of access and equal formal rights (with increasing pressure from marginalised groups such as women, disabled people and ethnic and racial minorities) and supported fair equal opportunities policies as opposed to just formal equal opportunities. The principle of fair equality of opportunity refers to when 'positions are to be not only open in a formal sense, but that all should have a fair chance to attain them' (Rawls, 1971:73). Thus liberal educationalists have supported policies which *enable* and *encourage equal participation* in education for marginalised groups. With equal participation, the aim is to ensure that marginalised groups will be able to participate on equal terms with other groups once they enter the system. However, while this facilitates success it does not guarantee it. *Equality of outcome*, which would *ensure* equal rates of success for marginalised groups within the different systems of education, via such procedures as quotas or preferential appointments, is far less likely to be supported within the liberal position. *Equality of condition*, which would ensure substantive economic and political equality in the living conditions of all members of society, is clearly not part of the liberal agenda.

LIMITATIONS OF THE LIBERAL EQUAL OPPORTUNITIES APPROACH TO EQUALITY IN EDUCATION

Those who have been involved in teaching, research and/or policy initiatives relating to the elimination of social class inequalities in education are familiar with the outcome of policies devoted to the promotion of formal equality of educational opportunity; they have resulted in a trickle of social mobility between social classes but have had no real impact on the class structure (Clancy, 1988, 1995; Shavit and Blossfeld, 1993; Erikson and Jonsson, 1996). Both the weak and the strong versions of liberal equal opportunities policies fit comfortably with the interests of the dominant educational, economic and social order. In many respects, they legitimate existing structured inequality while offering selective mobility into elite positions for those who are selected out. There are a number of reasons why policies designed to promote both formal and fair equality of opportunity in a highly stratified society will not promote equality in any substantive sense.

In a highly unequal society, someone has to occupy the subordinate positions even if the identity of those occupying them may change from white to black, from male to female, or from citizen to migrant worker. The concepts of both formal and fair equality of opportunity are premised on the assumption that the social hierarchies remain; all that differs between this and a system in which there is no emphasis on equality of opportunity is who ends up on top. The whole point of equality of opportunity is to 'regulate the competition for advantage': this does not alter the inequalities themselves (Baker, 1987:46). Liberal policies do not propose 'the absence of violent contrasts of income and condition but equal opportunities of becoming unequal' (Tawney, 1964:103). Indeed policies of equal opportunity are lauded from public platforms often on the understanding that this very limited notion of equality which they propose will be

> content with ceremonial honours. It retains its throne, on condition that it refrains from meddling with the profitable business of the factory and the market place. Its credit is good, so long as it does not try to cash its cheques. Like other respectable principles it is encouraged to reign, provided that it does not attempt to rule. (ibid.)

The problem stems from the fact that

> From its inception classical liberalism was identified with the 'free market' and opposed any intervention by the state to remedy the unequal consequences of market competition or to distribute goods, resources and opportunities more equitably between the competing classes. (Hall, 1986:41)

Classical liberalism has never opposed hierarchies or graduations in society except where these rested on legal privilege (Tawney, 1964:102). In fact, in many respects, the inequalities emerging from the meritocratic order are regarded as legitimate, inevitable and, indeed, even desirable. They are seen as desirable in so far as they offer an incentive to work and compete; they are seen as inevitable and legitimate in so far as they reflect the so-called 'natural' differences in talent (Davis and Moore, 1970).

The model of justice which underpins liberalism is devoid of a structural analysis. It is concerned with removing irrelevant considerations or barriers affecting individuals, but remains blind to the discrimination which lies within institutions themselves, the discrimination which is structured within them. It does not address the position of 'individuals-as-relational-actors' in institutional systems structured around inequality. It is not surprising to find therefore that moral approbation frequently follows educational success, while its opposite follows failure, for disadvantaged groups. Those who are structurally excluded find that they are held personally accountable for their own exclusion.

The abstracted individualism which underpins liberalism focuses analytical attention on personal character and individual attributes. Attributes such as gender, social class, ethnicity, religion, race, disability or sexual orientation are examined, not in relational terms for their equality impact, but rather in individualistic terms, what Bourdieu (1973) called 'atomistic terms'. The causes of inequality are sought within the attributes themselves rather than within the sets of social, economic, cultural and political relations which operate between these 'attribute-bearing' individuals. While there is a growing body of research and theory, especially in the feminist field, which challenges this orientation, it is still standard practice in educational theory and practice to locate the problem of inequality within the dominated rather than the dominant, within women rather than men, within black rather than white, within migrant workers rather than the host society, etc. (Mac an Ghaill, 1994).

Consequently when policies are introduced to promote equality in education, we tend to focus on ways in which the dominated rather than the dominant are problematic; the focus is on how women need to change in order to succeed in a male-dominated world, rather than how men and the education institutions they have constructed must be adapted and changed; it is on how working-class people must adapt rather than how middle-class values in education are to be challenged; it is on how 'to cope' with disability or cultural difference rather than invent non-disablist and truly intercultural systems.

Selective mobility for those who succeed at adapting to the dominant order is the goal. Liberal equal opportunities policies in education (in practice if not in theory) are very much about selecting out members of marginalised or disadvantaged groups to become socially mobile within the existing system. And the measure of success is to achieve equality of access, and perhaps participation, by marginalised groups within the dominant systems. Thus equality for many groups has been measured in terms of upward social mobility. If the proportion of working-class students who enter higher education rises, or if there is a rise in the proportion of women taking engineering, then it is assumed that equality objectives are being realised. The focus is not on the ways in which feminist forms of knowledge are structurally excluded from education itself. Nor is there a focus on how the ordering of economic and labour relations creates a stratified labour market which makes inequality in social class terms inevitable, and which thereby devalues the forms of knowledge associated with lowly paid occupations, including knowledge relating to caring and personal relationships.

While social mobility is a laudable goal from the perspective of those who are successful, it does not radically alter the pattern of inequality which exists. Logically, it is not possible to enable all those who are disadvantaged to succeed, both because there are not sufficient places at the top of the privilege pyramid for all who might be technically eligible to occupy them, and because those who currently occupy elite positions will resist substantial displacement. Also, without equality of condition selective mobility from within any marginalised group will inevitably favour the most advantaged within that group.

MERITOCRACY

Within the liberal tradition, equality of educational opportunity is normally defined in meritocratic terms. And within this frame of reference, equality is an issue principally for those who are deemed talented; Young's (1958) famous dictum is the ideal: IQ + Effort = Merit. Yet to develop talent (ability + effort), access to privileged resources is essential. In a hierarchically and patriarchally stratified society, one cannot draw a clear dichotomy between ascribed and achieved qualities. Students who have prior access (via their homes/habitus) to the cultural talents that schools value are the most likely to be labelled intelligent, and those who know that they have most to gain from the education system are the most likely to work hard and be ambitious. Lack of developed talent is a function, in many ways, of the hierarchical orderings of society itself, while lack of effort is a function of the lack of visibility and availability of opportunity (Tumin, 1970).

The net outcome of equal opportunities policies based on meritocratic principles, therefore, is the sponsoring of the 'talented' into elite positions; and given the structure of opportunity in society, the talented and the privileged are closely related. It is those who have the resources to develop talent who gain most, both within a given group and in a comparative group context.

Because liberal policies based on the principles of equalising opportunities presuppose the existence of social hierarchies, they do not pose a serious threat to patriarchal, disablist, ethnocentric or capitalist values. The identity of those who compete for privilege may change, but the individualistic competition and the anti-community values which this entails remain the same (Baker, 1987). Thus, a culture based on meritocratic principles is basically anti-communitarian as each person is rewarded constantly for maximising self-interest. Divisions between the successful and the unsuccessful, between the haves and have-nots, are merely exaggerated in a system guided by the principle of equal opportunity as it is now assumed that those who get to the top 'deserve to'; they owe no debt to their inferiors. This is one of the most divisive features of meritocratic systems, and of equal opportunities policies premised on such principles within societies without equality of condition.

Another problem with a liberal equal opportunities approach to equality issues is that it assumes wrongly that the successes and failures of one generation can be separated from the life chances of the next without altering the structural conditions under which success and failure are created. This may be a logical possibility but it is not generally a social possibility. One cannot give equal opportunities to children whose parents own vastly different resources; when governments try to do this, all that happens is that those parents who have extra resources use these to offset the effects of equal opportunities policies designed to help the disadvantaged. Financial, power and other differentials operating outside of education maintain educational differentials within the system.[4] We will have equality in education and in society at large only when we have what Tawney has termed practical or economic equality. 'In the absence . . . of a large measure of equality of circumstances, opportunities to rise must necessarily be illusory' (Tawney, 1964:107).

Because the middle and upper classes of society (especially men within these classes) are closely integrated into the educational decision-making machinery of most states, both directly, through their own representative bodies (such as political parties), and indirectly, through the mediating bodies which manage and control the day-to-day running of educational services (such as managerial bodies, curriculum and assessment bodies, trade unions, local authorities, etc.), they can order the pattern of educational relations in their own class (and/or gender or racial) interest (Lynch, 1990). There is no hidden hand guiding the educational system as the bodies which seek to influence and define the educational agenda are usually overt and direct in their interventions. This is evident in Ireland in the ways in which powerful interest groups succeeded in radically altering the terms of the original Education Bill (No. 1) 1997 for the Education (No. 2) Bill 1997.[5]

What is being suggested therefore is that most equality policies in education are framed in terms of liberal notions of equality of opportunity. The focus of attention is on promoting equality of opportunity between the dominated and dominant groups. The aim is not to eliminate hierarchies of knowledge, power, wealth and privilege which create unequal structures and positions, but rather to enable people to compete more equally for the unequal positions.

This is not to suggest here that there is no gain for anyone in promoting liberal equal opportunities policies. There is gain for the relatively advantaged within the marginalised or excluded group who are selected out into more privileged positions. However, the myth of liberalism is that the selection or success of the few will become the pattern for the many.

BEYOND LIBERALISM: EQUALITY OF CONDITION

What equality of condition involves is the development of an egalitarian society which is committed to equality in the living conditions of all its members (both citizens and non-citizens) taking due account of their heterogeneity be it arising from gender, ethnicity, race, disability, religion, age, sexual orientation or any other relevant attribute. It involves equality of economic and political conditions, and equality of respect. It means having substantial equality in working conditions, job satisfaction and income across different occupations; an educational system devoted to developing equally the potential of every member of society; a radically democratic politics which is aimed at the equal participation and influence of all persons; and a restructuring of family and personal life for the sake of enriching the personal relationships of every individual. Policies based on the second and third criteria of equal status could clearly contribute substantially to satisfying this fourth criterion, although they would continue to fall short of it.

The structures and mechanisms required to promote equality of condition would involve widespread changes in constitutional and legislative frameworks, as well as in the political, economic, social and cultural infrastructures of the society. Taxation, legislation and education would be among the many mechanisms required to bring about change.

Those who argue for equality of condition also recognise that the solution to the problem of inequality does not rest with changing the attributes and attitudes of particular individuals. Inequalities do not arise from the intrinsic nature or characteristics of marginalised or excluded groups but from the way in which their unique characteristics are handled. Moreover, they persist because positions are differentially rewarded or resourced in terms of wealth, power and privilege, not because of the character of the people who occupy these positions. Yet most policies treat the marginalised or excluded group as the problem when the problem lies with the structures of the institutions and systems which people occupy and the attitudes of those who control them.

While the limitations of models of equality focusing on equality of access, participation and outcome are intrinsic to the objectives themselves, the limitations of equality of condition are extrinsic to the objective. The difficulties are primarily political and institutional, namely the difficulty of realising equality of condition in a society which is already structured around income, power and wealth inequalities, and where such differentials are protected by a variety of legal, institutional and other political and social supports.

Within education, the dilemma arises in relation to credentialising forms of cultural capital (namely knowledge and understanding) and utilising modes of assessment which are not the forms of capital and modes of assessment legitimated by those who control the cultural markets both within and without education. The reality of educational power relations is that the status, power and, in certain cases, income differentials of those who manage and mediate educational services[6] are contingent on maintaining the existing hierarchies of cultural relations. And while the identity of these mediators changes from country to country, in all countries these proximate decision-makers within the machinery of the state exercise considerable power to direct policy and determine the forms of knowledge which will or will not be credentialised and how they are assessed. In particular, university professors, teachers, educational managers, researchers and related professionals have all benefited substantially from the ideology which proclaims the superiority of so-called mental labour over manual labour — their pay differentials are tied to it. And as the educational currency in which they deal has placed a high value on linguistic and mathematical coinage, any devaluation of these intelligences and related modes of assessment poses a threat to their professional and career interests (Bourdieu, 1993).

While there is no readily available solution to this dilemma, it can be addressed by developing a strong politics of presence for marginalised groups within all decision-making systems and government departments within the state, including decision-making systems in the Department of Education, and in other education bodies such as the National Council for Curriculum and Assessment, the National Council for Vocational Education and the Higher Education Authority, to name but a few. This issue is discussed in more detail below.

In addition, what can be recognised and made more visible to existing elites and power holders in society is that the cost of inequality, politically, socially and economically, is high (Glyn and Milliband, 1994). That is to say, while it may be unrealistic to expect privileged groups or individuals to support egalitarian aims on the grounds of principle or on the grounds of compassion, what is possible is that they may come to support them on the basis of enlightened self-interest. Wastage of educational ability, poverty, unemployment, ethnic tensions, gender tensions, and other by-products of inequality create political and social instabilities and conflicts in a given society. These instabilities result in both direct costs and opportunity costs which are considerable. Such costs if enumerated and publicised could contribute to developing a commitment to equality even among those whose immediate self-interest may not be visibly served by equality of condition.

Even if a given society does not adhere to the principle of equality of condition, a recognition of its importance does influence the way in which objectives are framed and targeted. For example, a move to promote greater equality in the distribution of income and wealth through the promotion of greater equality in taxation structures would move society towards this objective; the introduction of systems and structures which promoted participatory democracy in decision-making would also help in the realisation of equality of condition.

The failure to recognise the importance of equality of condition, on the other hand, means that powerful interest groups who own and control dispropor-tionately large resources of wealth, power and income in society will always be in a position to use these to circumvent or challenge equality policies developed within a purely liberal framework. This, in turn, will put considerable expense and onus on the state and its agents to defend the policies it has enacted.

Having identified the parameters and weaknesses of a liberal perspective and then outlined in a general way the principles which would underlie a more radical principle of equality of condition, the chapter will go on to explore tentatively some solutions to the problems of inequality in the light of radical thinking. It will focus on institutions and structures especially. It will begin by examining some limitations of the distributive approach to equality which has dominated both liberal and radical thinking.

EQUALITY AS DISTRIBUTION AND EQUALITY AS RESPECT FOR DIFFERENCE

Although radical and liberal interpretations of equality have been presented above as being quite polarised, much of what has been written about equality in both traditions aligns the practice of equality with the practice of distri-bution (Young, 1990). Liberals have focused on equalising access to education, while radicals (such as Bowles and Gintis, 1976, for example) have been princi-pally concerned with equalising wealth and incomes as a way of promoting equality within education itself.

The limitations of the distributive approach to equality is that it is based, in part, on the assumption that education itself is an implicitly unproblematic good (Connell, 1993). The content, process and structures of education are subjected to critique or required to change only for secondary reasons, namely in order to promote an exterior objective such as equal access, participation or outcome. The hierarchies of cultural practice which are institutionalised in the curricula of schools, and the hierarchies of power which are institutionalised in the modes of assessment and in organisational and pedagogical practice, are not required to change except and in so far as change is necessary to achieve equal access, participation or outcome for a particular target group.

The issue of equality, however, is not just a distributional one, it is also an issue of ensuring equal respect for all groups and individuals. This demands that the culture, lifestyle and values of minority and other groups are given full and equal recognition within a given education system and that systems for equalising the distribution of power are also introduced. The issue of equality is not just about getting working-class or other marginalised groups and individuals 'in and out of the system' successfully; it is about changing the nature of education itself in both its organisation and its curricular substance. Radical views of equality in education must complement the distribution model with one which is centred on equality of respect.

CHANGING THE ORGANISATIONAL AND PEDAGOGICAL RELATIONS OF SCHOOLING: FROM HIERARCHY TO PARTNERSHIP AND DIALOGUE

The practices and procedures which govern the organisation of the school as a social system, and which determine the nature of pedagogical relations in classrooms, are crucial in determining the outcomes of equality policies. Unfortunately our schools are remarkably similar both in the structure of their power relations and in the nature of their pedagogical practice to what they were in the nineteenth century. The banking concept of education (Freire, 1972a) with its implicit belief in the superior knowledge and authority of the teacher and its passive view of the learner is still highly pervasive. Such hierarchical relations are antithetical to the development of an egalitarian perspective as they habituate both pupil/student and staff consciousness to a mode of educational and organisational relations in which dominance and subordinacy are naturalised. If schools are not participatory democracies in their organisation, and dialogical in their pedagogical practice, then it is likely that equality goals pursued through the curricula (e.g. about democracy and rights) will be self-defeating as the hidden curriculum of schooling will contradict the message of the formal curriculum. And students are subjected more systematically and consistently to the equality message (or the inequality message) of the former rather than the latter (Lynch, 1989).

Equality of condition would require a deconstructing of the hierarchies of organisational and pedagogical practice in schools and colleges. It would require changes in styles of management, discipline and organisation to make schools and colleges truly democratic and accountable to children and young people, and not only to so-called educational partners, be these teacher bodies, parents or whoever, all of whom are adults. More open and democratically structured pedagogical, organisational and management styles, taking account of the basic dialogical pedagogical principles developed by Freire (1972a, 1972b, 1973), would therefore be a prerequisite for equality of condition. It is truly amazing how children and young people are so rarely consulted in matters and decisions that directly affect their lives. They are not defined as legitimate partners in education (Lynch, 1998). Yet there are very few adult interest groups that one would dare to speak about without consulting directly with them. Would men hold a conference on women without consultation? Would disabled people be ignored in developing policies relating to themselves? Even if such events happened, it is not politically acceptable to act in this way. We have not yet begun to take young people and children seriously as legitimate partners in their own education. Yet the UN Convention on the Rights of the Child (ratified by Ireland) states that

> The States Parties shall assure to the child who is capable of forming his or her own views the right to express those views freely in all matters affecting the child, the views of the child being given due weight in accordance with the age and the maturity of the child. (Article 12.1)

CHALLENGING CURRICULUM PRACTICE AND MODES OF ASSESSMENT

Schools and colleges are the principal institutions in our society for transmitting and legitimating cultural forms. Yet most of what is incorporated in the formal curricula of schools and colleges does not take a full account of the diverse cultures in our society. The lifeworld of working-class people, ethnic minorities, disabled people, Travellers, women, or groups such as linguistic minorities, are given little space in the formal curriculum. At present, only two forms of human intelligence are given full recognition in most formal Western educational systems: linguistic and logical-mathematical (Hanafin, 1997). All the other intelligences, including spatial, musical, the personal intelligences (intrapersonal and interpersonal) and bodily kinaesthetic intelligence, have a relatively lowly place in education (Gardner, 1983, 1993). The failure to take on board cultural diversity and ability-related differences is not only a problem for the people concerned, however, it is also a problem for society. Much talent and commitment is lost when schooling does not recognise cultural difference. The high drop-out rates among young working-class people, and more especially among Travellers, is perhaps the most visible proof of this. In terms of ability, it is self-evident that much of the work that people do in life, especially service work, such as teaching, nursing, marketing, etc., and all caring work, requires personal intelligences yet there is no place for the development of these within the present system. An egalitarian policy would mean devising a new curriculum, one in which all types of human intelligence, and different cultures, were given equal recognition. This would mean bringing about changes in the nature of what is taught within syllabi, introducing new subject matter and altering modes of assessment.

The preoccupation of so much of formal education with credentialising those forms of knowledge and human understanding which can be assessed and measured through the medium of written language and mathematics is, in fact, a factor creating inequality and disability in education. For example, many people have insights, competencies, skills and abilities which cannot be measured through the linguistic medium, yet such people are heavily penalised and often labelled disabled or failures in schools; examples include people whose primary interest is in the visual/spatial sphere, those who work through the oral rather than the written medium, those who are primarily oriented to the bodily kinaesthetic sphere, and those whose principal competencies are in the interpersonal and intrapersonal areas. The problem is not that such people are unwilling to learn or are educationally disabled, but that the education system does not allow them the means of expression or the opportunity to develop the fields of competency and interest which they have (Gardner, 1983, 1993). Neither the curricula nor the modes of assessment allow fully for the differences in intelligences between pupils. Not only do certain forms of knowledge predominate in education, so also do the modes of assessment associated traditionally with these forms of knowledge, namely pencil and paper tests of linguistic and mathematical capabilities. In effect, equality of condition would mean changing the school, the curricula and modes of assessment, not just making minorities or other marginalised groups fit the system as it stands. Equality of condition would require not just that various groups were enabled to access, participate and succeed on equal terms with others, but that the organisation of school life, and the formal curriculum, took account of their lifestyle and culture and included it fully in the school/college. It would mean mainstreaming differences into the curriculum, organisation, culture and life of the school. To do this would require considerable research investment as there has been very little research on how to develop musical, personal or visual-spatial intelligences on a truly universal scale.

THE IMPORTANCE OF PRESENCE FOR THE REALISATION OF EQUALITY: EQUALITY OF POWER

In an economically and politically stratified society, such as that which operates in most of the welfare capitalist states in Europe, the state itself is seriously constrained in its ability to act against powerful and political economic interests, not least because its own survival is dependent on taxation and returns on accumulated capital from such interests (Offe, 1984). In addition, the mediators and managers of educational (and other) services have career, status, power and income-related interests vested in the status quo (Lynch, 1990). Liberal reformers frequently ignore these contradictions at the heart of state action. The response is not just to ask teachers to become transformative intellectuals, as Giroux (1981, 1983), McLaren (1989) and other critical theorists suggest, but rather to develop a counterforce of political action by mobilising the marginalised and excluded groups both inside and outside education. Only through organised and systematic democratic action, based on principles of participatory democracy, will change occur.

Partnerships and dialogue are crucial therefore not only for the promotion of equality within schools and classrooms (Freire, 1972a), but for the development of effective equality policies at regional, national or international levels. A dialogical relationship is essential because of the dangers inherent in any equality process that the targeted 'marginalised group' becomes the object of charitable desire or professional career interest; in either case, the danger is that the interest of the professional or the philanthropist will take precedence over the interest of the target group. In other words, a form of colonisation can take place whereby the goal of equality becomes the project of an outsider group (mostly professionals in the case of education), and ultimately the professional group's self-preservation can and does take precedence over equality considerations for the target group. The net outcome of this process is frequently the enactment of liberal reforms which give legitimacy to the work of the professionals but which have only marginal impact in terms of equality outcomes for the people in question. Without power-sharing between marginalised groups, policy-makers and professionals, colonisation of the marginalised is often the unforeseen by-product of policy action. What is being suggested here is that liberal equality policies have come to predominate, not simply because these are the policies which are most politically palatable to the existing power-brokers in education, but also because the marginalised peoples and groups at which these policies are supposedly directed are not an integral part of the decision-making process. Their voices, if represented at all, are mediated by professionals (such as teachers, psychologists, researchers, doctors, social workers, health care workers, etc.) and other service workers outside their control. And mediated voices are not, by definition, organic voices. To move beyond the liberal agenda, it is essential that the oppressed groups, which have been marginalised in educational decision-making, are brought into the policy-making process at all stages as equal partners with full and adequate rights of self-representation. If equality policies in education are developed without the direct and immediate involvement of the target group (for example, disabled people, working-class people, refugees, gay or lesbian groups) then there is a strong likelihood that the types of issues which are addressed, or the way in which they are addressed, will not be in line with the real needs of the group. It is essential too that such groups be resourced and supported (and trained if necessary) — be these women, children, racial, or other minorities — if they are to be effective. Partnerships will only add to the oppression if those representing marginalised groups do not have the training, resources, time and skill to operate as equal partners in the negotiation or consultation process.

All institutions and systems, including education, are structured around institutional lethargy. And bureaucratic lethargy is in the interests of the status quo. Even where resistance is not organised, the prevailing elites can rely on the lethargy of the educational decision-making processes to forestall change, or to introduce minimalist changes at a given time. To ensure that egalitarian policies are promoted in education within a reasonable time-frame, the inertia of bureaucracy and vested interests must be confronted. Only the marginalised and oppressed groups themselves will have the energy, insight and commitment to demand this, although they may, of course, benefit from alliances and support.

In addition, the question of politics and alliances comes into play. If 'resistance for equality' takes place only within the education site, and, within this context, the principal actors are professional educators, then the scope and the nature of the equality impact will be very limited. The promotion of equality in education must be linked in strategically with interventions by the primary actors for equality, namely community and other grass-roots groups representing the oppressed and marginalised at local, regional and international level. It must also link in with work in other sites (such as in the taxation area, the media and the law) and with other states. Localised action needs to be complemented by national and international action.

The system of representative decision-making which has built up around education means that those with the best resources and organisation are most effective in having their voices heard. (We can see this happening now at a grand scale within the European Union where large companies and interest groups hire full-time lobbyists to try to influence decisions of the European Commission and, eventually, of the European Parliament. On a smaller scale, it is evident in the draft Education Bill (No. 2) 1997 published in Ireland. The partners in education defined in this bill did not include any community or grass-roots groups, although there is reference to 'voluntary bodies' in section 32.) Marginalised and vulnerable groups often have no formal channels to engage in an effective and ongoing way in decision-making; women's groups, ethnic minorities, migrant workers, Travellers and Gypsies, refugees or disabled people are left without a direct voice in education decision-making. Professionals or voluntary workers frequently speak on their behalf. Others claim their voice and mediate their message. This results in the build-up of an array of professionals or voluntary agencies which provide second-hand information on inequalities but which cannot be a direct voice, by definition. Moreover, their own professional interests can often cut across the interests of the group. We have direct evidence of this for many years in the fields of education dealing with learning disabilities.

If there has been any lesson learned from the work of the South American educationalist Paulo Freire, it is that the process is part of the outcome in any educational endeavour; the medium is part of the message. If the process for realising change or promoting equality is fundamentally inegalitarian, then the outcomes achieved will also be inegalitarian. Freire links political outcomes with pedagogical form in particular. He highlights the way in which educational practice is infused with political objectives; in a hierarchically organised society which is fundamentally inegalitarian, the resulting social, cultural, economic and political relations of oppression and exploitation are reproduced in schools. The job of education in this context is to develop a dialogical pedagogy 'in which learners and teacher engage in active interaction with knowledge in conditions of mutuality and respect' (Silva and McLaren, 1993:39). This is the position adopted by a host of critical theorists, especially in the US, including Aronowitz and Giroux (1991), McLaren (1989) and Apple (1982, 1986). While I do not assent to the position of many contemporary critical theorists with regard to the claims they make about the power of liberatory educational practice to create radical change (such as the claims made by Aronowitz and Giroux, 1991), the Freirean insight that the medium is a large part of the message is a fundamental principle which would reorient educational practice. Moreover, the medium includes the nature of organisational practice in schools, and procedures for developing policies at national level with the Department of Education and other state appointed and assisted boards and institutions.

EQUALITY OF ECONOMIC CONDITION

To have equality of condition within education, it would be essential to have equality of condition in the economic and political spheres as well. As education is, in a number of respects, 'a cultural commodity' which can be bought, the pre-existence of large income and wealth differentials allows relatively privileged classes and groups to gain differential access to education in its credentialised form, both in terms of the nature of the award (degrees, diplomas, certificates, etc.) and the level at which these are attained. Economic capital can be translated directly into cultural capital (Bourdieu and Passeron, 1977). Without an equalisation of income and wealth differentials, those with superior resources can always use them to improve their rates of achievement above and beyond that of less privileged groups (Erikson and Jonsson, 1996).

Moreover, a dialectical relationship exists between economic value and cultural value. The low economic value placed on activities such as caring for others (which is badly paid and of low status, especially within the home) feeds back into the cultural market and education and reinforces the low status of the knowledge base on which caring is based — notably interpersonal and intrapersonal intelligence. Thus knowledge about how to develop satisfying, emotionally rewarding and supportive personal relationships is not a subject for analysis in most schools (or if it is, it is part of the secondary rather than the primary knowledge system). The gendered nature of this exclusion is self-evident.

It is often argued by liberals that the state can make up the differentials between groups through intervening to subvent and support marginalised groups in education to the level that they will be able to compete equally with more privileged groups. The experience of a number of countries suggests, however, that intervening within education alone is not sufficient (Shavit and Blossfeld, 1993). Unless the state intervenes simultaneously in the economic system to reduce wealth and income differentials, those with access to superior resources can use these to maintain their relative advantages in education. Moreover, if wealth and income differentials are not addressed at source, the state must spend a considerable proportion of its time and resources collecting and redistributing moneys, so the amount available for direct interventions is reduced accordingly. The net outcome therefore is that the scale of the intervention required is not commensurate with the resources available; and the resources could not be made available without eliminating the very differentials which make the redistribution necessary in the first place.

CONCLUDING REMARKS

Liberalism consigns us to a narrow reformist view of educational change — one which, at best, will bring limited gain for the relatively advantaged among the disadvantaged. Moreover, the internal logic of liberal policies does not allow for anything more radical. It treats education as an autonomous site with an ability to promote equality internally irrespective of external forces. By ignoring economic and power inequalities outside of education in particular, it endorses social and economic systems which perpetuate inequality within education. In a global context of structured inequality, the promise of liberal equal opportunities policies is realisable therefore for only a small minority of relatively advantaged people within a given disadvantaged group. The radical egalitarian perspective offers an alternative to the liberal model, one which confronts inequalities both within and without education in distributive terms, and one which focuses also on radical policies to promote equality of respect, in terms of how schools, curricula, planning and policies in education are devised and negotiated.

REFERENCES

Apple, M.W. (ed.) (1982). *Cultural and Economic Reproduction in Education.* London: Routledge & Kegan Paul.

Apple, M.W. (1986). *Teachers and Texts: A Political Economy of Class and Gender Relations in Education.* London: Routledge & Kegan Paul.

Archer, M.S. (1982). *The Sociology of Educational Expansion.* Beverly Hills: Sage.

Arendt, H. (1984). The revolutionary tradition and its lost treasure. From *On Revolution* (1963). London: Viking Penguin. In M. Sandel (ed.), *Liberalism and Its Critics.* New York University Press.

Arnot, M. (1991). Equality and democracy: a decade of struggle over education. *British Journal of Sociology of Education,* 12:447–66.

Arnot, M. (1992). Feminism, education and the new right. In M. Arnot and L. Barton (eds.), *Voicing Concerns: Sociological Perspectives on Contemporary Education Reforms.* Wallingford, Oxfordshire: Triangle Books Ltd.

Aronowitz, S., and Giroux, H. (1991). *Post-Modern Education: Politics, Culture and Social Criticism.* Minneapolis: University of Minnesota Press.

Baker, J. (1987). *Arguing for Equality.* New York: Verso.

Baker, J. (1998). Equality. In S. Healy and B. Reynolds (eds.), *Social Policy in Ireland: Principles, Practices and Problems.* Dublin: Oak Tree Press.

Bourdieu, P. (1973). Cultural reproduction and social reproduction. In R. Brown (ed.), *Knowledge, Education and Cultural Change*. London: Tavistock.

Bourdieu, P. (1993). *Sociology in Question*. London: Sage.

Bourdieu, P., and Passeron, J.-C. (1977). *Reproduction in Education, Society and Culture*. London: Sage.

Bowles, S., and Gintis, H. (1976). *Schooling in Capitalist America*. London: Routledge & Kegan Paul.

Breen, R., et al. (1990). *Understanding Contemporary Ireland*. Dublin: Gill & Macmillan.

Clancy, P. (1988). *Who Goes to College*. Dublin: Higher Education Authority.

Clancy, P. (1995). *Access to College: Patterns of Continuity and Change*. Dublin: Higher Education Authority.

Cobalti, A. (1990). Schooling inequalities in Italy: trends over time. *European Sociological Review*, 6:199–214.

Cohen, G.A. (1995). *Self-Ownership, Freedom and Equality*. Cambridge University Press.

Connell, R.W. (1993). *Schools and Social Justice*. Philadelphia: Temple University Press.

Coolahan, J. (ed.) (1994). *Report on the National Education Convention*. Dublin: Government Publications Office.

Da Silva, T.T., and McLaren, P. (1993). Knowledge under siege: the Brazilian debate. In P. McLaren and P. Leonard (eds.), *Paulo Freire: A Critical Encounter*. London: Routledge.

Davis, K., and Moore, W.E. (1970). Some principles of stratification. In M. Tumin, *Readings on Social Stratification*. New Jersey: Prentice Hall.

Delphy, C., and Leonard, D. (1992). *Familiar Exploitation: A New Analysis of Marriage and Family Life*. Oxford: Polity Press.

Department of Education (1992). *The Green Paper on Education*. Dublin: Government Publications Office.

Dworkin, R. (1984). Liberalism. In M. Sandel (ed.), *Liberalism and Its Critics*. New York University Press.

Equality Studies Centre (1995). Equality proofing issues. Paper presented to the National Economic and Social Forum (NESF), 25 January, Dublin Castle. Dublin: Department of the Taoiseach (NESF).

Erikson, R. and Jonsson, J. (eds.) (1996). *Can Education be Equalised? The Swedish Case in Comparative Perspective*. Oxford: Westview Press.

Freire, P. (1972a). *Pedagogy of the Oppressed*. New York: Penguin.

Freire, P. (1972b). *Cultural Action for Freedom*. New York: Penguin.

Freire, P. (1973). *Education for Critical Consciousness*. New York: Continuum.

Gardner, H. (1983). *Frames of Mind: The Theory of Multiple Intelligences*. London: Penguin.

Gardner, H. (1993). *Multiple Intelligences: The Theory in Practice*. New York: Basic Books.

Giroux, H. (1981). *Ideology, Culture and the Process of Schooling*. Philadelphia: Temple University Press.

Giroux, H. (1983). *Theory and Resistance in Education*. London: Heinemann.

Glyn, A., and Milliband, D. (1994). *Paying for Inequality*. London: IPPR/Rivers Oram Press.

Hall, S. (1986). Variants of liberalism. In J. Donald and S. Hall (eds.), *Politics and Ideology*. Milton Keynes: Open University Press.

Halsey, A.H. (1991). Educational systems and the economy. *Current Sociology*, 38 (2/3):79–101.

Hanafin, J. (1997). Unfreezing the frame: implications of multiple intelligences theory for curriculum and assessment. In A. Hyland (ed.), *Issues in Education*, vol. 2. Dublin: ASTI.

Lynch, K. (1989). *The Hidden Curriculum: Reproduction in Education, A Reappraisal*. Lewes: Falmer Press.

Lynch, K. (1990). Reproduction: the role of cultural factors and educational mediators. *British Journal of Sociology of Education*, 11:3–20.

Lynch, K. (1998). The status of children and young persons: educational and related issues. In S. Healy and B. Reynolds (eds.), *Social Policy in Ireland: Principles, Practices and Problems*. Dublin: Oak Tree Press.

Mac an Ghaill, M. (1994). *The Making of Men: Masculinities, Sexualities and Schooling*. Milton Keynes: Open University Press.

McDonnell, A. (1995). The ethos of Catholic voluntary schools. Unpublished Ph.D. thesis, Education Department, University College Dublin.

McLaren, P. (1989). On ideology and education: critical pedagogy and the cultural pedagogy of resistance. In H. Giroux and P. McLaren (eds.), *Critical Pedagogy, the State and Cultural Struggle*. Albany (NY): SUNY Press.

Nielsen, K. (1985). *Equality and Liberty: A Defense of Radical Egalitarianism*. Totowa (NJ): Rowman and Allanheld.

Offe, C. (1984). *Contradictions of the Welfare State*. London: Hutchinson.

O'Neill, O. (1977). How do we know when opportunities are equal? In M. Veterling-Braggin et al. (eds.), *Feminism and Philosophy*. Littlefield (NJ): Adam and Co.

Organisation for Economic Co-operation and Development (OECD) (1995). *Education at a Glance*. Paris: OECD.

Raftery, A.E., and Hout, M. (1993). Maximally maintained inequality: expansion, reform and opportunity in Irish education, 1921–75. *Sociology of Education*, 66:41–62.

Rawls, J. (1971). *A Theory of Justice*. Oxford University Press.

Shavit, Y., and Blossfeld, H.P. (eds.) (1993). *Persistent Inequality: Changing Educational Attainment in Thirteen Countries*. Boulder (CO): Westview Press.

Tawney, R.H. (1964). *Equality*. London: Allen & Unwin.

Tumin, M. (1970). Some principles of stratification: a critical analysis. In M. Tumin (ed.), *Readings on Stratification*. New Jersey: Prentice Hall.

Young, I.M. (1990). *Justice and the Politics of Difference*. Princeton University Press.

Young, M. (1958). *The Rise of the Meritocracy, 1870–2033*. London: Pelican.

NOTES

1 And it is important to note the emphasis here on equality in the living conditions of all members of society rather than citizens. Frequently rights are accorded only to citizens with attendant negative consequences for those who are defined as non-citizens.

2 Rule 155 (4) (a) of the Rules for National Schools formally excludes a person from entering primary teacher education colleges unless she/he 'is of sound and healthy constitution and free from any physical or mental defect likely to impair his (her) usefulness as a teacher'.

3 Direct discrimination occurs when someone is treated differently when they should be treated the same and when, as a result, they experience a disadvantage. **Indirect discrimination** refers to the differential impact of the same treatment where the differential is not justified. It occurs when a condition or requirement is set such that a considerably smaller proportion of one than

of another group can comply with it, which is to the detriment of the person(s) concerned and where the person using the condition or requirement cannot show it to be justified.

4   We have ample evidence of this in Ireland. The private education market has now become a key context in and through which inequality is reproduced (see chapter 6 above). Those who have resources can buy services in the private education market which will ensure that they maintain or gain relative advantage in education. The lack of any constitutional or legislative provision guaranteeing any form of equality in education means that there is no mechanism through which the state can be held accountable for its failure to address persistent social class differentials in educational opportunities.

5   The Education Bill (No. 1) 1997 proposed new regional structures for primary and second-level education which would have eroded the powers of the existing stakeholders in education considerably, notably the churches, the teacher unions, managerial bodies and the vocational education committees. The revised bill has introduced a whole series of provisions whereby these groups have certain rights to be consulted by the Minister before any major policy initiative is adopted.

6   In Ireland these include teachers, the churches, senior civil servants and inspectors, parent bodies, academics and vocational education committees. (See Lynch, 1990 for a discussion of the role of mediators.)

INDEX